Reconstructing the Society of Ancient Israel

LIBRARY OF ANCIENT ISRAEL

Douglas A. Knight, ***General Editor***

Reconstructing the Society of Ancient Israel

PAULA M. MCNUTT

SPCK
LONDON

WESTMINSTER JOHN KNOX PRESS
LOUISVILLE, KENTUCKY

First Published in the United States in 1999 by
Westminster John Knox Press
100 Witherspoon Street
Louisville, KY 40202-1396

First published in Great Britain by
Society for Promoting Christian Knowledge
Holy Trinity Church
Marylebone Road
London NW1 4DU

Book design by Publishers' WorkGroup
Cover design by Kim Wohlenhaus

This book is printed on acid-free paper.

PRINTED IN THE UNITED STATES OF AMERICA
99 00 01 02 03 04 05 06 07 08 — 10 9 8 7 6 5 4 3 2 1

Library of Congress Cataloging-in-Publication Data

McNutt, Paula M.
Reconstructing the society of ancient Israel / Paula M. McNutt. — 1st ed.
p. cm. — (Library of ancient Israel)
Includes bibliographical references and index.
ISBN 0-664-22265-X (alk. paper)
1. Jews—History—To 70 A.D. 2. Judaism—History—To 70 A.D. 3. Bible O.T.—History of Biblical events.
4. Excavations (Archaeology)—Palestine. I. Title. II. Series.
DS121.M385 1999
933—dc21 98-31938

British Cataloguing-in-Publication Data

A catalogue record of this book is available from the British Library.

ISBN 0-281-05259-X

Contents

Foreword

The historical and literary questions preoccupying biblical scholars since the Enlightenment have focused primarily on events and leaders in ancient Israel, the practices and beliefs of Yahwistic religion, and the oral and written stages in the development of the people's literature. Considering how little was known about Israel, and indeed the whole ancient Near East, just three centuries ago, the gains achieved to date have been extraordinary, due in no small part to the unanticipated discovery by archaeologists of innumerable texts and artifacts.

Recent years have witnessed a new turn in biblical studies, occasioned largely by a growing lack of confidence in the "assured results" of past generations of scholars. At the same time, an increased openness to the methods and issues of other disciplines such as anthropology, sociology, linguistics, and literary criticism has allowed new questions to be posed regarding the old materials. Social history, a well-established area within the field of historical studies, has proved especially fruitful as a means of analyzing specific segments of the society. Instead of concentrating predominantly on national events, leading individuals, political institutions, and "high culture," social historians attend to broader and more basic issues such as social organization, conditions in cities and villages, life stages, environmental contexts, power distribution according to class and status, and social stability and instability. To inquire into such matters regarding ancient Israel shifts the focus away from those with power and the events they instigated and onto the everyday realities and social subtleties experienced by the vast majority of the population. Such exploration has now gained new force with the application of various forms of ideological criticism and other methods designed to ferret out the political, economic, and social interests concealed in the sources.

This series represents a collaborative effort to investigate several specific topics—societal structure, politics, economics, religion, literature, material culture, law, intellectual leadership, ethnic identity, social marginalization, the international context, and canon formation—each in terms of its social dimensions and processes within ancient Israel. Some of these subjects have not been explored in depth until now; others are familiar areas currently in need of reexamination. While the sociohistorical approach provides the general perspective for all volumes of the series, each author has the latitude to determine the most appropriate means for dealing with the topic at hand. Individually and collectively, the volumes aim to expand our vision of the culture and society of ancient Israel and thereby generate new appreciation for its impact on subsequent history.

The present volume by Paula McNutt sets for itself a task that is at the same time fundamental and far-reaching. At one level, she engages the methodological problems involved in trying to recover and frame the history of ancient Israel's society. The question of sources looms large in this regard, as well it should. Yet she is above all interested in the ways in which social-scientific disciplines have extended the discussion by directing attention to aspects of society not readily apparent in the sources—the subsistence strategies, the kinship structures, the environmental factors, the regional and social diversity. Sociology and social anthropology, she argues, provide conceptual models to aid the interpretive process. At a second level, McNutt moves stage by stage through ancient Israel's main historical periods—settlement, "tribal," monarchic, and colonial. In each she describes the varying nature of Israelite society, focusing especially on demographic patterns, economic circumstances (e.g., labor, commerce, property ownership, and technology), sociopolitical affairs, and religious institutions. The resulting overview of societal conditions presents the reader with a cross-sectional picture of each period, but just as importantly it also provides a means for comparing the periods with one another in terms of the longitudinal developments that occurred over time. McNutt's attention to the difficulties presented by the textual and material sources as well as to important disputes associated with the application of social-scientific models gives her discussions the necessary critical edge. The result is a cogent and insightful portrait of Israel's social worlds—and of the complicated process of reconstructing them.

Douglas A. Knight
General Editor

Acknowledgments

The research for this book was facilitated by two grants from the National Endowment for the Humanities—an NEH Summer Stipend and an NEH Fellowship for College Teachers—and Faculty Fellowship Awards from Canisius College. I thank both the Endowment and Canisius College for this support.

There are many individuals who have provided me with encouragement and support in my journey through the labyrinth of information, models, and theories that has resulted in this study. First and foremost, my gratitude extends to my family. I also owe special thanks to a number of colleagues who over the years have stimulated and nourished my interest in the social world of ancient Israel, some of whom generously read and offered comments on earlier drafts of the book—Jim Flanagan, David Gunn, Dennis Duling, Jon Berquist, Shawn Kelley, and, of course, Doug Knight, who has so patiently guided me through the final stages of preparing the manuscript with his helpful comments and direction.

I am also indebted to the participants in various American Academy of Religion, Society of Biblical Literature, and American Schools of Oriental Research-sponsored groups and seminars over the years (especially the Social World of Ancient Israel Seminar, the Sociology of Monarchy Seminar, and the Constructs of the Social and Cultural Worlds of Antiquity Group), many of whom have influenced my thinking and the directions it has taken along the way. In addition to those I have already mentioned, these include Norman Gottwald, Frank Frick, Philip Davies, Keith Whitelam, David Hopkins, and Tom Overholt.

Many others were also invaluable in providing me with moral support as I worked on this project. Among them are my colleagues, friends, and students at Canisius College, my friends from William Goodenough House in London, and the members of the religion department at the School of

Oriental and African Studies at the University of London, who offered me hospitality and resources during my sabbatical year in London.

Finally, I thank those individuals at Westminster John Knox Press who were instrumental in helping to bring the manuscript through its various stages of production.

Abbreviations

AJA	*American Journal of Archaeology*
ARA	*Annual Review of Anthropology*
AUSS	*Andrews University Seminary Studies*
BA	*Biblical Archaeologist*
BARev	*Biblical Archaeology Review*
BARIS	British Archaeological Records International Series
BASOR	*Bulletin of the American Schools of Oriental Research*
BRev	*Bible Review*
CBQ	*Catholic Biblical Quarterly*
IEJ	*Israel Exploration Journal*
JAAR	*Journal of the American Academy of Religion*
JBL	*Journal of Biblical Literature*
JNES	*Journal of Near Eastern Studies*
JSOT	*Journal for the Study of the Old Testament*
JSOTSS	Journal for the Study of the Old Testament Supplement Series
NEASB	*Near Eastern Archaeology Society Bulletin*
PEQ	*Palestine Exploration Quarterly*
SBLDS	Society of Biblical Literature Dissertation Series
SJOT	*Scandinavian Journal of the Old Testament*
SWBAS	Social World of Biblical Antiquity Series
VTS	Vetus Testamentum Supplement
ZDPV	*Zeitschrift des deutschen Palästina-Vereins*

Archaeological Periods

Early Bronze I	ca. 3500–3000 B.C.E.
Early Bronze II	ca. 3000–2700 B.C.E.
Early Bronze III	ca. 2700–2200 B.C.E.
Early Bronze IV	ca. 2200–2000 B.C.E.
Middle Bronze I	ca. 2000–1750 B.C.E.
Middle Bronze II	ca. 1750–1550 B.C.E.
Late Bronze I	ca. 1550–1400 B.C.E.
Late Bronze II	ca. 1400–1200 B.C.E.
Iron IA	ca. 1200–1150 B.C.E.
Iron IB	ca. 1150–1000 B.C.E.
Iron IC	ca. 1000–900 B.C.E.
Iron II	ca. 900–586 B.C.E.
Babylonian Exile	586–539 B.C.E.
Persian Period	539–332 B.C.E.
Hellenistic Period	332–63 B.C.E.
Roman Period	63 B.C.E. to 360 C.E.

Chapter 1

"Unscrambling Omelets" and "Collecting Butterflies"

Sources, Methods, and Models

Much of the recent research on the history of ancient Israel has given attention to understanding the nature and development of society. To date, there has been no single-authored general synthesis of these studies that both gives attention to methodology and covers the periods extending from the tribal period through the period of Persian domination. This volume represents an attempt to provide such a synthesis. Examining the approaches and conclusions of recent reconstructions of the social and cultural contexts and processes out of which the literature of the Hebrew Bible arose during the course of ancient "Israel's"[1] history is one of my purposes here. Another is to provide a general overview of constructs of the processes and elements of Israel's social dimensions. Although belief systems are an essential part of culture, and are thus certainly relevant to society, the emphasis here is on elements that comprise society and the relationship of these elements to the social system and social organization, and to social processes associated with change.

"Unscrambling omelets" and "collecting butterflies" are metaphors used by anthropologist Edmund Leach to describe some of the methods that have been central to the task of reconstructing the history and society of ancient Israel.[2] Trying to recover earlier forms of biblical texts, in Leach's estimation, is like trying to unscramble an omelet. And cross-cultural comparison based on social structure and organization, which involves classifying and organizing things according to type and subtype, amounts to nothing more than collecting butterflies. Leach's views stand at one end of the spectrum in recent debates about how much confidence can be placed in the Bible as a source of history and about the validity of using cross-cultural comparison as a tool for understanding the nature and development of Israelite society.

I introduce this chapter with Leach's pessimistic stance not because I agree with him fully, but rather to emphasize that in this age of poststructuralism and postmodernism (post-postmodernism?), the approaches we use in interpreting the past, and the sources we depend on, are more than ever before subject to scrutiny.

Examining the nature of recent methodological shifts and assessing the value of both traditional and new approaches are the subjects of many recent works.[3] One significant shift in the last several decades is a more intentional application of social-scientific methods, models, and theories as tools for reconstructing ancient Israel's social world, along with a concern for refining methods for interpreting and relating the ancient information.[4] These developments have significantly expanded the field of questions it is possible to ask about the nature of ancient societies, and thus allow us to view the nature and function of their literature in a new light. The current emphasis among Syro-Palestinian archaeologists on recovering as much material information as possible about all aspects of ancient life has also had an effect on expanding the field of inquiry.

This book is as much about the problems and processes associated with constructing the past from the sources available to us as it is about the social world of ancient Israel itself. Thousands of years stand between the social worlds of the ancient Israelites and modern interpreters, and the information upon which we depend is fragmentary and often, to our sensibilities in the twentieth century, inconsistent and contradictory. In addition to this gap between the twentieth-century investigator and the ancient sources, the gap between the sources, both textual and material, and the ancient societies they represent must also be taken into account. In a sense, then, history is understood here more as an "ongoing conversation" between past and present than as what we know or think we know about past events and peoples.[5]

Another factor that affects the construction of history, and consequently influences the way in which we read historical constructions such as those in this volume, is the acknowledgment among modern interpreters that complete objectivity is a goal never reached by the historian—the types of questions we bring to our investigations, as well as our individual biases and presuppositions, necessarily affect how our research proceeds and influence the reconstructions we propose. This ultimately requires us to be more and more critically conscious of our own biases, assumptions, and aims, particularly in dealing with a source like the Bible. As a cultural and religious artifact for Western societies, the Bible is a part of our fundamental cultural frameworks (and thus our tacit assumptions), which in turn affect our interpretations. Grounded in these cultural frameworks are presuppositions we generally leave unexamined and uncriticized because, as part of our collective worldview, we assume them to be "the way things are." As fundamental shifts in our worldviews occur, they necessarily affect the ways in which we go about doing our research at every level and stage, and thus also our interpretations, that is, we constantly revise our understanding of the past in light of current developments, understandings, and attitudes.[6] These factors, no doubt, account in part for the wide variety, and sometimes radical differences, in constructions of ancient Israelite history and society, some of which are considered in this volume.

SOURCES

The sources available to us for reconstructing the social world of ancient Israel include the Hebrew Bible in its various early versions, other ancient Near Eastern texts and documents, and material information recovered through archaeological excavations. Historical geography, technology, and demographics have also been important in a number of recent studies. Although traditionally the Hebrew Bible has been the primary source for interpreting the social contexts out of which the literature contained in it emerged, many recent studies have placed more emphasis on archaeological information and theories and models from comparative sociology and anthropology. There is, in fact, some controversy at present relating to the issue of the relative value of the various sources, particulary with respect to the Bible. This has to do both with the question of the degree to which the Bible contains actual historical and social information and with the argument of some scholars that depending too heavily on the biblical texts for social and historical information involves engaging in a kind of circular reasoning—that is, generating a cultural and historical "reality" from a text and then turning around and trying to understand the same text in relation to the background that was reconstructed from it.[7]

The Bible

Like all texts, the Bible grew out of sociopolitical realities and cannot be fully understood apart from them. Narratives and other literary genres are often grounded in what anthropologist Victor Turner called "social dramas," that is, sociocultural processes, which have an interdependent and dynamic relationship with genres of "cultural performance" (ritual and literature).[8] Because of their relatedness to social dramas, the biblical texts are potentially useful sources of social and cultural information if used critically. But it is important to emphasize that, as is the case for any text, the biblical traditions are *models* or *constructs* of reality. Although they can tell us something about general cultural "notions" about reality, they also reflect the individual biases and assumptions of their various authors and editors. They do not record "history" in the sense that history is understood in the twentieth century. There is, in fact, no claim in the Bible itself that the writers intended it to be an objective representation of historical or social reality. It is religious and political literature in which the past is constructed from a religious perspective—written, edited, and arranged in its present form long after the collapse of the two nations on which the stories contained in it focus. In terms of content, it represents a wide diversity of values and viewpoints; and the laws, stories, genealogies, prophetic speeches, wisdom sayings, and so forth relate to a host of social institutions and practices associated with social and political experiences that spanned many centuries. Furthermore, many of the events related in the stories are cosmic in dimension, clearly more "mythological" than "historical."

The "history" recorded in the biblical narratives, therefore, whether they contain accurate information or not, must be understood first and foremost as representing notions, beliefs, and myths constructed to serve some purpose in the social and historical contexts in which they were written, edited, and arranged in their present form—that is, the *meanings* conveyed in these texts must be interpreted in relation to the "social dramas" that prompted their writing and editing. The past, for the biblical writers as well as for twentieth-century readers of the Bible, has meaning only when it is considered in light of the present, and perhaps an idealized future. For this reason, it is important to take into account the symbolic intentions of the texts as myths that convey some essential truth about social and religious values, principles, and identity at the time they were written and/or edited but not necessarily "facts" about the history they purport to be relating.

Any reconstruction of the history and society of ancient Israel must rely, then, on interpretations of the history and development of the texts themselves before we utilize them as sources of historical and social information. The Hebrew Bible's development has involved a complex literary process spanning over three thousand years. This process, in very general terms, probably included the formation and combining of independent oral and literary units, *possibly* beginning as far back as ca. 1200 B.C.E., the final formation of these literary units into an authoritative collection of writings, and the preservation and transmission of this collection, both in the original languages and in translations.

The independent units making up this rich collection of literature would originally have been addressed to the immediate situations and needs of diverse communities during different periods in Israel's history. Many may have circulated independently before being progressively grouped together into narratives and collections of stories, sayings, poetry, prophetic oracles, and so forth. Those traditions that originally circulated in oral rather than written form were most likely transformed in some way once they were written down.[9] In order to glean from the Hebrew Bible any information about the social worlds in which it was produced, therefore, it is necessary first to ask such questions about a given text as: Who might have written this text? When was it written? Where was it written? Why was it written? What was the audience to whom it was directed? It is also necessary to consider the forms and functions of the various texts. For example, narratives that treat important ancestors or religious figures may have been intended *not* as historical accounts of what particular people actually did at particular times for particular purposes, but rather to explain *symbolically* something about origins, institutions, customs, or relations with other peoples. The answers to all these questions are necessarily hypothetical, but without such hypotheses about the texts themselves it is not possible to propose in a responsible way hypotheses about the nature and development of the society and culture in which they were produced.

In using the Bible as a source for historical and social reconstruction it is also important to consider who may have been responsible for having *collected* and *edited* the independent literary units over time, as well as when and why they may have been collected and edited. Particularly in crisis situations such as political subordination or exile, or periods of rapid social change, the biblical writers in various periods would have appealed to and reinterpreted sacred history (myth) to legitimate claims about the present and to encourage others to accept these claims, with such intentions as strengthening national identity or emphasizing the superiority of Israel's God. This type of response is well documented by anthropologists in societies experiencing rapid cultural change or crisis brought on by other factors. The past as remembered, interpreted, and recounted in light of a present crisis, and the symbols used in the recounting, would have functioned to reaffirm shared values or to reinterpret these values and legitimate them by reinterpreting the symbols.

That portion of the Bible we tend to refer to as "historical," for example (Joshua, Judges, 1 and 2 Samuel, 1 and 2 Kings), probably reached its final form in the context of the Jewish religious community sometime after the fall of Judah to the Babylonians, that is, after it had ceased to be an independent state. It therefore reflects more the concerns and social world of the peoples of the postexilic Persian period than those of the "times" to which the narratives refer. The process of collecting and editing these traditions likely occurred because of a need to explain the tragedy of Judah's loss of national identity and to reaffirm the religious past in light of the present situation. Those responsible for gathering and editing this material would have been deliberately selective in what they chose to include, therefore providing us with a skewed view of Israel's past. Behind these literary traditions there must have been some kernels of genuine historical memory, but the genuine is difficult to distinguish from that which was constructed at a later period.

Another important consideration is the social locations of those responsible for writing and editing the texts, as well as of the audiences toward whom they were directed.[10] Because the literature of the ancient world was the product of scribal activity, it did not necessarily represent the ideals of the whole society. In typical agrarian societies such as Israel, those who can read and write well constitute less than 5 percent of the population. This means that the remaining 95 percent, as well as many who may have been literate, would not have had access or been exposed to this literature. The authors of the biblical literature were most likely male, and would almost certainly have been from a small and elite class (probably based in the Jerusalem Temple and perhaps also in the governor's court). The literature they constructed, then, most likely reflects more the concerns of their own gender and their own class consciousness than that of the society as a whole.

From what we know about societies, both ancient and modern, different groups would have had different, often competing interests (whether these are articulated or not) and different worldviews. It follows that whatever actual religion and ideology the biblical literature reflects, it is not necessarily the religion and ideology of the people outside this class. Nor can we even claim with any certainty that the members of the class responsible for writing the biblical texts themselves practiced the kind of religion that the biblical literature could be taken to represent.

The intentionality of the writers/editors is another factor that is important to consider. It is likely, for example, that in their original social contexts some of the biblical materials may have been intended in part as propaganda.[11] Ruling elites in socially stratified states often seek to maintain their power through persuasion and propaganda, as well as by repression. In the ancient Near East propaganda assumed various forms, some written (such as royal inscriptions), some oral, and some even architectural (for example, in the form of monumental buildings). No royal inscriptions or iconic representations of Israelite or Judean kings, and only modest public buildings dating to Iron Age II, have been uncovered by archaeologists in Palestine.

But propaganda is almost certainly present in the Hebrew Bible, much of it probably deriving from times of social tension or upheaval.

The Bible as a Historical Source

Reconstructing the social world of any ancient society is essentially interrelated with understanding its history. Although accuracy in portraying "reality" is one of the primary goals of the historian, in actuality our knowledge of whatever "the reality out there" is depends on historians' *constructions* or *images* of it, which in turn depend on a wide range of variables.[12] Ancient history and society are unfortunately unobservable and beyond the reach of our experience, so we necessarily depend on different types of information that open up a window into that world. But the images of the past we see in that window (which we create) are *not* the same thing as the information from and about the past. The images we accept as more, or less, reliable tend to be a matter of consensus, and the consensus is continually shifting. In a sense, history is not so much what "really" happened in the past as it is what historians can convince us "probably" happened. But this "probably" is always subject to revision.[13]

The question of the degree to which it is possible to construct an accurate account of history based on ancient sources, especially the Bible, is one that has been hotly debated in recent years.[14] Because historical context is important for understanding the nature and development of Israelite society, it is worth presenting the general gist of the debate. At one end of the spectrum are those who insist that the Bible is literally accurate in all historical details. At the other end are those who view the overall value of the Bible as a historical source with great skepticism. Most biblical scholars fall somewhere between the two extremes, but the skeptics' voices in recent years have been loud enough that they have generated some heated responses from some who hold the middle ground or are closer to the other end of the spectrum.

Although he is considered an "outsider" by many biblical scholars, and thus is not always taken seriously by them, Edmund Leach had a strong interest in the question of what kinds of information can be gleaned from biblical texts. Leach denied the validity of using the Bible for historical investigations of any kind, and thus is clearly at the "skeptic" end of the spectrum.[15] The patterns and structures in the text *can,* he argues, reveal something about the storytellers (in the case of the Bible, the editors) and their worlds, but only those responsible for the *final* form of the text. As stated at the beginning of this chapter, for Leach trying to recover any earlier forms of the biblical texts is like trying to unscramble an omelet. As a structuralist, he argues that anthropology's contribution to biblical studies has been to show that the Bible is mytho-history and that therefore "no part of the Bible is a record of history as it actually happened."[16]

Among biblical scholars, one of the most vocal skeptics is Philip R. Davies.[17] Davies argues that it is difficult to understand what the criteria are that biblical scholars use to distinguish "fictions with real historical settings" from historical accounts.[18] He further asserts that the argument that the literary construct (the Bible) is a historical one that confirms itself is, as has been noted above, a circular one.[19]

Davies argues that the Hebrew Bible was the political and cultural product of the Jerusalem power structure during the Persian period, created by professional scribes who constructed an idealized and fictitious entity, "Israel." This ideological construct, "Israel," provided a model for establishing a new identity as "Judahites" or "Jews" in that period, and as such, it has little historical value for preceding periods.

Davies asserts that scholars have naively confused this *literary and ideological construct* of "Israel" with the *actual reality* of the Iron Age inhabitants of Palestine, and that what we call "ancient Israel" is a *scholarly* construct. This scholarly construct is *not* the same as the Israel of the biblical literature.[20] It is something that lies *between* literature and actual history, and is the product of making a *literary construct* the object of *historical* investigation. Along with other "skeptics," then, Davies would agree with Leach's assessment of the biblical literature—any material that may predate the Persian period is so transformed and embedded in the text that it is impossible to unravel its intricate structure. Setting aside the presuppositions that cause us to confuse the literary constructs with actual history, he argues, would free us to view the evidence of text, archaeology, and history from a more tenable perspective.

Keith Whitelam,[21] agreeing with Davies to some degree in his estimation of the historical value of the Hebrew Bible, asserts that it is necessary to renounce the priority of the biblical narratives for historical reconstruction, and to relegate them to a secondary position in relation to social archaeology in research strategy. Although he does not deny the significance of the biblical traditions for the study of particular individuals or aspects of Israel's history (allowing that they provide one important though restricted source), he argues that it must first be demonstrated, rather than assumed, that they offer information useful to the historian.

Other scholars remain much more optimistic than Davies and Whitelam about the relative historical value of the Bible, and regard their skepticism as overly pessimistic. Baruch Halpern, for example, is very critical of what he calls their "minimalist" view—a view he associates with claims that the history of the Israelite monarchy was "made up" after the Jews went into exile in Babylonia, and, in its most extreme form, with the appeal to archaeology to "subvert" the validity of the biblical traditions.[22] Arguing that these "minimalists" are not "real" historians, Halpern sets out in a recent article to test the validity of their assertions by checking the extrabiblical textual material (which, he claims, the "minimalists" ignore) from the monarchic period against the traditions recorded in the books of Kings. He concludes that the books of Kings preserve a large amount of accurate historical information—for example, in relation to the names and dates of foreign kings and international affairs. He further argues that the "facts" from the archaeological record clearly indicate that the biblical traditions about the premonarchic period of settlement and expansion are "perfectly reasonable," pointing to archaeological evidence such as the extrabiblical reference to Shishak/Sheshonq's military campaign in Palestine at the end of the tenth century, and the existence of systems of defense and fortifications, also dating to the late tenth century B.C.E., that indicate a centralized government authority (contra the "minimalist" argument that a centralized state did not exist in Israel until the ninth or eighth century). Halpern does not deny that some of the "history" in the Bible presents a distorted picture, but he does claim that it is possible through "reasoned deconstruction" to approximate historical reality from it.

I do not intend here to take a stand on this issue, or to offer any solutions. Each perspective is worth considering, and reconsidering, as we engage in the task of constructing and reconstructing histories of ancient Israel and trying to look behind the evidence to catch a glimpse of what Israelite and Judean society may have been like. What I would argue, however, is that in using the biblical traditions as sources for historical and social reconstruction, it is necessary to keep in mind at every step that they are "myths," and that as myths they functioned, and continue to function, as myths function in other cultures and their religions. They answer such fundamental questions as: What were our origins? Who are we and how are we related to each other and to God? How are we related to the land? Why is Israel the way it is? What are the origins of our system of justice, and why is this system legitimate?

Other Ancient Near Eastern Texts and Documents

The Hebrew Bible and other ancient Near Eastern texts from Syro-Palestine, Egypt, Mesopotamia, and Anatolia share a broad cultural heritage as well as some common literary forms and themes. There are a number of different types of literature from ancient Near Eastern contexts that provide us with potentially useful historical, social, and cultural information—inscriptions, ostraca and letters that record information about events and political relationships, mythological literature and cultic inscriptions that reveal something about religion, worldview, customs, practices, and the like, inventories that give us a glimpse of economic systems and relations, and legal texts that reflect beliefs about social values and concepts of justice.

Comparison of these texts to those in the Bible has contributed in a number of ways to our understanding of ancient Israel and its literature, history, and culture. Mythological texts, for example, have made it possible in some cases to distinguish biblical texts that are clearly of little use for historical reconstruction, but in some cases can nevertheless provide us with information relevant to understanding something more about ancient Israelite culture and society. Although relatively few in number, references in other ancient Near Eastern texts or monuments to events and/or individuals mentioned in the Bible, on the other hand, allow us to place some confidence in the historical value of the biblical traditions relating to the monarchic and Persian periods. These also provide us with additional information about Israel's and Judah's historical and political relations with the surrounding regions. The earliest extant texts that make reference to Israel or Judah, however, date to the ninth century B.C.E. This means that there is no clear extrabiblical evidence for events or individuals predating the reign of Omri of Israel—that is, we have no extrabiblical information about prominent biblical figures such as Abraham and Moses, or even David and Solomon. Although there are two possible ninth-century references to the "house of David"—on a stela recently discovered at Tel Dan and one of King Mesha of Moab—we cannot take this as evidence for David himself. Both date to the ninth, not the tenth, century and there is substantial controversy over what the references actually mean.[23]

As is the case with the biblical literature, the available extrabiblical texts from the ancient Near East yield very selective kinds of information, are often ambivalent, sometimes making conflicting claims, and are sometimes simply unbelievable. It is necessary, therefore, to observe the same kinds of cautions identified for the biblical material in evaluating the historical value of this material—for example, the possibility that royal inscriptions were intended as propaganda, and thus present a distorted picture of real events and relationships.

Care should also be taken at the interpretive level of comparing biblical texts with texts from other geographical, social, and historical contexts. These also must be understood first and foremost in the context of the social dramas that gave rise to their production.

Archaeological Information

> Archaeology, in the strict sense, i.e. the study of the material remains of the past, is only an auxiliary science, which helps us to reconstruct the actual setting in which [Israel's] institutions functioned: but it reveals to us the houses in which families lived, the towns administered by the elders of the people or the king's officials, the capitals where the court resided, the gates where justice was administered and the merchants set up their stalls, with their scales and the weights they kept in their purses. It shows us the ramparts which armies defended, the tombs at which the funeral rites were performed, and the sanctuaries where the priests directed worship.[24]

Roland de Vaux's reference to archaeology as "only an auxiliary science" reveals his belief that the Bible is the primary source of information about ancient Israelite social institutions. This belief is apparent in his study of Israel's social and religious institutions, a work that deals in a comprehensive way with the relevant biblical material and cites archaeological information only when it illuminates what he has concluded on the basis of the texts. Although most today would agree with what de Vaux lists as the types of information yielded by archaeological excavations, many would dispute his assertions about the relative value of archaeology, arguing either that priority should be given to archaeological information or that each should be given equal consideration.

Archaeology as a discipline includes both the systematic recovery and the study of the material remains of the past. In interpreting these remains archaeologists draw inferences and propose hypotheses regarding the nature of the culture, society, and history of the peoples with whom they were associated. They are concerned, then, not only with investigating how people lived in the past, but also with how and why changes took place over time.

In the past, archaeologists working in the Middle East were typically interested in illuminating the biblical text and clarifying the relationship of Israel to surrounding cultures. Thus, historians used the material remains of ancient Israelite culture revealed through excavation to supplement (and often to corroborate) the biblical texts in their reconstructions. In recent years, however, more emphasis has been placed on the kinds of information they contribute to reconstructing the total range of ancient Israel's social world—the world out of which the biblical texts were produced. Of particular significance in this regard is the shift in research strategy of many recent excavations, surveys, and archaeological studies—from an almost exclusive concern with the chronology and monumental architecture of large sites and sites thought to be associated in some way with the biblical traditions, to a consideration of smaller sites and the type of remains that provide us with information on everyday life. The attention now given to excavating and surveying smaller sites is especially important given the fact that rural life has not been as well documented archaeologically as has city life. The past emphasis on the latter has left us with a rather lopsided view of ancient life, particularly given the fact that about 90 percent of the population probably would have lived in small towns and villages. Many types of archaeological materials, for example, can help the interpreter define the economic and technological bases of a settlement or region. The arrangement and size of structures, and the distribution of resources, prestige items or valued commodities, and the like indicate something about social structure and organization and relations with neighboring groups. The patterns of settlement distribution, artifact and building distribution within a settlement, distribution of resources, distribution of artifacts among graves in a cemetery, and regional distribution of exchanged items provide insights into aspects of the social and economic structures of ancient societies that are not necessarily revealed in texts.

Archaeology, then, provides an impressive range of information that has advanced our knowledge and understanding of the physical, technological, economic, social, and intellectual life of the peoples of the ancient world, as well as how, and why, change occurs. Archaeology also allows us to reconstruct ancient Palestine's environment (for example, topography, climate, land and water resources), subsistence systems, exchange networks, settlement patterns, demography, and the like which cannot be reconstructed on the basis of texts. It allows us to compare the material culture of ancient peoples as well as the beliefs and ideas encoded in texts. For ancient Palestine, it has also provided an important corrective to the biblical picture of ancient Israel's origins, the transition to a state form of sociopolitical organization, the internal structure and external relations of Judah and Israel, and the nature of society in Palestine following Judah's restoration. It allows us to go beyond focusing on the impact of individual heroes or the role of religious ideology in trying to understand the dynamics of social and cultural change.

As is apparent in discussions throughout this volume, textual information from the Bible and archaeological information do not always appear to tell the same stories. Considering the relationship of archaeological and textual materials, then, is an important part of the interpretive task.[25] Archaeological evidence is considered by many to be more reliable and accurate than the biblical texts as a source of historical information. The argument is that, in contrast to the Bible, there is no intentional selectivity in what has been left behind for archaeologists to find. In a sense there is actually some selectivity (although not intentional) in archaeological remains, resulting, for example, from such things as the arbitrary nature of human behavior and accidents of preservation—for example, iron corrodes over time and wood disintegrates, and unless the excavator is especially careful to notice the scant signs left of such artifacts, their presence and thus potential information about such things as technology, economy, and trade are lost, and the reconstructions of scholars distorted. But many nevertheless argue that the remains of material culture, by their very randomness, are more objective and neutral and thus more representative of what really happened in the past. In contrast to the Bible, archaeology also provides us with a continually expanding source of new data. But it is important to recognize that our individual biases, along with contemporary ideologies and social ideals,[26] are likely to influence our interpretations of the archaeological data, just as they do when we interpret biblical texts; that is, a certain amount of subjectivity is inevitable in interpreting material culture, just as it is in interpreting texts.

The types of questions we ask also affect our hypotheses and interpretations. W. F. Albright, for example, an American archaeologist whose work was crucial in the development of Syro-Palestinian archaeology in this century, set out in much of his research to prove that the Bible was an accurate portrayal of ancient Israel's history. With this goal in mind, he was able to point to archaeological evidence that he believed supported this assertion. Recent reevaluations of the evidence Albright used, however, suggest that many of his arguments are in fact not valid.[27] Another good example of this principle is the past tendency to assign ethnic and/or ideological value to artifacts on the basis of assumption rather than critical assessment of the material remains. This is an issue that will be discussed more thoroughly in chapter 2, but it is worth noting here that interpreters are now much more careful about making such assertions.[28]

The value of much of the archaeological information that has come to light in the past century must also be considered seriously. Much of it comes from excavations carried out before adequate methods of excavation, recording, and dating were developed, and is therefore either lacking context altogether or the reconstructed contexts are questionable. Much of it also comes from excavations of large sites in which there was an emphasis on uncovering monumental architecture and museum-quality artifacts, with little attention given to more mundane material remains such as botanical or osteological material.

Archaeological information, then, is an important source for understanding the nature of Israelite society and its transformation over the course of many centuries. But like the biblical literature and other ancient Near Eastern texts it *mediates* between what actually happened in the past and what is represented through it as having happened, and thus it must be interpreted. Any resulting interpretations must be recognized as hypotheses that are subject to change as new information or different methods of interpretation are applied.

ANTHROPOLOGY AND SOCIOLOGY

Anthropology and sociology have informed many of the recent reconstructions of ancient Israel's social world, so it is useful to include a general discussion of their varied emphases. Although models and theories from both disciplines have played important roles in recent reconstructions of ancient Israel's social world, I have chosen to concentrate here on summarizing the various approaches used by anthropologists. One reason is my own familiarity with anthropology. Another is that there seems to be a move toward more dependence on anthropology in the more recent reconstructions. This may be due in part to the fact that sociologists have tended to concentrate on evaluating industrial and postindustrial societies, and anthropologists on the types of societies that are closer in structure, technological complexity, and so forth to ancient Israel. This has never been a hard and fast distinction between the two disciplines, however, and in recent years the distinction has become increasingly blurred.

Anthropology is concerned with studying both contemporary and historical societies. As an academic discipline, it is somewhat difficult to define, in large part because there is no clear agreement on a central paradigm for research or on the nature of the questions anthropologists should be asking. Like other disciplines in the social sciences, it depends on data as a means of constructing hypotheses about larger wholes.

One emphasis in anthropology is on analyzing social structure and organization, particularly in relation to observed regularities, and how they relate to such things as social inequality, gender relations, and political authority.

Anthropologists and sociologists are also concerned with studying social institutions such as kinship, community, and tribe. Institutions are "customary, accepted ways of doing things in a given society . . . the culturally shared patterns of meaning and mutual expectations which underlie such conventions,"[29] that is, they are *subjectively* held ideas about social relations that are shared by members of a society, represented in rules, customs, symbolic actions such as ritual, and the conduct of everyday affairs.[30]

A more recent emphasis is on studying cultural symbols and patterns of meaning, that is, on the ways in which people think about their worlds and construct systems of meaning that are expressed through symbols, and the ways in which these influence social and cultural change.[31] This approach to studying cultures shows a concern not only with the *behavior* of human populations, but also with their notional models for generating behavior and for perceiving and interpreting their material environments, that is, the interrelationship between modes of thought and modes of action. It includes consideration of how people generate, maintain, modify, and reproduce symbols as a way of making sense of the world and determining how to act in it. Trying to get at the shared meanings of such symbol systems can be especially problematic when studying societies such as ancient Israel whose basic concepts of time, space, and person, along with other aspects of the social order, differed significantly from our own. Contributing to this problem for the interpreter is the fact that such notions are often taken for granted to such an extent that they are never fully articulated. This is less of a problem for anthropologists who are able to make sense of such notions through observed behavior than it is for someone whose concern is with ancient societies, and who can depend only on written and material remains, without the advantage of being able to observe directly the society being studied.

Also important in the study of symbol systems is comparing how the organization and development of complex systems of meaning and practice relate to the contexts of political domination and economic relations among groups and societies of different levels of complexity and in different periods. This, again, is an important question for biblical scholars to ask, given ancient Israel's multiple experiences of political and economic domination by outside powers.

Traditionally, one of the goals of anthropologists has been to develop universal "laws" of social organization or of cultural order. But many studies focus on specific societies and cultures within particular historical contexts, and so it is possible to argue that anthropology shares many common features with the discipline of historical studies, and that, in fact, they complement each other. Historians, for example, may seek primarily to explain specific events, but they nevertheless rely, even if only implicitly, on sociological or anthropological conceptions about such things as the nature of religious beliefs and political relations. And although anthropologists may be concerned primarily with studying recurrent regularities in a society, such as the relationship of certain systems of belief to social action, the nature of symbol systems, or the relationship between types of political authority and ideas about social inequality, their expression is necessarily related to specific historical events. Both historians and anthropologists, then, seek systematically to infer what is known or knowable about beliefs and social order, whether of contemporary societies or of societies in earlier periods.

Ethnohistory and ethnoarchaeology are subdisciplines in anthropology that combine the methods of historians and anthropologists. These subdisciplines provide an important framework for the work of social historians concerned with ancient societies that cannot be observed in the same way ethnographers can observe living societies.

For the ethnohistorian, both oral traditions and traditional history, which form a part of a people's social life and culture, are accepted as legitimate data for reconstructing cultures and their histories.[32] Ethnohistory has been described as a kind of documentary ethnology, encompassing a set of methods and techniques employed for "reducing all classes of documentation to raw ethnographic data applicable to the study of human behavior with an anthropological theoretical framework."[33] For the ethnohistorian, then, the "document," either oral or written, or material plays the role the informant plays for the ethnologist.

Ethnoarchaeology is an approach that is similar to ethnohistory in highlighting the complementarity between anthropological and historical approaches to studying culture and society.[34] This approach emphasizes integrating historical and archaeological data, and using ethnographic information from contemporary societies and anthropological models as a way of illuminating this information. It operates on the assumption that some behavioral elements of sociocultural systems have material correlates. Those material correlates that are part of the archaeological record are used to develop inferences about the *behaviors* with which they were associated.

HISTORICAL BACKGROUND OF SOCIAL-SCIENTIFIC APPROACHES

Serious ventures on the part of biblical scholars to fathom the complexities of the ancient Israelite social world from a social-scientific perspective began over a century ago.[35] The earliest interpreters showed particular interest in social data such as legal texts and lists and summaries of political administration, and in comparing Israelite society to other societies. Most of their studies were oriented toward solving literary and historical puzzles rather than social ones, though, and those who were more concerned with social reconstruction were hampered by undeveloped anthropological and sociological methods and models. Although attempts were made before this time to explain the nature of social life and religion in ancient Israel by drawing on comparisons with contemporary "primitive" societies,[36] it was not until the publication of W. Robertson Smith's *Lectures on the Religion of the Semites*[37] in the late nineteenth century that this type of approach began to have any lasting impact on biblical studies as a developing discipline.

In spite of Robertson Smith's pioneering work, and subsequent occasional studies of ancient Israel with somewhat of a social-scientific orientation, his approach did not have a direct impact on the directions taken in biblical studies throughout much of this century, and it did not gain recognition as a valid approach by most biblical scholars until several decades ago. But both his approach and some of his conclusions have had an indirect influence on the recent renewed interest in the social world of ancient Israel through his influence on the development of method and theory in the social sciences, notably sociology of religion (through Émile Durkheim) and psychology (through Sigmund Freud), but also anthropology (through, for example, E. E. Evans-Pritchard). Durkheim's work on sociology of knowledge and symbolic forms was inspired by Robertson Smith's conviction that symbolic behavior is related to the nature of social groups. Evans-Pritchard's influential study of segmentation among the Nuer of the southern Sudan (on which some studies on segmentation in early Israel have depended) was also influenced by his work. It was not until the recent renaissance of interest in the potential worth of social-scientific approaches, particularly comparative studies, for illuminating ancient sources that Robertson Smith's work was recognized in biblical studies for its pioneering significance.

Robertson Smith has been criticized frequently both for his methods of interpretation and for theoretical arguments that, in retrospect, are considered faulty. For example, the gross comparative method and evolutionary model, reflecting the state of the social sciences at the time, led to simplistic conclusions that discouraged others from attempting to improve on the approach. He assumed that bedouin society was a holdover from the time in which the Hebrew Bible was produced and was relatively unchanged. And his overall interpretation was based on the prevailing assumption that historical societies in the ancient Near East had evolved out of pastoral nomadic societies (like the bedouin). The assumption that Israel was a pastoral nomadic society was accepted uncritically until the last several decades and was perpetuated in other early studies.[38] Despite such problems, however, Robertson Smith touched on many of the basic issues of anthropological inquiry and his contributions, both to the social sciences generally and to biblical studies specifically, cannot be ignored.

Following Robertson Smith, the next major contribution to the social-scientific study of ancient Israel was made by Max Weber in *Ancient Judaism*.[39] Weber, a sociologist, was the first to apply comprehensively to the study of ancient Israel the methods and approaches of sociological analysis.

His aim was to identify the relationship between social organization and (1) the groups of which it is composed and (2) religious beliefs and practices in ancient Israel. He was particularly interested in the connection between religion and economics. Although not a biblical specialist himself, Weber was able to present an impressive analysis of the texts in the Hebrew Bible, while simultaneously applying sociological methods of inquiry. In addition to his evaluation of the relationship between religion and society, Weber's contributions included analyses of Israel's cult, the covenant, early Israel's "charismatic" type of leadership, the social role of the Levites, Israel's diverse socioeconomic groups, and the nature and role of prophecy as related to conflict between religious ideals and socioeconomic organization. Weber distinguished four basic types of social structure in ancient Palestine—nomadic bedouins, seminomadic herders, peasant farmers, and city dwellers—and three basic types of societal authority—legal, traditional, and charismatic. Weber's "ideal type" model has also had a strong influence, not only in biblical studies but in the social sciences in general.

Although there are certainly problems with Weber's models and interpretations, he nevertheless raised questions that have been important in subsequent studies, and his work is often still cited. He perceived relationships in the Israelite social world not previously recognized, and his work stimulated new insights into the changing economic and social conditions underlying the literary sources that had been identified by earlier biblical scholars. In particular, he stimulated new ways of looking at the role of Israelite religion in maintaining economic stability and in transforming Israel's economic ideals during times of crisis.

Following these early attempts at reconstructing ancient Israel's social world by appealing to the social sciences, there was a hiatus (until the 1970s) during which biblical scholars turned away from them, although there was continuing interest in the types of questions posed by social scientists. For example, studies by Johannes Pedersen (a 1926–40 psychological study of ancient Israel that included some attention to the nature of Israelite society)[40] and Roland de Vaux (a 1961 study of Israel's social and religious institutions)[41] emphasized the importance of ancient Israel's social institutions, but with little use of sociological methods. De Vaux's study is perhaps the most comprehensive to date in terms of its survey of biblical material, and is still particularly useful as a source for identifying those passages in the Hebrew Bible that relate in some way to the social and religious institutions of ancient Israel. But it is lacking in attention to the possible changes in these institutions over time and the social processes associated with change. Hermann Gunkel's emphasis at the turn of the twentieth century on identifying the *Sitz im Leben* of literary genres was continued by other scholars[42] throughout this period and is still an important aspect of form-critical studies today. After Gunkel, however, there was increasing emphasis on identifying the social settings of the *language* used in biblical texts, with little attention given to the social roles that these genres played in Israelite life as a whole. Other examples of important early studies that emphasized social organization are those by Adolphe Lods[43] and Antonin Causse. The works of Albrecht Alt and his student Martin Noth,[44] who is particularly known for his hypothesis that in early Israel the tribes were organized in an amphictyonic cultic league, and W. F. Albright[45] also attest to a continued interest in trying to reconstruct the social organization of ancient Israel. But their work was not markedly informed by sociological method or theory either.

The move away from direct dependence on the methods of anthropology and sociology for reconstructing ancient Israelite social history was a consequence of a number of interacting factors. Among these were an increasing attention to archaeological material, a move toward greater concern with theological questions, and a recognition that the works of the early advocates of social-scientific approaches shared the weaknesses of the contemporary anthropological and sociological research on which they depended.

Interest in applying social-scientific theories was nevertheless kept alive by a few biblical scholars concerned with reconstructing Israel's religion. Perhaps the most prominent were those associated with the controversial British Myth and Ritual School founded by S. H. Hooke. This "school" was influenced particularly by the notion of "patterns" of culture proposed by anthropologist A. M. Hocart.[46] In agreement with diffusionist theories popular at the time, Hooke and others in the Myth and Ritual School asserted that culture change is the product of cultural contact rather than evolution and, thus, that the common ritual pattern they claim to have identified throughout the Near East had diffused from one cultural center.

Other studies predating the 1970s treated the subjects of social, political, and religious offices, practices, and institutions, but little attention was given to reconstructing their cultural contexts. Biblical scholars have now come generally to recognize the importance of relating the literature of the Hebrew Bible to its varied social contexts, and of applying social scientific approaches and theories to this end. This is related to the growing awareness that this literature was shaped by social, religious, and ideological factors that were influenced by social forces as well as by the historical phenomena that were emphasized in the past. The availability of a wider range of social-scientific data and approaches combined with attention to methodological rigor has contributed to generating new theories with the potential of opening up new perspectives on biblical material. An especially significant development in recent studies is the emphasis on the importance of diachronic and processual studies for understanding culture and society, an orientation that is necessary for understanding both the nature of the biblical literature and the sociocultural contexts that underlie it.

The social-scientific approach as it is now applied in biblical studies is represented by different methodological currents. These studies appeal, for example, to sociological and anthropological models of nomadism, tribalism, and state formation. Advances in archaeological theory have contributed to these developments by giving more attention to the use of ethnographic analogies (ethnoarchaeology and ethnohistory) and to such factors as settlement patterns and means of subsistence.

A number of the studies cited in this book are *functionalist* in orientation. The major source of the functionalist tradition in anthropology and sociology is the work of Émile Durkheim,[47] whose writings influenced A. R. Radcliffe-Brown and Branislaw Malinowski,[48] who are particularly identified with this approach to studying culture. Essentially, the premise of functionalism is that the *parts* of any cultural system must be understood in relation to one another and to the overall structure of the system as a whole. Radcliffe-Brown in particular saw parts of the cultural system (for example, religious practices, belief structures, mechanisms for dealing with conflict) as contributing to the maintenance or perpetuation of the system, assuming that social systems, like organisms, have a tendency toward equilibrium. Conflict is often considered by functionalists to be a natural element in a society's development, resolving itself within the modified but coherently "functioning" unity. *Conflict models* (associated, for example, with Karl Marx and Max Weber),[49] on the other hand, tend to view social structure and change as related to the ways in which different groups within a society pursue their own interests, emphasizing the conflicts among different worldviews and ideologies rather than accepting the functionalist view of society as a self-maintaining organism. The distinction maintained between these two approaches, which was important in sociological theory in past years, is now more blurred, and some reconstructions of ancient Israelite society have incorporated both.

Functionalism enjoyed great prominence in the field of anthropology until the last two decades, but as an approach in and of itself it is now considered by many anthropologists to be problematic. This has essentially to do with the fact that it has a built-in bias of treating societies as if they were closed systems existing at only one historical moment. Because the theoretical frameworks of functionalism are static, they are difficult to correlate with the processes associated with transition and change. This limitation is particularly apparent when functionalist theory is applied to complex, historically known societies such as ancient Israel. Whatever its shortcomings as social theory, however, it is still considered useful as a practical framework for organizing research because it encourages viewing societies in their totality and identifying interrelations among kinship, myths, politics, economics, and other aspects of social life.

Another approach that has played a part in recent developments in social-scientific approaches to reconstructing ancient Israelite society is the ***historical cultural materialist approach*** (or techno-environmental/techno-economic) of anthropologists such as Marvin Harris and some French neo-Marxists.[50] This approach, advocated in biblical studies especially by Norman Gottwald, developed in part as a reaction against structural functionalism and its inability to account for social change. The emphasis is on relating social forms to their roots in a society's economy and environment and the role of economy, environment, and technology as important factors in social change.

The interdisciplinary *la longue durée* approach of the French Annales school of social and economic history, associated particularly with Fernand Braudel,[51] has been considered in recent years to be a particularly useful one among Near Eastern archaeologists. The emphasis in this school is on generalization and searching for broad insights without regard for the kind of "disciplinary territorialism" that is often allowed to control analysis. The *longue durée* approach is considered particularly suitable to archaeological research.[52]

Some recent studies have focused on *institutional* aspects of ancient Israelite social life, looking at offices or roles and administrative structures represented or implied in biblical texts, often with attention to other ancient Near Eastern parallels or broader comparisons from anthropological and sociological studies. Such studies are similar to, but more sophisticated from a methodological standpoint than, those of earlier scholars such as Albright and Alt.

Many social-scientific analyses of ancient Israel consider particular historical periods. The period that has received the most attention is the enigmatic *transition from the Late Bronze Age to Iron Age I.* Both the controversy over the reasons for the substantial increase in settlements in the hill country of Palestine and the recognition that Martin Noth's amphictyonic hypothesis inadequately explained the organization of the tribes have contributed to a growing interest in appealing to social scientific models for possible insights.

Recent social-scientific methods and theories have also been applied to interpreting the social world of the *early Israelite monarchy.* Studies focusing on the rise of kingship and the state have used anthropological theories and models on state formation to reconstruct this transitional period in Israel's history, during which tribal organization began to move toward state organization and the establishment of kingship. The transition is examined in light of cultural evolution and social anthropological descriptions of the processes involved in succession to high office. Factors such as kinship, politics, religion, and economics and their contributions to the rise of monarchy are considered. Archaeological information and literary images are illuminated with comparative anthropological studies, and constructing *models* for using and interpreting various types of information is important in some of these recent studies. Of primary import in these studies is the recognition that factors internal to the social world of ancient Israel may have played, in the adoption of a state form of sociopolitical organization, a role equal to, if not more significant than, such external forces as the Philistine threat emphasized in the biblical narratives.

The period of the *divided monarchy* is not well represented among the recent studies with social-scientific orientations, perhaps because the texts that deal with this period are generally believed to contain more accurate historical information, and thus have not drawn the same amount of attention as the transitional periods at the beginning and end of Iron Age I. This relative lack of representation may also have to do with the fact that there is little theory available that is appropriate for analyzing small, village-based states like Israel and Judah.

The social world of the *Persian period,* on the other hand, is receiving more attention. This may, again, be due to a relative lack of biblical information relating directly to this period. In any case, there are a number of recent studies that focus on such issues as ethnic identity, social organization, religion, demography, and the status of women.

In addition to studies associated with particular periods and transitions, there are a number of useful studies that focus on particular subjects such as the institution of prophecy, women's roles, social and religious movements, and types of leadership.

Although it is clear that the social-scientific approach has now been accepted as a valid approach that is making valuable contributions to our understanding of the social world of the ancient Israelites, it has not avoided criticism.[53] One criticism is that social science models and theories are often used uncritically, with the result that their conclusions are reductionist, explaining that which is complex in overly simplistic terms. Some have also fallen into the trap of treating models and theories as if they were *data* for ancient Israel, rather than as hypothetical entities, as a way of filling in the gaps in the existing sources. Other studies are criticized for their tendency to use jargonistic language that is unfamiliar to many biblical scholars; their tendency to deal with such a broad range of factors at such an abstract and theoretical level that it is difficult to relate them to specific events and peoples; their tendency to be determinist in their assumptions that history unfolds in a predictable manner that is largely dependent on environmental factors; and their assumptions that specific events and individual initiative are only incidental in the broad sweep of social change.

Each of these criticisms is to some extent valid in relation to particular individual studies, and in some cases the problems they point to are unavoidable. But our response to the criticisms should be to consider them as possible correctives rather than as reasons to abandon the approach altogether.

THE INTERPRETIVE PROCESS

Many levels of interpretation are involved in the task of constructing the social worlds and processes of any ancient society. Each of these requires a unique background and set of skills on the part of the interpreters. Each step in the interpretive process is crucial to the shape of the historian's conclusions, and most historians must depend in a number of ways on the interpretations of others. Interpretation at a number of levels, then, has already occurred before social-scientific models and theories are applied. Before using literary sources, for example, translating the languages is a necessary first step. Already at this level interpretation comes into play, influenced by the translator's assumptions and biases. Because language is always implicit and subject to interpretation, translations of words do not necessarily provide us with their full meanings within their original cultural contexts. Thus, it is always necessary to postulate meanings.[54] It should come as no surprise that written texts from the distant past pose particularly great difficulties, with a high risk of misunderstanding their meanings, in large part because of their temporal and cultural distance, but also because our knowledge of the languages in which they are written will always be incomplete. The deficiencies in our abilities to grasp fully the meaning of ancient languages are exacerbated by other problems connected with the texts being interpreted and a lack of knowledge about the authors' background assumptions and intentions, and about the contexts or purposes of texts (which must be reconstructed hypothetically).

Another level in the interpretive process involves identifying the literary conventions and genres of ancient texts and how these relate to both their cultural-historical and literary contexts. Ultimately, the way in which a text is classified will determine how we read it and how we determine its value as a source of historical and cultural information. Related to these issues is trying to understand the author's intentions and the possibility that the text was intended to persuade, conceal, or otherwise deceive the reader in some way, or that it was intended to have more than one meaning.

At yet another level in the interpretive process is determining the place and role of a particular text or set of texts in the overall development of the whole. This task is further complicated when there is more than one version to consider. This necessitates considering how the versions are related to each other and whether one or another is more reliable as a source of historical and cultural information.

Material remains must also be interpreted. As Ian Hodder has noted, "It is . . . one of the central paradoxes of archaeology that the objects dug up are concrete and real things, yet it is so difficult to ascribe any meaning to them."[55] There are also many levels in the process associated with interpreting them. Interpretation takes place, for example, in the choices made about what sites to excavate and what portions of those sites to excavate, about what kinds of information to record in the field books and computer databases and what kinds of material to send off to specialists for analysis, in the reports written by the excavators and specialists, and in the choices made about what reports to consult in resolving a particular historical problem. Interpretation is greatly affected, therefore, by the question of who makes what decisions in what context. Certain objects or places, for example, may be considered important for one interpreter and not worth bothering about by others.

As is the case with textual interpretation, the assumptions and biases of the interpreters will ultimately influence the conclusions they draw. Our understanding of past culture always has its context in the present. In some cases, politics and ideologies can have a significant influence on how archaeological materials and their relation to literary sources are evaluated. Ian Hodder points to the importance many political leaders often attach to legitimizing their positions through the "evidence" of the past. In some cases this has involved conscious manipulation of the past for national political ends. In some cases the archaeological "evidence" of cultural continuity, as opposed to discontinuity, may make a difference to indigenous land claims or the right of access to a site or region.[56]

Conclusions will also vary according to the interpreters' theoretical orientations. Archaeologists, like scholars in any other discipline, are influenced in their interpretations by the received wisdom of their times, both in the sorts of classificatory schemes they consider appropriate to their subject, and in the way the dating of their material is affected by their assumptions about the capabilities of the people concerned. Nowhere is archaeological explanation immune to changes in interpretive fashion.[57] Syro-Palestinian archaeologists in general have not moved significantly beyond the "New Archaeology" of the 1960s in terms of theory. This "school," in which positivism, functionalism, ecological adaptationism, systems theory, and unilinear evolutionism were emphasized, has recently been described as "an intellectual embarrassment in the history of archaeology,"[58] particularly because of its rejection of historical method. Its primary enduring contributions to archaeology are mainly its attention to research design and quantitative methods. And many Syro-Palestinian archaeologists still depend heavily on comparing archaeological remains with the "history" presented in the Bible. But the wide variety of theoretical orientations developed in the last two decades (postmodern, structural, poststructural, structural-symbolic, post-processual, material culture studies[59]) are sure to have an impact on the way archaeological evidence is interpreted in the future. The recent trend toward the crumbling of boundaries between disciplines is also affecting the way archaeologists evaluate the material remains of the past.

Whatever the nature of the sources being used, the historian's primary aim is to reconstruct the human past as accurately as possible. But despite the *ideal* of objectivity, the relationship between the available material and the variety of aims and interests of the interpreter necessarily involves subjectivity and creativity on the interpreter's part. Historians' choices about what is significant are crucial, as is the kind of history being written. These choices may reflect wider interests than simply constructing an accurate picture of history—any political, social, economic, or religious history is likely to be colored by the historian's own views on politics, society, economics, or religion. But, fortunately, this does not have to be viewed negatively, if we accept that viewing the past from different perspectives and engaging in constructive debate can contribute in a positive way to our understanding.

METHODS AND MODELS

> Social world studies do not offer a single method or theory in the usual sense of the term. Their dependence on standard methodologies, archaeology, and comparative sociology make them derivative and eclectic in ways that defy methodological purity. They comprise an approach—in fact, many approaches. These seek to illumine hidden and overlooked information in ancient material and written sources. This means, in effect, that they endeavor to formulate hypotheses and to understand less known ancient societies by illuminating them with comparative information from better known ancient and modern societies.

> The "better knowns" are drawn from general and theoretical social studies, from ethnographies of societies with ecologies similar to those in the ancient world. . . . They [social world studies] rest on the assumption that knowledge of history requires imagination, but disciplined imagination, and that critical thinking is aided and made less arbitrary by integrating archaeology, literatures, and cross-cultural comparisons.[60]

As is suggested in this definition, there is no general agreement among scholars about which social-scientific models are particularly relevant for use in reconstructing ancient Israelite society; nor is there necessarily any agreement on how they should be used. The use of models as a means of illuminating the ancient information has become an essential element in studies of ancient Israelite society, particularly in trying to understand the relationship between various types of information.

The debates regarding appropriate versus inappropriate methods are complicated by the fact that the word "model" can be understood and used in a number of different ways. Sometimes it refers to an explicit use of a carefully defined research practice or taxonomy, sometimes to a rather flexible use of sociohistorical categories, sometimes simply to the unidentified presuppositions of the interpreter.[61] And some scholars feel that models have too often been anachronistically applied, imposing modern sociological categories uncritically on the ancient information.

There are, of course, limitations imposed by using models. The most obvious is that, once within the model's terms of reference, it is difficult to consider other issues or viewpoints. On the positive side, however, a model forces us to be methodical and to be conscious of the fact that we do have a viewpoint.

Among the other potential problems associated with model building is the danger of becoming fixated on particular models, especially in terms of trying to force the data to fit the model. Unless one is able freely and deliberately to choose between models, one is not in control of them. Models should have the effect of expanding, rather than inhibiting, the interpreter's sense of the possible in research. Not only must the interpreter apply a model in a self-critical way, but he or she must expect constant refinement and updating of available models.[62]

Other problems inherent in attempting to reconstruct any ancient society, including ancient Israel, have to do with the nature of our sources and how to categorize and integrate them. As Gottwald[63] has noted, it is important to consider not only the nature and scope of the various kinds of evidence we have, but also how far the evidence goes in providing a picture of the elements and dynamics of a society, how the different types of evidence are read—both on their own terms and in conjunction with other types of evidence, and how the different kinds of evidence are brought together to form a composite picture of the society. Particularly at points where the textual and archaeological information are insufficient or contradictory, it is necessary to hypothesize through the use of models. And the model or models a particular interpreter uses will affect the conclusions he or she draws. A related factor is the range of the interpreter's skills. Because each type of evidence requires particular kinds of methodological skills, it is necessary for the interpreter to become conversant in a number of different methodologies. Engaging in this type of research necessitates crossing over traditional disciplinary boundaries, so scholars at home in one set of skills must learn how to read the evidence sifted and the hypotheses generated by other sets of skills.[64]

One of the problems it is necessary to consider in the research process is how to relate different types of ancient information, especially when they appear to be contradictory. This involves, first, decisions along the way that relate to gathering, sorting, and interpreting information within the appropriate discipline according to the specific questions being raised. The second step is to attempt to integrate the separate conclusions in a reconstruction.[65] A partial solution to dealing with information that appears to be contradictory is simply to recognize, as anthropologists do, that in all societies there is often a distinction between people's "notions" (related to an ideational system) and their "actions" (related, for example, to social structure)—that is, what people *say* they do is not necessarily the same thing they *actually* do. What people say about the way things are is not necessarily, in reality, the way they are.[66] An example of this distinction can be seen in the way in which segmentary lineage structure is conceptualized in tribal societies.[67] Segmentary lineage structure as it is constructed by anthropologists is not a model that members of such societies necessarily use in actual political processes, but an ideology or representation of what they perceive as being an enduring form of their society. Such lineage ideologies are by nature flexible. Assertions of lineage structures and relationships assume invariance and uniformity in the makeup and relations of different units, but in reality allow for and tolerate internal differentiation, cohesion, and development, as well as rationalizations of departure from them, depending on circumstances. This raises the question, then, of whether cultural constructs like genealogies reflect what really happens in a society, or whether they rather reflect more accurately what people think, hope, or want others to think happens.

James W. Flanagan proposes a "holographic" interpretive model for understanding the relationships among different types of evidence. In this model he assigns textual and literary studies primary responsibility for ancient information from the domain of *notions* and archaeology responsibility for the physical/material world and the ancient domain of *actions*.[68] This is not, of course, a hard-and-fast distinction, as actions do reflect notions—archaeology does yield information about notions, ideologies, and symbols; and stories are sometimes set in actual physical time and space, and therefore provide us with information about actions. But the distinction, he argues, is nevertheless useful for analytical purposes. In this proposed model, comparative sociology illuminates the relationship between these domains and the worlds behind them.

Comparative approaches have been the subject of some criticism. The dangers inherent in using such approaches for reconstructing history and society are well known. In a recent study of ancient Israelite religion and early Judaism, Howard Eilberg-Schwartz points to several traditional perspectives within biblical studies from which comparative inquiry is viewed with skepticism.[69] "Contextualists" tend to argue that cross-cultural comparisons are problematic because religious concepts or customs that are *perceived* as being similar *actually* have different meanings and purposes in different religions. Proponents of this perspective assume that cultures or religions must be understood *on their own terms* and *in their own context,* and assert that contextualist and comparative models of cultural interpretation are essentially incompatible. Comparative inquiry, it is argued, extracts cultural elements from their contexts, distorting their meanings, functions, or character. In response to such assertions, Eilberg-Schwartz asks whether this problem is by definition intrinsic to comparative inquiry and suggests that, in theory, comparativists today are more likely than their predecessors to take account of the larger cultural contexts of the elements being interpreted.[70] He concludes that this approach is no more problematic than others and that a pure ethnography or history that is uncontaminated by generalizations based on comparative inquiry is an ideal that cannot exist in practice.[71]

Diffusionists, although they *do* engage in a type of comparative method, are skeptical of similarities between cultures that cannot be explained in terms of diffusion. According to S. Talmon, the general principle applied is that "Comparison can be applied to societies which lie in the same 'historical stream' as biblical Israel," but that "Comparisons on the 'grand scale' are best avoided."[72] Talmon further argues that comparison with other societies should be undertaken only *after* considering all of the relevant biblical material.[73] But in making such an argument, Talmon succumbs to the type of circular reasoning of which Philip Davies is so critical—constructing a cultural and historical reality out of a text and then trying to understand the text against that reconstructed background. Comparative analysis is one way of avoiding this type of reasoning.

Other problems to which skeptics of the comparative approach point include: the dangers inherent in adopting ethnological models from a discipline in which the average biblical scholar is essentially an amateur;[74] the fact that primary data, which themselves require interpretive sophistication, are not amenable to simplistic cross-disciplinary theoretical treatments;[75] or problems associated with the uncertainty and multiplicity of meanings in the biblical texts themselves, which undermine straightforward application of social theory.[76] Patching together scattered bits of texts in order to construct patterns that match comparative models, described as a "case of too much theory chasing too little data," has also been cited as a way in which comparative inquiry has been abused.[77]

From quite a different perspective, Edmund Leach is suspicious of cross-cultural comparisons based on social organizations, and rejects their utility as a historical tool. Classifying things according to type and subtype is, in his estimation, comparable to "collecting butterflies,"[78] that is, almost useless, because the possibilities for human diversity are limitless.

To disregard completely the comparative approach in studying ancient culture is to engage in what Eilberg-Schwartz refers to as "Parallel-anoia."[79] Regardless of the problems it poses, comparative inquiry provides new ways of thinking about issues for which traditional approaches are ill equipped. It offers new models and theoretical insights for thinking about Israelite practices and beliefs. Awareness of the potential problems associated with engaging in comparative analysis, and acknowledgment that comparative information cannot be used as a substitute for inadequate historical and social data, are certainly important. Temporal and spatial distance militates against drawing definitive conclusion on the basis of comparative information. The symbol systems, for example, of any society, whether ancient or modern, must certainly be interpreted in the overall context of that society's particular situation. But because literary and material remains provide only a fragmentary picture of the lost whole, comparative inquiry and anthropological models and theories are indispensable for interpreting and reconstructing past cultures. We should be careful, however, not to use anthropological material simply to "fill in the gaps" in our knowledge of ancient society.[80]

Reducing complexity by appealing to models and typologies always entails a certain methodological risk, and they should be used with conscious regard for their limitations. It is important to keep in mind at every level of the interpretive process that a "type" or "model" is not "real"—they are hypothetical entities. They should be used to analyze the existing data, not as substitutes for evidence in the absence of data. Neither should data that do not mesh with the model be shoved aside or forced to fit the model. In such cases the interpreter should investigate why it is that the data and the model diverge. Models do *not* provide definitive answers.

There are, in spite of its problems, a number of advantages in approaching the study of ancient Israel from a social-scientific perspective. Comparative inquiry forces implicit assumptions to the surface, providing fresh ways of conceptualizing the relations among the phenomena in question. From anthropology and sociology biblical historians have drawn valuable information on structural and processual forms in other societies that can shed light on the social organization and institutions of ancient Israel and on the religious foundations underlying the biblical texts. Application of the "ideal type" construct—models of social roles and institutions—has helped us to understand more about the nature of such things as prophecy, charismatic leadership, and sects. The "type," which is constituted from a large number of cases, does not correspond exactly to any specific entity, but it sheds light on character and social function. The social sciences also illuminate the sociological dimensions of the interpretive process, providing ways of identifying the origins, transmission, and meanings of texts, and relating these to social roles, social groups, and social structures. They offer analogies from modern and historical societies that help us to interpret the oral traditions underlying the biblical texts and the functions of the literary forms in the Hebrew Bible. The significance of using a social-scientific approach to interpreting ancient Israelite history, therefore, lies *not* in providing further evidence to the biblical scholar—analysis of the text itself and the archaeological information must provide the criteria for supporting, disproving, or modifying hypotheses generated by anthropological material—but rather in introducing tools for analyzing and raising questions about the ancient information and applying theories about the ways in which societies in general are organized and develop. This type of approach provides an important corrective to traditional historical reconstructions that conceive of history as the story of deliberate action on the part of discrete persons or groups of persons. It balances the tendency to concentrate on Israel's political and religious history with attention to economic, social, technological, and other aspects of daily life. It also introduces a stronger concern for the general as well as the specific, for the social world as well as isolated events and single individuals. The complexity of interactions in any society cannot be subsumed under the thoughts and activities of a few individuals. Reconstructing social history involves consideration of the relationships between events and processes as well as the roles of individuals, a concern with the interconnectedness of events and the structure of ideas, values, and social relations. This is particularly important for understanding periods of rapid social change (for example, the rise of monarchy in ancient Israel and periods during and after the Babylonian exile). Although Edmund Leach is perhaps overly pessimistic about the possibilities of reconstructing any of Israel's social history in the periods preceding the exile, his caution that raising detailed historical questions about the Bible contributes to misunderstanding the nature and purpose, and distorting the meaning, of the biblical literature[81] is worth keeping in mind. This is important, as he argues, because the meaning in these sacred texts lies not in the history they may or may not have recorded, but in the use that religious groups have made of them. In this sense, there is no correct interpretation.

At present, there are numerous, often conflicting, theories and hypotheses about the nature and development of ancient Israelite society. We cannot know with any certainty which of these theories and hypotheses are more or less valid. Because historians' interpretations are not scientifically testable assertions, their hypotheses offer plausible explanations, guide further reflection, and are subject to constant revision, but they can never be "true" or "false." As Eilberg-Schwartz has noted, the ancient Israelites themselves would certainly consider our reconstructions bizarre.[82] All we can say with any confidence is that one or another hypothesis or theory seems more or less convincing or adequate in light of the evidence, and that these hypotheses and theories will continue to be reevaluated and adjusted in the future. We must continually question what social explanation (hypothesis/model) makes the most sense of the relevant evidence, at the same time acknowledging that all interpreters approach their object of study with assumptions, dispositions, and tools of analysis that lead them to single out and emphasize particular aspects of their object of study. The reconstructions surveyed here as representative of the direction social-world studies has taken are not comprehensive by any means.

ORGANIZATION

The book is organized chronologically, beginning with the question of the origins of "Israel" and ending with the Persian period. Chapters 2, 4, and to some extent 6 focus on the social processes associated with major transitions in ancient Israel's history (that is, they focus on the diachronic dimension of Israelite society). And chapters 3, 5, and 6 are more synchronic, in the sense that they deal more with identifying and describing social institutions, social structure, and social organization. The material in chapters 3, 5, and 6 is somewhat artificial in the sense that it is presented as if it represents single static moments when all the elements and relationships described existed at the same time, when in fact each of the three periods spans hundreds of years, over which much of what is described must have changed to some extent.

Each of the chapters is introduced with a general overview of the available evidence associated with the period in question. Chapters 2 and 4 focus on discussions of the processual models that have been proposed for these transitional periods. Chapters 3, 5, and 6 are basically organized around the social dimensions of these periods: demography and settlement patterns, economy (subsistence strategies, patterns of labor, systems of exchange and trade, land ownership and distribution of wealth, technology), sociopolitical organization and structure, and social and political institutions (leadership, government, the judicial system, religion).

Chapter 2

Iron Age I

The Origins of Ancient "Israel"

DEFINING "ISRAEL"

The problem of Israel's origins is one that in recent decades has been intensively scrutinized and hotly debated. Who were the earliest "Israelites"? When and why did "Israel" come into being? Where did the Iron Age I settlers of the Palestinian highlands come from—geographically, socially, and ideologically? When did the peoples of ancient Palestine begin to think of themselves as "Israelite"? Was the worship of the god Yahweh integrally related to these peoples' initial self-identification as "Israelites"? Did the designation "Israel" consistently refer to the same entity throughout the Iron Age and subsequent periods? By what criteria did people identify themselves as "Israelite"? What made one an "Israelite," especially in the early period before the establishment of the state? These questions, it is now generally agreed, can no longer be answered adequately by appealing simply to the biblical traditions.

There is a great deal of discussion in recent anthropological literature regarding group definition, particularly in relation to the nature of ethnicity,[1] and this is having a significant impact on the ways in which historians of ancient Palestine are evaluating Israel's origins and development. Most anthropologists would agree that ethnicity involves the creation and maintenance of social boundaries,[2] which are often based on such factors as geographical proximity, common descent (often from a mythical ancestor) or other types of affiliation, common values and religion, shared systems of communication (for example, languages or accents), codes of dress or diet, material symbols, or a combination of these and other factors.

The traditional view of ethnicity, defined somewhat statically as an ascribed affiliation linking groups through common ancestry, and as being essentially synonymous with culture, has been succeeded in recent years by an approach that views ethnic identification as a much more fluid phenomenon, which is responsive to different situations and circumstances. Ethnicity in this view is a flexible label employed by groups of intentioned individuals in diverse contexts, rather than an "objective" fixed component of identity, which is used by individuals seeking to establish and justify social boundaries either for themselves or for others. The "us/them" distinctions that are made in order to establish and justify social boundaries typically have strong political overtones and may be either imposed from outside the group or employed from within. As such, they are subject to reinterpretation as historical realities change, and will have very different implications according to context. In this view, then, notions of ethnicity are *social constructs* that react to modifications in group goals and interests, and are integrally related to a society's more general cultural assumptions about the nature of the social world and social relationships, as well as to the specific historical contexts in which they are maintained, transformed, and reproduced.

Understanding the ways in which ethnic identification is conceptualized even among contemporary groups is a very complex enterprise. In dealing with ancient groups such as "Israel" the complexities are multiplied, because we do not have the option of asking individuals to clarify for us what it is they believe makes them "Israelites," or what "non-Israelites" would identify as the distinguishing characteristics of "Israelites" as opposed to how they conceive of their own identities. Nor can we observe the actions of groups that could provide us with some clues. We must depend on the implicit notions represented in ancient texts and the implied actions behind the material remains that may indicate something about group identity. So we must be careful to recognize that the propositions we make about group differentiation in the ancient world are hypotheses that may be subject to further adjustment. Given the fluid nature of group identification, it is highly likely that the notions about what it meant to be "Israelite" were quite different, for example, in premonarchic Iron Age I than they were during the period of the monarchy or the Persian period. This is something that is now generally recognized among biblical scholars, and has been the subject of a great deal of discussion and debate, particularly in relation to Iron Age I. More attention is now being given to determining the factors that might have shaped Israel's peoplehood and the specific boundary markers by which this people distinguished itself from others in its formative years and later. This shift in the discussion is apparent, for example, in recent studies such as G. W. Ahlström's *Who Were the Israelites?*[3] and Philip R. Davies's *In Search of "Ancient Israel."* Ahlström concludes that the name originally was a label for all peoples of a certain *territory* irrespective of ethnicity, eventually becoming a designation for *national identity,* and later an *ideological* characterization. Davies lists ten ways in which the designation is used in the biblical literature, classifying each according to three possible categories—ethnic, political, and religious (acknowledging that the term is generally used in more than one of these senses simultaneously): (1) as the name of the ancestor Jacob (ethnic); (2) as the name of a sacral league of tribes (ethnic); (3) as a united kingdom with a capital in Jerusalem (political); (4) as the name of the Northern Kingdom after the United Kingdom was divided (political); (5) as another name for Judah after the decline of the Northern Kingdom (political); (6) as a name for the socioreligious community in the Persian province of Yehud after the exile (religious, ethnic); (7) as the name of a group within the postexilic community—the laity as distinct from "Aaron" (ethnic); (8) as a name for the descendants of Jacob/Israel (ethnic); (9) as a premonarchic tribal group in Ephraim (ethnic); and (10) as adherents of various forms of religion (religious).[4]

The problem is particularly acute in dealing with the period preceding the rise of the state, not only for determining what "Israel" was at that point, but also what its relationship was to other local populations, especially those designated as "Canaanites" or "Amorites" in the biblical traditions,[5] where they are identified with a number of different named groups—for example, Hittites, Perizzites, Hivites, Girgashites, and Jebusites. Many archaeologists now argue that there is no clear nonbiblical evidence of ethnic distinctions among these groups or of their being culturally different from other occupants of Palestine. Others argue further that given the lack of evidence it is not possible to identify Israel as a distinct ethnic or cultural entity until after the Israelite state in the northern highlands came into existence, when being Israelite was essentially defined as belonging to a political entity.[6] But even then, according to the biblical stories, "Canaanites" were also residents of the "Israelite" state, so we are still left with the dilemma of what the distinction was based on in the minds of the writers.

Given the ca. 1207 B.C.E. reference to "Israel" in the Merneptah stela, it is probably safe to assume that sometime during Iron Age I a population began to identify itself as "Israelite" through some process of ethnic boundary marking, though it is still not clear what the nature of that entity was. But there are clear signs of a long process of intentional boundary marking on the part of the biblical writers for later periods, represented, for example, in the persistent assertion that Israelites are not Canaanites and should not marry them, and in the emphasis on family history and genealogy and, of course, religion.

The question of how and when religion became part of this process of self-identification has been an important consideration in the discussions of Israel's origins. Once considered the primary basis of Israelite identity, because it is what the biblical texts themselves emphasize, many now maintain that although religion *may* have been an important factor in the early boundary-marking process, at present there is not sufficient evidence outside the Bible to make this argument with much force. The likelihood that the eventual solidarity of the peoples settling in the highland villages was due more to *social* and *economic* than to religious factors, and that Yahwism emerged later, is now emphasized by a growing number of scholars. Ultimately, the factors emphasized by any one scholar, though, will depend on how he or she conceives of the social processes that led to Israel's establishment.

GEOGRAPHY OF ANCIENT PALESTINE

Two important factors in understanding Palestine's history are its strategic location on the trade and military routes of the ancient Near Eastern world and its regional variation. Serving as a kind of land bridge between Egypt to the southwest and Anatolia and Mesopotamia to the north and east, the peoples of Palestine were constantly throughout their history subject to outside influence and often political control. Much of the region was controlled by Egypt during the Late Bronze Age, by Assyria and Babylonia during Iron Age II, by the Persians during the period that is named for them, and in later periods by the Greeks, the Romans, and more recently, the Turkish Ottoman Empire.

The influence of Egypt and Mesopotamia, and other smaller states bordering on Israel and Judah (for example, Aram, Ammon, Moab, and Edom), certainly affected the sociopolitical organization of the Palestinian states as well as their economies. The facilitation of international trade in particular would have entailed diplomatic relations, the establishment of alliances, and often struggles for supremacy among states. Religion also played a role in these interactions, serving as an ideology for legitimating the existing social and political order and for establishing relationships among states. The small states of Israel and Judah were often drawn into diplomacy and warfare, and thus into arenas of conflict between the imperial powers that surrounded them.

The region now generally referred to as Palestine or Israel is the immediate area in which the social history of the ancient Israelites was played out. But it was sometimes known as "Canaan" before the establishment of the states of Israel and Judah, a term that is used inconsistently both in the Bible and in other ancient Near Eastern sources. In second-millennium B.C.E. texts, it seems to refer roughly to the regions of the modern states of Lebanon and Israel. The Bible defines it as the territory east of the Mediterranean, and extending from the "Wadi of Egypt" south of Gaza to central Lebanon in the north (Deut. 34:1–3; Josh. 12:7–8; Ezek. 47:15–20). The northern and eastern limits in the biblical traditions vary, and appear to be idealized, but in general they are the Jordan Rift Valley on the east and the Lebanese Bekaa Valley in the north.

The geography of Palestine is strikingly varied given its relatively small size,[7] with a number of very different ecological niches. Geographically, it has been described as a "meeting place,"[8] where several of the earth's plates meet, three major natural vegetation zones meet, and arid and wet climates meet. These variations would have affected the nature of local settlement and production patterns and supported a broad range of different economies, residential strategies, and lifestyles among the different subregions.

The geographical variations within Palestine include radical changes in terrain, elevation, rainfall and moisture, soil, and vegetation from subregion to subregion. Its relief ranges from a height of +2815 meters on Mt. Hermon to −395 meters at the northern shore of the Dead Sea. Weather patterns also vary considerably from north to south and from the coastal areas to the mountains, valleys, and plateaus. This complex arrangement of microenvironments would have affected the amount of contact among the inhabitants of the different subregions, resulting in a large degree of local autonomy, self-sufficiency, and diversity. Rough terrain, varied soil types, and erratic rainfall distribution also contributed to diverse local and regional adaptations, which, in turn, tended to isolate regions from one another.

Although many different subregions have been identified, there are at least five general geographical zones in Palestine:[9] (1) the coastal plain, (2) the highlands, (3) the Jordan Rift Valley (4), the eastern plateaus of Transjordan, and (5) the Negeb.

The coastal plain extends north to south along the Mediterranean shore from Turkey to the Gaza Strip. Topographically, this region is characterized by beaches and sand dunes interspersed with wetlands. Settlements were typically located inland and, because the Palestinian coast was unsuitable for them, there were no major harbors there until the Roman period (although there is evidence of harbors at Ashkelon, Tel Mor near Ashdod, and Dor). Phoenicia to the north was the chief maritime power in the region because of the availability of good harbors. The primary significance of the coastal plain for Israel was that through it ran the Via Maris ("way of the sea"), one of the two major trade and communication routes. This road parallelled the Mediterranean Sea, extended northward along the Plain of

Sharon, where it turned northeastward and through the highlands to Damascus.

The highlands, occupying most of the territory between the coastal plain to the west and the Jordan Valley to the east, comprise several geomorphological zones and are characterized by a topography consisting of isolated narrow ridges, elevated plateaus, and dissected valleys and basins. Ecologically, the northern and southern portions of the central highlands differ significantly. The northern region of Samaria, with its hills separated by large valleys, relatively moderate topography, and comparatively fertile eastern steppe, was more amenable to human settlement than was the case for the Judean hills, whose harsh rock formations and steppe areas to the east and south were not conducive to agricultural activity. The ecological disparities resulted in demographic and settlement differences. Northern Samaria was more densely settled, with larger sites and very little evidence for nonsedentary activity. In contrast, the Judean hills were sparsely inhabited by sedentary peoples until Iron Age II, being more suitable for supporting pastoral groups. These ecological and demographic differences are also believed to have affected the nature of the political entities that developed in Iron Age II.

The Jordan Rift Valley is part of a rift system that extends north into Syria and south through the Red Sea and into eastern Africa. It includes the Sea of Galilee in the north (elevation −209 meters) and the Dead Sea (elevation −395 meters) and Arabah Valley to south.

Geologically, Transjordan, the region located to the east of the Rift Valley, is, in most areas, a continuation of the highlands west of the rift. Its western boundary is sharply delineated by escarpments, and to the east the plateau slopes gradually toward the Syrian desert. Wadis running perpendicular to the rift flow westward into it, some depositing large alluvial fans at the base of the escarpment. The other major communication route, the King's Highway, ran through the Transjordanian plateau from Damascus in the north to the Gulf of Aqaba in the south.

The Negeb is an extremely arid region extending south of the highlands as far as the Gulf of Aqaba. Geomorphologically, it is diverse, particularly from east to west. The eastern portion of this zone is defined by the Arabah Valley. North and east of the Gulf of Aqaba the landscape is rugged, with high angle slopes. To the north is a plateau that is mostly flat and slopes gently to the northwest. Midway between the Gulf of Aqaba and the Mediterranean, in the central Negeb, is a region of hills, and between these hills and the Mediterranean is a plain. The Negeb is what has been referred to as the "pioneer fringe" of Palestine, that is, a region of marginal resources and unreliable precipitation.

The general climate in Palestine has probably not changed significantly since around 6 or 7000 B.C.E., although it is subject to fluctuation. There are essentially two seasons—a wet season and a dry season—with two brief transitional seasons from September to mid-October and mid-April to the end of May. Conditions are more conducive to agriculture in the northern highlands, which are higher in elevation and rainfall (approximately 1,000 mm of rain per year), and temperatures are cooler. Accumulation of precipitation in the highlands is also significantly higher than on the coastal plains on average. Rainfall in Judah is typically lower and less regular than in the northern highlands (an average of 550 mm per year in Jerusalem). In general, rainfall decreases from west to east and from north to south. But the rainfall patterns are not consistent from year to year, and this very likely contributed to the changing patterns of settlement, particularly in the south, that have been identified in the archaeological record.

Agricultural patterns, including the types of crops planted in the various regions and the times of planting and harvesting, are dependent on precipitation. Water distribution was also one of the major determining factors in locating settlements. The most significant aquifers and springs occur in the hill country, particularly in the north. This may have been an important factor in favoring settlement in the highlands over the coastal plains in some periods.

A number of different soil types also occur in Palestine. Along with amount of rainfall, soil types affect the agricultural patterns in the different regions. Sandy alluvial soils characterize the coastal regions. There are four general soil types that occur in the highlands. Terra rossa soils, which support a wide range of crops, are particularly productive when they are located in areas that allow for the accumulation of humus. Otherwise, they are shallow and clayey, conditions under which cultivation is difficult. In the highlands, these latter soils could be productively farmed only by constructing terraces. Medium-brown forest soils are similar to, but not as rich as, terra rossa soils. Rendzina soil types are poorer in organic matter than terra rossa and medium-brown forest soils, but are more permeable and less susceptible to erosion. A fourth type of soil found in the highlands consists of brown basaltic soils. These soils, found primarily in the eastern parts of Galilee, are clayey in texture, and are normally fairly shallow, with minimal amounts of organic matter, and thus are relatively unproductive. The most productive soil types are the terra rossa, medium-brown, and alluvial soils.

Although the distribution of soil types is fairly complicated, in general the Judean highlands are composed of terra rossa and medium-brown forest soils, but contain some areas of less productive soils, particularly to the south and east, where there are relatively infertile desert soils (except in the wadi beds running into the Dead Sea). The northern highlands are composed primarily of terra rossa soils, with some areas of medium brown forest soils and rendzina-type soils. As is noted above, portions of Galilee are composed of the less productive brown basaltic soils.

Soil salinity is another factor that affects agricultural productivity. The soils in the highlands are for the most part free of salinity; soils in the plains regions tend to have moderate salinity; and the soils in the Negeb, parts of the Judean wilderness, and the lower Jordan Valley are fairly high in salinity.

The distribution of agricultural sites appears to have correlated with soil types. Those with the longest histories of settlement are associated with a variety of soil types, allowing for a diversity of crops and minimalizing the risk of crop failure.

Although the climate in Palestine appears to have changed little in the past eight thousand to nine thousand years, the landscape has undergone significant modification as a result of human activity. The change is particularly pronounced in what had at one time been forested areas, but where scrub vegetation is now prevalent. The major human causes of deforestation included cutting wood for use as fuel and in industry (for example, the production of metals required large amounts of wood), animal grazing, and clearing forest areas for agricultural purposes. This process of forest degradation probably began as early as the Neolithic period. As early as the Middle Bronze Age the forested slopes in the highlands were being replaced with terraces.

THE ORIGINS OF ANCIENT "ISRAEL"

Although there are many who would disagree, Iron Age I—the so-called tribal period or period of the Judges—is now generally recognized as the earliest possible period to which Israel's origins may be traceable. The working assumption is that peoples living in the region that eventually became Israel did not begin to form any kind of identity as a distinctive social entity called Israel until, at the very earliest, sometime during—and most likely toward the end of—Iron Age I. Although there is a growing consensus that Israel as a national phenomenon did not exist until the process of centralization had begun toward the end of Iron Age I, or even later,[10] there are some indications in the biblical texts that traditions from an earlier period (presumably associated with groups that eventually identified themselves with Israel), have been preserved and incorporated into the later national traditions (for example, Judges 5).[11] For that reason, along with the fact that "Israel," whatever entity it may refer to, is mentioned in the ca. 1207 B.C.E.

Merneptah stela, I begin my discussion of ancient Israelite society not with the Middle Bronze Age (a period in the past associated with the ancestral traditions), but with the transition from the Late Bronze Age to Iron Age I.

The Bible and the Origins of Ancient Israel

The biblical texts present us with an especially complex puzzle when it comes to determining their value for reconstructing how Israel came into being. According to the traditions in Genesis, God was actively involved in, and ultimately responsible for, the creation of the people Israel. This active intervention began with a promise to Abraham, a promise that was passed down through succeeding generations and finally fulfilled following the liberation of Abraham's descendants from their bondage in Egypt, as related in the books of Exodus, Leviticus, Numbers, and Deuteronomy. The book of Joshua describes this fulfillment as having occurred through a series of successful military campaigns against the local Canaanites in the hill country of Palestine, under Joshua's leadership. Once the Canaanites had been defeated and the land distributed among the twelve tribes, "Israel" was born.

Until the last several decades, historians of ancient Israel have tended to begin their accounts of Israel's history with the so-called "ancestral" or "patriarchal" period, dated variously to Middle Bronze I (ca. 2000–1750 B.C.E.), Middle Bronze II (ca. 1750–1550), or the early part of the Late Bronze Age (ca. 1550–1200). Underlying these histories is an assumption that the traditions recorded in the book of Genesis about Abraham and his descendants, those in the remainder of the Pentateuch about Moses and the exodus from Egypt, and those in Joshua and Judges about the conquest and settlement preserve some historical evidence of a period preceding the birth of Israel as a nation at the end of the early Iron Age. But it is now generally recognized that there is nothing specific in the Genesis stories that can be definitively related to known history in or around Canaan in the early second millennium B.C.E., and that there is, in fact, no solid evidence for any date. None of the kings mentioned is known from other sources. The identification of Abimelech as king of the Philistines could not be historically accurate, as the Philistines did not arrive in Palestine until much later in the second millennium. The pharaoh who enlists Joseph into his services is anonymous. Abraham is identified as coming from "Ur of the Chaldeans," but the Babylonians were not known as Chaldeans until a much later time. Laban is identified as an Aramaean, but there is no evidence that the Arameans were an identifiable political entity before the twelfth century B.C.E.

Attempts were also made in earlier historical reconstructions to relate the customs portrayed in the ancestral stories to those in texts from, for example, Nuzi (fifteenth to fourteenth centuries B.C.E.) and Mari (ca. 1800). But these have ultimately proved to be unconvincing, as there is ample evidence now that many of these customs were pervasive in the ancient Near East for hundreds of years, well into Iron Age II. And because the final editing of these traditions took place many centuries after the events they purport to relate, it becomes very difficult to judge whether, or how much of, the social world they portray reflects an early period in Israel's history.

The question of how the biblical account of the exodus from Egypt relates to the emergence of Israel is the subject of some debate. Some still maintain that there *might* be a historical core, or some kind of vague historical memory, in the Moses traditions, and others argue that they are completely fictional. But, again, there is no extrabiblical evidence that has established any historical correlations with the biblical texts. Given the nature of traditional stories in other societies, it is possible that many of the traditions about Moses' leadership were intended to legitimate certain offices and functions in later Israel. And it is worth noting that many peoples claim historical migrations in their origin stories, even those for whom the available evidence strongly suggests an indigenous origin.

In any case, it is now widely agreed that the so-called "patriarchal/ancestral period" is a later *literary* construct, not a period in the actual history of the ancient world. The same is the case for the "exodus" and the "wilderness period," and more and more widely for the "period of the Judges."

The constructs of ancient Israel's consolidation as a people and a "national" entity are represented primarily in the books of Joshua and Judges, part of the so-called Deuteronomic History (Deuteronomy, Joshua, Judges, 1 and 2 Samuel, 1 and 2 Kings), which traces Israel's "history" from the "conquest" of Canaan to the Babylonian exile.[12]

In its present form, the Deuteronomic History is the product of the end of the monarchic period at the very earliest. It is clear that the editors of this portion of the Hebrew Bible were looking back at Israel's history from a perspective colored by the events of their own times, writing a "history" that must have been aimed primarily at coming to terms with their current situation and articulating their sense of identity in that situation, particularly in relation to the exilic experience. This is apparent in the repeated emphasis on the rebellious nature of the Israelites from the time Joshua led them into the land to the time they were led off into exile by the Babylonians, and the repeated exhortations that obedience to God's commandments would lead to blessings, whereas disobedience would result in punishment or curse.

Although there is a general consensus that the "history" recorded in these traditions cannot be taken at face value, there is nevertheless a broad spectrum of opinion regarding the extent to which they can be regarded as preserving accurate social and historical information. In spite of the obviously imposed structure in the Deuteronomic History, the optimists argue that its editors nevertheless preserved older chronicles and popular stories, although they would have taken on new meanings in their present literary contexts. They agree that there are problems with getting at the information that may be valid, but for them the major problem is determining what criteria should be used for sorting this information from that which derives from later periods. Those who are more skeptical, although often granting that there may be some early traditions in the Bible, contend that these can be retrieved only through evaluating them against extrabiblical textual and archaeological information.

The books of Joshua and Judges played an important role in earlier interpretations of ancient Israel's origins. In the book of Joshua, Joshua first leads the united tribes of Israel in the conquest of the highlands in three swift and decisive campaigns (Joshua 1–12), emphasizing an almost total extermination of the local Canaanite population. Some of these traditions (particularly those recounting the destruction of Jericho and Ai) are believed now to be etiologies deriving from later periods when those towns were in ruins. In the remainder of the book (Joshua 13–24) Joshua divides the conquered land among the tribes. This section of the book consists largely of a series of lists containing inventories of the territorial holdings of the tribes, with some scattered accounts of battles, seizures, or occupations of cities and regions, and—contrary to chapters 1–12—failure to expel some of the Canaanites. The subject of each of these stories is a single tribe (not the united Israel of Joshua 1–12). The book ends with a narrative recounting an assembly of tribes and a covenant ceremony at Shechem, over which Joshua presides.

Judges 1 depicts the military and political struggles either of individual tribes or of two tribes collaborating to gain control over the hill country. In contrast to Joshua 1–12, Judges 1 describes both the successes and failures of individual tribes in displacing the Canaanites, challenging the oversimplified view of rapid conquest in Joshua 1–12. The emphasis is on the tribe of Judah, which is portrayed as having been successful in taking possession of its allotted land, in contrast to the northern tribes, who failed to gain control over theirs and were not able to expel the Canaanites. The chapter ends with reference to the people giving in to the temptations of idolatry, thus beginning the formalistic cycle of apostacy, punishment, deliverance, and judgment repeated throughout the book. The general picture in this chapter is of a partial conquest by independent clans and tribes, without a national leader or any kind of all-inclusive tribal unity.

Information from Extrabiblical Literary Sources

There is very little in the way of textual material dating to this period that can help us sort out the problem of who the early Israelites were or where they came from. The few potentially relevant sources date to the Late Bronze Age and are difficult to assess in terms of their direct relatedness to ancient Israel's emergence. One of these is the Merneptah stela, a monument viewed by many as the key to dating the arrival of the Israelites in Canaan. In the long run, however, this monument has ended up being one of those pieces of evidence that raises a number of interesting questions but thus far has not provided any definitive answers. The stela (discovered at Thebes and now dated to ca. 1207 B.C.E.) is a monument that recounts the military exploits of the Egyptian pharaoh Merneptah and contains the earliest known reference to "Israel" ("Israel is laid waste, its seed is not"), which is included in a list of conquered peoples.

At one time it was assumed that the reference is evidence for dating the "conquest" of Canaan as described in the book of Joshua to a time before Merneptah's campaigns in Syro-Palestine. But if we accept the argument that the stories in Joshua are a later fiction, and are thus not representative of Israel at the beginning of Iron Age I, we are left with the question of what is meant by "Israel." Although there seems to be little doubt that Merneptah's Israel was located somewhere in Palestine, the reference does not make clear exactly what kind of entity is being referred to. The problem stems from the determinative that occurs in connection with the word "Israel" and identifies it not as a nation or a city-state (as is the case, for example, for Ashkelon, Gezer, and Yanoam) or even as a group that is associated with any particular land (as is the case in the reference to Canaan), but simply as a people.

There are a number of ways in which the reference has been interpreted.[13] Some have proposed that Merneptah's Israel was a *socioethnic or sociopolitical entity* in Canaan,[14] some that it consisted of a *territory* within Canaan,[15] and some that it was *both* a *people* and a *territory* within Canaan.[16] And some argue that it was a *nomadic tribal entity,*[17] and yet others that it was *sedentary.*[18]

Another issue relates to the term *prt,* "seed," in the reference, which is variously understood as referring either to Israel's "descendants/offspring" or to its "grain." If it means the former, it could refer to either a settled group or a nomadic one. If it means the latter, it may indicate Israel's food supply, implying that Israel was some type of sedentary agricultural society.[19]

The Merneptah stela, then, provides us with evidence that some entity called Israel existed in the latter part of the thirteenth century B.C.E., but at present it provides no clear answer to the question of what that entity was, what its size or internal organization was, what the sources and socioeconomic status of its members were, or how, or even if, this "Israel" is related to the Israel depicted in the stories in the Pentateuch or the books of Joshua and Judges.

A related Egyptian source is a series of reliefs from a temple at Karnak that possibly illustrates the military successes of Merneptah.[20] Some of the panels have been interpreted as representing Canaanite cities mentioned in the Merneptah stela, and two have been identified as possibly depicting "Israelites." But this interpretation is still debated and thus, again, we are left with interesting questions rather than answers about what this Israel of the late thirteenth century B.C.E. was.

Another Late Bronze Age source that has been important in some of the recent reconstructions of Israel's origins is the fourteenth-century B.C.E. (ca. 1390–1362) collection of letters recovered from Tell el-Amarna in Egypt. These letters were written by Syro-Palestinian rulers and tell us something of the social and political milieu of Palestine during the Late Bronze Age. Among them are letters that contain appeals to the Egyptian overlords for garrisons and reinforcements, suggesting that the Late Bronze Age in Syro-Palestine was a time in which conflict and competition among the leaders of city-states resulted in struggles for power and economic resources, in addition to competition over succession within city-states.

The letters further provide information about tribute, trade, taxes, and slave labor, which appear to have increased as leaders sought to promote their personal standing with Egyptian overlords, and to have resulted in political and economic instability. Demands on the part of the Egyptians for increased tribute appear to have led to conflict between city-states, internal conflict among classes, unrest among contenders for succession to leadership positions, and inefficiency and low productivity.

A number of the letters make reference to the threatening activities of a group called the *'apiru*. It is fairly clear from these references, as well as those in other Late Bronze Age texts, that this designation refers not to a nation or a particular ethnic group, but to a marginal social stratum that seems to have been composed of outsiders, gypsy-type wanderers, raiders, mercenaries, and slave labor.

While it has not been definitively established that the term *'apiru* is linguistically cognate with the biblical "Hebrews," as has sometimes been suggested, a number of scholars have proposed either that the marginalized *'apiru* constituted a significant portion of the population of Iron Age I "Israel"[21] or that they took part in an Israelite "movement."[22]

In any case, the Amarna letters provide us with information about the unrest in the ancient Near East during the Late Bronze Age, which may have contributed in some way to the weakening of the Palestinian city-states about a century later and the subsequent emergence of Iron Age I culture.

A number of New Kingdom Egyptian toponymic texts that describe general conditions and even specify various groups in Late Bronze Age Palestine also figure in some reconstructions, especially those texts that refer to the *shasu,* a group concentrated in southern Transjordan, but also referred to as having been active in the northern part of Sinai and possibly some parts of the Negeb, who appear to have been pastoral nomads and to have been troublesome to the Egyptians. There is no indication in the texts of what the sociopolitical organization or the economic system of the *shasu* was like, except that they kept small cattle.

Archaeological Information[23]

The most recent models of Israel's origins tend either to subordinate the biblical material to archaeological evidence or to exclude it almost completely from consideration. But tracing the origins of ancient Israel in the archaeological record also poses difficulties. The material evidence has proved ambiguous and inconclusive in relation both to the issue of the Iron Age I settlers' identity and to that of their geographical and socioeconomic origins. The problem is compounded by the fact that the social disruptions of the Late Bronze Age were so extensive that contemporary literary documentation from Iron Age I is scarce.

In the past, archaeologists and historians depended heavily on the Hebrew Bible for sorting out the complex puzzles the Late Bronze Age and Iron Age I peoples left behind in the archaeological record. But the biblical descriptions of invasion and conquest from outside Canaan are not supported by the archaeological information. Although there is evidence that some of the major Bronze Age centers were destroyed at the end of the period, the biblical assertions about conquest and destruction do not correspond with the archaeological record in some important ways. For example, a number of the sites said to have been conquered by the Israelites, or mentioned in some other context (for example, Heshbon, Arad, Hebron, Gibeon, and especially Jericho and Ai), have not yielded any significant signs of occupation in the Late Bronze Age. It is also clear from the archaeological record that the decline of the Late Bronze Age urban centers was a gradual process, lasting more than a century, not the swift military defeat depicted in Joshua 1–12. Many of the lowland sites, in fact, were destroyed in the late twelfth, rather than the thirteenth, century B.C.E. It is also telling, given the clear indications in the archaeological remains of a strong Egyptian influence in Palestine well into the twelfth century, that there is no mention of any Egyptian presence in the biblical stories. And there is the fact that the Transjordanian kingdoms of Ammon and Moab, which in the biblical traditions are already present at the time of the conquest, were not established until late in Iron Age I.

One of the things we can say with some certainty on the basis of the archaeological information is that there was a major cultural shift in Palestine between the end of the Late Bronze Age and the beginning of Iron Age I and that Palestine was not unique in this respect. The labels we attach to the major historical periods of the ancient world are technological, but the advent of the Iron Age (ca. 1200 B.C.E.) in Palestine, and throughout the Eastern Mediterranean world, appears to correspond more directly with the social, political, and economic changes than with technological innovations. The Late Bronze Age was a time of prosperity and extensive international trade. But the end of this prosperous age presents quite a different picture. It drew to a close with a series of social, political, and economic upheavals that have defied any kind of definitive explanation. Migrations, dislocations, and movements of diverse peoples are referred to in Late Bronze Age texts and inscriptions. And mass destruction of Late Bronze Age cities and towns is documented in the archaeological record. This tumultuous period of decline, then, is characterized by destruction, disruption of international trade routes, shifting populations, and a redistribution of power throughout the Eastern Mediterranean and Near East. Whether these contemporary crises were related is unknown, but the Eastern Mediterranean was plunged into a dark age characterized by material poverty and isolation. These crises marked the end of the great Late Bronze Age empires and of the palace economies that had developed around their urban centers. Egypt's loss of control over Palestine was also a part of this process.[24]

The most telling evidence of a major social transformation in Palestine itself during this period is a significant increase in the number of occupation sites in the central highlands. Recent archaeological surveys have established that settlement in this region was sparse during the Late Bronze Age (about twenty-five known sites) but that by the end of Iron Age I more than three hundred sites were occupied, some of which had been occupied in previous periods, but most of the sites had never been settled before. New settlements were also established in the agriculturally marginal areas on the eastern and southern desert fringes of Transjordan and the arid and semiarid regions of the Negeb, all zones that required either labor-intensive cultivation, such as terrace farming and storage, or pastoralism, or some combination of these subsistence strategies.[25]

Settlement was most intensive in the regions of Ephraim and Manasseh and the eastern part of Benjamin, somewhat less in Galilee, and much more sparse in Judah and in the Negeb, where permanent settlements were sporadic. The recent survey of Ephraim indicates that about 75 percent of the early Iron Age I sites there are located in the desert fringe and eastern part of the central range, with expansion to the western slope occurring in a later phase of Iron Age I and in Iron Age II.[26]

Surveys and excavations indicate that the populations of these highland villages during the twelfth century B.C.E. were small, most of them probably supporting no more than a hundred individuals, and the largest no more than three hundred. The settled population in the territory west of the Jordan River has been estimated at approximately twenty thousand in the twelfth century B.C.E., and double that number in the eleventh century.[27] These figures, of course, contrast sharply with the biblical tradition in Ex. 12:37 that records a number of "about six hundred thousand men on foot, besides children," which would mean that the total number of individuals fleeing Egypt would have been somewhere in the vicinity of two and a half million.

In contrast to the Late Bronze Age cities in Palestine, typically situated along the major north-to-south and east-to-west trade and communication routes, the new Iron Age I sites tended to be removed from these routes, and thus isolated and protected. Most were established in previously unoccupied areas rather than on the ruins of destroyed Late Bronze Age Canaanite sites, and many were located in places where there were no permanent sources of water in close proximity. Most were also very small, comprising in many cases no more than three or four multiple-house clusters, and lacking walls.

On the basis of his Ephraim survey, Israel Finkelstein[28] notes that most of the larger villages dated to the eleventh century were concentrated in the central range and northern slopes, locations with obvious economic advantages. Smaller villages, on the other hand, were located on the desert fringe, on the southern slopes, and in the foothills, areas that because of climate and other factors were not conducive to the development of larger settlements. The larger sites tended to be relatively widely and evenly spaced, in many cases with one or two small sites situated in close proximity to them, suggesting a settlement pattern of prominent central sites with peripheral populations connected to them. Some of the smaller sites with only a few houses each (49 percent of the sites surveyed) could have been either very small permanent villages or possibly seasonal campsites.

Volkmar Fritz[29] identifies three general settlement types: (1) ring-shaped villages, (2) agglomerated villages, and (3) farmsteads. Characteristic of the first type—ring-shaped villages—is the arrangement of houses in a closed circle or oval, with an open area in the center, an arrangement that possibly functioned as a means of defense, as well as providing an open area for keeping animals. The agglomerated village type consists of individual buildings, or complexes of several buildings, with streets of varying width and irregular open areas left between the individual units. The edges of this village type are open, and living space is relatively close and restricted. The third type of settlement—farmsteads—consists simply of single buildings or groups of buildings surrounded by a widely extending wall, which may have functioned as an enclosure for animals.

None of the excavated sites in the central hill country that date to Iron Age I was urban in character, and there is a kind of homogeneity to the material culture that suggests a relative absence of specialized elites, as is also indicated by the absence of monumental and public structures.[30]

One of the architectural styles typical of these sites is the so-called "four-room" or "pillared" house, a style that began to become common in the twelfth century B.C.E. and continued to be used down through the sixth century.[31] Its basic layout consists of a long narrow room with three "rooms" extending out from it. In many examples, however, there are more than four rooms, with some of the rooms subdivided and others added around the periphery. Thus the more recent designation "pillared" house seems more appropriate. It also seems likely that the central room of the three extending out from the fourth is a courtyard area rather than a room, and that this particular type of structure had a second floor, adding yet more rooms. This is a style that, at one time, was considered to be distinctively Israelite.

The pillared house is not, however, the only architectural type found in the new Iron Age I settlements. Apart from numerous buildings that cannot be classified according to any particular type, Fritz[32] identifies two more that are typologically similar to the "four-room" type: broad-room houses and what he calls pillar houses (which are distinct from the "four-room" type that others call pillared). Common characteristics of the broad-room type are the position of the entrance on the long side of the structure and uneven subdivision by a row of pillars along its length. Fritz's "pillar house" is relatively rare and consists of a building which is divided along its length into three units by two rows of stone pillars, with the entrance leading into the middle unit (probably a courtyard), which is wider than those on the sides.

Iron Age I highland sites are characterized by a simple and relatively meager ceramic repertoire consisting primarily of large store jars (*pithoi*) and cooking pots (as much as 80 percent of the entire ceramic assemblage at some sites), suggesting a subsistence economy in which the storage of food and water were basic concerns. Although the assemblages are similar throughout the highland settlements, regional differences are nevertheless apparent in forms and sometimes variety.[33]

There is some debate about the extent to which the ceramic assemblage, as well as other types of material culture, of the Iron Age I highlands is continuous with Late Bronze Age forms. Some argue that continuity is clear.[34] Others maintain that although there may be some peripheral influence, the differences are more pronounced than the similarities, particularly in relation to the poor and limited character of the Iron Age I assemblages as compared to the rich, decorated, and varied assemblages of the Late Bronze Age.[35]

Adherents of both positions agree, however, that in evaluating the ceramics and other material culture, environmental conditions, the socioeconomic status of the populace, relations with neighboring regions, and the background and influences from the preceding period of the group under discussion should all be taken into account. But the ways in which the evidence is interpreted has strong implications with regard to how the origins of the Iron Age I highland settlements are understood. The problem has to do with whether the peoples who settled there derived from the Late Bronze Age urban centers of the lowlands or from some other group or combination of groups.

Stone-lined or rock-cut silos and lime-plastered water-storage cisterns were also typically present in the new Iron Age I settlements, as is evidence for terracing in some areas. These suggest that strategies were being developed for making the marginal zones in which the villages were situated economically viable by opening up new areas to agriculture.[36] There is some question about how much of an impact these technologies had on the settlement process and about how early in the process terracing was used. The answers to these questions also have implications for how the settlement process is interpreted. If terracing was used early in the process, for example, this may suggest that the settlers came from a sedentary agricultural background, as some have argued. If it was later, on the other hand, this could be construed as indicating that the original settlers were not experienced farmers (that is, they were nomads), and that the settlement process began in areas that did not require terracing, as Finkelstein argues, with terracing being introduced only as the settlers eventually expanded into regions that required it.

In spite of the label we attach to this period, it is unlikely that iron technology had any role in the survival strategies of the Iron Age I settlers, as has sometimes been asserted in the past. Recent surveys of the evidence indicate that iron technology was adopted gradually during Iron Age I over a period of several hundred years and that the earliest possible date for the intensive use of iron for manufacturing functional tools and weapons in Palestine is sometime in the tenth century B.C.E. or even later.[37] There is evidence of the sporadic use of iron for ritualistic and perhaps utilitarian purposes before the tenth century, but it was not sufficient to have had any impact in either warfare or agriculture. Bronze remained the dominant metal throughout the period, although, as is the case with material culture in general, there is a clear decrease in metal luxury goods and in some areas a deterioration in craftsmanship.

There is very little material evidence relating to religious practice in Iron Age I highland sites. Possible cultic places have been identified at Shiloh, Mt. Ebal, and the so-called "bull site," but there is some debate about whether these sites actually functioned as cultic sanctuaries during this period. There is also no evidence from this period that tells us anything about whether or to what extent the worship of the god Yahweh played any part in the processes that occurred in the transition from the Late Bronze Age to Iron Age I in Palestine.

Archaeology and Ethnic Identity

> Throughout the history of archaeology as a discipline material culture . . . has been taken to reflect activities of specific social groups or "societies" whose physical movements across a geographical stage have often been postulated on the basis of the distribution patterns of such objects, and whose supposed physical or ethnic identity . . . has often been assumed to correlate with such artefactual groupings. More recently archaeologists have been forced to recognize . . . that a distinctive material culture complex may represent the activities of a vast variety of social groupings and subgroups, and that archaeological classification may often serve to camouflage the more subtle messages of style and technique . . . which probably symbolize complex patterns of behaviour, as well as individual aspirations—within any society.[38]

Anthropological studies on the relationship between ethnic identity and material culture in living societies indicate that understanding their interrelationship requires consideration of a complex web of relationships both within and between societies.[39] As was indicated at the beginning of this chapter, many of the defining "traits" of ethnic identification are subjective, based on individual and social perceptions, and "ethnic boundaries," even when they can be isolated in material culture remains, are flexible and constantly changing.

It is apparent in the varied models discussed below that issues having to do with the identity of those who established the new Iron Age I settlements, the nature of their relationship to the surrounding peoples and with each other, and the point at which they began to regard themselves as "Israelite" have stood at the forefront of recent scholarly debate about Israel's origins. In the past the tendency among Syro-Palestinian archaeologists was simply to assign ethnic identity at a particular site on the basis of biblical references and the presence of particular types of pottery or architecture. But it is now clear that neither occasional literary references nor isolated archaeological discoveries are conclusive evidence for identifying the ethnicity of populations.[40] "Canaanite" and "Israelite," for example, are clearly and intentionally distinguished in the biblical literature but are not so easily distinguished in the archaeological remains.

Two types of archaeological remains were assumed in the past to be evidence for attaching the ethnic label "Israelite" to the new settlements in the hill country. The first is the so-called "four-room" or "pillared" house,[41] and the second the "collared-rim" store jar.[42] But both are now recognized as types that are also found at sites outside the central highlands, in regions associated with the Canaanites and Philistines in the biblical literature, and in Transjordan.

More complex factors are now thought to underlie the presence or absence of certain types of material remains at these sites, and some of the differences are now attributed to social and economic complexity rather than ethnicity—for example, urban sites naturally yield different kinds of assemblages than rural sites. From this perspective, the pillared house and collared-rim type storage jars are simply common features of Iron Age I material culture in Palestine, significant not so much as ethnic markers, but for their practicality in relation to the socioeconomic structure of the highland villages. Those features of Iron Age I highland material culture that differ from the urban assemblages are, therefore, best explained as socioeconomic adaptations to agricultural village life in the highlands, as differences between the socioeconomic lifestyles of urban and rural Palestine, not as *ethnic* differences.

Some nevertheless still argue that it *is* possible to identify a distinct new ethnic group in the material remains.[43] For them, the question is whether this group can be labeled "Israelite" and, if so, on what basis. Even if the distinctive features of the Iron Age I material culture from hill country sites largely denote the functional differences between urban and rural "lifestyles," it is argued, they can also convey significant information about the development of distinctive lifestyles in different population groups and thus about the tangible dimensions of the behavior associated with ethnic boundary marking.

Israel Finkelstein argues that the only material clue for ethnic affiliation in Iron Age I Palestine appears in the evidence for food consumption. He notes that pig bones are absent in the faunal assemblages of Iron Age I hill country sites, but *are* present in Late Bronze Age sites in this area and at Iron Age I sites in both the lowlands and Transjordan.[44]

Models

The biblical construct in which Israel's origins are traced back to a miraculous liberating event in Egypt and an equally miraculous conquest from outside Canaan was accepted by biblical scholars as historically accurate in general terms until early in the twentieth century. Once archaeology became a well-established discipline, however, and archaeologists began trying to correlate their discoveries with the events described in the biblical traditions, confidence in the Bible as a historical source for understanding Israel's origins began to deteriorate. Questions began to be raised, for example, about why there is no evidence in the archaeological record of an exodus from Egypt or of significant Late Bronze Age occupation at sites such as Jericho, Ai, and Gibeon—all sites that play a central role in the Joshua account of the conquest—and why, if the early Israelites were outsiders who came in and destroyed the Canaanites, there is such strong evidence of cultural continuity with Late Bronze Age Canaanite culture.

The models that dominated throughout the first three quarters of this century, however, did depend on the biblical material as a primary source of information. The most prominent of these models were those proposed by William Foxwell Albright and Albrecht Alt.[45] Albright and a number of his students had set out to prove the historical accuracy of the Bible, and his model, the so-called "conquest theory,"[46] argued in favor of the historical soundness of the Joshua account. Evidence of destruction in Late Bronze Age strata at some sites supported this to some extent. But this model was called into question as more and more contradictory evidence came to light through further excavation and reevaluation of the evidence from sites originally believed to support the theory. Although the dating of destruction layers in Late Bronze Age urban centers is still controversial and constantly being revised, archaeologists have, for example, pushed the date of Hazor's destruction back to ca. 1250 B.C.E., a date that is earlier than the conquest is supposed to have occurred according to this model. And Lachish's destruction has now been dated later—to ca. 1150 B.C.E. The point is that neither destruction layer (or any other, for that matter) can be attributed with any confidence to a group of people called Israelites, led by an individual hero named Joshua.

In contrast to Albright's model, the "peaceful infiltration" model, first formulated by Albrecht Alt[47] and supported particularly by Martin Noth and later by Manfred Weippert,[48] argued that Judges 1 is a more reliable rendering of the events associated with the settlement, and that essentially it consisted of the sedentarization of pastoral nomads infiltrating Palestine from outside, who intermarried and entered into treaty relationships with the local Canaanite population. In addition to the traditions recorded in Judges 1, Alt's model was based on an examination of the political and demographic situation during the Late Bronze Age as reflected in New Kingdom Egyptian sources. Although Alt's model is still one that is supported to some extent, it is one that is particularly difficult to document in the archaeological record—pastoral nomads do not leave behind the kinds of material remains that lend themselves to easy interpretation, and there is no convincing archaeological evidence of any movement of peoples from Transjordan westward into Palestine.

As a result of such problems as the apparent contradictions in the biblical and archaeological records, in addition to the recent emphasis in archaeology on regional surveys and excavating smaller sites, a number of new models have been proposed. No definitive reconstruction of Israel's origins has replaced those of Albright and Alt, although among the hypotheses proposed in the last two decades there does seem to be some movement toward consensus. Careful and critical consideration of all the relevant evidence and use of comparative ethnographic information and social anthropological models have been particularly important in these recent attempts to understand the social world of Palestine in the centuries preceding the rise of monarchy.

The model that initiated and further stimulated the search for new models was the so-called "peasant revolt" hypothesis, first proposed by George Mendenhall[49] and later reworked and considerably expanded by Norman Gottwald.[50] Mendenhall and Gottwald evaluated the problem of Israel's origins from quite a radical, and therefore controversial, perspective. Although they differed significantly in their arguments and approaches, the basic premise they shared was that early Israel was composed primarily of peoples from the local Canaanite population who, because they were dissatisfied with their oppressed situation in the Canaanite city-state system, revolted and moved to the marginal highlands—that is, the bulk of the population settling in the hill country during Iron Age I did *not* come from outside Palestine proper, as in the biblical construct. Both Mendenhall and Gottwald suggest, however, that a group of infiltrators from outside, the exodus group, joined forces with these local Canaanites.

In his ambitious and controversial *The Tribes of Yahweh,* Gottwald uses the biblical books of Joshua and Judges as a foundation, arguing that, when critically evaluated, they contain trustworthy sociological information.[51] The traces of social revolution he discerns in these biblical books—and in the Pentateuch—are, from his perspective, evidence of peasant unrest among diverse but collaborative peoples who eventually became Israel.[52]

Gottwald relies heavily on the stream of sociological scholarship associated most closely with Karl Marx, which many critics find suspect because it rests so heavily on ideological assumptions unacceptable to them. He also uses both structural-functional (synchronic) and cultural-materialist (diachronic) models to facilitate his reconstruction. Although he relies on Mendenhall's earlier proposal of a peasant rebellion against the oppressive Canaanite city-state system, Gottwald differs significantly from Mendenhall in arguing that the forces underlying historical change are economic and social rather than ideological (as had been asserted by Mendenhall). Religion is also understood in materialist terms, and Gottwald concludes that Israelite social and economic relations were more significant in initiating the movement than Yahwist religion, which functioned rather as a kind of legitimator and facilitator.

Gottwald identifies his primary conclusions as follows: (1) Early Israel was a heterogeneous formation of marginal and oppressed Canaanite peoples that included "feudalized" peasants, mercenaries and adventurers, transhumant pastoralists, tribally organized farmers and pastoral nomads, and possibly itinerant artisans and disaffected priests—social groups that were identified in the fourteenth-century B.C.E. Amarna letters; (2) Israel emerged from a fundamental breach in Canaanite society brought on by a common opposition to Canaanite imperialism; (3) early Israel's social structure was a deliberate and conscious "retribalization" process; and (4) the Yahwistic religion was a crucial societal instrument for supporting political and economic equality at the individual and tribal levels.[53]

This picture is supported, Gottwald argues, by the Amarna letters, which reveal social unrest and rebellion within city-states, and thus an earlier stage in the process of civil disorder from which Gottwald sees Israel as having emerged.[54] The exodus group was the final catalyst that brought the social revolution to fruition. The religion of this group, with its emphasis on the delivering god Yahweh, became the socioreligious ideology and organizational framework that helped forge these rebellious peoples into an effective revolutionary movement and allowed them to establish a loose egalitarian tribal system of free peasant agriculturalists in place of the hierarchical and oppressive system they had rejected.

In contrast to other Canaanite farmers, who were subjected to taxation and debt payments, then, the early Israelites became free agrarians with complete control over their own surpluses, defenses, administration of justice, and so forth.

In recent years, Gottwald has introduced a number of adjustments into his model, although he still supports the idea of a social revolution.[55] Initially, for example, he presupposed some fundamental social unity, having accepted Noth's proposal that the Pentateuchal themes developed in the context of the centralized cult of tribal Israel (without subscribing to his amphictyonic model).[56] He now concedes that cultic unity in premonarchic Israelite society can no longer be considered certain. He has also abandoned the terms "peasant revolt" and "egalitarian society" as imprecise and misleading explanatory categories for early Israel, replacing them with "agrarian social revolution" and "communitarian mode of production." He still maintains, however, that Israel emerged as the result of an intentional social movement to oppose city-state control and to develop a countersociety—but not so much a cataclysmic peasant uprising as a sustained military, economic, and cultural struggle.

Gottwald's model, and his interpretations of the archaeological and biblical material, remain controversial, and there are numerous examples of scholars who disagree with him for various reasons. Many argue, for example, that there is no archaeological or biblical basis for his hypothesis that there was conflict between peasants and urban elites in Palestine during the Late Bronze Age. And his assertions that irrigation agriculture was an important factor in the settlement and that the knowledge of how to build terraces was the most important factor,[57] have also been refuted.[58] His study is nevertheless important, and represents a watershed in the development of social-scientific approaches to interpreting the history of ancient Israel.

Stimulated particularly by Gottwald's detailed analysis and the new evidence archaeological excavations and surveys are constantly bringing to light, the problem of Israel's origins is being considered anew, with a recognition that the processes must have been much more complex than any of the earlier models allowed. Consistent in almost all of these models is an agreement with Mendenhall and Gottwald that the origin of most of the Iron Age I highland population was indigenous to Palestine itself.

A number of reconstructions have also followed Mendenhall and Gottwald's lead in proposing that the settlement involved some type of withdrawal on the part of some portion of the Canaanite population, but without the emphasis on social revolution. Another characteristic of recent models is a concession that, in addition to the "urban refugees," other groups were probably also represented among those who moved into the highlands—*'apiru,* resedentarized pastoralists, the *shasu* mentioned in Late Bronze Age Egyptian texts and other immigrants from Transjordan, and even some newcomers from Syria and Anatolia.

In his critique of the peasant revolt hypothesis, Niels Peter Lemche,[59] for example, agrees that Israel emerged from among the indigenous inhabitants of Canaan, but suggests that its formation may have resulted from a *long-term* development associated with the *habiru* (*'apiru*), spanning the whole of the Late Bronze Age or longer. According to his proposal, the central highlands were occupied during the Late Bronze Age by *habiru,* a "para-social element" of the Canaanite population who had withdrawn from the city-states in the plains and valleys and were not necessarily sedentary. This withdrawal weakened, but did not destroy, the city-states. The new settlements at the beginning of Iron Age I are identified by Lemche as evidence of the emergence of new social and political structures among these groups, which resulted from the development of an agrarian economy made possible by certain technological innovations. In a sense, then, the settlers were returning to their old way of life, though "in other areas and on other terms than would previously have been possible."[60] Arguing that a lineage structure characterized Canaanite society in general, Lemche suggests that this same structure among the nonsedentary highlanders provided the basis for their (re)tribalization, political integration, and development of a tribal organization once they had adopted a settled, agricultural lifestyle. Thus tribal Israel, which is attested by Merneptah's reference to Israel, evolved from the nonsedentary inhabitants of the hill country through the processes of *resedentarization and retribalization.*

The two most highly developed models proposed in recent years are those that have been referred to as the "peaceful transition" or "transformation" model and the "symbiotic" or "internal nomadic settlement" model. The "peaceful transition" or "transformation" model, associated particularly with Robert B. Coote and Keith W. Whitelam,[61] is similar to the models introduced above, but focuses on identifying social *processes.*

Coote and Whitelam base their analysis primarily on anthropological and social scientific theories and models and on analysis of settlement patterns because, in their estimation, the issue of how ancient Israel emerged has been influenced too much by interpretations based on the biblical texts.[62] The emphasis in this model is on *gradual evolution* and *cultural continuity* rather than "destruction" or "collapse," with the transition manifest in the Iron Age I highland settlements being viewed as a process, probably lasting at least half a century if not more, that can only be understood as part of longer-term trends in the history of the region.[63] From this perspective, the increase in highland rural settlements is regarded as having been similar to shifts in other areas of the eastern Mediterranean in a centuries-long cycle of growth, stagnation, decline, and regeneration in Palestine's history, not as a unique event.

Coote and Whitelam build on Fernand Braudel's notion of *la longue durée,*[64] which emphasizes examining the long-term, slow, and subtle change that occurs over the course of centuries within a particular geographical and ecological setting. For them, understanding the type of social change that occurred in this period of transition involves investigation and comparison of settlement patterns over long periods of time and consideration of historical demography. The domination of this area by outside political powers is considered to be a particularly important constant of Palestinian history, and to have had a profound effect on settlement patterns. This is related to Palestine's geography, also a crucial factor, in large part because of its strategic place in the Eastern Mediterranean trade routes, which made it particularly vulnerable to any disruption or decline in the major centers.[65]

Coote and Whitelam also find Gerhard and Jean Lenski's sociological model of "agrarian society"[66] useful in constructing their own model of Iron Age I society, although they recognize that the Lenskis' exclusion of nomadic societies is problematic in considering the situation in ancient Palestine.

Israelite origins are explained in this model, then, as a pattern of settlement and agriculture in the highlands that is analagous to the cyclical settlement history of the region, in which Early Bronze II-III, Middle Bronze II, Iron I, and the Roman-Byzantine period were times of expansion, and Early Bronze IV and the Late Bronze Age were periods of major retraction.[67] These cycles were influenced by a variety of factors that include urbanism, interregional political and economic relations, and local sociopolitical structures—that is, Palestine's situation in relation to wider economic and political systems and the dynamics of the economic, social, and political interrelationships among urban elites, the peasantry, pastoralists, and social bandits.[68] Urban elites, pastoralists, and bandits are viewed as central, the elites because they were more closely connected with external political powers and trade, and the pastoralists and bandits because they defined the boundaries of state power. In periods of political stability high levels of trade and external investment stimulated dense settlement in the highlands, while a collapse of these conditions reversed the situation. The Iron Age I settlement of the highlands does not fit this pattern, Coote and Whitelam argue, because it occurred after the decline of the Late Bronze Age imperial world order. Although Late Bronze Age Canaan was characterized by urbanism, external political control, and trade in coastal areas, the nonurban highland region was unstable. Instead of supporting a large peasant population, as in Middle Bronze II, the highland population consisted largely of bandits and pastoralists whose well-being depended on urban elites and trade.

The catalyst, although not necessarily the primary cause, of the shift in settlement patterns during Iron Age I, in Coote and Whitelam's model, was a disruption in international trade at the end of the Late Bronze Age, not social conflict brought about by class struggle or external invasion or infiltration—that is, the growth of highland settlements needs to be viewed as a *result* of the urban economic decline rather than its *cause* (contra Gottwald).

The decline of the trade and economy that had sustained the power structures of the Palestinian city-states, along with the many circumstances that accompanied it, were thus fundamental to the economic, political, and social transformations in Iron Age I Palestine. The urban elite and their means to power were negatively affected, thus creating the conditions that led to the establishment of new settlements in the highlands and marginal areas of Palestine. Rural groups—nomads, bandits, and peasants also economically and politically dependent on trade, could no longer maintain profitable relations with the cities, and out of necessity turned to local production in areas that had previously been part of a general pattern of seasonal transhumance, where they established agricultural village settlements and became more politically independent. The normal intraregional social divisions were replaced by an interregional class distinction opposed to urban elites and state authority, whose resulting lack of control in these areas would have contributed to the increasing political independence.[69] The resulting "Israel" was a segmentary society, consisting of a loose federation of highland villages and towns, pastoral nomadic groups, and previous bandits. But rapid population growth, uneven productivity of agricultural land, regional intensification of production, and revival of international trade soon led to the reintroduction of centralized power.

Characteristic of this model is a rejection of models that propose massive population withdrawal from Canaanite urban centers and internal nomadic movement as explanations in and of themselves, even though such factors are acknowledged as having been involved. The settlement in the hill country and the consequent increase in population are attributed, rather, to the demise of urban life in the lowlands, which permitted greater expansion and population growth within the villages *naturally* over a period of several generations.

The "symbiosis" or "internal nomadic settlement" model[70] is somewhat like Alt's in that it emphasizes a nomadic origin for the Iron Age I settlers.[71] The significant difference is that the early Israelites are understood as having been descended from the *local* pastoral nomadic population, rather than from a nomadic population that migrated into Palestine from outside.

In his reconstruction, Israel Finkelstein emphasizes analogies with the settlement patterns of early twentieth-century Arab villages and modern pastoral nomads in the process of sedentarization, in addition to close analysis of the archaeological data and ecological, geographical, and environmental factors. He argues that the process of settlement was intimately connected with the nature of the land itself—the landscape, the climate, and the land's economic potential.[72] Anthropological studies of the situation in Palestine during the period of Turkish rule indicate, Finkelstein argues, that sedentary peoples tended to become nomads in times of upheaval, but were often forced later to settle down again as a result of crises in the production of agricultural goods.[73]

As in the "peaceful transition"/"transformation" model, the "symbiosis" model considers broad historical context.[74] Focusing on the central highlands areas associated in the biblical texts with the tribes of Manasseh and Ephraim, it also contrasts village Canaanite and pastoral "Israelite" societies *within* Palestine, but assumes long-term contacts between them throughout the Late Bronze Age. The pastoralist "Israelites," according to this model, had lived in close proximity to, and in symbiosis with, villages and cities (what is referred to in the anthropological literature as "enclosed nomadism").[75] The origins of these pastoralists are traced to a period of urban collapse at the end of the Middle Bronze Age (ca. 1600–1550 B.C.E.), when they migrated to the highlands and a substantial element of the population subsequently became "retribalized" throughout the Late Bronze Age, living on the margins of the settled areas or perhaps even in their midst. As the Late Bronze Age urban centers declined, these highland pastoral nomads lost the trading market on which they had depended for agricultural products, the pastoralism constructed around symbiosis with the Late Bronze Age urban settlement systems became impossible, and thus out of necessity during the late thirteenth through twelfth centuries B.C.E. they became sedentary farmers and established villages. This occurred in the central hill country because the more favorable areas became overcrowded (that is, population pressure was the primary causal factor).[76]

The bulk of Finkelstein's 1988 study is a review of the archaeological evidence. In support of his argument for a pastoral background, he cites as evidence:[77] (1) survey data which suggest that the earliest stage of the settlement was most dense in regions suitable to cereal crops and pasturage and relatively sparse in areas appropriate to horticulture and mixed agriculture,[78] (2) the "oval courtyard" layout of settlements in the earliest stratum which, he argues, corresponds with the way in which the modern Bedouin sometimes arrange their tents in encampments to protect their flocks,[79] (3) the form of the "four-room" pillared house, which he compares to the living arrangement of a typical Bedouin tent, the pillars being a later development related to the structural requirements of hill-country sites,[80] and (4) the lack of variety in the early highland assemblages.[81]

On the basis of survey data that suggests a pattern of movement from the eastern desert fringes toward the forested slopes of the west, the spread of this new culture into the highlands is construed as having occurred at a gradual pace. Finkelstein points to his Ephraim survey, which indicates an initial concentration of settlement sites in the eastern part of the hill country—an area suitable for a mix of limited dry farming and animal husbandry—followed by a slow spread of occupation westward into the foothills. The spread of settlement to the southern slopes of Ephraim, a region suitable for horticulture, occurred only later in Iron Age I and in Iron Age II.[82] This demographic shift is cited as evidence that in the early stages of the settlement the population was still in transition between pastoral nomadism and sedentary life, as is his interpretation that the circular layout found at earlier sites no longer occurs in later phases, where there is also an increase in the number of silos, indicating that the inhabitants had become fully settled by that time. The geographical and economic expansion, then, involved a gradual shift from regions adapted for an economy based on growing grain and herding (the desert fringe, the eastern flank of the central range of the central hill country, the foothills) to one that was based primarily on horticulture (the western slopes of the central range), a shift that also brought about significant sociopolitical change. The argument depends in part on the assumption that settlement in areas suitable for horticulture presupposes a sedentary populace prepared to wait a number of years before harvesting the fruits of its labor, whereas a subsistence base of cereals and pastoralism did not require year-round occupation at permanent sites.

Arguing against the hypothesis that the Iron Age I settlers were of urban "Canaanite" origin, Finkelstein asserts that the ceramics from the earliest stratum are completely different from the Late Bronze Age Canaanite repertoire and thus can be identified as early "Israelite." While he acknowledges some connection with Canaanite types, Finkelstein explains this by arguing that these ancient pastoral nomads (his "Israelites") assimilated Canaanite ceramic traditions, just as modern pastoral nomads do when they settle down and become farmers. The signs of continuity with Late Bronze Age traditions, then, indicate nothing more than some influence from Iron Age I lowland sites. Both the continuity and the discontinuity are interpreted as indicating environmental and socioeconomic conditions rather than direct roots in the Late Bronze Age lowlands.

In contrast to Coote and Whitelam's broad-ranging study, Finkelstein's 1988 study focuses primarily on a particular region and very close analysis of the archaeological evidence. He gives little attention to evaluating the place of the lowland urban communities and the wider interregional forces involved in the transition from the Late Bronze Age to Iron Age I. In a later analysis, however, he considers these forces more directly, arguing that regionalism played an essential part in Iron Age I cultural and demographic developments, but that each region was also influenced to some extent by either proximity to or isolation from the various urban cultures of the lowlands.[83]

Finkelstein's hypothesis remains controversial, particularly in relation to the way in which he interprets the data in his arguments for lack of continuity with Canaanite culture and for pastoral nomadic origins. Many archaeologists see a marked continuity in material culture between the highland settlements and longer-settled "Canaanite" sites from the very beginning of the expanded settlement, and the evidence from 'Izbet Ṣarṭah and other sites is interpreted by others as indicating that the people who had settled them were not pastoral nomads, but experienced stockbreeders and efficient farmers, able to produce significant surpluses, as is indicated by the presence of silos and storage pits.[84] Finkelstein's model has also been faulted for concentrating so much on the sedentarization of pastoral nomads that he neglects considering other groups that must have also been a part of the process.[85] This is considered especially problematic given his acceptance of Rowton's model of "enclosed nomadism," which emphasizes the economic, social, and political connections of nomads with settled populations and state power, on the one hand, and his denial that there is any direct derivation of the Iron Age I highland population from the Late Bronze Age urban centers, on the other.

In spite of the controversial nature of his model, Finkelstein's documentation of the Iron Age I settlement as an indigenous, complex *gradual* process of social and economic change is acknowledged as a welcome emphasis, and his work is often cited as the most thorough and sophisticated analysis of the archaeological evidence for the Israelite settlement yet published.[86]

There are a number of differences between the models proposed by Coote and Whitelam on the one hand and Finkelstein on the other. Finkelstein's model, for example, is supported by close analysis of the archaeological data from Palestine, whereas Coote and Whitelam's gives less attention to this data, but has a much broader scope. Coote and Whitelam also emphasize the interrelationships of the various social types, factions, and forces in the region, as well as their interactions with the wider world, throughout Palestine's history. Finkelstein, on the other hand, emphasizes the isolation and exclusivity of the Iron Age I settlers, and their freedom from the influence of external forces. But in spite of the fact that these models are elaborated to different degrees and contain different emphases, the reconstructions are not in total disagreement.

Most of the recent social-science-oriented models, in fact, share certain fundamental perspectives both in their approaches and in their interpretations.[87] And as Gottwald has recently noted,[88] they are, in a sense, constructs along a continuum that simultaneously share some interpretations of the evidence and disagree on others. Typically, however, there is more dependence in these models on archaeological information than on the biblical traditions. There is more openness to using models from anthropology as a way of illuminating the ancient information. The highlands are now generally viewed as a frontier that is sensitive to changing circumstances. A long-term historical perspective is an important element in the most recent models. And there is general agreement that the majority of the Iron Age I highland population was indigenous and diverse. In general the internal origin of the highland settlers first proposed by Mendenhall and Gottwald has endured, although their argument for social revolution has not.

The data we have at present, however, are too ambiguous to produce certainty and consensus, and thus the models should be viewed as inconclusive and in process. There is still, and is likely to continue to be, considerable debate concerning which, if any, of them is most representative of the processes that occurred in the transition from the Late Bronze Age to Iron Age I in Palestine. But the general acknowledgment of the complexities associated both with the interpretive process and with processes of social development brings us closer to constituting a more accurate, even if less definitive, construct of early "Israel."

Chapter 3

Iron Age IA and B

The "Tribal" Period

Iron Age I is the period on which most recent social-scientific investigations of ancient Palestinian society have focused. This is due in part to its chronological association with the "settlement," and in part to the growing lack of confidence in the biblical traditions as direct evidence for "Israel's" early history and social life. As a consequence of the latter, more scholars are appealing to comparative studies and models developed by anthropologists and sociologists in their reconstructions of this period. Many of these reconstructions have also been motivated by Gottwald's monumental work,[1] which considers Iron Age I social life in addition to the processes associated with the settlement in the highlands.

BIBLICAL INFORMATION

The biblical books traditionally regarded as providing information about the so-called "tribal period" or "period of the Judges" are Joshua, Judges, and 1 and 2 Samuel. Many of the traditions recorded in the Pentateuch, however, are also believed by some to have preserved ancient traditions from the period preceding the rise of the state in ancient Palestine, and thus have been used as sources for reconstructing its social world during this time.[2] Until recently, the so-called "source hypothesis" provided a means for determining what traditions in the Pentateuch were older, and thus more reliable. But this hypothesis has now come under fire, and by many is no longer considered to be valid for determining which texts may actually reflect ancient traditions.

Although we cannot make definitive assertions about whether these narratives contain any historical nucleus deriving from the period preceding Iron Age II, it is nevertheless possible that some of the traditions, even if they do derive from later periods, preserve some fragmentary information about fundamental features of the Iron Age I social world, particularly given the likelihood that at some levels of society (for example, family and kinship structure at the village level) there may have been very little change over time.

It is worth considering briefly the ancestral traditions in Genesis, because they clearly encode social information, even if it is not possible to pinpoint the extent to which they are truly representative of the early period.[3] They include most prominently stories about Israel's eponymous ancestors and the nature of their relations with the eponymous ancestors of other groups. In their present form as a continuous narrative, they consist of a kind of narrative genealogy that focuses on one line of purported biological descent bearing a divine blessing. They also portray a kind of "family tree" through brief references to groups who are claimed to have branched off from the main "trunk" and are immediately lost to the ongoing story. Most of these stories are also written in the form of saga, a genre that often serves as an expression of national, racial, or religious identity. They appear, however, to have been linked together only secondarily by means of genealogies and itineraries. Thus, what moments in time the relationships in these stories symbolize are probably impossible for us to determine, although it is likely that they represent to some extent notions about how groups interrelated with one another at the time they were written and/or edited.

The books of Joshua and Judges purport to relate the "history" of Israel during this period that preceded the unification of the tribes under a single king. Joshua, as indicated in chapter 2, contains a heavily idealized portrayal of Canaan's conquest and the subsequent distribution of land among the "Israelite" tribes. As is the case with all the traditions incorporated into the Deuteronomic History, the extent to which the information relating to tribal structure and organization provided by these narratives is representative in any way of the real situation during Iron Age I is still open to debate.

In the scheme represented in the book of Judges, this period was a time when Israel repeatedly turned to apostasy, was subsequently given into the hands of oppressing nations, and ultimately delivered by "judges" raised up by Yahweh once they had repented. The book is primarily composed of stories about these leaders, some of whom are said to have judged "all Israel." Most of them, however, portray localized conflicts, in which no more than a few of the tribes are involved.[4] The leaders in the stories are individuals whose primary roles are military defense in the struggles of subgroups to secure a firm hold on the land in the face of repeated threats from enemies such as the Canaanites, Moabites, Ammonites, Midianites, and Philistines, or in internal struggles among groups. Explicit etiological motifs also appear in some of these sagas.

Some scholars[5] place more confidence than do others in the historical and social value of the traditions preserved in this book, in spite of the apparent editorial framework and imposed ideological agenda that derives from a much later period. Even if they are not accurate in their portrayal of historical events, they argue, they may nevertheless preserve some valuable data about social, political, and economic structure and organization, institutions, and customs. Some of the details in the stories also seem to correspond somewhat with the information exposed through archaeological excavations and with anthropological models of tribal societies.[6]

The books of Samuel depict the rise of the "united monarchy," but are potentially relevant, in that the stories are about transition and thus in some respects relate to both Iron Age I and Iron Age II. As part of the Deuteronomic History, they are also the product of later editing. But, as is the case for the book of Judges, some scholars believe that they may contain traditions that are ancient, and thus may be useful for understanding the social situation at the end of the tribal period and on the eve of the rise of statehood.

ARCHAEOLOGICAL INFORMATION

As indicated above, the archaeological material from early Iron Age villages[7] provides an assemblage of material culture that seems to agree in some respects with the social conditions implied in Judges and Samuel. The plan and layout of the houses at Iron Age I highland sites, which often share a common courtyard with other dwellings, may, for example, correspond with the bits of information we can glean about socioeconomic organization from the book of Judges—the compounds formed by these groups of houses perhaps represent the extended family mentioned in biblical texts, and the entire village, with perhaps a dozen of these clusters of buildings, may have comprised the biblical *mišpāḥāh* or "kinship group" mentioned in the texts.[8]

As was indicated in chapter 2, Late Bronze Age material culture continued to exist and evolve during Iron Age I, although with regional variations. New forms were also introduced, some from internal and some from external sources. The latter is most clearly evident in the Mycenean influence on the material remains of the "Sea Peoples," which begin to appear in the southern coastal regions in the twelfth century B.C.E. The indigenous materials are typically locally produced forms deriving from the Late Bronze Age material culture, but they lack the high-quality craftmanship of earlier artisans.

Surveys indicate that village populations during Iron Age I were small, and that the villages themselves, for the most part unwalled, were built in isolated and protected areas away from major trade routes. The typical settlement pattern seems to have consisted of more prominent central sites surrounded by smaller peripheral ones, some of which may have been campsites rather than permanent settlements. The homogeneity of the material culture, in addition to the absence of monumental and public structures, in general suggests a relative absence of specialized elites.

The simple and relatively meager ceramic repertoire, consisting mainly of large storage jars and cooking pots, suggests a subsistence economy in which the storage of food and water were basic concerns. Other evidence for the economy and subsistence strategies—stone-lined or rock-cut silos, lime-plastered water cisterns, and evidence of terracing in some areas—indicates that agriculture was an important component of the economy.

The construction of the so-called "four-room" or "pillared" house has been interpreted as being particularly suitable to a subsistence-based agricultural economy.[9] The ground floor of this house type typically contained large numbers of storage jars and cooking pots, as well as implements such as large stone saddle querns and stone mortars and pestles that would have been used for processing cereal products. Fragments of flint blades from sickle tools used for harvesting cereals also point to a dependence on agriculture. The ground floor was probably also used for storage and small craft production.

In addition to the presence of the faunal remains of sheep and goats, some of the architectural features of the house type have been interpreted as indicating that the ground floor, in addition to being the locus of food-processing activities, was also used to shelter animals.

A second story, which would have been the living and sleeping area, has been postulated on the basis of the fact that the foundations and pillars would have been sufficient to support a second story, and the presence of stone stairs that were preserved in several Iron Age II examples.

Each of these structures probably housed a nuclear family, as the typical size is too small to accommodate more. The clustering pattern of two or three individual houses has been interpreted as possibly representing family organization and residency at the level of the extended family.

Tel Masos is often cited in the literature as a unique site that does not fit the Iron Age I pattern.[10] The site is three times larger than the typical sites in the hill country, and ten times larger than other sites in the Beersheba Valley. The ceramic assemblage and other objects also point to the possibility that the people living at Tel Masos had trade relations with urban sites on the Mediterranean coast and with southern Arabia and the Transjordanian plateau (there is little evidence of trade in the remains of other village sites dating to this period). It is also different from other sites in that some of the houses are larger than others—although there is still no evidence of monumental architecture and no walls, palaces, or temples—suggesting more differentiation in wealth and status, and perhaps the presence of public buildings. Egyptian and Canaanite influence is apparent in the architectural features of several structures.

Overall, however, the picture we can construct on the basis of excavations and surveys of early Iron Age I hill-country villages is of a society that was somewhat isolated, with a very simple material culture.

There is very little indication in the archaeological record of literacy during this period (for example, a late thirteenth- or early twelfth-century inscribed jar handle from Raddana, an abecedary on an Iron Age I ostracon from ʿIzbet Ṣarṭah, and the tenth-century Gezer Calendar),[11] and it is unlikely that more than a small fraction of the populace could (or needed to) read or write.

There is little Iron Age I material evidence relating to religion, although excavations have uncovered some materials that may provide some insight. One example is a fragmentary inscription of a poem from Kuntillet ʿAjrud, a site in the northern Sinai.[12] Although the site itself has been dated to the ninth century B.C.E., there is general agreement that the poem, which is similar in many respects to the archaic poems in the Hebrew Bible, was probably composed earlier. The geographical references in the poem have led some scholars to hypothesize that the worship of the deity referred to had its origins to the southeast of Israel and Judah, somewhere in the region of northwestern Arabia. This hypothesis corresponds with one based on the Midianite tradition in the book of Exodus that describes Moses' first encounter with Yahweh as taking place while he is resident in Midian (Exodus 3; cf. Ex. 18:11).

Also supporting this argument, according to some scholars, is a shrine that was uncovered at a twelfth-century site in the Timnaʿ Valley, which is considered to be similar to the tabernacle described in Exodus 25–30 and 35–40. In the vicinity of the shrine there was evidence (large quantities of cloth and pole holes) that a large tent had been erected over the temple court. The shrine also contained a row of *maṣṣebôth* and round incense altars, Midianite pottery, and a copper serpent (cf. Num. 21:6–9) with a gilded head.[13]

Although the biblical construct of Iron Age I refers to a number of operating sanctuaries in the area of the highlands, only a few possible shrines have been uncovered through excavations, and even these are controversial. Shiloh, a site that according to biblical tradition was a tribal center where the Ark of the Covenant was kept (1 Samuel 1), has yielded no definitive evidence of any kind of religious shrine from the Iron Age I, although some argue that there is enough evidence to postulate the presence of a cultic center that may have served as an interregional cult center in the central hill country and its vicinity.[14] The evidence cited includes a building complex that is composed of atypical buildings, a large number of storage jars, fragments of a cult stand and two vessels ornamented with animal heads, and numerous animal bones believed to be evidence of sacrificial offerings.

Two other sites, dated to the late thirteenth or twelfth century B.C.E., have been identified as possible shrines. These are an installation uncovered at Mt. Ebal near Shechem and the so-called "bull site." The installation at Mt. Ebal dates to the twelfth century B.C.E. and was identified by the excavator as a sacrificial altar associated with the shrine described in Joshua 8:30–35.[15] But there is a great deal of controversy over the structure's function, some asserting that it was an isolated fort,[16] and others that it was a farmstead.[17]

The "bull site" is located near biblical Dothan in the hill country of Samaria,[18] and also dates to the twelfth century B.C.E. Among the remains recovered at the site were *maṣṣebôth* and a small bronze bull figurine. The bull's presence has prompted the suggestion that the site was associated in some way with Canaanite religion, as the principal epithet of the Canaanite god El was "Bull El."

DEMOGRAPHY AND SETTLEMENT PATTERNS

Historically in the Middle East, what appear to be isolated communities are always linked in some way to communities elsewhere. Because of the interdependent, complex, and ever-changing ways of life in this region, social groups have not always fallen readily into neat classificatory niches such as villagers, pastoral nomads, or city dwellers.[19] Although this was probably the case during Iron Age I, as it has been in other periods, only the villagers left behind sufficient remains for us to determine the character of their settlement patterns.

The archaeological evidence for Iron Age I demography and settlement patterns has already been presented in chapter 2, so only a brief summary will be included here. Recent surveys have identified more than three hundred sites in highland Palestine that date to Iron Age I. Some of them had been occupied in previous periods, but most were in locations that had never been settled before. New settlements were also established in the agriculturally marginal areas on the eastern and southern desert fringes of Transjordan and in the Negeb.[20]

The populations of these villages were small, most of them supporting no more than a hundred individuals, and the largest no more than three hundred. The settled population for the twelfth century has been estimated at approximately twenty thousand, and for the eleventh century double that number.

Settlement was most intensive, and villages were larger, in the northern regions of Ephraim and Manasseh. It was much sparser to the south, in the areas of Judah and the Negeb, where the villages were also smaller. In many cases one or two sites were located in close proximity to the larger sites, suggesting a possible pattern of more prominent central sites with peripheral populations connected to them.

None of the excavated sites from this area was urban, and at present there is little, if any, material evidence for pastoral nomadism (although, as has been noted, it almost certainly existed).

ECONOMY

In general, the economy in ancient societies was intricately interrelated with other social institutions, particularly those that we would associate with politics and kinship, but also with religious institutions. This would almost certainly have been the case in ancient Israel as well.

Environmental features would also have had some effect on the economies of this region during Iron Age I. These probably included: (1) the distance of the highland villages from both maritime and overland trade, (2) their relative isolation and separation by topographical barriers, and (3) their constant struggle with ecological constraints. This isolation probably allowed for relative freedom, economic and otherwise, from the centralized powers that in many periods dominated the lowlands.[21]

Subsistence Strategies

Studies of Middle Eastern economies indicate that both in the recent past and in earlier historical periods, agricultural, pastoral, and trade activities have typically formed a single interdependent economic system.[22] Subsistence strategies have also varied from region to region—dry farming in the flat, open areas, horticulture in the mountainous areas, animal husbandry in the desert fringe, and summer pasturage in other parts of the highlands.

As is typical of many preindustrial societies, the dominant economic activities in Iron Age I Palestine were associated with agriculture. In settled communities, agriculture would also have been supplemented by stockbreeding and the production of simple handcrafts. As is the case in this region today, agriculture was based on regional mixes of grains, wine, oil, fruits, and vegetables. Wheat, barley, and millet are the typical crops planted in the autumn to ensure maturation in the late spring or early summer. Vines, tubers, and bulbs are also cultivated. Often olive trees, grapevines, cereals, and vegetables are planted together in a single field in order to make good use of limited land resources, spread the risk of crop failure, and add variety to the diet. Types of crops differ according to ecological zones. In the coastal Mediterranean zone, vines, cereals, and olive and fruit trees were typical commodities. Crops in the highlands of Judah included wheat and barley, grapes, and olives. Sheep and goats, kept for milk and its byproducts, wool, and leather and for use in sacrifices, were extensively bred over the whole area.[23]

The environment during Iron Age I was also ideal for pastoral activity—particularly what is referred to as "enclosed nomadism," which involves routine migrations between the steppe in the winter and the highlands in the summer.[24] Pastoral nomadic groups have an economy based primarily on the intensive domestication and herding management of animals, usually camels and/or sheep and goats. This mode of life requires movement in a seasonal cycle dictated by the need for pasturage and water. Most Middle Eastern pastoral societies also cultivate some crops. In some cases the same community has pastoral nomadic and farming segments. In other cases a whole group alternates pastoral nomadism with crop cultivation in half-year cycles.[25] The extent to which members of a pastoral nomadic group themselves engage in farming depends on factors such as erratic rainfall and political and economic circumstances. The apparent exceptions to this pattern are the deep-desert camel herders of the Arabian Peninsula, but even they maintain some type of symbiotic relationship with settlements. Although it is often the case, nomads do not always live only in marginal areas, as is typically assumed, and in fact there are no particular zones that are especially suited to nomadic life. Rather, nomads tend to adjust their social and economic organization to the political realities in the regions with which they are associated at any given time.

The degree of self-sufficiency and isolation of pastoral nomadic groups also varies, and a broad spectrum of complex relations exists between them and settled peoples.[26] These range from integrating completely, except for periodic movements with the herds, to frequent or periodic contact between them for the exchange of goods and mutual services. Contact of this sort is more often friendly than hostile, but can sometimes involve pillaging or force. On occasion, pastoral nomads also control trade routes and impose tribute. Gottwald suggests that this may have been the case, for example, with the Midianites in Sinai and Transjordan in the eleventh century B.C.E.[27] It is also not unusual for farmers to take up pastoral nomadism and then return to farming when economic and political circumstances change.

The amount of surplus produced in either agricultural or nomadic pastoral contexts during Iron Age I is difficult to determine on the basis of the archaeological information. It is likely that production was sufficient to sustain the population and generate limited surpluses, as long as appropriate social, economic, and political mechanisms were maintained. The populations in the marginal regions would almost certainly have had a fairly low level of economic productivity, with few surpluses. They would also have had a more pressing need for spreading risks and applying alternative strategies for exploiting the environment, such as increased pastoralism and labor-intensive terracing, possibly some irrigation, and the development of storage systems.

Patterns of Labor

In general terms, labor in antiquity, like other economic pursuits, was embedded in other institutions, especially those related to kinship and household contexts. Industry was normally small-scale and conducted within the context of families.

The Iron Age I village community was most likely economically self-sufficient and independent. The basic socioeconomic unit within the village community is considered by some to have been the nuclear family,[28] and by others to have been the extended family.[29] Each family (or extended family) was autonomous, producing its own economic necessities, cultivating and harvesting its own fields, and selling its surplus produce if there was any. It is possible that family and village networks of mutual aid were extended to larger social groupings in times of need.[30]

Ideally, the entire populace had equal access to resources, although this was probably not always the case. With a few exceptions (for example, Tel Masos), the archaeological record indicates that the socioeconomic relations of the Iron Age I villagers was relatively egalitarian, in the sense that there is no clear evidence of division of labor.

Systems of Exchange and Trade

Reciprocity was probably the primary system of exchange during Iron Age I. The most elementary form of exchange, occurring mostly in tribal and simple societies, reciprocity is based primarily on kinship relations and is characterized by a kind of social give-and-take, with a wide range of gradation, mutuality, and balance, depending on the in- or out group status of the parties in the exchange and on the nature of the commodities exchanged. Reciprocal exchange functions to bond intergroup relations, in addition to ensuring relatively equitable distribution of goods and assistance in hard times. "Full reciprocity" occurs among members of a family, where goods and services are freely given. "Weak reciprocity" is typical among members of a clan, where gifts are given, but an account is kept of the balanced returnflow of countergifts. Where distant tribal kin are involved, "balanced reciprocity" is practiced, and the concern for keeping track of gifts and countergifts is greater. Outside the tribe in this type of system mutuality ends, and "negative reciprocity," where outsiders are "fair game" in the exchange process, is the norm.[31]

Luxury goods in a reciprocity system tend to be associated with trade relationships. In trade, when goods are reciprocated, trading partners relate as guest-friends to each other's clans (or lineages) and tribes. Reciprocity also allows for the exchange of agricultural surplus, if there is any, in terms of weak or balanced reciprocity under the protection of the tribes concerned.

The socioeconomic effects of trade are the subject of a recent study by Israel Finkelstein, which attempts to account for the unique character of Tel Masos. On the basis of the archaeological evidence from Tel Masos, Beersheba, Tel Arad, and Tel Esdar (sites located in the Beersheba basin) and Negeb highland sites, Finkelstein argues that during the eleventh century B.C.E. desert nomads in these regions participated in, and perhaps monopolized, trade with Arabia. This brought about a dramatic change in the economy, and a gradual shift from pastoral nomadism in this area to a subsistence based more on trade and seasonal agriculture. According to his construct, some of the population settled and an urban trade center (Tel Masos) emerged, along with an increase in social stratification. Eventually, however, the loss of the trade monopoly caused the abandonment of settlements and a process of renomadization.[32] Whether or not this construct is accurate,[33] it nevertheless provides a possible scenario for how Iron Age I nomads participated in the systems of exchange during this period.

Land Ownership and Distribution of Wealth

Because land was the major factor in production in antiquity, wealth was measured in land, and control of land was an important issue (cf. Lev. 25:23, 25–28; 1 Sam. 8:14; 1 Kings 21). Some of the economic models of Iron Age I highland Palestine postulate that there was a communal type of land ownership, in which land was distributed among individual or extended families. Niels Peter Lemche notes that this type of system seems to be confined to societies whose economies are based on the cultivation of grain and that it probably served to strengthen solidarity within the framework of the village or lineage; that is, cooperation was necessary in order to carry out distribution. But he also cautions that we cannot assume that all land was common property, since horticultural land (that is, orchards and vineyards) is not suitable to this type of apportionment.[34]

In his study of the social structure of ancient Israel, S. Bendor argues that flocks probably belonged to individual nuclear families, but were pastured in common village land, that is, the fields for grazing belonged to the public and were open to public use. He also suggests that patterns of land possession and use differed in regard to fields and vineyards (or olive orchards). Although both were part of the extended family's inheritance, the ownership rights of the nuclear unit were not limited with regard to the vineyard (except in selling it), while with regard to the field they were limited to the right of *using* it.[35]

Ideally, land would have been evenly distributed among families. It is unlikely, however, that there was a truly egalitarian socioeconomic structure in Iron Age I, as Gottwald argued. Ethnographic studies indicate that even in societies with an egalitarian ideology, there is some differentiation in status, power, and wealth (see the discussion of segmented systems below).

Technology

The production of food, clothing, and shelter involved a number of technologies that included woodworking, metallurgy, ceramic technology, brick making, and leather and stone working.[36] The items produced by these technologies were probably manufactured in the context of each self-sustaining village, or perhaps in villages that specialized in the manufacture of particular items.

Agricultural success in Iron Age I was facilitated by technologies that included waterproof cisterns and rock terracing. Terracing, in particular, was essential to the farming pursuits of the Iron Age I villagers, as without it, farming the rugged, steep hills of Palestine would not have been possible in some areas. Terracing also increased the carrying capacity of the land, transforming the natural slopes into a series of level steps, held in place by retaining walls built of dry-laid stones, that served as fields suitable for farming. Most village compounds had one or more bell-shaped cisterns situated beneath the floors of houses or in courtyards. These were necessary particularly in those settlements that were not located in close proximity to water sources.

There is a great deal of uncertainty about the role of metallurgy in economic productivity during this period, but it is fairly clear that bronze remained the dominant metal for manufacturing tools and weapons.[37] Iron did not come into common use in Palestine before the tenth century B.C.E. The earliest examples of objects made from iron were primarily ornamental, and were found in contexts that suggest either ritual or ceremonial functions or some precious or special status (tombs, temples, graves, palaces). Although it was increasingly employed for the manufacture of utilitarian implements from the twelfth century B.C.E. forward, 1200–900 was a transitional period during which iron eventually replaced bronze as the predominant working metal.

Contrary to the common interpretation based on 1 Samuel 13:19–22 (in which iron is *not* mentioned), the Philistines also used more bronze than iron, and there is no evidence that they could have had a monopoly on iron's production. Most of the iron objects recovered from Iron Age I Philistine sites are ceremonial rather than functional tools and weapons. And there is little evidence of carburization, which is the necessary prerequisite for producing *functional* iron tools and weapons.

SOCIOPOLITICAL ORGANIZATION AND STRUCTURE: TRIBES AND SEGMENTED SYSTEMS

There was a clear break in type of sociopolitical organization between the Late Bronze Age and Iron Age I. The Late Bronze Age was characterized by complex and socially stratified urban settlements that were centers of petty kingdoms or city-states. In contrast, social organization in the new highland settlements during Iron Age I was much more limited in complexity and stratification, with very little commercial activity or craft specialization.

The biblical traditions emphasize the tribal structure of this period preceding the rise of the state. Nowhere in this material, however, do we find an explanation of how the notion of tribe was conceptualized, what the composition of tribes was, how the tribes related to one another on the economic and political levels, or the structure of society in general. In some traditions there is emphasis placed on the number of tribes composing early Israel as being twelve (for example, Judges 1).[38] Judges 5, on the other hand, lists only ten. There are also tribes introduced in the narratives that are allied with "Israel," but are never included in the lists (for example, the Calebites and the Kenites). Neither is there any evidence of precise geographical boundaries for the tribes. The city lists associated with the description of land distribution in Joshua 13–19 are now believed to reflect the situation during the monarchic period, and thus their value for determining the original settlement patterns of the Iron Age I highlands is limited. They may provide information about patterns at the dawn of the monarchy, when the tribal regions were transformed into administrative districts for purposes of taxation and recruiting labor for public projects and military service. But even for this period, the lists may be idealized.[39]

In relation to social structure, only very schematic and superficial representations occur. Examples are found in Joshua 7:16–18, where society is divided into families, lineages or clans (see below), and tribes, or in census reports such as that in Numbers 26.

Although we have no descriptions, there are a number of terms that occur in the biblical texts that point to conceptualizations of different levels of organization in the tribal structure. As is clear in the discussion below, there is no clear consensus on exactly what these terms mean or what level in the organization they refer to. There is also a good bit of skepticism regarding whether they in fact represent the reality of the early social organization or were later imposed by the writers of the monarchic and postexilic periods.

The difficulty in understanding the meanings of these terms can be variously explained. First, the terms we, or ancient peoples, use to identify social categories refer to *ideal* and not necessarily *empirical* categories. In this respect, members of Israelite society themselves (at whatever time) were probably not precise in their use of these terms. It is also likely that in the course of the texts' transmission the meanings of the terms changed as tribal organization became subsumed under the centralized state, and that individuals in the circles that preserved them were not familiar with their earlier usage. Another possibility is that the Israelite societies (synchronically and diachronically) did not adhere to any single system.[40]

Kinship and Genealogies

Kinship systems and genealogies are ways of organizing and expressing relationships within a social system. In the modern Middle East, a wide variety of personal relationships are expressed in the language of family relationships.[41] How people regard themselves in kinship terms and how they behave toward one another as "kin" and "family" in tribal societies, therefore, cannot be accounted for entirely in genetic terms.

Kinship is expressed through genealogies. As an organizing principle, kinship relations are significant in terms of how people understand economic and political, as well as social, relationships and their relationships with outside groups. For example, village and family property and the formation of political and economic alliances among families and among villages are kinship-based. Kinship also operates as a kind of code in which relationships of power are defined. The primary function of genealogies, then, is not to produce and transmit accurate lists of biological relationships through time, but to define social, political, and economic relations, which are always open to revision, thus representing a fluid mixture of genuine and fictitious kinship connections.

Genealogies, especially those in segmented systems, also serve as memory devices for keeping track of the relationships among individuals and groups and for ranking them in terms of inheritance and succession rights. When relationships or statuses change, genealogies fluctuate in order to maintain their usefulness. When individuals or groups decline in prominence, their names are dropped. Thus, omissions are also important in understanding the dynamics of social relationships. As a result of such omissions, contrasting genealogies may exist that derive either from different times in a group's life or from different spheres of social life. Written forms are more resistent to fluidity than oral forms, but both may be adjusted as a way of keeping them functional and "true" in relation to the existing set of relationships. Variants of written genealogies such as those in the Hebrew Bible, therefore, may not necessarily be the result of copyist error or textual corruption, but signs of the ongoing life of the genealogy.

Tribal genealogical systems have been studied extensively by anthropologists, and their conclusions have been applied to ancient Israelite society by a number of scholars.[42] In some cases, we have different versions of a genealogy, which give us some clues about how different groups in different time periods and social contexts chose to construct their understandings of a particular set of social relations according to their particular biases and agendas. The genealogies in the so-called Priestly traditions, for example, are very likely stereotyped conceptions of the social structure of early "Israel" that are meant to legitimate the writer's ideals about social relations at the time they were written down. Many of the genealogies in the Hebrew Bible are no doubt the result of such secondary and fictive systematization, constructed at the time they were written down, and later incorporated into the narrative framework. Whether any of them actually date as far back as Iron Age I is probably impossible to determine. But investigating them can nevertheless provide us with clues about the varied ways in which social, political, and economic relations were understood in some periods.

In spite of problems having to do with dating the genealogies in the Hebrew Bible, anthropological models have allowed us to approach their investigation with new questions. Particularly useful in helping us to understand the nature and function of biblical genealogies are: (1) the typical distinctions in composition between oral and written genealogies; (2) the existence in tribal societies of contrasting types of genealogies with different functions—*segmented* genealogies, which have segments or "branches" and are often preserved orally, and *linear* genealogies, which represent only a single line of descendants, linking the last named to those that are named before; (3) the tendency of genealogies to be fluid and flexible, with names often being moved onto, within, and off lists; and (4) the multiple functions served by genealogies in the socioeconomic, domestic, political, and religious spheres of life.[43]

Early Israel as a Segmented Social System

It is now widely accepted that the highland population of Iron Age I Palestine probably consisted of nomads, seminomads, semisedentary peoples, and sedentary farmers and village residents, all types of societies that would in one way or another have been engaged in symbiotic relationships with one another. Segmentation is a typical organizational principle in all these types of societies in the Middle East.

Recent descriptions of classical segmented systems include a variety of characteristics.[44] Ernest Gellner identifies the two essential characteristics of a segmented system as: (1) the primary means of maintaining order at every level of segmentation is opposition between groups; and (2) the criterion by which groups are defined is "coextensive society itself."[45]

More specifically, in a segmented system society is composed of "segments" and is characterized by considerable flexibility. Segments are units within the system that have the same structure—for example, families, clans or tribal sections (sometimes called lineages), and tribes. Individuals can have overlapping membership in more than one segment in the system at a time, as their economic, social, political, and religious affiliations do not always coincide, and their regional and supraregional identities can be based on different allegiances. Every individual is enmeshed in multiple, sometimes conflicting, affiliations and alliances, related, for example, to factions, age, or gender. An individual segment is usually autonomous and tends to align itself politically so as to obtain maximum advantage for itself. This results in a continually changing organization. If the political conditions change, the subgroups may change their political and familial relationships with other subgroups within the tribe, or even with other tribes.

Individuals within this type of system conceive of relationships among themselves on the basis of shared common descent and are related *situationally* to one another. In the classic segmented system an ancestor represents political unity in a group, and symbolizes its limits. Everyone "descended" from the ancestor is considered to be a member of the particular segment and is responsible, for example, for protecting it. Any "segment" of society—from individuals to small, cooperative groups of close patrilineal relations, tribal sections, and tribes—"sees itself as an independent unit in relation to another segment of the same section, but sees both segments as a unity in relation to another segment."[46] Segments at the same "level" are ideally equal and are defined by "balanced opposition" toward one another.

The Rwala bedouin, for example, have five tribal "sections" with genealogies that are essentially fixed. Below the level of these tribal "sections," genealogies are more flexible and reflect the situations of actual living groups. The named groups below the level of the tribal section ("minimal sections") are call *ibn 'amm* by the Rwala, and are said to be descended from a male line five generations distant. The minimal sections are essentially economic units, whose members cooperate very closely with one another.[47] The composition of descent groups below the level of tribal section changes slowly over time to accommodate shifting economic and political realities. Intermarriage is one of the ways in which individuals can claim new ties to other segments. The fact that women do not appear in the formal genealogies provides the necessary latitude for this flexibility.[48]

In segmented societies, there is no permanent "governmental" authority (according to theory). In the absence of centralized power, political order is dependent on the ways in which communities relate to one another through the segmentary principle, and efforts are made to control conflict and maintain order at the lowest possible level. The bottom "level" in a segmented system is composed of discrete camping clusters or rural local communities that claim common identity and may share residence in a common territory or herd together, and expect other group members to support their interests. Many households within such a community, but not necessarily all, claim common kinship ties. Conflict with other groups is understood in relation to collective honor, and members of individual groups, which are *situationally* defined, are expected to support one another. High value is placed on the autonomy and honor of individuals, as is a "balanced opposition" of honor-bearing individuals and groups. Cultural notions of persuasion, mediation, honor, and negotiation, rather than use of force, are emphasized in conflict resolution and the maintenance of social order. Thus one becomes a man of honor in such societies by learning how to be persuasive.[49] The balanced structure of segmented systems also helps to contain violence by maintaining the ideal of equality, even though in actuality egalitarianism is not absolute.[50] Even so, political leadership can exist, as long as it remains personal and is not institutionalized into an office, so that the ideal of egalitarianism can be upheld in spite of political inequality on the ground.

As an example of *flexibility* in a typical segmented group, Eickelman points to the Bni Bataw of Morroco.[51] As is the case for other segmented societies, the rural local community is the most important "level" in terms of everyday activity. Individuals in a rural local community claim patrilineal kinship to one another (among other ties), but cannot specifically identify how all members of a group are mutually related. They often point to an unspecified *ahistorical* past as a way of legitimizing present-day alignments. What counts, then, is not how individuals are in reality related by blood, but who acts together with whom in a sustained way on various ritual and political occasions.

Flexibility is also apparent in the makeup of the community's council. The council is an informal body constituted by male heads of households, who consult on such issues of mutual concern as transhumant movements, quarrels over water and pasture rights, and other types of collective obligations. When circumstances permit, individual households or groups of households who are dissatisfied with membership in a particular local community may break away to join another rural local community or to form their own in a process of fissioning and fusing.

Marriage ties, a wife's inheritance, or purchasing land in another rural local community can serve as the basis for a realignment. Normally, the realignments occur only within the context of nearby local communities, and often households are not even physically relocated. What is of primary significance, then, is not a person's actual physical location, but who is aligned with whom in what circumstances.

The next "level" in the Bni Bataw system, the *section,* is usually composed of three or four local communities and is somewhat more stable in composition over time, although composition and formal identity do tend to change gradually. The greater stability of the sections over against the lower levels in the system is connected with their recognition as administrative entities. Prior to the colonial period, for example, sections were responsible for constructing fortified compounds for collective defense against intertribal raids, making collective arrangements for grazing rights to pastures controlled by neighboring groups, and arranging "ritual alliances" between rural local communities and sections in the same or different tribes, in which groups agreed to refrain from fighting and raiding one another and, at least in principle, to aid one another when there were threats from third parties. Such alliances were generally based on exchange of herding rights.

At the level of "tribe," coalitions of various sections and rural local communities within the tribes often occurred, but the tribe appears to have existed more as a means of providing a range of potential identities than as a base for sustained collective action.

Interpreters of early Israel's social world continue to debate the issue of whether segmented social organizations, systems, and ideologies existed and whether the segmented model is appropriate.[52] In making a determination about the utility of this model, it is important to note the distinction between segmentation and "segmentary lineage theory." Segmentation involves *culturally* maintained *principles* that *inform* social action in many tribal contexts, not actual observable actions and relationships. This principle should not be confused with "segmentary *lineage* theory," which *does* attempt to identify real actions and relationships. Segmentary lineage theory has been criticized for its tendency to ignore cultural principles, along with its implication that political relationships of *actual groups* are formed primarily or exclusively on the basis of lineage descent, at each "level" of society being balanced by others with roughly equal strength.[53] Objections to the model's application to the situation in early Israel, as far as I can tell, are related, then, not to the *principle* of segmentation, but to segmentary lineage theory.

In any case, this model does seem to accord well with the archaeological information from Iron Age I, and some of the texts in the Hebrew Bible seem to embody notions associated with the cultural principles of segmentation as outlined below. Even though we cannot really argue that they reflect historical reality, they nevertheless possibly tell us something about how these principles were understood by the writers and editors of the texts.

Anthropological Models of Tribal Organization

In his recent anthropological survey of contemporary Middle Eastern societies, Dale F. Eickelman notes that a common "family resemblance" is identifiable among Middle Eastern notions of tribe, in spite of variations from region to region. Because of this it is possible, he argues, to make general statements about common elements or "family resemblances" in these notions without presuming that they all must fit into a neat typology. He conceives of these common elements as "partial similarities that can meaningfully be compared and contrasted, rather than exact, nearly botanical identities asserted by simpler but less accurate theoretical assumptions."[54]

Defining what a "tribe" is, and how tribes are organized, has proven to be a notoriously complex task. Part of the problem in earlier attempts to come up with a broad, all-encompassing "ideal type" is that tribes from different regions of the world often have little in common.[55] This has also been a problem in some of the studies of tribes in ancient Palestine that have depended on models developed in studies of African tribes rather than on those relating to the geographical context of the Middle East. The concepts of tribe refer to real relations and have social and economic significance, but these are highly variable, as tribal structure and membership change constantly. Within the context of a particular tribe, as practical definitions of self-identity change, so do factional alignments over land rights, marriage strategies, access to resources, and other aspects of society. Power and leadership also shift according to current membership in changeable descent groups.

Another complicating factor is that the context and goals of the person engaged in defining "tribe" affect the ways in which a tribe is conceptualized. *Administrative concepts* (that is, concepts developed by administrators of states into which tribes have been incorporated), for example, frequently assume a corporate identity and fixed territorial boundaries that many "tribes" do not possess.[56] Tribe members themselves, on the other hand, do not necessarily think of themselves primarily in relation to the state, and their social and political alignments frequently shift, even as the ways in which they conceive of boundaries tend to be blurred and flexible.[57]

It is too simplistic, then, to view tribalism as a single phenomenon, or as an undifferentiated whole, a peripheral social system, or simply a stage in the evolution of human civilization, as is often done. Rather, it is a complex system that brings people together for many different purposes, in the context of many different competing or alternative principles of alignment.[58]

Nevertheless, as Eickelman argues, it is possible to identify some "family resemblances" among Middle Eastern tribes. In general, a tribe is a group that is conceptualized in terms of genealogy, and may be either a *part* of a "nation" or identical with a *whole* "nation." Tribes are found in a wide range of socioeconomic settings, including pastoral nomads, settled farmers, or even urban dwellers, and their members are often, although not necessarily, politically unified.[59]

The composition of segments in social structure and the ways in which the structure is articulated vary from tribe to tribe and will also vary depending on whether the group is nomadic or sedentary, or a combination of both. For example, in a sedentary tribe, the village might be an identifiable segment in the system, whereas in a pastoral nomadic tribe, the "camp" would be the corresponding segment. In terms of articulation, sedentary groups tend to develop more rigid lineages than is the case for nomadic groups. Because kin groups put a great deal of energy into working and protecting particular plots of land, their sense of ownership and investment, along with feelings of in-group loyalty and obligation, tend to be stronger. Kin groups in nomadic societies, on the other hand, tend to have looser, more flexible lineages because of their dependence on being able to gain access to widely dispersed areas. Flexible and cooperative alignments that allow them to move beyond the social and territorial boundaries of smaller, blood-related kin groups offer advantages in this respect. By means of such processes as "telescoping," "fusioning," and "grafting," pastoral nomads continually generate loose and flexible networks of cooperation and alignments, through which they maintain control over widespread rangeland pastures, watering places, camping sites, storage depots, and burial grounds. Complicating matters further is the fact that it is not unusual for a certain amount of sedentarization and nomadization to occur among individual households, depending on their personal circumstances and shifts in economic and ecological conditions.[60]

There are also numerous variations with respect to political organization. Some tribes are organized without strong or centralized apparatuses of power, while others are governed by a supreme tribal leader or chieftain.[61] Tribal elites tend to think of themselves as egalitarian and making decisions collectively. But in reality egalitarianism rarely exists.

Ideologies relating to tribal identity also vary, but are generally based on a concept of *political* identity formed through common patrilineal descent, as expressed through genealogies. Political actions in such tribes (the patterns in which groups of people actually come together or come in conflict with one another in a political manner) are generally explained by anthropologists in terms of *segmentary theory*, as has been indicated above, although other grounds for political action may coexist with segmentary ones. Ideologies are elaborated in varying degrees by individual members of a tribe, depending on their social positions and particular situations. Individuals who are socially and politically dominant often elaborate such ideologies in more complex ways than others, using them, for example, to solidify political alliances with members of other tribal groups and to enhance their own positions in relation to state authorities.[62]

Another problem that arises in attempting to present a general description of tribal organization is that the terminology used to designate organizational levels varies from scholar to scholar. The use of the term "lineage," for example, is often avoided now because of its connection to segmentary lineage theory, which implies a rigid system in which unilineal descent is associated with actual blood ties. It is also sometimes difficult to distinguish between a "lineage" and a "clan." Both lineages and clans are unilineal groups that perceive themselves as being descendants of a particular individual. But they are different in that the genealogy of a lineage is more permanent, reflecting both real and postulated kinship between its members, while a clan genealogy varies according to particular clan segments, and its members, who assume common ancestry, cannot demonstrate their genealogical connections.

As is indicated in the discussion of segmented societies above, a tribe is typically segmented into at least two or more subdivisions (referred to variously in the literature as sections, moieties, subtribes). The form, function, and significance of these subdivisions correspond in most respects to those of the tribe, but they apply to only a section of it. A section may be segmented into a number of "clans" which, again, in terms of structure and function resemble both the subtribe and the tribe. On all three of these levels of integration it is the *concept* of blood relatedness rather than actual blood relations that motivates common activities. A clan may be segmented into a number of maximal lineages which are in turn composed of lineages and minimal lineages. In some tribes, the village or camp is also an identifiable segment in the system. Finally, the lineages themselves are subdivided into extended and nuclear families (although the extended family is not always a significant social unit).

Integration and cooperation are typically strongest at the lowest level of the nuclear or extended family, weaker in higher levels of organization, and weakest at the level of "nation" or tribal confederacy (if one exists). The smaller units in a tribal system (for example, clans or lineages) rarely unite with each other politically. When they do, it is normally because of some threat or crisis that requires it. In between times of threat, some sense of solidarity and unity and loose bonding are maintained through economic and religious ties (for example, trade and ritual). A sense of unity is further supported by myths of common descent, fictitious kinship links by means of mythical or assumed ancestry.

Lemche's summary of the social structure of nomadic societies in the Middle East offers a good example of how individuals relate to the various levels in tribal social structure. Lemche notes that one common feature of all nomadic societies in the Middle East is that the family is the basic social and economic unit, although politically it has little significance. Extended families with up to three generations sometimes live together, but such families, he indicates, are relatively few in number. The family is exogamous, and the ideal marriage is between agnates (relatives related through male descent or on the father's side). In actuality, however, this is not necessarily the case, especially in "princely" families, where political concerns motivate alliances outside the paternal line.

The family in nomadic tribal societies is economically autonomous, each owning its own livestock. In terms of inheritance, there is ordinarily no strict rule dictating that the oldest son must inherit a larger share than others, so ideally all sons have equal rights of inheritance.

The camp, composed of families who travel together through the annual cycle, is the next level in the structure. The camp is usually a cooperative unit in which all members share in caring for the animals and, in cases where agriculture is practiced, in farming. Its organization and the principles that govern it, and the extent of its political significance in the larger structure, also vary.[63]

The next level in the characteristic social structure of Middle Eastern nomadic societies is the lineage, which consists of a number of related families who claim descent from a single tribal ancestor. The lineage tends to be a fairly stable social unit, in that it almost always bears a name that it retains for long periods of time. But, as has been emphasized above, it is not completely inflexible. Divisions sometimes occur that may lead to the emergence of new lineages, and the genealogies are always susceptible to adjustment when circumstances require it. The actual form of a genealogy represents the ideological basis for the composition of the lineage in question within particular situational contexts. An individual male's political and economic status within the system is also established through his position in the lineage system. Ordinarily, rights to such things as pasturage and water are connected to lineages, and the lineage is responsible for defending the rights of its members and for protecting individual members. The lineage is typically endogamous, that is, marital ties are usually formed within the lineage. Within the larger system, some lineages may have more power and status than others, and the status of the individuals within a given lineage is relatively homogeneous. Tribal leadership, if any, usually operates at the lineage level, or within the families comprising the lineage. Often, there is an officially acknowledged leader whose role is usually confined to how his lineage relates to other segments in the structure rather than governing within the lineage itself.

Maximal lineages, clans, and subtribes are all above the level of the lineage, but have decreasing importance in relation to daily life. It is rare, for example, for the tribe to function collectively.[64]

Models of Tribes in Iron Age I Palestine

One of the characteristics of earlier studies that considered the nature of the tribe in Iron Age I Palestine following the "settlement" was the assumption that a number of its features were "survivals" of nomadic ideals.[65] As indicated above, however, recent studies of tribal societies have shown that many tribes in the recent history of the Middle East share a number of similar features, whether nomadic or sedentary. And more and more among biblical scholars there is a consensus that a significant portion of the population comprising Iron Age I highland Palestine derived from sedentary groups.

C. H. J. de Geus's more recent work on tribes in ancient Israel was particularly important because he argued that biblical scholars should abandon the notion that the Semites, and thus the ancient "Israelites," were originally nomads who came from the Arabian desert in successive waves of invaders.[66] He also points out the important distinction between transhumance, which is associated with agriculture, and pure nomadism. Contrary to earlier studies, he is also aware of the fact that tribal organization is not associated *only* with nonsedentary societies. For him, then, the evidence for tribal organization in sedentary societies, such as those portrayed in the biblical texts, is not evidence of survivals from an earlier nomadic stage. He also deals with the issue of the political significance of the tribe in relation to other levels of tribal organization, and concludes that the most important political group, and thus the locus of the real power in society and the basis of political organization, was not the tribe, but the *mišpāḥāh* or "clan." This level of Israelite social organization, he proposed, was made up of the population of a small town or, in some cases, several clans in the same town. The tribe, composed of groups of clans, was primarily a *geographic* concept that served as a means of enabling individual Israelites in a given region to define their relationships to other Israelites in other parts of the country. The tribe, therefore, had no significance in isolation from the entirety of Israel.[67]

One of the issues concerning Iron Age I sociopolitical organization that has yet to come to any kind of consensus is the question of how the various tribes in Palestine related to one another (socially, economically, politically, and religiously). In his extensive study of the tribal period, Norman Gottwald agreed with de Geus on most questions of detail in relation to social structure.[68] But he attributed more significance to the level of the tribes and their participation in an intertribal organization, which he perceived as being of central importance.[69] "Israel" as a "confederacy or league of tribes" was, in Gottwald's estimation, "the widest societal and culture-bearing unit of associated egalitarian Yahwistic tribes."[70] The basic characteristics of this confederacy were a common concern for the Yahwistic cult, shared laws and ideology, a commitment to economic egalitarianism, and a readiness to organize military opposition against external, threatening forces such as those of the Canaanites and Philistines. For Gottwald, then, the tribe was "the primary organizational segment,"

> an autonomous association of segmented extended families (*bēth-'āvōth*) grouped in village/neighborhood protective associations (*mishpāḥōth*), averaging about 50 per tribe, functionally interlocking through intermarriage, practices of mutual aid, common worship, and a levy of troops.[71]

What shaped these tribes into such units was their common experience of oppression and rebellion, as well as their territorial grouping in areas that were determined by factors such as terrain, climate, or enclaves of Canaanite city-states.[72]

In his more recent studies, Lemche[73] agrees with de Geus that the Israelite tribes were primarily territorial units. On this basis he argues that the individual tribes identified themselves particularly with their respective geographical territories, and postulates that the variations in the descriptions of tribal territories in the texts correspond to the normal fissioning and fusioning processes of traditional tribal societies.

The composition of these tribes, in Lemche's estimation, essentially included the lineages and clans inhabiting the regions with which the names of particular tribes were associated. They maintained a sense of social identity on the basis of shared interest in keeping the territory in their own hands. Tribal affiliation, which would have been flexible and expressed in terms of kinship, could have been based also on any number of other factors—for example, actual or fictitious blood ties, common history, common economic interests, or common external enemies.

Lemche agrees that there were probably tribal alliances, but argues that they would not necessarily have been stable and fixed. There is not, he asserts, a single concrete bit of evidence dating from the second millennium B.C.E. that indicates that Israel was ever constituted as a permanent coalition during this period, as is implied in the "all-Israel" construct of the Deuteronomistic traditions, or that there was any single sanctuary that might have been the center of such a league, as such scholars as Noth and Gottwald have argued. The picture presented in the biblical texts, in his estimation, suggests that the tribes may have been united religiously in some way, but it is not certain that there was a central shrine that represented this unity. There were probably economic ties as well, expressed, for example, through trade.

Constructs of Tribal Period Social Structure

Anthropologists have noted a tendency for tribal structure to remain intact even after a tribal territory has been incorporated into a state system, and a number of biblical scholars continue to maintain that the basic tribal structure of Iron Age I persisted, at least in rural areas, throughout Iron Age II.[74]

It is possible, then, that portions of the biblical construct may reflect to some extent the Iron Age I situation.

The three Hebrew terms that occur most frequently in the biblical texts that clearly refer to levels of social structure are *bêt 'āb, mišpāḥāh,* and *šēbeṭ* (or *maṭṭeh*). It is far from clear, however, what each of these terms means in many of the contexts in which they occur.

The terms in question are normally understood to designate the nuclear or extended family (*bêt 'āb*), the clan or lineage (*mišpāḥāh*), and the tribe (*šēbeṭ* or *maṭṭeh*). Another term that is sometimes used is *'eleph* (for example, Judges 6–8), which in some contexts may refer to the same level as *mišpāḥāh* or perhaps even to another level.[75] A close examination of the writers' use of these terms, however, indicates that they very likely have a variety of different meanings, depending in part on the literary contexts in which they are used.

The term *bêt 'āb,* which occurs frequently in the ancestral narratives, seems to overlap in some instances with *mišpāḥāh*.[76] In some cases it appears to refer to the nuclear or extended family, but in others to "lineage" or "clan."[77] In Genesis 7:1 and 45:10–11, for example, *bêt* clearly refers to the extended family. But in other passages it is not clear whether it refers to extended or nuclear families or to lineages.[78] Even in passages in which *bêt 'āb* occurs together with *mišpāḥāh,* it is not easy to distinguish their relative meanings.[79] Sometimes *mišpāḥāh* occurs but *bêt 'āb* does not, and, again, the meaning is ambiguous.[80] There are also passages in Judges 6–8 in which *bêt 'āb* possibly refers to lineage rather than family or extended family, and one in Judges 9:1 where "mother's house" also seems to refer to a lineage. "David's house" clearly refers to a lineage, as does "Saul's house."

The term *mišpāḥāh* occurs most often in census lists and genealogies, many of which are Priestly, and much more rarely in narrative contexts.[81] The term *bêt 'āb,* on the other hand, is not normally used in Priestly genealogies and census lists.

The census list in Numbers 26 indicates one way in which the internal organization of the tribes was conceived in the Priestly traditions. Reference to the *bêt 'āb* occurs only once in this list (v. 2), where Israel's leaders are assigned to take a census of the people according to their *bêt 'ābôt*. Thereafter, the use of the term *mišpāḥāh* suggests that it represents the same basic unit as the *bêt 'āb*.

In Numbers 1, where Moses is instructed to take a census of the *mišpāḥāh* of *bêt 'āb,* the census does not penetrate below the level of tribe. The emphasis is on determining the number of grown men in the various tribes according to the various subdivisions of the tribe in question, but the nature of these subdivisions is not revealed. Numbers 1, then, does not really provide any information about how these two segments of society were understood. Neither of the census lists in Numbers, then, tells us much more than that at this stage in the formation of the traditions there seems to have been some uncertainty about how the terms related to social reality and to each other, and that the boundaries between them were fluid and overlapped somewhat. The stereotypical use of *mišpāḥāh* in the Priestly lists, therefore, may be a Priestly systematization of kinship units that is secondary and has no relation to the social reality the term may at one time have been associated with.

Because of this confusion in the texts, anthropological models have been useful in attempts to reconstruct what the social reality might have been, even though a number of different constructs have resulted. The most thorough treatment to date of the biblical references relating to social structure is that of S. Bendor.[82]

Bendor sees the structure of Israelite society as having remained essentially the same from the time of the "settlement" until the end of the monarchic period.[83] He emphasizes in his study the difficulty posed by the blurring of boundaries in the biblical texts among the levels in the sequence *bêt 'āb/ mišpāḥāh/ šebeṭ*, which is especially prominent as indicated above in the usage of *bêt 'āb* and *mišpāḥāh* (which he translates "extended family" and "sib" respectively).[84] Part of the difficulty, he suggests, may be due to varying perspectives from which the *bêt 'āb* would have been viewed: for example, the synchronic perspective of the *bêt 'āb* as constructed by its component generations would have differed from the diachronic perspective. Generational differences would also have affected the perspectives from which the *bêt 'āb* was viewed: father, son, and grandson would each have seen the *bêt 'āb* and its familial relations differently.[85] One of Bendor's aims, then, is to construct a general framework in which the dynamic balance of kinship relations can be viewed both synchronically and diachronically (that is, statically and dynamically).[86] He acknowledges that in attempting to do this he is presenting "abstractions," and quotes Evans-Pritchard:

> [The anthropologist] seeks to discover the structural order of the society, the patterns of which, once established, enable him to see it as a whole, as a set of interrelated abstractions. Then the society is not only culturally intelligible . . . but also becomes sociologically intelligible . . . the social anthropologist discovers . . . its basic structure. This structure cannot be seen. It is a set of abstractions, each of which, though derived, it is true, from analysis of observed behaviour, is fundamentally

> an imaginative construct of the anthropologist himself. By relating these abstractions to one another logically so that they present a pattern he can see the society in its essentials and as a single whole.[87]

Most reconstructions of ancient Israelite social structure subscribe to the interpretation that the *bêt 'āb* consisted of the extended family, with as many as three generations living together as a residential group,[88] that this segment of society was the primary social and economic unit, and that it was exogamous,[89] although there are differing nuances in their arguments. Lemche, for example, acknowledges that the emphasis in the Hebrew Bible is on extended families rather than nuclear families, but suggests that this has to do with the fact that the figures portrayed in most of the narratives are great men—that is, although the extended family was probably the *ideal,* in reality the nuclear family was probably more persuasive in day-to-day existence.[90] The centrality of the nuclear family is reflected in the custom of Levirate marriage (Genesis 38; Ruth; Deut. 25:5–10), which emphasizes the survival of the nuclear family, which is threatened by extinction when the father of the house dies without having left sons.

Bendor agrees with the consensus that the *bêt 'āb* was a self-sufficient social and economic unit consisting of three or four generations, including the head of household ("father"), who had authority over it, and his wives, their sons and their wives, their unmarried daughters, the sons' offspring, and nonrelated dependents.[91] The *bêt 'āb* was patrilineal (descent was reckoned through the male line) and patrilocal (the wife left the *bêt 'āb* of her father to reside in the *bêt 'āb* of her husband). This segment of society, then, was composed of nuclear domestic units that consisted of the households of sons within the *bêt 'āb*.[92] This household constituted a unit in its own right, although it was dependent upon the *bêt 'āb*.

The status of the individual male in a nuclear unit, according to Bendor, was dependent on his position in the *bêt 'āb* in relation to his father and brothers, especially with respect to his portion of the *naḥala,* or patrimony. This consisted of the land belonging to the kinship group as a whole, which was divided into plots inherited by the sons.[93] The plot was the basis for the nuclear unit's status in the *bêt 'āb,* just as the *naḥala* as a whole was the basis of the *bêt 'āb*'s status within the *mišpāḥāh* and of the *mišpāḥāh* in the larger society.[94] These nuclear units were not necessarily uniform or equal in terms of distribution of wealth and status. Although grazing pastures were shared by all member of the *bêt 'āb,* for example, flocks were the property of each nuclear unit, and the vineyards and fields belonged to the units that inherited or planted them.[95]

It is very typical in Middle Eastern tribal societies, as Bendor suggests for ancient Israel, for some individuals to be accorded more prestige than others. Even though ideally they regard themselves as equals, there are nevertheless considerable differences in social status and prestige that are associated with such qualities as wealth, warlike accomplishments, and eloquence.[96]

Bendor identifies the social functions of this segment of society as: protecting, cultivating, and developing inherited land; clearing and preparing new land; passing knowledge from generation to generation; bearing responsibility for daily existence and survival; arranging marriages; avenging blood; maintaining internal order; redeeming land that had fallen into the hands of creditors and kinsmen who had sold themselves; safeguarding the *mišpāḥāh*'s rights of inheritance; allocating resources and dividing the obligations of the *mišpāḥāh* among its units; and performing the rituals associated with sacrifice, holidays, marriage, birth, death, and burial.[97]

In terms of the diachronic dynamics affecting social structure and status, Bendor argues that the distribution of inheritance would have determined to some extent the ways in which relations within a particular *bêt 'āb* would have shifted over time. A *naḥala* of regular size and resources, if repeatedly divided over several generations, for example, would have been reduced to a series of plots that could not support everyone in the *bêt 'āb*. Over time a point would have been reached when subdivision among heirs was no longer possible because of the limited availability of property. The *bêt 'āb* might have responded to such a situation by occasional fissioning. Or it might have responded by passing the inheritance to only some of the brothers, or only the eldest, in which case the others would be called by the name of their brothers in their *naḥala*, that is, they would no longer be units in their own right within the *bêt 'āb*.

In Bendor's construct, the *bêt 'āb* was interrelated with the *mišpāḥāh*, the next identifiable level in the social structure, in the following ways: the head of household participated in the institution of "elders"; the *bêt 'āb* appealed to and accepted judgment from the *mišpāḥāh* in conflict situations that could not be resolved within the *bêt 'āb* itself; the *bêt 'āb* requested assistance from the *mišpaḥāh* in times of crisis and participated in periodic land distribution; it appealed to the *mišpāḥāh* for assistance in relation to blood feuds and marriages; and it participated in communal rituals.[98]

The *mišpāḥāh* is typically understood to have been composed of a number of extended families ("father's houses") that resided together in a village or small town.[99] A territorial identity for the *mišpāḥāh* is suggested in the tribal boundary lists in Joshua 13–19, where the tribes are allotted land according to their *mišpāḥāh*. Some scholars equate it with "clan,"[100] a view that is generally based on Joshua 7:17, where a lot-casting procedure follows the order of *mišpāḥāh, bêt 'āb,* and an individual and his immediate family. Others view it as being closer in definition to lineage (a descent group composed of a number of residential groups in Lemche's definition[101]), and yet others as "sib."[102]

Gottwald defines the *mišpāḥāh* as a "protective association of families," consisting of:

> a cluster of extended families living in the same or nearby villages . . . providing socioeconomic mutual aid for its constituent families, contributing troop quotas to the tribal levy, and indirectly serving alone or in concert to provide a local jural community.[103]

In addition to the *mišpāḥāh,* Gottwald suggests that there were also "cross-cutting" associations, or sodalities, in the Iron Age I social structure. These included: protective associations that provided mutual aid and mustering a citizen army, the ritual congregation, the Levite priests, and probably the Kenites (itinerant metalworkers). In his construct, groupings of protective associations and other sodalities, tribes, and an intertribal confederacy operated in various ways to provide mutual aid, external defense, and a religious ideology of covenanted or treaty-linked equals.[104]

Bendor disagrees in some respects with Gottwald's construct of the *mišpāḥāh,* arguing that there is no evidence that it was an "association" rather than a genetic group (especially given the fundamentally genetic concept prevalent in the biblical texts), even though some are artificial schemes. He agrees with Gottwald, however, that the *mišpāḥāh* probably was not exogamous (that is, members of the same *mišpāḥāh* were marriageable partners), but this does not prove that it was a "protective association" with no genetic ties.[105]

Lemche hypothesizes that the term *mišpāḥāh* is more likely to refer to the levels of lineage and maximal lineage than to a clan, although the formal similarities between "clan" and "lineage" make it difficult to determine whether the Iron Age I tribal social structure included clans. None of the biblical references to the *mišpāḥāh,* in his estimation, can clearly be identified as fitting the clan model, although neither do they, he concedes, provide enough information to argue definitively in favor of the lineage model.[106]

In the biblical traditions, especially as portrayed in the Genesis narratives, the ideal Israelite marriage was endogamous within this level.[107] Some traditions, particularly those in Genesis, suggest that polygyny was an acceptable practice at some points in Israel's history—probably for the purpose of acquiring more children or more prestige and power—although on the whole monogamy is the norm in the biblical construct. As in many societies, the arrangement of marriages involved an exchange of gifts to cement the relationship between the families, particularly in the form of gifts given to the bride's father.[108]

In his discussion of the relationship between the *bêt 'āb* and the *mišpāḥāh,* Bendor suggests that much of the dynamic of the *bêt 'āb* occurred in the blurred boundaries between the two. The demarcation between them varied according to particular situations and the points of reference of the individuals or groups concerned. This constituted a continuous process in which the *bêt 'āb* renewed itself and the *mišpāḥāh* grew, changing the points of reference for each generation.[109] Sometimes this resulted in the creation of new *mišpāḥôt* as *bêt 'ābôt* naturally increased and branched out in a kind of continuous segmentation. These new *mišpāḥôt* would have continued in some cases to be associated with the traditional *mišpāḥôt,* whose territory they regarded as their patrimony. This would have been one of the factors that contributed to the continual overlap between places of settlement and *mišpaḥôt*. In other cases, the new *mišpāḥôt* would have expanded into new settlements. In such cases, as a sign of the segmentation that had occurred, a link would have been added in the genealogical record, horizontally as a "brother," and vertically as a "son." In this way the collective responsibility of the *mišpāḥāh* was maintained, since the *mišpāḥāh* and *bêt 'ābôt* continued to exist as active kinship groups. The kinship group may also have been reduced in size at times. Either strategy would have contributed to the maintenance of demographic stability.[110]

In considering function in his reconstruction of this level in the social structure (maximal lineage or possibly clan), Lemche argues that it is unlikely that it was more important socially or politically than the *bêt 'āb* (a designation that was applicable to a variety of groups). It was the economically independent family (whether nuclear or extended) that was of decisive importance. The lineage was probably significant when irregular situations arose—for example, economic misfortune that entailed the loss of communal lands, external political pressure, or conflicts among the members of the lineage. Conflicts within lineages would have been internally resolved, and conflicts between families not affiliated by marriage would have been resolved either through negotiations or by feuds.[111]

In the biblical text, just as the *bêt 'āb* is considered part of the *mišpāḥāh,* so the *mišpāḥāh* is considered part of the *šēbeṭ* (or *maṭṭeh*) ("tribe"), the next level in the social structure. The term appears primarily as a component in "the twelve tribes of Israel," in the organizational schemes including the sequence *bêt 'āb/ mišpāḥāh/ šēbeṭ,* and in texts concerned with tribal boundaries. It is portrayed as an active social unit primarily in the literature concerning the period of settlement and the beginning of the monarchy. The names of the tribes often have geographical significance, in that they tend to appear in conjunction with geographical terms such as "land" or "mountain." These references have led to the proposal that the tribe functioned primarily, although not solely, as a territorial-demographic entity, and was the least active level in terms of affecting the everyday lives of individuals.[112]

Women

Women are an essential part of any social system. Until recently, however, there has been a tendency to ignore them in most fields of inquiry, including biblical studies, archaeology, and anthropology. But in the past several decades there has been a significant increase in studies that focus on this sometimes forgotten gender. In archaeological and anthropological bibliographies, we now see such titles as *Engendering Archaeology*[113] and *Dislocating Masculinity;*[114] and in biblical studies, such titles as *Gender and Difference in Ancient Israel.*[115]

The biblical traditions introduce us in an indirect way primarily to the domestic status and roles of women. Women are almost always portrayed in relation to men—who are the main characters—as wives, daughters, sisters, mothers, or widows. Occasionally, other roles are represented: women as prostitutes, as having some special wisdom or skill, as foreigners, as prophetesses, and as queens (although in this role the status as *wife* or mother of the king is what is emphasized). Very little is revealed concerning how women participated in social, political, and religious institutions outside the domestic sphere.

Whether the status and roles of women changed in any significant way throughout the course of Israel's history is difficult to determine on the basis of either the biblical or archaeological information, although it is likely, at least in rural areas, that they remained consistent.

The traditions in Genesis clearly portray a patriarchal society, in which it was perfectly legitimate for men to marry more than one woman, and to have concubines as well. References to women in the Pentateuchal legal traditions treat women in a manner similar to the treatment of other kinds of property. The picture is of a society in which a woman has no power if she is not protected by a family, and even less if she is unable to participate in ensuring family continuity by providing her husband with children, especially male children to carry on the family name. According to the biblical construct, then, a woman's proper realm of influence was in relation to the family and related domestic pursuits.

The most thorough construct to date of women's roles and status in Iron Age I Palestine is that proposed by Carol Meyers.[116] Considering biblical texts, along with archaeological information and anthropological studies of women in preindustrial societies,[117] Meyers postulates that the absence of any sign of female dominance in the biblical texts does not necessarily mean that women were dominated. Nor, she suggests, is the apparent exclusion of women from such roles as the priesthood necessarily a sign that women were perceived as being inferior to men. And the fact that women are less visible publicly does not necessarily mean that they were submissive, or less important to the community. In support of her argument, Meyers points to anthropological studies that have drawn a distinction between "power" and "authority." In this distinction, authority is understood as requiring cultural legitimation, whereas power is seen as deriving from an ability to control, regardless of whether it is socially sanctioned. Women in Iron Age I Palestine, she suggests, could very well have had power, even if subordination to men with authority was what was officially sanctioned. The unauthorized power of women, then, was as important as male rights, and male authority would have been affected by female power. In further support of this argument, Meyers points to Edmund Leach's assertion that although "myth" does express a certain kind of "truth," it is not necessarily a "truth" that is based on everyday reality (that is, actions do not necessarily correspond to notions). The public "myth" of male dominance as expressed in the biblical traditions, then, according to Meyers, could well have been imposed on a situation that *functionally* was nonhierarchical.[118]

An important factor in Meyers's construct is her evaluation of the roles of women in relation to subsistence. She appeals to studies that have shown that the type of subsistence strategies in a given society affect the ways in which labor is distributed along gender lines, as well as how power is allocated within a community. These in turn affect the quality of relationships between men and women. Among the three factors she identifies as contributing to group survival in preindustrial societies—reproduction, sustenance, and defense—reproduction is the exclusive arena of women, sustenance requires contributions from both men and women, and defense is exclusively male. Meyers postulates that because it was necessary for men to give so much time and energy to terrace construction, it was also necessary for women to participate in the farming activities. This was in addition to attending to other responsibilities such as rearing and educating children, food preparation, sewing and weaving, and pottery production (possibly) in the domestic sphere (where women were dominant), all of which were also highly demanding in terms of energy. Because of the large amounts of energy required on the part of both men and women in order to survive in the Iron Age I "frontier" settlements, then, gender became blurred to some extent, and thus gender hierarchy in work roles was virtually nonexistent.[119]

Another issue that arises in relation to the role of women is the extent to which they were active in the cult. This, again, is particularly difficult to determine on the basis of the biblical traditions, which emphasize the religious roles of men. On the basis of archaeological information and comparative studies, however, it is possible to postulate that women in Iron Age I Palestine may have had a greater role than in subsequent periods. There is a growing consensus that during this period religion was practiced primarily in the context of the family, and that rituals were often carried out at household shrines. Meyers suggests that the father had the role of "priest" and "diviner" in this context, and that the mother functioned as a kind of wise woman, as well as a "diviner." Again, men very likely dominated in more public expressions of religion, but women would nevertheless have had important roles at the family level.[120]

Other Segments in the System

It is possible that the social structure in Iron Age I Palestine also included, as Gottwald has suggested, outsider or marginal groups that were considered by the dominant group to be structurally inferior, and that some memory of such groups is preserved in ancient Israel's traditions.[121] Structural inferiority is a state that exists for groups that are either (1) set outside the structural arrangements of a social system, or set apart in terms of status and roles ("outsidership"), or (2) simultaneously members of two or more groups who distinguish themselves from, and are even opposed to, one another ("marginality").[122]

Artisans and metalsmiths in particular in many societies, including traditional Middle Eastern societies, tend to exist either in a state of outsidership or marginality. Such groups tend to be regarded with ambivalence by the dominant social groups with which they are associated. There is, in fact, a clear incongruence between notions and actions with regard to such marginal groups—between the ambivalent attitudes directed toward them and a reliance on them for the production of economic and cultural necessities. The marginal character of such groups has in part to do with the fact that they do not participate in the primary economic activities such as farming and herding.

In the organization and structure of traditional African societies, for example, artisans and smiths tend to form groups apart. This separation may be radical, especially in East African pastoral societies where they are held in low esteem and are viewed with ambivalence and fear;[123] or it may take the form of endogamous families or guilds, as seems to be typical in agricultural societies in which they are honored, but also nevertheless feared. In either case, contact with them is avoided, and intermarriage with them is considered to be dangerous and polluting, and at least ideally is forbidden.

The pattern in traditional Middle Eastern Bedouin societies basically conforms with that identified for East African pastoral societies.[124] Artisans and smiths are marginalized, feared (they are believed to possess the "evil eye"), and shunned, and they form groups apart, which are typically fragmented and scattered, as is the case with the *ṣunna'* (tinkers and blacksmiths) and the *Ṣolluba*. Intermarriage with them is discouraged or forbidden.

In both East African and Middle Eastern Bedouin societies, smithing groups typically provide weapons for both parties engaged in warfare and are exempt from threats by either side. And in many societies they also function as mediators and ritual specialists, even where they are considered to have particularly low status.

Although none of the Hebrew terms used for identifying artisans or smiths in the biblical traditions is attached to the Kenites and Midianites (and we cannot definitively determine on the basis of the texts what the nature of these groups was), they are nevertheless portrayed in such a way that it is possible to hypothesize that they were structurally inferior to other groups in Iron Age I Palestine in ways that are very similar to the manner in which such groups are related to dominant groups in other traditional tribal societies. The Kenites and the related Midianites, for example, are portrayed as a people who were staunch supporters of Yahwism but never fully incorporated into the biblical construct of "Israelite" society. Their marginality is implied, for example, in Judges 4 and 5, where the "clan" of Heber the Kenite is described as having peaceful relations with Jabin, the king of Hazor (Judg. 4:17), but as nevertheless allied with "Israel." Some biblical scholars have argued that they were associated with activities that required moving between different geographic locations, either as caravaneers or as nomadic or seminomadic itinerant metalsmiths.[125] The biblical portrayal of the culture hero Cain,[126] who is identified as the ancestor of Tubal-Cain, the eponymous ancestor of metalsmiths, and may have had some association with the Kenites, may reflect the marginal status of such groups in ancient "Israel" and the ambivalent attitudes with which they may have been regarded.

It is also possible, as is the case in many tribal societies in Africa and the Middle East, that members of these marginal groups functioned as mediators and ritual specialists.[127]

As is evident from the models introduced in the previous chapter, it is likely that Iron Age I Palestine was characterized by variety and that, far from being static, the social situation continued to be dynamic in the sense that processes of fissioning and fusing of populations would have been common, as is typically the case in tribal societies.

SOCIAL AND POLITICAL INSTITUTIONS

Leadership

The biblical construct of the period preceding the establishment of a monarchic form of leadership in the book of Judges refers to tribal leaders called "judges." Those who are mentioned in lists (Judg. 10:1–5; 12:7–15) are said to have held office over "all Israel." Information is provided about their places of origin and burial, their families and wealth, and the lengths of their terms of office. But there is no information about what they actually did when they "judged" Israel, nor is there any indication of how they were appointed or what their roles and duties were.

Other "judges" are the central figures in the sagas about leaders who are said to have risen up to help resolve situations of conflict, either among the tribes of "Israel" themselves (for example, Judges 19–21) or with outsiders such as the Canaanites, the Midianites, the Moabites, and the Ammonites (for example, Judges 4 and 5). Each of these leaders is described with reference to his or her relationship to a particular tribe.

The role of the leaders in the sagas is primarily military. Only in the introduction (Judg. 2:16–19) are they called "judges." Otherwise they are said to have "judged" Israel (for example, Judg. 3:10; 15:20; 16:31), but are not called "judges." Othniel (3:9) and Ehud (3:15) are called "deliverers." Interestingly a woman, Deborah—who is also referred to as having "judged Israel" and is given the title "prophetess"—is the only leader who is portrayed as being involved in any way in administering justice.

In one case in the book of Judges (Judges 6–8), there is reference to permanent leadership. A military leader (Gideon, of the tribe of Manasseh) is asked by the people to rule over them, that is, take on the responsibilities of a king. He refuses, but one of his sons by a concubine in Shechem, Abimelech, makes himself king, although he is eventually overthrown and killed.

In 1 Samuel, Samuel is represented as administering justice in parts of

Benjamin (1 Sam. 7:15–17) and as having "judged" Israel by intercessory prayer and offering sacrifice (1 Sam. 7:5–14).

In spite of the clear reference to leaders in these stories, it is difficult to identify on the basis of their vague and stylized constructions what roles and statuses such leaders might have had in Iron Age I Palestine, or whether the construct had any basis in reality: Were they local leaders? leaders of all Israel? civilian leaders? military leaders? Here again, anthropological models have proved useful in determining the possible nature and function of leadership during this period.

One of the characteristics of segmented tribal societies is that there is typically no permanent, centralized power. Correspondingly, there are no specialized institutions of law and order or political office. Leadership is mainly confined to the status-bearing men of the community or clan/lineage and the family (often referred to as "elders"), and whatever authority a leader might have is without formal status. Choice of leaders above the level of family tends to be based on an individual's reputation and such personal qualities as "charisma," persuasiveness, and prowess as a warrior. This is the type of leadership that has often been referred to as "charismatic."[128]

At the tribal level in Middle Eastern nomadic societies there is often some sort of official leadership structure, usually a single designated leader whose functions vary widely from society to society. Such a position is often filled by members of a prominent family or lineage, who sometimes monopolize it for long periods of time. But this position is dynamic in the sense that members of the tribe can choose a new leader when they deem the former leader to be ineffective. Generally the person in this role is perceived as having some political influence and authority among outsiders as well as tribal members, and in most cases does not have enough power to execute decisions that are not supported by members of the tribe. The leader also has no authority over the economic affairs of families or in matters involving families within lineages.[129]

An example of the influence of tribal leaders outside the tribe can be found among the Rwala, whose the tribal "princes" (*amir*) are economically and politically influential beyond the confines of bedouin society. They live in towns and have greater access to government authorities than ordinary tribesmen. But within the tribe, Rwala sheiks have no formal coercive power, maintaining their leadership status through their skill in matters like encouraging consensus and representing the tribe to state authorities. Among nomadic pastoralists, the reputation and status of potential leaders are based on their display of bedouin virtues (honor, bravery, generosity, political acumen, mediatory abilities), rather than wealth or control over resources.[130]

Leadership in Iron Age I Palestine was certainly male-dominated (in spite of the reference to Deborah). As in contemporary tribal societies, decision making on the local level was probably the responsibility of elders, and perhaps of leaders associated with particular lineages. Although there is no positive evidence of a single stable leader over "all Israel" until the rise of monarchy, it is possible that on the tribal level there were chiefs, or chieftains, who mediated in situations that could not be dealt with on the local level. Memories of this type of leadership are possibly represented in the "judges" of the books of Judges and Samuel.[131]

There may also have been a tendency for individual leaders within some of the lineages to act as spokespersons for a whole kinship group, to coordinate battles with the assistance of other lineages, and probably also to help resolve conflicts between individual families within the lineage.[132] If this was the case, their status within their own group, as is typical in tribal societies, would have been based on the willingness of lineage members to take their advice and acknowledge their decisions, as long as they conformed to the members' expectations of them. There is no information on how such leaders might have been chosen, but in all likelihood the head of household of the most prominent family in the lineage would have served in such a capacity, although other individuals could have been considered as well. It is also possible that various functions were distributed among a number of individuals according to their respective gifts and abilities; it is characteristic of societies of this type that such leadership functions are not formally constituted, usually arising in connection with specific problems that need to be solved. The "elders" or "heads" referred to in the biblical traditions were possibly individuals who served as spokesmen for lineages.[133]

Government and the Judicial System

Little attention has been given to evaluating how law may have related to other institutions and social customs, and to social structure, in Iron Age I and II Palestine. Typically the focus has been on how law functioned in relation to religion, as is emphasized in the biblical traditions themselves. Our understanding of the judicial system, judicial authority, and the mechanisms by which laws may have been enforced, therefore, is minimal.

There is no consensus on the issue of whether any of the laws recorded in the Hebrew Bible date back to Iron Age I, just as there is no agreement on the nature of society during this period. In a recent study of the role of law, Robert R. Wilson argues that if it were possible to define more precisely what the nature of that society was, it might be possible to draw more conclusions about how law functioned.[134] Wilson constructs his proposals assuming that the social context was a segmented system composed of lineages. He agrees with others that a segmented system, in spite of the *ideal* of equality, has a hierarchical dimension that encourages the exercise of power by individuals or groups that have higher status. This kind of situation has the potential of creating resentment on the part of those who occupy lower-status positions along with aspirations for a new social position.

Wilson agrees that lineage legal systems function most efficiently at their lowest levels, where the lineage heads have the power to enforce decisions as long as they are in accord with customary law. In the case of disputes between larger lineages, where no "living" individual exists to play an authoritative role, justice would have been more difficult to impose, and the resolution of disputes would probably have depended more on achieving group consensus through compromise. The appearance of "judges" (if in fact they played any role in the judicial system) would, Wilson suggests, have created a situation in which tensions might have arisen between this customary judicial system and the judicial interests of the judges themselves.

Above the local level (perhaps the lineage, as Wilson and others have suggested), it is unlikely that there was any common political or juridical forum, either for a whole tribe or among the tribes. The exception may have been in cases of conflict with outside groups, but even then the whole tribe would not necessarily have been involved. It is likely, as many of the recent constructs have proposed, that the highland villages were politically independent throughout Iron Age I, and to some extent during Iron Age II, although there may have been some economic dependence on the city-states of the lowlands (Iron Age I) or the states within which they were situated (Iron Age II). Governance and justice, then, were most likely carried out on the local level of the *bêt 'āb* or *mišpāḥāh,* as Wilson and others have suggested.

In certain matters the head of household would have had the authority to act judicially without any reference to any authority outside the *bêt 'āb.* As well as having jurisdiction within their own households, the heads of household may also have functioned within the community as "elders," although the Hebrew Bible never specifies exactly who the elders were or what the qualifications for this role might have been. The functions of the "council" formed by these elders probably focused primarily on ensuring the integrity and continuity of the household productive units, as is indicated in Bendor's list of the functions of the *bêt 'āb* and *mišpāḥāh*. The elders probably applied customary laws and made decisions by consensus.

Religion

Reconstructing the religion of Iron Age I Israel has proved to be equally as difficult as reconstructing the social processes that were intertwined with its emergence. Until recently, much of the emphasis in attempts to understand the nature of religion during this period focused on what have been interpreted as being the earliest texts in the Hebrew Bible, and on comparing these with extrabiblical religious texts from other parts of the ancient Near East. In addition, reconstructions of Israel's religion in all periods have emphasized the systems of *belief* associated with the "official" religion represented in the viewpoints of the biblical writers, rather than on religious organization or action, or on the "popular" religions that more than likely existed alongside the one more closely associated with the king's court. Furthermore, little attention has been directed toward understanding how the different facets of ancient Israelite religion related to socioeconomic context.

It is probably impossible to excavate the many layers of religious ideology represented in the final biblical construct of Israel's religion to uncover what the religion in this area might have been like before the formation of the state. Because of this major obstacle, biblical scholars and archaeologists alike are now appealing more to the material evidence uncovered through excavations as an important source of information. But very little has been done in the way of applying anthropological models.

It is impossible to do justice to the broad range of studies that have focused on the religion of Iron Age I or subsequent periods in a work such as this.[135] Consequently, only a very general, and superficial, review of the issues that have been raised will be considered here.

One issue has to do with the extent to which religion as it was practiced in this period related to other ancient Near Eastern religions, particularly the "Canaanite" religion represented, for example, in Late Bronze Age religious texts from Ugarit and presumably the forerunner to Yahwism in Palestine itself.

Another question is when Yahwism itself emerged, and what its origins were. A great deal of attention has been given to the possibility that it originated somewhere in Arabia, possibly among the Midianites (see the discussion under "Archaeological Information" earlier in this chapter).

There is also a move in recent studies away from the "all Israel" of the biblical construct toward considering the relationship of religion to the family and to local populations (what has been referred to as "popular religion"), as well as the role that women may have played in these contexts. It is in relation to this issue that social-scientific approaches are most relevant.

Social-scientific approaches are also particularly relevant to the question of what types of religious specialists existed in the Iron Age I context. The biblical construct of the Aaronic and Levitical priests is generally held to be late, so the extent to which it represents earlier practices (or whether it reflects early practices at all) is open to debate. Aside from possible evidence of sacrifice at the excavated sites that may be shrines, there is no clear material record of the activities of religious practitioners. Even the biblical materials are mixed in their representation of who can and who cannot offer sacrifices. In some traditions it is limited to priests, but in others we see nonpriestly individuals offering sacrifices.

A number of prophetic figures also play a part in the biblical traditions about "Israel" before the rise of monarchy. Moses is called a prophet, as is Deborah. Samuel is called a seer, with the function of serving as a channel of communication between God and people, inquiring of God on behalf of the people and delivering oracles from God to the people. But, again, whether prophets actually existed or had any significant social function among the peoples who lived in Palestine during Iron Age I is an issue that is open to debate, depending on whether one perceives the traditions as reliable sources for this period.

It is likely, however, that there were "mediators" of the type Robert Wilson introduces in his study of prophecy and society in ancient Israel,[136] perhaps the types of specialists outlawed in Deuteronomy 18:9–14 (diviners, soothsayers, augurs, sorcerers, necromancers). But this is also a subject that requires further investigation.

Chapter 4

Iron Age IC:

The Rise of Monarchy

During most of Iron Age I, social organization in the highlands of Palestine was very likely segmented. Eventually, however, segmentation gave way to centralization. When this transformation occurred, and what the processes were that led to it, are now subject to as much debate as the transition from the Late Bronze Age to Iron Age I. At one end of the spectrum are those interpreters who remain confident that the biblical accounts of the rise of monarchy are largely reliable.[1] At the other end are those who feel that it is not possible to determine whether any of the traditions contain any accurate information about the processes of centralization and prefer to base their reconstructions on archaeological information, informed by social-scientific theory and comparative studies.

BIBLICAL TRADITIONS ABOUT THE RISE OF MONARCHY

The biblical material relating to the rise of monarchy focuses on the individual heroic figures of Samuel, Saul, David, and Solomon. In the books of Samuel, there are two opposing opinions regarding the question of whether centralized leadership, as represented in these figures, was acceptable. In one view, it is opposed as being contrary to the ideal of egalitarian social organization. In the story recounting Saul's rise to power, the elders approach Samuel (described variously in the traditions as a judge, seer, and priest) and request that he appoint a king to rule over them "like other nations" (1 Samuel 8). The stimulus for this request is the outside threat of the Philistines. Samuel is represented as having been displeased, but God gives his approval, even though in making this request the people are rejecting God as king. Samuel then warns the elders of the potentially oppressive consequences of kingship: their sons will be drafted into the army or forced to perform other duties for the king; he will tax the people, take their property, and give it to the nobility; he will make slaves of them. Samuel nevertheless selects Saul by lot from among the tribes.

The other version (1 Samuel 9–11) presents a more positive view. Saul, in search of his father's lost donkeys, goes to Samuel the seer for advice, and Samuel secretly anoints him. He is publicly acclaimed king only after a victory in battle against the Ammonites. In this version kingship is represented as being divinely inspired—the "spirit of God" comes down on Saul. Saul's role as leader is thus legitimated by God, by choice of the people, and by his successes.

Saul's reign as "king" is portrayed in 1 Samuel as a period of national trauma resulting from outside threats, particularly from the Philistines, and Saul's own personal instability. But in the portrayal of his role as leader he appears more like a "judge" than a "king." He is chosen because of his charisma—he is tall and handsome—and, more importantly, because of his military abilities. He has more authority than a "judge," however, retaining it even outside of crisis situations and gathering a permanent standing army with clearly assigned functions, not just a tribal muster for particular situations. But he does not have the characteristics of a king—he has no established and legitimated capital, no palace, and no class of officials outside his family and personal household, and there is no mention of any system of taxation or civil administration.

Saul ultimately fails in his role as "king," alienating not only Samuel and David, but also God, who withdraws divine support. His personal weaknesses ultimately contribute to David's success.

The Deuteronomistic themes of land, covenant, Temple, kingship, and Jerusalem are prominent in the Samuel traditions about David.[2] Like Saul, David initially has more the characteristics of a charismatic "judge" than those of a king. He is handsome, wise, and well-spoken; he is a musician and a successful warrior; he is popular and a champion of the oppressed. He creates solidarity among his followers and enhances his popularity by sharing booty with friends and allies and making alliances with other nations. He also marries into Saul's family (Michal) and befriends Saul's son Jonathan (1 Samuel 18–20).

As in Saul's case, there are conflicting accounts of David's rise to leadership in the books of Samuel. But essentially he is portrayed as having served in Saul's army and, as his companion, soothing his troubled spirit with his music. Eventually, Saul's jealousy prompts David to flee, and he becomes a vassal of the Philistines (1 Samuel 21–26), whom he later decisively defeats.

From his position among the Philistines, David begins creating alliances and is eventually acclaimed "king" over the southern tribes at Hebron (2 Sam. 2:11). (Earlier in the story he is said to have been anointed king by Samuel [1 Sam. 16:1–13], with the "spirit of Yahweh" descending on him, as it had on Saul.) The traditions imply that there was a struggle for power between the north and the south, but eventually the north also turns to him for leadership, because Saul's successor Ishbaal (Ishbosheth) is inadequate. He then moves his capital to Jebusite Jerusalem (2 Samuel 6), a geographically and politically neutral territory between the northern and southern tribes. This move is legitimized ritually by transporting the ark of the covenant there.[3] David's reign is then divinely legitimized through a dynastic oracle (2 Samuel 7). In 2 Samuel 7 he is informed that God has no need of a temple; nevertheless, in 2 Samuel 24 he purchases a threshing floor as the future site for a temple.

While in Hebron, according to the Samuel construct, David's government consists of David himself and the members of his household. After the move to Jerusalem, his government appears to be more diversified, and there is a collective designation for people at court who do not belong to David's family but are close to and dependent on him. Military, civil, and religious offices are separate, and there is a more complex political organization (2 Sam. 8:16–18; 20:23–26). David also has the authority to appoint priests and to make independent decisions about who will succeed him.

By the end of 2 Samuel, David is a king who appoints court officials, introduces slave labor, takes a census (apparently for purposes of taxation and corveé), supports a harem, creates an "empire" that extends as far as the Euphrates, and establishes an administrative capital at Jerusalem. In spite of the turmoil that occurs during the course of his reign, the picture in these stories is of a man who is successful in his role as king over "all Israel."

The Samuel traditions portray David as a man with human weaknesses. But in later traditions he became the "ideal" charismatic king, and his weaknesses are overlooked. The Davidic covenant and kingship eventually became an important part of the religious belief system. The king is idealized in these traditions as the mediator between God and the people, with responsibility for maintaining justice and acting as caretaker of the oppressed. Following the exile, and the loss of independence, increased disillusionment seems to have led to messianic hopes, and the ideal king came to be patterned after the ideal David—just, righteous, champion of the oppressed.

In Chronicles in particular, David is the ideal king who organized the worshiping community, established a religious capital at Jerusalem, made plans for building the Temple, organized the Temple's music, and assigned the priests and Levites their duties. Anything that might detract from David as ideal king is left out in the Chronicler's construct—there is no reference to David's time as an outlaw among the Philistines, to his adultery with Bathsheba (2 Samuel 11–12), to Absalom's rebellion and David's subsequent flight (2 Samuel 9–19). David is concerned with plans to build the Temple even on his deathbed, with no reference to his instructions to Solomon about executing those in his court whom he had come to see as enemies (1 Kings 2). For the Chronicler, David is also the model against which subsequent kings are judged.

The biblical genealogies relating to David provide some information for how relationships in various periods were understood.[4] Preserved in the extended genealogy in 1 Chronicles 1–9, for example, is the authors' construct of the continually fluctuating relationships in Judah's history as understood in the context of Persian domination. The genealogy can be understood as charting the fissioning and fusing typical of segmented societies, although only those principal characters perceived as having created unity and prevented further segmenting are included in the list.[5]

The genealogical materials relating to David's family in the Samuel traditions are a reference to his "sister" Zeruiah, daughter of the Ammonite Nahash (2 Sam. 17:24–26), the lineage of Bathsheba and Solomon (2 Samuel 11; 12:24–25), and lists of sons born at Hebron, in which mothers' names are included, and Jerusalem (2 Sam. 3:2–5; 5:13–16).

Solomon, ultimately appointed as David's successor after a series of power struggles among the potential heirs, is portrayed in the Samuel traditions as having consolidated the power of the kingdom, building on and strengthening the "empire" David had created. He builds a Temple and a palace in Jerusalem (1 Kings 6–7), whose construction is carried out by Phoenician craftsmen and the use of enforced labor (cf. 1 Kings 7:52; 5:27), with wood imported from Lebanon (1 Kings 5: 15–26). The resulting debts are said to have been settled by ceding land to Hiram of Tyre (1 Kings 9:10–14). The palace is described as an elaborate structure surrounded by its own wall, forming an independent unit within the city, and the Temple as a royal sanctuary situated in the area of the palace.

Solomon also builds fortresses in outlying areas (1 Kings 9:15–19), equips large chariot forces, reorganizes the administrative districts, appointing officials for each of them (1 Kings 4:7–19), and strengthens his network of alliances through marriage. He supports an extensive system of taxation, corveé labor, and tribute, as well as building an extensive trade network. And he establishes the Zadokite priesthood and centralizes the cult in Jerusalem. In effect, he is portrayed as having subverted the tribal structure by introducing drastic changes in the economy and creating class distinctions, which results in the kind of oppression Samuel had warned the elders about when they first requested the appointment of a king. Solomon's oppressive policies, we are told in 1 Kings 12, eventually led to the division of the kingdom.

EXTRABIBLICAL LITERARY SOURCES

The biblical "empire" of David and Solomon is not mentioned in any known extrabiblical texts, nor are any of its kings,[6] although the "house of David" is apparently referred to in a ninth-century inscription from Tel Dan. The earliest Assyrian and Babylonian records that refer to Judah date to just before the fall of Samaria (ca. 734 B.C.E.), when Tiglath-pileser III refers to Yehoahaz (=Ahaz) of Judah. The one contemporary inscription that sheds any light on this period is the late-tenth-century Karnak Relief, which commemorates the campaign of Sheshonq I, who appears in the Bible as Shishak (1 Kings 14: 25–26). The relief is accompanied by a list of the places plundered in the campaign, many of which cannot be identified with certainty. A fragment of a monumental stela from Megiddo and a fragment of the chair of a seated statue from Byblos also bear his name. Sheshonq's campaign appears to have been concentrated in territory in or bordering on Israel (though "Israel" is not mentioned), bypassing the territory occupied by Judah, although Edom seems to be mentioned. Signs of destruction in the archaeological record, extending as far as the Esdraelon and Jordan Valleys, are typically attributed to this invasion (ca. 920–918 B.C.E.).

ARCHAEOLOGICAL INFORMATION

In general, the tenth-century B.C.E. (Iron Age IC according to one chronological scheme, and Iron Age IIA according to another) material culture at most sites is continuous with that of the twelfth and eleventh century highlands—similarity in site type and size, a general absence of luxury goods, and little evidence of class distinctions (for example, distinctive residences built in preferred locations within settlements, nonuniform distribution of elite goods). The material dating to the end of the tenth century at some sites does suggest however, that there was a movement toward some form of centralized sociopolitical structure by that time. This includes in particular a number of fortresses. There is also some indication of the production of agricultural surpluses on more than a "subsistence" basis, and some evidence of accumulation of wealth.[7]

As was indicated in chapter 3, the earliest clear evidence of a movement toward centralization comes from Tel Masos in the Beersheba Valley. The material remains from this site have been interpreted as indicating that there was a movement toward social stratification (or at least minimal ranking according to affluence) and political centralization at the site by the mid-eleventh century, possibly as a result of trading activity with outside urban sites,[8] and that it became an administrative center for surrounding villages such as Tel Esdar.

Excavations in Jerusalem have produced very little in the way of materials that can be firmly dated to the tenth century, and thus have provided little evidence of the processes of state formation. Nevertheless, most interpreters argue that by the end of the century Palestine had developed into a Jerusalem-based centralized polity that was stable enough to promote the construction of monumental architecture and defense systems, such the fortification systems that have been uncovered at Gezer, Hazor, and Megiddo (cf. 1 Kings 9:15–19), and the Temple and palace in Jerusalem, which are described in the biblical text but are not archaeologically confirmed. The scholarly consensus is that Gezer, Hazor, and Megiddo were transformed in the mid-tenth century into complex fortified "administrative centers," each with a casemate wall system, six-chambered gateway, and palace complex (although a palace has not yet been discovered at Hazor).[9] Both Megiddo and Hazor appear to be lacking in domestic architecture, a feature that is also cited as evidence for a centralized state, as administrative centers were often set apart from the general populace.[10] The typical supposition, then, is that one centralized authority (that is, the king in Jerusalem) was responsible for the construction of these "administrative centers."

Syro-Hittite and Phoenician influence, particularly in building techniques (for example the use of ashlar masonry), is apparent in the remains of the palaces, fortifications, and elite buildings at these sites, suggesting some degree of communication and trade.

The original confidence that these sites confirm the biblical account of centralization, however, is now wavering. For example, the extent to which the "Solomonic" six chambered gates are really similar is now disputed.[11] Whether Megiddo even has a casemate wall is now considered to be unclear.[12] And some scholars have questioned the tenth-century date assigned to some of the relevant architectural features, proposing that at least some of the "Solomonic" fortifications at Gezer, Hazor, and Megiddo should be redated to the ninth century.[13]

The sites for these administrative centers, whatever their date, appear to have been chosen on the basis of their proximity to water sources and land suitable for agriculture, their potential defensibility, and their strategic location in relation to communication and trade routes.

Another indication in the archaeological record of some movement toward centralization is a marked increase in population from early Iron Age I to the tenth century. On the basis of recent surveys, the population for the whole of Palestine (including the coastal regions) in 1000 B.C.E. has been estimated at about 150,000. In the central highlands the population is estimated to have increased from approximately 20,000 in early Iron Age I to 55,000 by the end of the eleventh century (not including nonsedentary groups).[14]

Surveys in the Judean hill country indicate that the population there also was almost doubled from early Iron Age I to the end of the tenth century, the most significant increase in the settlement history of this region.[15] Settlement became denser particularly in the south and southern desert fringe and on the northern desert fringe. The only notable decrease in settlement activity is apparent in the northern part of the central Judean range, where an unprecedented increase in settlement had begun during early Iron Age I. The surveys indicate that the population in this area tended to be concentrated in relatively large and protected sites. Ofer suggests that the population increase was in large part due to the sedentarization of pastoral elements, particularly in the southern and northern desert fringe areas.[16]

Settlement also appears to have expanded in the Negeb and the Beersheba Valley, peaking at the end of the eleventh century.[17] In the Negeb, there is evidence that dozens of small farmsteads were founded and that populations were settling in more arid regions. In the southern portion of the Beersheba Valley there is also evidence that enclosed settlements were being established. At the beginning of the tenth century, however, the settlement pattern in the Beersheba Valley appears to have changed significantly. Tel Masos, the former "central place," was almost completely deserted, as were the enclosed settlements. There are no indications of total destruction by any kind of military campaign, and most settlements seem simply to have been abandoned, perhaps suggesting that in both the Beersheba Valley and the Negeb highlands the population reverted to pastoral nomadism.

The major new development in this region was the establishment of a chain of settlements in the Negeb that have been interpreted as fortified strongholds or administrative centers.[18] The change is typically attributed to the emergence of the monarchy and a concern with controlling the growing agricultural communities. Ze'ev Herzog points out, however, that the spatial distribution of sites and the demographic estimates do not support this model. Overall, there are fewer sites that date to the tenth century, and these are located in a restricted area. A large portion of each of the new sites is also covered by fortifications, storerooms, and other nonresidential units, which, along with the decline in number of sites, suggests a decline in settled agricultural population rather than growth. His counterargument is that the change in settlement patterns in this area should probably be attributed to environmental factors, which forced part of the population in the Negeb and the Beersheba Valley to abandon permanent settlements and shift to a nomadic life, while others were probably absorbed into state military and commercial services. The chain of fortresses, in his estimation, could have been built as administrative centers to diffuse the deteriorating relations between farmers and pastoral nomads that resulted from a lack of grain. At the same time they could have been intended to facilitate trade with Arabia in the south and Phoenicia in the north.

The archaeological record also indicates that by the end of the tenth century many of the trade systems that had been disrupted at the end of the Late Bronze Age were reestablished. This is apparent in the presence of foreign goods, which suggests contact and interregional trade with other peoples.

The material remains from sites associated with the "Philistines" or "Sea Peoples" have also played an important role in the various constructs of the processes of centralization in Palestine.[19] Most of the ceramics associated with these cultures are found in the southern coastal plains and Shephelah, although some are also found in sites traditionally identified with the "Israelites." This is variously interpreted as either evidence of contact and trade with the Philistines or, more often, evidence of Philistine encroachment on "Israelite" territory, and therefore of a Philistine threat that contributed significantly to the establishment of the monarchy. The archaeological evidence suggests that these peoples had access to natural and cultural resources that facilitated their becoming a formidable maritime and agrarian power in Palestine. They had access to the sea for fishing and shipping, and to the rich agricultural land of the coastal plains, which produced oil and wine as well as grain. Maritime trade appears to have been an important part of the Philistine economy—importing such necessities as timber and metal and exporting local commodities such as grain, wine, and oil.

The uniqueness of the Philistine material culture is identifiable in a number of ways. One is the distinctive style of their ceramics, which has clear Aegean roots. Another is their city planning models and concepts of urban organization, which are new to Palestine but similar to those of the Aegean world. At Ekron, for example, there are signs of urban planning in which industry was carried out along the perimeter of the city, but still inside the fortification walls. Public buildings were located at the center of the site, with a "palace shrine" complex at the very center. A hearth in a long, pillared hall was apparently the focus of the civic and religious center.

Philistine society also appears to have been centralized. There is evidence of a diversity of social roles that includes rulers, warriors, farmers, sailors, merchants, priests, artisans, and architects. Some industries (for example, at Ashkelon, Ekron, and Ashdod) appear to have been associated with administrative and religious centers.

MODELS

As is the case for social transition following the breakdown of the city-state systems of the Late Bronze Age, the processes connected with the rise of monarchy and the state in ancient Palestine are now recognized as having been much more complex than those identified in previous interpretations. In comparison to the problems associated with reconstructing Israel's origins, the possibility of constructing a fairly accurate picture of the period of the "united monarchy" is by some still perceived as being possible. But, for many, there has been a significant breakdown in confidence in the biblical construct. As is the case for much of the biblical literature, there is a move toward understanding these traditions as telling us more about Jewish culture during the Persian period (or later) than about the history and culture of the early Iron Age. Another problem, from the perspective of some scholars, is that there are no *clear* signs of full centralization in the archaeological record that can be firmly dated to the tenth century B.C.E.

The question of *when* centralization became a reality in Palestine was not really an issue until recently; that is, the biblical assertion that monarchy was introduced during the tenure of Saul's leadership toward the end of the eleventh century was generally accepted.[20] Also, the biblical traditions in 1 and 2 Samuel and 1 Kings were considered to contain essentially accurate historical information (the so-called "Court History" in 2 Samuel, for example, and the list of districts established by Solomon in 1 Kings 4:7–19).[21]

Perhaps the most radical argument relating to the issue of when full centralization was achieved is that of David W. Jamieson-Drake. Based primarily on an assessment of the archaeological material, Jamieson-Drake argues that full centralization in Judah, and Jerusalem as an administrative center, cannot be documented for any time earlier than the eighth century.[22] In his estimation, it is not until the eighth century that there is combined evidence for a significant increase in population, building activities, production, centralization, and specialization. Although he agrees that there is evidence of some form of administrative control dating to the tenth century, he argues that the evidence points to regional or local management of labor and resources, perhaps associated with chieftaincies, rather than to a centralized state administration.[23]

In spite of Jamieson-Drake's argument, however, the general consensus among biblical scholars and archaeologists is still that Judah and Israel were both centralized states by the end of the tenth century. But regardless of exactly when this was achieved, it is clear that there was at least some *movement toward* centralization during the course of the tenth century.

Although we cannot know the extent to which the biblical descriptions of the processes that led to the establishment of statehood in Palestine are accurate, we can now postulate with some certainty that both internal and external factors played roles. For example, internal pressures deriving from an increase in population—an increase clearly documented in archaeological surveys—would have contributed to a significant extent to this transition. This would have affected the society in a variety of ways, probably including the establishment of more clearly defined territorial boundaries and an increase and improvement in craft specialization. Such changes normally lead to social stratification and the creation of "classes" with differences in power and wealth,[24] and stimulate an evolution toward permanent centralized leadership.

The biblical construct asserts that it was outside pressure, consisting primarily of a threat on the part of the Philistines, who were starting to encroach on "Israelite" territory, that stimulated the need for a more permanent and stable type of leader than the "judges." Whether or not the threat was posed specifically by the Philistines, it is nevertheless possible that some form of external pressure also played a role in the processes that eventually led toward the establishment of a state form of sociopolitical organization in Palestine.

Until recently a number of scholars argued, on the basis of a passage in 1 Samuel 13:19–23, that a Philistine "monopoly" on iron technology was one of the contributing factors in this threat, an argument that is no longer considered viable. Not only does the passage in question make no reference to iron, but the archaeological evidence indicates fairly conclusively that the technology had not developed to an extent that it could have had any such impact. Bronze continued throughout Iron Age I to be the dominant metal used in manufacturing tools and weapons both in the highlands and in the regions associated with the Philistines.[25] Although there is evidence that iron objects were manufactured in this region, they occur archaeologically primarily in ceremonial and ritual contexts. The Philistines may have been technologically superior in some ways, but it is highly unlikely that iron was used to gain any kind of political or military advantage.

It is nevertheless possible that the development of this new technology did play some role in the transition toward centralization at the end of the tenth century, as this appears to have been the arena in which the new technology was finally accepted and adopted, and thus the time during which its impact might have begun to play a part in social, economic, and political processes. Because this was a time during which moves toward consolidation and centralization were apparently accelerating, it is plausible that the adoption of iron technology was a significant factor in the strategies employed by individuals who played crucial roles in the transition.

One of the mechanisms, then, by which the move toward centralization may have been effected was the control and distribution of important resources. We might postulate that the tenth-century leaders took advantage for the first time of the technological innovation of ironworking, gained control of the local sources of iron ore, and encouraged the adoption of the new technology for utilitarian use.

The social-scientific studies of the rise of monarchy carried out in the last two decades are grounded in anthropological theories and models on the nature and evolution of the state,[26] particularly "secondary," as opposed to "primary" or "pristine," states.[27] Pristine states develop in areas where there are no contemporaneous or previous centralized political entities. Secondary states, like those that arose in Iron Age Palestine, emerge in response to the collapse of other states or as the result of contact with neighboring states, and thus are a response to qualitatively different conditions than the formation of primary states. In this respect, secondary states may form in societies where evolution toward statehood would otherwise be unlikely.

Another issue that has played an important role in studies on the emergence of the monarchy in Iron Age Palestine has to do with identifying the evolutionary stages leading up to its establishment. Two of the most extensive studies propose that there was an intermediate stage of chiefdom as segmented tribal organization evolved toward statehood.[28] The evolutionary and processual models introduced below are organized chronologically and by author according to date of publication, as each builds on and/or is a response to earlier studies.

Processual and Chieftaincy Models

James W. Flanagan was the first biblical scholar to make a detailed argument for the presence of chiefly leadership during the tenth century.[29] In this study he analyzed the biblical texts in relation to anthropological theories on state formation and the processes involved in succession to high office as a means of reconstructing this transitional period in Israel's history.[30] After reviewing the relevant anthropological models, he proposed an intermediate stage of chiefdom for the reigns of Saul and David as one stage through which Israel's sociopolitical organization passed as kingship emerged. Considering factors such as kinship and genealogies, politics, religion, and economics, he argued that Saul and David were chiefs who provided leadership for family-based, but nonegalitarian, social groups. From the perspective of sociopolitical evolution, Flanagan proposed that Saul's leadership as portrayed in the biblical construct is typical of a chiefdom, that the traditions about David's reign reflect the transition from a chiefdom to a state, and that full statehood did not develop until the reign of Solomon.

One central element in this study is Flanagan's analysis of the biblical traditions in light of the list of traits Colin Renfrew identifies as distinguishing chiefdoms from egalitarian societies,[31] a list that Frank S. Frick also uses in his analysis of the archaeological evidence for the period (see below). These traits are: (1) a ranked society; (2) redistribution organized by a chief; (3) greater population density; (4) increase in the total number of individuals in the society; (5) increase in the size of residence groups; (6) greater productivity; (7) more clearly defined territorial boundaries; (8) a more integrated society, with a greater number of sociocentric statuses; (9) centers that coordinate social, religious, and economic activities; (10) frequent ceremonies and rituals serving wider social purposes; (11) rise of priesthood; (12) relation to a total environment (and hence redistribution), that is, to some ecological diversity; (13) specialization; (14) organization and deployment of public labor for agricultural or building activities; (15) improvement in craft specialization; (16) potential for territorial expansion; (17) reduction of internal strife; (18) pervasive inequality of persons or groups associated with permanent leadership; (19) distinctive dress or ornament for those of high status; (20) no true government to back up decisions by legalized force.

In a study that followed Flanagan's initial article on chieftaincy, Frank S. Frick also argues for a transitional stage of chiefdom in the evolution of the Israelite state.[32] Frick's approach differs from Flanagan's 1981 study, however, in that it is based more on an evaluation of the archaeological material than on the biblical traditions. As in other social-scientific analyses of ancient Palestine, Frick views models and theories from the social sciences, especially anthropology, comparative ethnographies of African societies, and ethnoarchaeology, as providing controlled comparisons for understanding the sociopolitical processes operating in the period immediately preceding the emergence of the state. He is careful to point out in defining his approach that he is not attempting to provide precise answers, and that the study is tentative in some respects and not uniformly tested against the biblical and archaeological data.[33]

Frick's perspective on the biblical narratives is that almost all the sources underlying them are documents that were either written under state sponsorship or reflect the concerns of people who lived under state rule. In using them as sources, then, Frick focuses on the ways in which social behavior and processes came to be expressed in them and the ways in which material remains can help set parameters for reading them.

Because Frick's concern is to understand the nature of the social change that occurred in the transition to monarchy, he begins his study by reviewing theories of cultural evolution,[34] particularly those relating to systems theory, a model used for analyzing complex social interrelationships. Although there is no overall agreement on a general evolutionary scheme, proponents of systems theory view societies as problem-solving systems in which an alteration in one part of the system affects other parts of the system. His particular interest in this type of theory is that its basic principles allow him to postulate the environmental factors that may have influenced the social transformations that occurred at the end of Iron Age I. He takes as his starting point the concept of ecological succession. Ecological succession refers to the classification of ecological systems in terms of increasing complexity over time, and the theory proposes that in different circumstances particular sociocultural forms are better adapted than others in the context of particular ecological niches.

He also introduces in this section of the study a summary of R. N. Adams's evolutionary model,[35] which he views as being particularly compatible with the concept of ecological succession. In this model, Adams postulates that there is a fundamental developmental sequence that repeats itself through the course of human evolution, and which consists of three phases: identity (that is, mutual awareness and a common sense of identity among individuals in a society), coordination (for example, Israel as a segmentary society), and centralization.

Frick also reviews several types of state formation theories, making the distinction noted above between pristine and secondary states. Noting that the Israelite monarchy developed as a secondary state, Frick suggests that studies of pristine states are nevertheless useful in that they identify classes of variables, and types of variable linkages, that may be applicable in particular cases of secondary state development.

Three basic types of state formation theories are summarized in the study—the conflict approach,[36] the integrative approach,[37] and the synthetic approach—and Frick indicates that he finds the last of these most useful. In the synthetic approach both structure and process are emphasized. State formation is viewed as a systemic process that can be affected by any one or more of a number of factors, with no presuppositions that there is a single unilineal trajectory or that there is a single cause that can be presupposed above all others. It is, therefore, a "multilineal" approach, which allows for the possibility of multiple trajectories to statehood. From this perspective, after the tendency to centralized control has been triggered, by whatever means, the hierarchical structure itself becomes a selective factor that feeds back to all other sociocultural features. The dependent variables in a system are viewed as constantly changing, yet remaining within certain limits. When a particular system is transformed into another system, one or more variables are understood as having exceeded the limits of the previous system. Although from the perspective of this approach there are differences in the ways in which primary and secondary states are set in motion, the internal interactions that are necessary for transforming a nonstate society into a state society do not vary significantly. State formation in both types of states consists of a multiple feedback system, in which prestate polities respond to selective pressures by, for example, changing some of their internal structures, subduing a competing group, or gaining control of water sources. The initial shift, whatever form it takes, sets off a chain reaction of other changes that result in the formation of a state.

Frick introduces three systemic models of secondary state formation that he considers useful for evaluating the situation in ancient Palestine. The first is Barbara J. Price's model, which builds on the concept of a "culture core."[38] In this model, some cultural traits, particularly those that are linked to energy, are understood as bearing more explanatory weight than others. The "core," then, consists of those institutions in a society that are responsible for harnessing, storing, and distributing the flow of energy within and between populations. From this perspective, anything that is made by humans is an important class of data that represents a transformation of energy. Another type of data that is central in this model is settlement patterns, which are considered to be the most reliable evidence for identifying processes of sociocultural change. Frick emphasizes these types of data in his analysis of ancient Palestine, focusing especially on intrasite clustering and intersite patterning as they reflect a combination of environmental and sociocultural factors.

The second systemic model Frick applies is that of William T. Sanders and David Webster,[39] a multilineal paradigm in which different evolutionary trajectories are understood to be related to variations in agricultural risk, diversity (including such factors as soil types), productivity (including cultural factors such as technology, social organization, and information flow), and the nature of the environment. The value of this model from Frick's perspective is that it avoids the artificial dichotomy often made between ecological and societal variables, as well as facilitating the integration of archaeological and comparative ethnographic data. In relation to the productivity variable, Frick examines the role of such technological factors as the impact of iron technology, water systems, and terracing in Iron Age I as a means of assessing whether surpluses were produced, and the ways in which any such surpluses may have been invested.

The third systemic model Frick introduces is Colin Renfrew's catastrophe/anastrophe theory, which is based on a mathematical approach to culture change.[40] Although he does not apply this model in any great depth, Frick suggests that it has potential for further investigation of the situation in Iron Age I Palestine. The theory postulates that sudden changes or discontinuities in a sociocultural system are produced by, and can be understood in terms of, gradual and continuous changes in the control variables within the system. Frick includes a list of what Renfrew views as the general features of system collapse (such as that which occurred at the end of the Late Bronze Age) and anastrophe (the aftermath of the collapse). The model suggests that under certain conditions following the catastrophe of system collapse, segmentary societies emerge and are then followed by the formation of a chiefdom and then a secondary state within a relatively short period of time.

The trajectory Frick suggests for Iron Age I Palestine on the basis of these models is state to segmentary society (the collapse of the Canaanite city-state system), segmentary society to chiefdom (at least by the time of Saul), and chiefdom to a small urban state (David in Jerusalem; a small rather than large state because of the topographical fragmentation of Palestine). In this construct, the transformation of the segmentary lineage system into a chiefdom was facilitated by agricultural intensification, and the establishment of a chiefdom allowed for the incorporation of outside groups.

In contrast to traditional interpretations, Frick also suggests that the Philistine threat emphasized in the biblical traditions was only one of the dependent variables in the formation of the state—one that accelerated the emergence of the state from a preexisting chiefdom.

After reviewing models of social evolution and the formation of the state, Frick examines the characteristics of chiefdoms, the stage that he argues Israel passed through before developing into a state.[41] Here, in addition to comparative ethnographic material and the narratives in Samuel, he considers archaeological information relating to demographics, settlement patterns, agricultural intensification, land use patterns, technology, public architecture, and associated features in religion and social organization.

Two organizational principles are identified as being basic to chiefdoms, and as differentiating them from segmentary societies: (1) the statuses of individuals within a local community are ranked; and (2) local communities are regionally centralized. Essentially chiefdoms represent a movement toward social differentiation, along with centralization of leadership in the person of a chief. Chiefs in different societies range considerably in power and influence, from being the heads of small tribes to positions as the leaders of kingdoms with populations in the hundreds of thousands, with corresponding variations in their secular and ritual powers.

Another diagnostic feature of chiefdoms is that the fissioning processes characteristic of segmentary societies slow down. This occurs when a chief moves from filling subordinate positions with close kin to appointing less-close kin and even non-kin—that is, forming a centrally appointed bureaucracy whose means of survival in the system depends on loyalty to the one responsible for making the appointments.

Once chiefly leadership develops in a society, its continued success and legitimation appear to depend on the chief's success in redistribution, in appealing to religious sanctions, and in building a clientship. In order to build and maintain a fairly broad range of support, a chief must obtain and accumulate some measure of wealth and then provide periodic redistribution. He is also dependent on the allocated power of individuals who are loyal to him because, for example, he is successful in obtaining and distributing resources or as a leader in war, or in being perceived as a charismatic person.

Eventually, the interests of increasingly powerful chiefs begin to diverge from those of their lineages, and conical clans, ramages, and other nonunilinear or cognate descent groups emerge. In a conical clan descent system, certain individuals are considered as being closer to a dominant line, and thus have greater status and access to resources. This type of system leads to a ranked society and away from the segmentary type of organization in which the segments are regarded ideally as equals. In a ramage descent group, membership can be determined by tracing descent through either male or female lines. The gradation of rank as represented by these types of descent systems is not a smooth progression from lowest- to highest-ranking individual. Rather, the chief and his lineage, and perhaps other proximate lineages, are qualitatively set off from the rest of the population.

Studies of chiefdoms also suggest that one of the most effective mechanisms employed in legitimating chiefly leadership is religion. Theocratic claims are made on behalf of chiefs that are lacking for leaders in segmentary societies. This is a way of establishing and maintaining a common sense of identity and political action among autonomous groups.

Frick postulates that in Iron Age I Palestine the growing pressure of population on limited resources led to agricultural intensification as well as political centralization under the sacral leadership of a chief. This change in turn stimulated traditionally sanctioned and increasingly institutionalized means for handling the interrelated problems of: (1) greater insecurity resulting from a reliance on fixed resources and from unpredictable variations in the environment; (2) an increase in competition for limited resources; and (3) a developing economic interdependence among specialized producers and ecological zones, which placed more value on the redistribution of goods, protected trade routes, and peaceful markets.

In the context of such conditions, Frick argues, following D. Webster, that warfare is an adaptive ecological choice,[42] whose major role in the formation of the state is in breaking down evolutionary constraints. Because it causes great adaptive value to be placed on stable military leadership, warfare also strengthens the political authority of the successful war chief. The gains from his military successes, resources that are external to the traditional system, also reinforce the chief's role as redistributor.

Clientship—the bond between a political superior and a person to whom he has delegated a part of his authority—also plays an important role in legitimating a chief's position of leadership. The establishment of such patron-client relationships is the principal process through which individuals begin to acquire power that is independent of the power granted by peers in a segmentary system.[43] The system of reciprocity is also affected, in that it is a relationship that further differentiates persons of higher and lower rank. The successful patron in this type of system is one who is successful in accumulating material wealth. Through having more to give away, he is able to gain more clients and thus more power. In the case of tenth-century Palestine, Frick suggests, this factor may well have figured into David's success in achieving paramountcy over Saul.

In his discussion of the characteristics of chiefdoms, Frick also introduces proposals by anthropological archaeologists that certain archaeological features can be interpreted as being diagnostic of chiefdoms. Here he lists the traits proposed by Colin Renfrew, the same traits that Flanagan cited in his interpretation of the biblical narratives (see above). Among these are evidence of ranking and redistribution, demographic data (evidence of population increase, site hierarchies, and central places), and evidence for cooperative production. Only about half of these traits, Frick suggests, are discernible in the archaeological record.

Another systemic archaeological model of chiefdoms (or ranked societies) that Frick considers is that of C. S. Peebles and S. M. Kus, who propose five major variables that they consider distinctive of chiefdoms: (1) evidence of ascribed ranking, which is most clearly distinguished in mortuary practices; (2) evidence of a hierarchy of settlement types and sizes; (3) settlements located in areas that assure a high degree of local subsistence sufficiency; (4) evidence of organized productive activities outside the household group—this is most apparent in evidence for monumental architecture, organized craft specialization, and trade; (5) evidence of organizational activity for dealing with unpredictable environmental factors—for example, some evidence of risk-spreading activities (such as mixed subsistence strategies, storage facilities). If warfare is one of the unpredictable environmental variables, there should also be evidence of defensive organization.[44]

The third archaeological model introduced by Frick is that of T. K. Earle, who identifies three general types of evidence for analyzing the centralized hierarchy of chiefdoms: (1) evidence of an organizational structure for a full range of cooperative productive activities, such as those requiring labor outside the extended family; (2) evidence for a system of central places, that is, site hierarchy; and (3) evidence of ranking provided by mortuary practices.[45]

In comparing these models, Frick points out that they all agree that chiefdoms are ranked societies, and that demographic data (especially as reflected in site hierarchies and central places) are important indicators of chiefdoms, as is evidence of cooperative production. Evidence of the management of a total environment (data related to agricultural activities) is an important variable in the models of both Renfrew and Peebles and Kus.

After introducing the relevant theoretical background and models, Frick turns to a reconstruction of the interrelationship between agriculture and social organization in the sociopolitical evolution of ancient Israel.[46] In this section of the study, he analyzes the ways in which the constraints imposed by varying levels of agricultural intensification, and the extent of agricultural risk and diversity, provided the setting in which the mechanisms and processes of centralization operated as strategies for coping with the types of problems that would have arisen in the environment of ancient Palestine. He describes the agricultural environment of the highlands, considers how the development of technologies (such as terracing, cisterns, and the use of iron tools) may have contributed to the intensification of settlement, and proposes ways in which technological variants may have affected and been affected by other elements of society and culture. This reconstruction draws on Leon Marfoe's work, which considers the effects of ecological relationships on social behavior in relation to the processes of centralization in

Lebanon.[47] Technologies are interpreted as indicators of the society's investment of energy, as Price argues. For example, terraces, which were attached to villages and existed prior to the formation of the state, not only reduced runoff, but also discouraged the tendency toward fissioning by encouraging cooperative labor and establishing socioeconomic relations within and between villages.

In relation to lime-plastered cisterns, Frick concludes that the degree to which these were necessary for the expansion of agriculture into the highlands must be left open to question. The widespread use of cisterns during the period, however, can probably be viewed as evidence for the settlement growth that accompanied agricultural intensification.

In his consideration of the impact of iron technology, Frick points to the apparent increase in the production of iron tools, and the increase in the types of tools made from iron, during the course of the tenth century, and suggests that this development accompanied agricultural intensification.

Agricultural productivity, demography, and settlement patterns are also considered.

Interpretation of the material remains from Tel Masos plays an important part in Frick's construct of the processes of state formation in Iron Age I Palestine.[48] Comparing the archaeological information to the characteristics of chiefdoms (or ranked societies) identified earlier in the study, he argues that there is evidence for an eleventh-century chiefdom at the site—evidence of ranking and that the village was a central site in a two-level settlement hierarchy in the region (in relation to other sites such as Tel Esdar).

Religion also enters into Frick's reconstruction. Just prior to the formation of the state, he suggests, Yahwism developed as a relatively flexible unifying ideology that satisfied the egalitarian ideals of the farmers, while at the same time empowering priest-bureaucrats to organize production and enforce laws. Religion, then, was a mechanism that functioned to maintain social solidarity and order on the village and intervillage levels and facilitated the integration of diverse communities.

In his synthesis,[49] Frick presents a construct that is grounded in the theoretical material and evidence introduced throughout the bulk of the study. Briefly summarized, he postulates that under conditions of agricultural intensification in the highlands during the course of Iron Age I, specialization in the kinds of tasks necessary for labor efficiency began to increase. When labor needs exceeded what could be supplied by productive specialization in the local household or residential group, a chiefdom, with an organizing principle based on a hierarchical social divisions, emerged. To facilitate labor needs, the chief and his clients organized and directed energy exchanges among the different segments of the society. The power and authority of the chief also made it possible for him to organize agricultural production in a way that ensured the stability of production, as well as the production of surpluses. As labor became more specialized, this in turn led to the more sophisticated and requisite controls of the state.

With the increase in population density that accompanied agricultural intensification, land became more scarce and thus more valuable. This would have led to competition over land control, to larger local and interlocal cooperative social units, and to a need to acquire additional land in the adjacent plains. Especially under the leadership of David, early Israel evolved from the type of lineage organization that characterizes segmentary societies to broader alliances in the form of nonlocalized clan units that facilitated multicommunity organization for cooperative competition, particularly in the form of war. In Frick's view, the conflict with the Philistines should be understood in this light—that is, on the one hand the Philistines were seeking to exploit and control the economic and population base that resulted from the agricultural intensification in the highlands, and on the other hand the highland population had a need to acquire new productive land resources for its growing population. David was responsible, Frick suggests, for leading a large cooperative group in warfare against the Philistines, and was successful not only in alleviating their threatening expansion into the highlands, but also in expanding his own group's land resources. As chief, David then paid his debts to his loyal clients by redistributing portions of the newly aquired territory. This in turn stimulated further differentiation in wealth because of limited access to such strategic resources. Those who had fought with David, his clients, eventually developed the kinds of values typical of agrarian elites, seeking to broaden their powers of taxation and control of the agricultural surpluses that had previously been redistributed among the freeholding peasants of early Iron Age I.

Coote and Whitelam's study of early Israel also considers the processes associated with the transition to statehood, and is similar in many respects to Frick's.[50] In accord with their *longue durée* perspective, Coote and Whitelam emphasize the emergence of monarchy as part of a continuum relating to processes and developments at the beginning of Iron Age I, not as a dialectical conflict, as is typical in most reconstructions. For them, then, the monarchy was not an alien institution imposed on Israel, but an outgrowth of the circumstances surrounding Israel's emergence, as part of a whole complex of processes that spanned many centuries.[51]

As do other recent social-scientific studies of the rise of monarchy, Coote and Whitelam point to the inadequacy of reconstructions that do little more than reiterate the biblical texts and that attribute it to the pressures of external forces. To portray the Philistine threat as the cause of the transition, as the biblical text does, ignores the importance of the internal processes and developments, in combination with external forces, that are a necessary prerequisite to significant social change. In agreement with other recent analyses, Coote and Whitelam also view the developments in both premonarchic and monarchic Israel as representing particular adaptations to social and environmental pressures.

The most suggestive anthropological theory for conceptualizing the transition, from their perspective, is Carneiro's circumscription theory of state origins.[52] Carneiro proposes that states arise in response to specific cultural, demographic, and ecological conditions, and emphazises the significance of environmental and social circumscription, that is, the limitations imposed by environmental and social factors, particularly as agriculture develops over the course of several generations.[53] In applying this model, Coote and Whitelam point out that the geographical setting of the Judean highlands was effectively circumscribed *environmentally* by semiarid steppe and desert regions. The loose federation of groups in the Iron Age I highlands was *socially* circumscribed by the network of lowland city-states, the incursions of hostile nomadic raiders (for example, the Midianites and Amalekites), and Philistine pressure from the Mediterranean coastal region. Combined with other internal and external factors, these factors stimulated the escalation of warfare, which in turn acted as an impetus to the formation of the state. According to the circumscription model, warfare is a necessary condition for the rise of the state, but not sufficient in and of itself.

Coote and Whitelam agree with the proposal that there was a transition from segmentary society to chiefdom to early state in Iron Age Palestine. In their review of other theories on state formation, they cite the systems approach of Cohen,[54] who argues that the decisive difference between prestate polities, particularly chiefdoms, and states is the latter's tendency to fission, and that the most important feature of the early state is the development of institutions that counteract the pressures that lead to fissioning. On the basis of Cohen's work, Coote and Whitelam suggest that states, including secondary states such as Israel, emerge where fissioning becomes impossible or unacceptable, or when one chiefdom opens up new economic resources and thus acquires an advantage over all others. They reiterate here, however, that no one factor is sufficient, or even consistently antecedent, to state formation. As Frick also points out, whatever triggers the process sets in motion a multiple and complex feedback system involving and acting on all forms of economic, social, political, and religious organizations. In this respect, Coote and Whitelam also suggest that the emergence of the state in Palestine needs to be understood in the wider context of the simultaneous state formations in Ammon, Moab, and Edom, which are as yet still little understood.[55]

Another model that is central to Coote and Whitelam's analysis is Renfrew's model of systems collapse (cited also in Frick), which they cite in support of their assertion of the importance of understanding the formation of the state in Palestine in relation to the previous economic decline and systems collapse at the end of the Late Bronze Age:

> Increasing marginality, whether arising from increased population, circumscription or whatever, may be one of the preconditions for the sudden anastrophic formation of a state society. Intriguingly it is likewise a necessary precondition for the catastrophic collapse of a highly centered political system.[56]

In Coote and Whitelam's construct, then, the society that emerged at the beginning of the Iron Age in the highlands and margins of Palestine was decentralized, with low production and low military costs. As agricultural production increased, at first because of the expansion of agricultural land into marginal areas, so did the population and a tendency toward stratification. As the land available for agricultural production declined, expansion became less cost-effective and growth became more dependent on increasing agricultural intensification. At the same time, there was a growing urban-based military threat from the lowlands that was related to an increase in social conflict and competition for declining resources. This in turn led to an increase in defense costs, which further contributed to a need for institutionalized intensification. This involved a formal political redefinition of issues such as dominion over arable land, distribution of produce, and labor arrangements.

The shifts that occurred, then, were not only political in terms of the movement toward centralization, but economic and social as well. From the beginning, the economic base steadily expanded along with the rapid increase in population and number of settlements, and social stratification became more pronounced with the growth of wealthy families and increasing competition for resources once the limits of the land were reached.

One of the major variables in this process was the nature of the farming strategies that had developed in the highlands, particularly the practice of terracing, which made marginal land available for farming. One of its effects was the necessity of long-term investment and continual maintenance. The tree crops typical of Iron Age I production also required long-term investments. Thus the maintenance of both terraces and tree crops necessitated residential stability, a crucial factor among the complex forces that led to chieftaincy and then statehood and acted as a buffer against the inherent tendencies of prestate societies to fission.

The difficulties of highland farming were overcome to some extent, in addition to terracing, by means of water management through the construction and use of cisterns. As arable land was depleted over time, however, new strategies were necessary—more marginal land had to be cultivated, tougher forests had to be cleared, and more labor was ultimately required. Depletion of the available resources and overpopulation also contributed to the development of the political forms associated with centralization, which were increasingly supported by wealthy farmers who had interests in increasing their land holdings and producing cash crops such as grapes and olives for urban markets, as well as preserving the power and privilege that accompanied their increasing wealth.

An escalation in interregional trade, as is suggested by the material remains at Tel Masos, was another potential factor in the economic growth and eventual centralization of Israel, as was the development of more local regional political and economic centers such as Phoenicia, Edom, Ammon, and Aram. Again, these factors acted and reacted with others in a multiple-feedback process which gave impetus to centralization.

Although there was certainly some differentiation in social and economic status from the beginning of Iron Age I on—as is suggested by the archaeological evidence from Ai, Raddana, and Tel Masos,[57] and the biblical references to village elders, judges, and debt service—socioeconomic stratification would have increased over time, especially at those sites that benefited from the gradual expansion of interregional trade.

The development of stratification was also affected by a number of interrelated factors. The social isolation of various groups that resulted from subregional geographic diversity contributed to economic diversification, based in part on varying degrees of proximity to trade routes and centers, and in part on the distinctive productive advantages of each region. Contact with urban centers and trade routes would have allowed some more opportunities than others to sell their produce, labor, or military service. Even populations that were located along marginal routes had the potential of benefiting economically from traders searching for trade routes alternative to those which had been disrupted at the end of the Late Bronze Age.

Different families, groups, and areas would also have had varying types of relationships with nomadic groups, some of whom certainly played some role in the systems of trade and commerce. Some would have been in a position to benefit, for example, from raids carried out along trade routes or by controlling passes. Others would have suffered economically through being in the position of having to pay tribute to either urban or nomad elites while others did not. As villages fissioned, other complex relations of dominance and subordination would also have developed. Given these kinds of situations, there were probably a number of rich rulers or chiefs—either established villagers or bandits—and some kind of network of elite clans.

Social conflict and political centralization, which accompanied the increased tendency toward stratification, are also suggested by the apparent destruction or abandonment of a number of sites toward the end of the eleventh century at rural and marginal as well as urban sites, and by evidence for the presence of the two-level hierarchy type of settlement pattern characteristic of chiefdoms. Although admittedly fragmentary, the evidence is interpreted by Coote and Whitelam as being consistent with Carneiro's theory of state formation in circumscribed areas—population pressure on limited resources led to competition for arable land. This in turn led to social conflict, which resulted in an increase in the size and degrees of organization in territorial units. As these territories increased in size they would have decreased in number, eventually leading to the formation of a chiefdom and ultimately to the state.

The increase in production in the highlands that accompanied the move toward centralization appears also to have attracted lowland elites such as the Philistines, who presumably also benefited from the expansion in trade and enlarged their own lowland dominion. The resulting pressures from the lowlands presumably compounded the social circumscription being experienced in the highlands, adding significantly to the regional costs of defense. Those in the highlands who bore the greater defense burden because of their wealth also would have shifted the burden back down to the village smallholders. Seen in this light, centralization functioned as a means of "redistributing" the cost of defense. The emergent landed class would also have attempted to retain among themselves (over against the lowland population) political control over trade, which would also have been facilitated by centralization.

Coote and Whitelam conclude their analysis by suggesting that the highland population centralized and expanded at the expense of surrounding areas because of the pressures of social and environmental circumscription. The lowland populations failed to compete, they argue, because they did not experience the pressures of circumscription to the same extent. Lowland farming strategies, for example, did not depend as much on residential stability, and when confronted by social or political pressure, rural populations were able to move more easily to pastoralism and the more marginal areas as a means of escaping effective state control. This in turn created greater pressure on the resources of the marginal regions, leading to further competition and eventually to centralization.

In a more recent study that focuses on the figure of David, Flanagan builds on his earlier proposal on the processes of state formation in Iron Age I Israel.[58] Here, he extends his study on chieftaincy by including an analysis of the archaeological information (not considered in the earlier study) and illuminating archaeological and literary images with comparative studies based largely on Middle Eastern ethnographies. One of the features that differentiates this analysis from those of Frick and Coote and Whitelam is the greater attention given to interpreting the biblical texts. Another is his focus on understanding the nature of leadership.

Flanagan uses the technology of holography—the stages in the process of holographic encoding and illuminating, as well as the holographic image—as metaphors and models for several aspects of his approach. First, it serves as a metaphor for the processes and relationships that constituted the ancient social world. These include: (a) ideas, opinions, aspirations, and motives, (b) physical and material resources, (c) social norms and systems, and (d) the relationship among them. Second, the historian's constructs of the past can also be viewed as holograms because they reconstitute past meanings through the reconstruction of relationships. Third, the technical processes of holography serve as a model for Flanagan's research design—interpreting the different types of information (literary and material) and using information drawn from comparative studies to illuminate the ancient information and the relationships among the types of information.[59]

This model fulfills for Flanagan what he argues is the need for an approach to interpreting ancient societies that separates archaeological information from literary information analytically, as a means of allowing each to be interpreted independently. In the model, the Iron Age I archaeological material represents primarily the "domain of actions," and the biblical narratives the "domain of notions."[60] One of Flanagan's aims in using this model is to illuminate the relationship between the two types of information.

The model, then, incorporates two stages of analysis. In the first stage, standard methods of interpretation in the disciplines of textual and archaeological studies are used to establish separate images of the domains of notions and actions. At the second level of analysis, these images are integrated, illuminated, and interpreted in light of comparative anthropological studies.[61] The comparative materials are the "illuminating beam" of the hologram.

Flanagan's thesis in this study is "that the 'Israel' of the time was transitional and in the betwixt and between religiously, socially, politically, economically and that tradition casts David in a mediator's role in each of the domains."[62] He suggests that the chiefly leaders of the beginning of Iron Age IC were mediators who used their skills to pacify and reduce fissioning among the disparate peoples of the Iron Age I cultures and eventually to unify them in a single centralized polity. He also argues that *dynasty,* not monarchy, is the basis of the David tradition.

One of the emphases in Flanagan's analysis, as in those of Frick and Coote and Whitelam, is that the social processes in Iron Age I Palestine were more complex than those identified in previous constructs. Whereas most explanations emphasize the collapse of Canaanite cultures and the emergence of "Israel" as more or less sequential processes, Flanagan proposes that there were sociopolitical and religious processes of devolution and evolution that were occurring simultaneously and continuously in a single, open society, which was composed of a diversity of peoples who were struggling to maintain their equilibrium in the face of economic and political change.

In his examination of the archaeological material,[63] Flanagan begins with a description of the topography and ecological zones of ancient Palestine. Next, he analyzes occupation patterns, and argues on the basis of his review of the material information that there was no universal pattern of discontinuity and continuity in the transition from the Late Bronze Age to Iron Age I, nor was there a single date for the transition. With a *longue durée* perspective typical of many of the recent studies of the social world of ancient Palestine, Flanagan points to the several dramatic shifts that occurred in population between Middle Bronze I (ca. 2000 B.C.E.) and Iron Age IC (the tenth century), when contemporary populations in each phase were interacting constantly and symbiotically. In this light, he interprets the material culture of Iron Age IC as incorporating forms and traditions from a variety of continuous cultural traditions, rather than building on a single culture or society identified with an Iron Age IA or "Israelite" population.

In his interpretation of the archaeological material, Flanagan also appeals to comparative anthropological studies, including Marfoe's systemic analysis of the relationship between land use and social patterns in Iron Age Lebanon (see Frick above). According to this model,

> agricultural risks are reduced by mixing cultivation and husbandry and by forming social networks that extend across production zones at various elevations on the plains and in the mountains . . . that could save agriculturalists and pastoralists in times of drought or political devastation. The unpredictable and uncontrollable nature of affairs produce dynamic rather than static traditional societies whose basic socioeconomic instability and demographic fluidity are related to the ecology.[64]

In such a situation, security is more important than profit, economic and residential patterns compete and change at each other's expense, and classifications of relationships are constantly shifting.

Flanagan points to modern ethnographies of Middle Eastern and North African societies as examples of how such strategies function to spread risks and establish relationships among segments of a society. On the basis of these models, he identifies four overlapping ecological zones that during Iron Age IC supported distinctive but complementary residential and economic subsistence strategies:[65] (1) seafaring mercenary traders (the Philistines); (2) sedentary agrarians; (3) semisedentary/seminomadic, semiagrarian/semipastoral groups; and (4) pastoral nomadic groups. In proposing this construct, Flanagan assumes that there were symbiotic relationship among these groups, with reciprocal exchanges and relocations. This model, from Flanagan's perspective, accounts for the tensions and transformations in tenth century Palestine that were interrelated with the symbiotic relationships that existed among disparate segmented groups living in varied environments.

In relation to leadership, as is the case in other preindustrial societies, access to resources was probably more important than having formal control over them or than defining clear boundaries. It is thus unlikely that the geographical limits of a leader's dominance were precisely delineated, especially in regions where peoples were continually relocating or changing allegiance. It is probably better, he suggests, to think in terms of access to territory and subjugation of peoples rather than control or governance of lands.

Because of the tension and competing interests that would have existed between those who tended toward centralization because of, for example, potential economic advantages, and those suspicious of potential tyranny and living with a lack of surpluses, the role of the leader in Iron Age IC would have been mediatory and homeostatic.

Flanagan concludes in this section that Iron Age IC was a time of pacification, reduced fissioning, and centralization. The new state that developed by the end of the tenth century was a secondary state that included both peoples who had previously lived in centralized polities and those for whom statehood, centralization, and nontribal organizations were new. The archaeological evidence—few signs of destruction and evidence from sites that were rebuilt after a hiatus in occupation—also suggests, in his estimation, that the transition to statehood was relatively peaceful.

In the next section in his study,[66] Flanagan focuses on examining the literary images of David presented in the biblical texts, looking not for specific historical information, but for the patterns and structures in the texts that tell us something about the storytellers and their worlds. Raising specific detailed historical questions about biblical texts, he believes, is to misunderstand their nature and purpose and to distort their meaning. He emphasizes that there cannot be any correct interpretation of such texts, and that therefore his approach is to attempt to interpret the past "adequately," not "truly" or "correctly."

Flanagan focuses, therefore, not so much on the "historical" David as on the question of what qualities the ancient writers saw in David. His aim is to distinguish between the variables and invariables in the biblical models of David in the Psalms, Chronicles, the Deuteronomic history, and the books of Samuel—between those qualities and actions that are represented in all the traditions (the invariables) and those that the writers changed, omitted, or added to (the variables).[67] He argues that each of the models can be viewed as an "ancient hologram" containing an image of the whole David figure. Although they differ in emphasis, and in their constructs of events and diachronic sequences, Flanagan argues that each model nevertheless illuminates the same fundamental transitions. The primary invariable in the different models is David's role as a ". . . mediator always remembered for being in the betwixt and between"[68] and as the founder of the Yahwist religion's tradition in Jerusalem.

Flanagan further suggests that when the literary sources are approached without presupposing monarchical ideals, many of the details can be interpreted differently than they have been traditionally, and a very different picture of David emerges. If stripped of the Yahwist roles imposed by the biblical writers, the core image of David in the text is that of a paramount chief, not a king, a mediator who would have been acceptable as a leader to most of the varied social groups of the time—including those that continued the Late Bronze Age cultures, who sought to halt the devolution from monarchical statehood at the level of chieftaincy, and the emerging Iron Age groups, for whom the limited centralization of chieftaincy was compatible with their level of social development and religious values.

The Samuel model traces the development of centralization through the use of genealogical and administrative lists as well as narrative. These, Flanagan suggests, represent a patronage network that had gradually, but not completely, replaced the segmentary tribal structure. As the "official" view of the genealogists and administrators, however, the traditions subsume and obscure much of the diversity of tenth-century Palestine.

Flanagan's general construct of the evolution toward centralization is similar to Frick's—from familial, village, and tribal leadership, toward urbanized patronage and administrative bureaucracy. In the Samuel traditions, the movement toward centralization is manifest in David's image as an outcast and fugitive from the northern groups; as a southern warrior-chieftain, whose followers are portrayed as economic, social, and political refugees who joined one of their own kind (David) for the purposes of protection and support; and finally as paramount leader in a centralized Jerusalem. Interests in the story also shift from the politics of marriage typical of segmented systems, reflected in the references to descent that identify wives, to a stronger concern for succession to office and centralized administration.

Flanagan also draws a distinction between the ways in which David's attitudes and actions are portrayed in relation to Yahwists and to non-Yahwists and foreigners. In relation to the latter (for example, in the stories about Goliath, the Ammonites, and the Philistines) he is depicted as fearless and cunning, aware of his advantages, and skillful in choosing the most effective responses to situations. In relation to the Yahwists, he is equally astute, but less authoritarian. For example, he does not respond forcefully in the face of Saul's hostility, aggression, and tyranny, and does not get actively involved in conflicts. Flanagan argues that this represents a deliberate strategy, the type of check and balance mechanism used in segmented systems for resolving conflicts and maintaining order.

Resistance to centralization is represented in the story about David's ordering a census, in which he acts as a tyrannical monarch capable of taxing production and conscripting soldiers and forced labor—an intolerable assertion of political power which, from the perspective of this model, would have drained economic resources, replicated foreign politics, and violated religious egalitarian values. David submits to the divine response (sending a plague), the limits of legitimate centralization in the model are established, and the redistributive economy of chieftaincy is maintained (in contrast with the Solomonic model).

Flanagan hypothesizes that the Samuel model focuses on David's personal legitimacy and the legitimacy of his house. While it explains developments and metamorphoses, it also opposes full centralization in favor of a chieftaincy model. David's house is affirmed, but without full centralization. The evolutionary trajectory is from tribalism to chiefly dynasty and succession to monarchy (*not,* as others have portrayed it, from tribalism to monarchy to dynasty to succession).

Flanagan also considers the texts in light of anthropological studies of succession to high office. Because there are constant rivalries and competition for paramountcy in segmented systems, neither personal nor dynastic legitimacy is affirmed simply by accession to office, and succession within a kin group is not automatically presumed on the basis of a single, successful paramountcy. Being chosen as a leader, then, is only a step toward legitimation. True leadership has to be demonstrated repeatedly and sustained in order to retain its legitimacy.

From the perspective of the biblical model, centralizing in Jerusalem (2 Samuel 5 and 6), submitting the new administration to Yahweh's control (2 Samuel 21–24), determining whose dynasty will legitimately prevail (2 Samuel 7), and deciding who David's legitimate successor will be (1 Kings 1–2) are separate issues. Succession is not an issue until David's abilities deteriorate; then the model is updated and succession by appointment within David's kin group is incorporated in the traditions.

Flanagan suggests that the biblical portrayal of David's struggle with Saul and Saul's followers can also be understood in light of studies of succession in segmented systems. In such societies, when leadership passes from one segment to another, competition within and among groups is likely to occur simultaneously. Competition between the one who has displaced a previous leader and other outside groups (such as the Philistines in the biblical construct) continues, while at the same time members of his own segment vie for power during the unstable transition period (for example, Absalom). Paramount leaders, especially when they are only marginally eligible for positions of leadership, must continually safeguard their power against contenders from outside, within, above, and below. In the Samuel model, where rules for succession do not appear to be clearly defined, the transition periods following Saul's death, during David's later years, and even after Solomon's reign are all marked by conflict and rebellion. The model's view is that legitimate leaders are those who survive and are successful.

In the traditions specific to David, his legitimacy as leader in the north depends in large part on his marriage into Saul's family, whereas in Judah it does not. The rise of a leader in a segmented system often includes marriage into another segment, even that of an incumbent chief. In the absence of heirs, rights may sometimes pass through daughters to their husbands, who then rule on behalf of the wife's father's line for a generation, or until succession returns to the central line through the daughter's children or a grandchild by another mother. Michal's childlessness, the house arrest of Meribbaal and Mica, and the death of all other sons and grandsons in the direct line curtails the possibility of succession being passed on within Saul's line.

The genealogical and narrative traditions indicate that David also marries other women outside his kin group, taking wives among both Yahwists and non-Yahwists, a tactic that is often used by pastoralists who are seeking to expand their network of relationships to groups that are economically, socially, and politically beneficial to them in some way.

David's flight from Saul and his residence among the Philistines is interpreted by Flanagan as typical of the kind of migration that allows a rival for a position of leadership a convenient means of escaping problems by withdrawing to a peripheral area away from where the acting leader has authority. Being in the peripheral area also facilitates his ability to demonstrate and develop his leadership skills and to create a power base of his own before making another attempt at high office.

Such maneuvers in outlying regions also typically affect descent lineages and genealogies, which are readjusted to reflect the actual social relationships that result. Flanagan points to the genealogical material associated with Hebron (2 Sam. 3:2–5; 5:13–16), in which David is at the head and his sons are listed according to their mothers' positions, and there is no hint of a connection with Saul's family. This implies, Flanagan argues, that the legitimation of David's position as leader in Judah is independent of his association with Saul and his marriage to Michal. This conclusion is supported by the narrative traditions about David's service among the Philistines and his roles as protector and redistributor in the south, both of which suggest that he is understood as having earned his position in Judah from a Philistine base, by rallying support among individuals and groups who were seeking the benefits of personal allegiance to him.

The accounts and lists of David's marriages also suggest to Flanagan something of how the biblical writers perceived David's strategies. David marries both upward into chiefly and royal houses and outward among many segments of society, building an increasingly secure network of alliances—spreading his risks in terms of geography and social class.

In the concluding section of his study,[69] Flanagan's aim is to look beyond the information provided by texts and tells and to seek

> a coherent multidimensional image—and for the processes that shape it—by integrating the separate analytic and systemic images from archaeology and literature by illuminating their intersections with relationships from better known and observable societies.[70]

He is explicit in asserting that he makes no attempt to "synchronize" the details in the sources or interpretations of them. Instead, information from the ancient domains of actions and notions are allowed to "interfere" and are illuminated in a way that enables multidimensional images (hypotheses) to be proposed. The result is "a hologram of the early Iron Age."

Again, Flanagan uses information on the nature of segmented societies for illuminating the sociopolitical situation in which David was able to rise to power. He proposes that as the monarchical city-states of the Late Bronze Age devolved, segmentation functioned to maintain peace and social stability, as eventually did the limited centralization of chieftaincy represented in the traditions about David's rise to power through a careful building of alliances.

Flanagan asserts that the archaeological evidence for the processes of change corresponds with the general construct of movements within the biblical stories. According to the cumulative composite myth in the Bible: (1) a pre- or non-Yahwistic Israel, in which Samuel played a role, merged with Yahwists in Benjamin to form "all Israel" under Saul; (2) David rose as a leader among the Philistines; (3) eventually he was accepted by a council of elders as leader of a federation consisting of Judah and the Philistines; (4) later he assumed leadership over the northern group and simultaneously led the two segmented moieties,[71] Judah and Israel, turning against the Philistines; (5) his legitimacy was continually threatened until first he, and then his house, were legitimated. David thus displaced first Saul, then Saul's house, then the Philistines, and finally the ark of the covenant. Only afterward, following the plague that resulted from the census, does David submit himself and his model of leadership to the Deity, and become therefore religiously legitimated.

Both the archaeological and the literary models also suggest simultaneous processes of devolution and evolution similar to the types of symbioses that exist among sedentary, seminomadic, and nomadic peoples documented in the anthropological literature. The model of David that is idealized portrays a pastoral nomad who first rises to leadership among the Philistines, whose role as mediators and traders in the literature between pastoral and agrarian peoples and between nomadic and sedentary groups corresponds positively with the roles of such groups as presented in ethnographic literature on the Middle East. The social role of David the literary figure (or historical individual if such a person existed) is most at home, Flanagan suggests, with the traditions about the Philistines. But David successfully adapts to Benjaminite, Israelite, Judahite, Transjordanian, ruling class, and peasant expectations and needs as well. Ideologically, his role is that of a Yahwist pastoral, nomadic chieftain and a former *'apiru,* who adapts to the needs and aspirations of all segments within the system.

Flanagan conceives of the process as taking something like the following trajectory: Separately, nomads and seminomads in southern Palestine and Transjordan formed a moiety with sedentary groups and sought to encapsulate, suppress, or associate in some way with the Philistines and related groups (the Sea Peoples) in the area (with the latter probably having been the early pattern). Towns of the two groups coexisted with minimal harmony, with the administrative skills of the Sea Peoples being appropriated to some extent by the other groups. Ultimately, the leader of the trading/agrarian/mercenaries in Ziklag (David) became the head of a religiously mixed moiety centered in Hebron. Facing the dilemma of allegiances and loyalties, David eventually sought (according to the model) to align himself more closely with the pastoral nomads. Flanagan proposes that the pressure to make this move was contained until the northern Yahwist moiety sought alliance with him. The suzerain-vassal, patron-client relations with the Sea Peoples were then reversed. Leadership was then relocated in Jerusalem and all the disparate groups became affiliated with the new leadership there.

Several patterns of adaptation were employed in making this move. Jerusalem, sociopolitically an artificial center, was the personal holding of the royal family. The specific ways in which the various groups related to the new center depended in large part on their historical and ecological circumstances. The complexity of political arrangements necessary in such a situation required skill on the part of the leader. The biblical perspective of these arrangements is that of the northern and southern moieties as interpreted by the Jerusalemite leaders. But the tensions among the various groups are not completely hidden in the biblical model. Tensions arising from differences in economic and sociopolitical interests, between the ruling and laboring strata of society, among geographical zones, and in historical development, on the one hand, militated against harmony and permanent centralization. But on the other hand, and paradoxically, they also contributed to unification, because leadership was emerging from within.

As a means of illuminating the role of religion in these processes, Flanagan applies Roy A. Rappaport's systemic ecological model of religion.[72] On the basis of this model, he suggests that rituals functioned as a means of regulating and mediating change by adjusting egalitarian religious values. Religion also served an integrative function in legitimating David's paramountcy as a single leader, while at the same time allowing for a variety of distinctive economic and social systems to remain intact as they were integrated politically. But conversely, religion also functioned to inhibit change, as is implied in the prohibition against building a temple in 2 Samuel 7, which reflects the bias on the part of segmented groups against centralization, while at the same time supporting the establishment of a nonmonarchic dynasty.

The prohibition against building a temple is also related to economic interests. The types of rituals associated with temples would be expensive—they consume large quantities of goods and labor, and require specialists who must be trained and economically supported—and would have placed too much stress on a system that was not equipped to bear the weight of such economic demands. The prohibition thus functioned in part to prevent potential economic collapse.

The myth was later adjusted in order to accommodate the later developments of centralization, imposition of force, and temple building in the idealized Davidic model.

Early State vs. Chieftaincy

Although most recent social-scientific studies of the processes of centralization in the tenth century tend to postulate that kingship/the state had not developed in Palestine until the "time of David" at the earliest, if not later, and that it is not possible to rely too heavily on the biblical texts as representations of accurate history, a recent study by Christa Schäfer-Lichtenberger looks to social-scientific models of the characteristics of states in support of her argument that the biblical stories *do* reflect the historical reality of the processes leading to statehood, and that an early form of the state developed during the reign of Saul.[73] She also argues in this study against the likelihood that chiefdoms developed in this area, in part because of the close proximity to primary states and in part because, in her estimation, the conditions necessary for the development of chiefdoms—geographical isolation in particular—are not present in Palestine. Thus, from her perspective, the chiefdom models that dominate the studies summarized above are inappropriate for understanding the formation of political associations in tenth-century Palestine. In contrast to these other studies, Schäfer-Lichtenberger also does not consider the *processes* associated with centralization. Rather, she focuses on comparing the biblical texts with the *characteristics* identified in models of the early state.

In her evaluation of biblical materials,[74] Schäfer-Lichtenberger notes that she is not convinced by arguments that the themes in 1 Samuel 8 through 1 Kings 11 (legitimacy of the governmental system of the state, continuity of leadership, legitimacy of succession, political enemies) were contrived in the late postexilic period and projected back into the eleventh to tenth centuries, especially given what she sees as their appropriateness in relation to social-scientific models that describe the structures in the early stages of the state. These models demonstrate, in her estimation, a correspondence between the structural development described in the biblical record and the logic of the early state's development. In further support of this position, she points out that these themes do not occur in Chronicles, which proves that the portrayal in Samuel and Kings is not a retrospective projection from a later era.

She begins her analysis with a discussion of the problems associated with defining the term "state." In considering the argument that there is a lack of archaeological evidence for the existence of the state before the eighth century, particularly the absence of royal inscriptions, she concludes that archaeology cannot demonstrate the *absence* of the level of economic activity congruent to what we call a "state."

In relation to the lack of inscriptions, Schäfer-Lichtenberger argues that because larger and smaller ancient Near Eastern states probably differed structurally, monumental inscriptions should not necessarily be expected for tenth-century Israel. If there were monumental inscriptions in this period, they would be found only in Jerusalem, where the probability of finding them is minimal. The absence of other texts can be explained by the likelihood that administrative texts were written on papyrus, a material that would not have survived in the archaeological record.

Schäfer-Lichtenberger proposes that part of the problem with past constructs of the rise of monarchy in ancient Israel has to do with modern preconceived notions of what a state is. Another has to do with the contradictions that exist among the various paradigms for state formation, particularly between "conflict" and "consensus" models. She nevertheless agrees that Israel belongs to the category of secondary state formation.

After looking at the problems associated with defining the "state," Schäfer-Lichtenberger reviews several models that she perceives as being relevant to the situation in Iron Age Palestine. The first is Weber's model of premodern states. She contrasts this with his normative model of the *modern* state, which he identifies as having three essential characteristics—legislation, administration, and monopoly on power. The latter, she argues, seems to have particularly dominated the discussion of the nature of the Iron Age state in Palestine, in spite of the fact that the premodern model is more suitable. According to Weber, the premodern states belong to the category of patrimonial states, states that are based more on *regulatory* than normative concepts. In a patrimonial state, ruling power is based on agreement between the ruler and the ruled. Political administration serves primarily to provide for the ruler's household, which in turn is responsible for providing for its officials. Obligations to pay taxes and to render services are thus *politically* based. The authority and legitimacy of officials, and the tasks for which they are appointed, are grounded in personal relationships with the ruler, and because they are personally dependent on the ruler they do not constitute a separate social stratum. Once property is appropriated by officials through heredity, however, they become independent of the ruler's household, and a kind of permanent decentralization, and limitation on the governing power of the ruler, is maintained.

Schäfer-Lichtenberger also reviews Claessen, Cohen, and Skalnik's models of the early state and, along with Weber's patrimonial state model, finds them to be appropriate to the situation in tenth-century Palestine as it is represented in the biblical traditions. The typical characteristics of the early state, according to Claessen and Skalnik, are:

1. The population is large enough that socioeconomic stratification and specialization develop, establishing a need for coordinating daily activities. The minimum population is five hundred.
2. The early state has a definite, regionally distinct, territory, but borders that are loosely marked.
3. The early state has its own political organization and central government with one governmental center and one royal court, and keeping civil order is largely based on authority. Specialists exist only at the highest administrative level, if an administrative hierarchy has been established. There is no codified law, professionalized justice system, or police force.
4. The state is de facto independent, and the government has the power to prevent the permanent separation of territorial regions, and to counteract outside threats. The ruler is the supreme military leader, and the population is obligated to military service.
5. Social stratification is minimal: the group of rulers is distinct from the majority of the population.
6. The level of production is high enough to attain a regular surplus that serves to maintain the state organization. The ruler's income consists primarily of taxes in the form of services and gifts, and these are imposed only on specific occasions (the imposition of regular taxation appears first in the fully developed early state, but in general is not common). The state's function of redistribution is ordinarily limited to distributing surpluses to the administration and providing sacrifices. Otherwise, individual social units are economically autonomous. Rights of land ownership are typically associated with larger social units such as clans and villages. Groups who have no right of land ownership include artisans, servants, slaves, and traders.

7. The ruler's position is legitimated on the basis of an existing ideology of reciprocity and, in his capacity as military commander-in-chief, his role as protector. He compensates his subjects by distributing gifts among them, and by providing celebrations and public buildings. The state ideology is supported and spread by the priesthood.[75]

Other typical characteristics of the early state, Schäfer-Lichtenberger suggests, cannot be verified for early Israel (for example, the urbanization and documented writings of all administrative levels).

The early state is distinct from the chiefdom in its ability to permanently prevent territorial regions from separating, and by a pronounced ideology of legitimation, which, as a rule, is more distinct than that of the chiefdom. The ideology of reciprocity, and the sacral legitimation of the ruler's position and the state's order, correlate in an explicit state-ideology. The genealogical legitimation of the ruler's position is less important in the early state than in the chiefdom, although the kinship system still prevails over the society as a whole.

According to Claessen and others, the ethnological data suggest distinguishing three developmental phases at the stage of the early state: (1) the inchoative early state, (2) the typical early state, and (3) the transitional early state.

The *inchoative early state* is characterized by the continued dominance of kinship and community ties in its political structures. The economy is still based on common ownership of land, with little emphasis on trade and markets and few full-time specialists. Taxes consist of occasional labor for the state, voluntary contributions, and tributary gifts. The ruler and ruling stratum are economically dependent on income from their own land. Thus, the dominance of the ruling stratum is more politically and ideologically than economically based. Officials receive compensation for their services in the form of natural produce and land allocations. Succession to political office is hereditary, and the judicial system is informal, with no codification of laws or full-time judges. Ideologically, the social differences between the ruling stratum and their subjects are denied, and they are minimized by the practice of reciprocity. The influence of the prestate communal and tribal ideologies continues alongside that of the state. The emerging state ideology thus revolves around the problem of justifying the differences between the ruler and his subjects, and of perpetuating the state beyond its immediate cause. The legitimation of the state as a social establishment is largely carried out by religious specialists.

In the *typical early state,* kinship relations are counterbalanced by local relations. Trade and markets develop on a supralocal level, and regular taxes in the form of natural produce and obligatory services are imposed. Competition and appointment, rather than descent, become essential in filling administrative positions. In addition to traditional forms of compensation, officials begin to receive pay. Alongside reciprocity, redistribution determines the relationships between the social strata. Private ownership of land is still limited at this stage, but the state is moving toward the role of an influential landlord.

In the *transitional early state,* kinship relations affect only marginal aspects of political activity. Private ownership of the means of production becomes more pervasive, and a market economy begins to develop, leading to the development of open antagonism among social classes. The administration is controlled in the transitional early state by appointed officials, and the government slowly evolves into a relatively independent political force. The tax and contribution system is fully developed, and is maintained by a complex system for ensuring a continual flow of taxes. The law is codified, and is primarily overseen by the authority of full-time judges.

The essential features of these early state models are similar, Schäfer-Lichtenberger proposes, to Weber's patrimonial state model, the primary difference being the way in which the relative status of the ruler and his officials is understood to develop. In Claessen's model, the state's officials function as the political counterbalance to the ruler and act as political mediators between the ruler and the ruled. They inherit their offices after the second generation, and in the third phase, appointments become predominant. In Weber's model, on the other hand, officials are appointed to their offices initially, and later appropriate them through descent.

Ultimately, Schäfer-Lichtenberger concludes on the basis of the biblical texts that Saul's reign was an "inchoative state," and David's (in Jerusalem) was a "transitional early state" in some respects (in terms of population, size, territory, political independence, and ideology), and an "inchoative state" in other respects (centralized government, stratification, and surplus economy).

Although one of Schäfer-Lichtenberger's intentions in this study is to counter the proposals of others that chiefdom was one of the stages in the processes of centralization in Iron Age Palestine, the models of the early state that she deems most appropriate, particularly that of the inchoative state, are very similar to the chiefdom models to which others have appealed. This is perhaps indicative of the influence the model or models one chooses have on the way in which information is viewed in the interpretive process.

None of the constructs of the transition to monarchy and centralization summarized here considers in any comprehensive way the role that might have been played by Solomon in these processes. There seems to be a general assumption that by the end of the tenth century the state apparatus was firmly in place. Perhaps by this time, as the biblical construct of Solomon and the archaeological evidence such as the construction of fortresses and increased trade suggest, full centralization had been achieved. Or perhaps Jamieson-Drake and others are correct in their assertions that centralization did not occur until later. This is certainly an issue that deserves further attention.

Chapter 5

Iron Age II

The Period of the Monarchy

Although changes in the social systems of both Israel and Judah occurred throughout the course of Iron Age II, the constructs introduced in this chapter are essentially synchronic in nature, that is, they focus on identifying and describing social institutions and social organization rather than social processes. Some of the constructs are based primarily on the evaluation of biblical texts, some on archaeological information, and some on both. Fewer constructs of the social worlds of this period have appealed to anthropological models than is the case for the preceding periods, for reasons already discussed in chapter 1.[1]

BIBLICAL INFORMATION/HISTORICAL SETTING

The transition from tribal organization to centralized state is believed by many scholars to have been accompanied by the rise of a literary court culture alongside oral forms of transmitting traditions. This is typically understood in terms of a rapid increase in literary activity, with earlier oral forms being set down in writing and often arranged in larger compositions. In these new literary contexts, the older oral forms acquired new life settings, in which their form and content were changed to some extent. But issues concerning which traditions are early, and whether these traditions did in fact originally circulate in oral form, along with the question of how early they were written down, are, even for the monarchic period, the subject of much debate.

The traditions about the monarchy contained in 1 and 2 Samuel and 1 and 2 Kings were, until recently, considered to contain largely accurate historical and social information about both Israel and Judah, even though some of the stories, such as those about Elijah and Elisha, were acknowledged to contain some legendary material. Although later in date, and in spite of their obvious bias in favor of Judah, 1 and 2 Chronicles were also considered to be reliable to some extent. Prophetic materials have also been used as sources for understanding the history and social world of this period.

As was indicated in chapter 1, the so-called "minimalists" have challenged the view that it is possible to place any great confidence in the accuracy of these texts, arguing that it is impossible to distinguish the later editorial overlay dating to the Persian period from those traditions which may actually have their origins in the earlier period of the monarchy. The exceptions are those references which have been confirmed by extrabiblical texts.

As was noted in chapter 4, some scholars have gone so far as to argue that a true monarchic or state system did not exist in Israel or Judah until possibly as late as the eighth century B.C.E., and thus the notion that there were true "kings" earlier than this is a later construct. This is of course not the consensus, but it is nevertheless a position that is worth considering as we continue to try to understand the nature and development of the Iron Age II social world.

Traditions about the monarchic period in the books of Samuel through Kings are stamped with the so-called Deuteronomistic historian's strongly biased interpretation. As Lemche has put it, "we see all of the events of the Israelite monarchy through the glasses of the Deuteronomists."[2] The general consensus is that the editors of these traditions had access to materials from a variety of sources: independent traditions about Samuel, Saul, David, and Solomon, administrative documents from the united monarchy, the royal archives of the divided kingdoms of Israel and Judah and the Jerusalem Temple archives, and cycles of prophetic tales.

First Kings 12 describes the division of a single kingdom into two—Judah in the south and Israel in the north—as resulting from Solomon's oppressive policies, reinforced by his son Rehoboam after his death, which prompt rebellion and secession by the north. Following the rebellion, Jeroboam becomes king in the north, establishes his own capital at Shechem, and sets up shrines at Dan and Bethel. The southern state of Judah retains Jerusalem as its capital. Whether or not this is an accurate portrayal of events, this and other traditions suggest that tensions between north and south were already deeply rooted.

The formulaic descriptions in 1 and 2 Kings of the reigns of the kings in both the north and the south following the secession of the north include such information as the years in which they reigned, their relationships to previous and succeeding kings, policies that are said to have been instituted during the course of their reigns, and the location of their capitals. There are also references to the "Book[s] of the Annals [Chronicles]" of both kingdoms. Although there may be some historically and socially accurate information in these traditions, none of them can be accepted at face value, particularly considering the strong theological overtones. These include particularly a conviction that obedience to the covenant yields blessings of welfare and peace, whereas disobedience leads to divine judgment in the form of suffering and even expulsion from the land, and an emphasis on centralization of worship in Jerusalem and condemnation of worship at other sanctuaries. There is also a strong polemic against the northern kings, especially Jeroboam, who is credited with establishing what the writer(s) considered rival sanctuaries at Dan and Bethel. Although Judah's kings fare somewhat better, both northern and southern kings are judged according to the standard of covenant obedience.

The stories assert that the Davidic dynasty remained relatively stable throughout Judah's history as an independent state, with the line of David remaining in power until the time of the Babylonian exile in the sixth century. In addition, the capital of Judah and an officially centralized cult are said to have been located in Jerusalem for the entire period.

Israel, on the other hand, is portrayed as being much less stable sociopolitically and religiously than Judah. Several short-lived dynasties are identified (for example, the Omrid and Jehu dynasties), but no single stable dynasty, as is the case for Judah. The picture presented for Israel is one of a state with a great deal of political intrigue associated with succession to the throne, often including the massacre of the previous king's family. A number of northern kings are also portrayed as having been singled out by prophets as leaders.

The "Chronicler" (1 and 2 Chronicles) borrows some passages directly from the books of Samuel and Kings, but ignores or changes other traditions. "History" is reinterpreted in light of the postexilic situation in Judah in which there was no longer a king, and politically neither Israel nor Judah was any longer an independent nation. The emphasis in the Chronicler's construct is on Judah as a worshiping community, with the Jerusalem Temple playing a central role. In spite of apparent biases in these books, some scholars believe that they preserve some reliable details of genealogies, topography, and political administration that can be used to supplement material in Samuel through Kings.

Israel is portrayed in the biblical traditions as having been at its height of power and wealth during the reign of Jeroboam II (786–746), who is said to have extended the boundaries of the kingdom northward into Syria and southward into the area of Judah. At the same time in Judah, Uzziah (783–742) is said to have expanded his territory east into Transjordan, south into the Negeb, and west into Philistia. Archaeological excavations at Samaria, Israel's capital, have been cited as evidence of the wealth and prosperity of this period, as have the prophetic books of Amos and Hosea, with their emphasis on social and economic injustice in Israel, presumably in reaction to an increase in class distinctions. These books are also believed to provide some indication of what popular religion may have been like during the eighth century in Israel.

We know from extrabiblical texts that after Jeroboam II's reign, Tiglath-pileser III (745–727 B.C.E.) ascended the throne in Assyria, and Assyrian power began to rise and threaten the security of both Israel and Judah. Part of the threat was grounded in the Assyrian policy of controlling conquered peoples through exiling them to remote parts of the empire. This situation must certainly have had a major impact on the sociopolitical situation in both states, even though ultimately they were affected in different ways. In Israel, the biblical texts imply, there was a period of internal chaos characterized by a rapid turnover of kings, accompanied by murder and intrigue, assassination, and conspiracy.

Tiglath-pileser III set up a system of provinces governed by Assyrian officials, and on the peripheries of the empire vassal states were bound to Assyria by treaties. In 738, Israel was reduced to vassal status, and ca. 722 lost its status as a state and was incorporated into the empire as a province. Presumably, some of its population was deported to other parts of the empire, and foreign groups moved in.

Judah was also forced into vassalage by the Assyrians, but during the period of Assyrian dominance did not completely lose its status as a state. Nevertheless, its position as vassal to a dominant state must certainly have had a strong effect on its political structure and functioning, at least on the state level, but probably on the local level as well. Presumably, for example, the necessity of paying tribute would have increased the tax burdens on the village populations.

The biblical traditions also assert that there were several major religious reforms in Judah, one during the reign of Hezekiah in the eighth century and one during the reign of Josiah in the seventh century. The focus of these supposed reforms is on abolishing the worship of foreign gods and centralizing worship in the Temple in Jerusalem. But how much these descriptions reflect reality is open to question—again, given the strong theological biases of the later editors.

Toward the end of the seventh century, the political dominance of Judah by Assyria was replaced by Babylonian control, when the Assyrian Empire fell to the Babylonians during the reign of the Babylonian Nabopolassar (626–605 B.C.E.). Judah remained under vassalage to the Babylonians until, during the reign of Nebuchadrezzar (605–562 B.C.E.), its status as a semiindependent state came to an end—the Jerusalem Temple was destroyed, some portion of Judah's population was deported, and the Davidic dynasty came to an end.

EXTRABIBLICAL LITERARY INFORMATION

A number of extrabiblical texts have aided in reconstructions of the histories of Israel and Judah. Some also provide information about sociopolitical organization and structure in other ancient Near Eastern states that may offer some insight into the situations in Israel and Judah.[3] "Ahab the Israelite" is mentioned in an Assyrian inscription on Shalmaneser III's (858–824 B.C.E.) "Kurkh stele" (ca. 853 B.C.E.), where he is said to have provided two thousand chariots and ten thousand foot soldiers (very likely an exaggerated number) at the battle of Karqar to help a coalition of kings fight Shalmaneser's forces. The inscription of Mesha, king of Moab (ca. 840 B.C.E.), refers to Israel and its king Omri (Omri's son is also mentioned, but not by name). "Jehu son of Omri" is mentioned and depicted on the "Black Obelisk" of Shalmaneser III, paying tribute to the Assyrian king (the Bible does not mention this). He is also mentioned in three other Assyrian inscriptions describing events that took place in 841, all associated with Shalmaneser III: the Aleppo Fragment, the Kurba'il Statue, and the Safar annals. According to these inscriptions, Israel became a loyal Assyrian vassal when Jehu came to the throne.

The Nimrud slab inscription, which records Adad-nirari III's expedition to Palestine in 803, mentions Hatti-land, Amurru-land, Tyre, Sidon, the land of Omri, Edom, Philistia, and Aram, but not Judah. And his "Rimah stele" mentions Joash of Samaria.

Tiglath-pileser III (745–727 B.C.E.) mentions "Menahem of Samaria" together with a list of other north Palestinian and Syrian kingdoms. And Sargon II mentions his conquest of Samaria and of "the whole house of Omri" (the typical Assyrian name for Israel is "house of Omri" or "land of Omri").

References to Judah and to Judahite kings appear less frequently in extrabiblical literary materials. Hezekiah is mentioned in Assyrian records and reliefs of Sennacherib's siege of Jerusalem in 701. It is interesting to note that the Assyrian and biblical accounts of this seige are similar in some respects, thus permitting us to make a reasonable guess that the Assyrians devastated Judah, that Jerusalem was not captured, and that Hezekiah ended up paying tribute to the Assyrians. The Babylonian invasion of the Shephelah and the Judean highlands is documented in the Lachish ostraca. And Jehoiachin (of 2 Kings) is referred to in a Babylonian text as being given rations at the Babylonian court.

From within Palestine itself, very little in the way of literary materials has been recovered through excavations, and what little there is takes not the form of monumental inscriptions, as in the surrounding states, but mostly ostraca. There is one inscription dated to the ninth century from Tel Dan that refers to the "house of David,"[4] and another from the Siloam tunnel in Jerusalem, dated to the eighth century.

ARCHAEOLOGICAL INFORMATION

Most of the archaeological information relating to Iron Age II dates to the ninth and eighth centuries B.C.E.[5] The material culture of the late seventh to early sixth century is more fragmentary, as is material from late-eighth- to early-sixth-century contexts in Jerusalem.

Archaeological surveys have indicated that there was a significant increase in Palestine's population throughout the course of Iron Age II. There is also corresponding evidence of centralization, and an increase in social complexity.[6] One of the clearest indicators is the development of an urban-based hierarchical settlement pattern (cities, towns, villages, hamlets). In addition, there is a greater variety of architectural forms (palaces, sanctuaries, store facilities, stables, both simple and complex structures, private houses, and small industrial installations), which suggest a larger range of services offered by some sites (for example, Hazor, Megiddo, Gezer, Beersheba, and Lachish), and thus the possibility of their having been regional or administrative centers of some type.[7] These sites are characterized as administrative centers on the basis of such features as: a highly centralized, planned layout; impressive city walls and multiple entryway gates; a palace and/or administrative complex near the city gate or elsewhere; monumental, well-engineered water systems; and large, colonnaded buildings that were possibly government storehouses.

At the opposite extreme are sites consisting of little more than a series of domestic structures, with perhaps a local leader's house and a few "industrial installations" (for example, olive presses or storage pits). These were very likely villages or hamlets that were dependent in some ways on the larger sites. In the middle of the spectrum are the town sites. These probably offered a limited range of services (more than villages, but less than the larger sites), and were ultimately dependent on either a regional or a major administrative center.

Domestic architecture in all Iron Age II sites is characterized chiefly by the further development of the "four-room"/"pillared"/"courtyard" house (the literature lacks consistency in the terminology used to identify this house-type). Social stratification is apparent in the fact that some of these houses are more spacious and well laid out than others. In addition to these relatively isolated dwellings, there are also large multiroom residencies, mostly at sites identified as administrative centers, and, in some cases, citadels. Ashlar masonry characterizes the most impressive of the structures, especially at ninth-century Samaria. These large buildings, some of them containing imported furnishings, were most likely residences of the ruling elites.[8]

Also differentiating Iron Age II from Iron Age I is the presence of fortified towns, some with "Solomonic" casemate walls, monumental city gates, and in some cases water tunnels (for example, Megiddo, Hazor, and Gezer), and frontier defenses (for example, at Tell el-Jib, Tell en-Nasbeh, Lachish, Arad, Beersheba). A number of other similar fortified cities, towns, and villages were also built, many of them in the highlands. Along with the centralization of Israelite royal functions at Samaria, the presence of fortified towns along the border between the northern and southern regions has been interpreted as archaeological evidence of the divided monarchy.[9]

In addition to the clear evidence represented in the large residencies at some sites, social stratification is indicated in the presence of such items as the ninth- to eighth-century carved ivory inlays, a distinctive Israelite art form with Phoenician prototypes and found mostly at Samaria (cf. 1 Kings 22:39; Amos 6:4; 3:15), and the seventh- to sixth-century stamp seals. Seals have been found in large enough numbers that nonelites may have possessed the plainer varieties that were manufactured from nonprecious stones. A number of seals, however, were most likely the property of elites, as they are made from precious stones and have ornate designs carved in them. They bear inscriptions that include titles such as "priest," "servant of the king," and "prince," among others.

Iron Age II tombs also provide some evidence of social stratification.[10] Most of the excavated tombs are monumental, with repositories for earlier burials. In several cases, there are Hebrew inscriptions with standardized warning and blessing formulas. The objects found in the tombs can be classified as luxury goods, and include jewelry and other items of personal adornment, costly metals, imported Cypriot and Egyptian pottery, juglets for perfumes, scarabs and seals, model furniture, and terra-cotta figurines. The long use of the repositories, number and quality of tomb offerings, chronological range of the pottery, and names in some of the inscriptions all suggest that these tombs belonged to elite families and were used over several generations. They have been found throughout Palestine, but are concentrated in eighth- to seventh-century Judah, with the most elaborate located in and around Jerusalem. Commoners were presumably buried in simple pit graves, although these are not well attested in the archaeological record.

Centralized bureaucracies are represented primarily in the capitals of the two states, Samaria and Jerusalem, and in the various types of evidence relating to economy.

The centralized economies of Israel and Judah are believed to have been dependent on a system of tribute, taxes, and tolls (see below), and to some extent on trade. The Mesha stele provides evidence of the payment of tribute, and the eighth-century ostraca from Samaria, evidence of taxation. Found in a building next to the palace, and comprising notations about deliveries of oil and wine, most of these ostraca appear to be receipts for taxes, apparently paid in kind into government warehouses. The names of individuals, possibly the owners of large estates, appear on a few of these documents.[11] Numerous examples of weights, measures, seals, silver hordes, and stamped jar handles indicate growth and standardization in trade and probably a systematically planned national economy administered from the capitals.

In addition to the Samaria ostraca, redistribution of tribute, taxes, and tolls is suggested by the presence of silos or granaries (that is, storage facilities) at sites that are believed to have been administrative centers, and by the hundreds of late-eighth-century stamped jar handles with seals reading *lmlk* ("belonging to the king") found in various places in Judah.

The relatively scant (compared to other ancient Near Eastern states) evidence of writing also points to centralization. Although very few royal or monumental inscriptions have been found in Palestine, hundreds of ostraca, inscribed pottery and stone vessels, ivories, weights, seals, and several tomb inscriptions have been found. Among the epigraphic finds are also a number of abecedaries. The apparent widespread ownership and use of seals, used primarily for sealing rolled papyrus documents, has been cited as evidence of a relatively widespread literacy, even among women, whose names appear on some of them. But even if this was the case and many people could read and write in an elementary fashion, relatively few—probably only the well-educated elite—would have been truly literate.[12] As has already been noted, anthropological and sociological studies of preindustrial agrarian societies indicate that the typical literacy rate is about 5 percent.

In spite of the biblical construct of Judean religion having been centralized in Jerusalem, there is archaeological evidence that other sanctuaries existed—for example, at Lachish and Arad, and possibly Beersheba, where a horned altar was uncovered. Hundreds of female figurines have also been recovered from sites throughout Palestine, suggesting the possibility of reverence for female deities.

DEMOGRAPHY AND SETTLEMENT PATTERNS

Magen Broshi and Israel Finkelstein argue that, demographically, the first half of the eighth century was an important turning point in Iron Age II Palestine, postulating that the population reached its apex during this time—approximately 460,000—350,000 in Israel and 110,000 in Judah. They calculate that Israel was more densely populated than Judah at this time, but that a larger proportion of the population lived in the southern capital in Judah than in the northern capital of Samaria.[13]

The settlement pattern of the preceding centuries, before 734 B.C.E., indicates a gradual increase in population and relative stability and peace, which allowed for the foundation of many small and undefended settlements. The proportion of the population that lived in larger settlements is calculated as having been similar in both kingdoms: 32 percent in Israel and 29 percent in Judah. But the population of Israel decreased dramatically after Assyrian domination was imposed on Palestine, and signs of destruction are discernible in almost every site excavated in the area of the former kingdom of Israel. At other sites there is clear evidence of decline.

The demographic balance between different regions also changed significantly according to this survey. Jerusalem expanded to three times its former size, possibly as a result of immigration from the north, and there was a corresponding increase in the number of settlements in the Judean hills, the Judean desert, and the Beersheba Valley. After the seige of Jerusalem in 701, the "suburbs" surrounding Jerusalem were destroyed, as were a number of other sites.

Urban vs. Rural Settlements

One of the major characteristics of the Iron Age II settlement pattern that distinguishes it from Iron Age I is the development of urbanization, which probably occurred as the result of a complex interplay between such factors as a growth in population and political and military power, an increase in division of labor and social stratification, and a corresponding increase in numbers of administrators, military forces, artisans, and possibly merchants.

City population levels were much lower than today (a large city would have had a population of approximately two thousand according to some estimates). City life would also have been markedly different from village life in rural areas, where peasant farmers most likely had a distinctive subculture of their own. And the lives of nomadic groups and border dwellers would have differed as well.[14]

Demographic studies often cite the relationship between urban and rural settlements in terms of an opposition between "center (urban) and periphery (rural)." Although in centralized societies urban centers do tend to dominate in terms of politics and economics, setting them as the central points of reference, and other regions as peripheral to them, tends to undermine the significance of the majority. Understanding the relationship as one of "opposition" also undermines the mutual interdependence of urban and rural populations. In the Middle East today, the relationship between city and village is not a "dichotomy," but a continuum. Furthermore, there are many types of social, economic, and political relationships between peasant populations and urban centers.[15]

The vast majority of the Iron Age II populations of Israel and Judah lived in rural, rather than urban, settings. Broshi and Finkelstein's estimation that about 30 percent of the population lived in the capitals of the respective kingdoms is higher than what is typically expected for preindustrial agrarian societies (usually between 80 and 95 percent of the population is estimated to live in nonurban settings), but nevertheless agrees on the question of where the majority resided. But even in urban settings, a large portion of the population was probably composed of farmers.

Villages were small, as in Iron Age I, most supporting populations of between two hundred and three hundred people, but frequently fewer. In most of the habitable and densely populated regions, they were often spaced about 2 to 4 kilometers apart.

A modified "Central Place Theory" for analyzing site size, character, and location in terms of "rank-size hierarchy," has been postulated as a useful model for understanding the character of urbanism and its relationship to other settlement types in Iron Age II Palestine.[16] The typical configuration that defines "urbanism" according to this model is a settlement pattern that has a "three-tier hierarchy," comprising: (1) a few large urban centers that function as administrative and economic centers (in Iron Age II Palestine, probably Jerusalem, Samaria, Dan, Hazor, Gezer, Lachish, and Hebron); (2) a much larger number of middle-size towns ("nodes" in the network), which are relatively evenly distributed geographically and participate in the exchange of goods and services both with one another and with the administrative centers; and (3) a still larger number of small villages, hamlets, and farmsteads in rural areas. The bulk of the population, according to this model, lives in the middle- and lower-tier sites, but administrative control is centralized in the hands of a few elites in the more urban administrative centers.

The three ninth- to eighth-century "city"-types identified by Volkmar Fritz basically correspond to this model.[17] They are: (1) the residential city, (2) the city with a limited administrative or military function, and (3) the city as an administrative or military center. The residential city is characterized by lack of planning, with streets that followed an irregular course, houses that stood close together in clusters, and an absence of identifiable public buildings.

The second type differs from the residential type in having been more carefully planned and in that it contained a small number of public buildings, normally situated near the city gate. Houses were arranged in rows or blocks, on streets oriented in more or less straight lines (except for a ring road that followed the city wall). Most of the streets opened into a square in front of the city gate. The schematic layout of the public buildings and the alignment of streets in this city-type probably, Fritz surmises, derived from a central authority rather than from local planners.

The third city-type in Fritz's construct was built for administrative and defense purposes. Although there were a certain number of private houses in such cities, the larger official buildings, typically located in the center of the city, appear to have been more important. These large official buildings also seem to have been positioned as a result of planning, in contrast to the unplanned layout of the rest of the city.

Power was almost certainly concentrated in the two national capitals—Jerusalem in Judah and, eventually, Samaria in Israel (according to the biblical traditions the capital of the Northern Kingdom changed location several times—1 Kings 12:25; 14:17; 16:24). Both have produced evidence of a monumentally fortified lower city, a separate and well-defined acropolis citadel, a sacred precinct, and (in the case of Samaria) an impressive palatial complex. The royal palace complex at Samaria, which was separated from the rest of the city by a strong encircling wall, included buildings probably connected with royal administration.[18]

Providing access to water sources was also an important feature of city/town planning. Three different solutions to this problem are identified by Fritz: (1) access to the groundwater supply was located within the city (for example, at Gibeon, Gezer, Hazor); (2) a spring located outside the city was reached by a hidden passage from the city (for example, at Megiddo);

and (3) water from a spring outside the city was brought into the city through a system of underground channels (for example, in Jerusalem).[19]

ECONOMY

As David Hopkins has emphasized,[20] there never was "an ancient economy" in ancient Israel, but rather a *multiplicity* of economies grounded in Israel's complex and fragmented geography. In this diverse landscape, there were two major economic zones: (1) rural areas and small villages, and (2) the more fully developed and interregionally integrated town- or urban-based economy.

Subsistence Strategies

The economy during Iron Age II, as in Iron Age I, was based on a system of mixed agriculture, primarily cereal crops in the basin areas and mixed agriculture, arborculture, and viticulture in the highlands.[21] Agriculture was combined with keeping small domestic flocks and herds of sheep, goats, and sometimes cattle, both as a matter of diversification and risk spreading and as a means of accumulating surpluses. Multicrop risk-spreading strategies involving herds and crops, cereal and garden farming, and the cultivation of vines and fruit trees contributed to the survival of the nuclear (or extended) family in its localized village setting.[22] On the local level in rural communities, then, food production essentially fulfilled the requirements of those involved in the production.

The question of the extent to which surpluses were generated, and if so what they were used for, is debated. Some argue that it was mostly taxed away, while others assert that they would also have been exchanged for other necessities, such as pottery, tools, and weapons, that could not be produced within the context of the household. The answer to these questions is difficult to determine on the basis of the archaeological record—except for palace granaries (Samaria) and large grain silos and granaries located near stables, there is a little evidence of mass/public grain storage. In any case, peasant society in general in antiquity seems to have had a subculture of its own, and thus the Israelite peasant's primary goal was probably self-sufficiency, in spite of outside pressures in the form of tax or rent extraction.[23]

Concentration of land ownership among fewer individuals and increased commercial opportunities over time may have led to increased cash crop specialization, primarily horticultural products, but again this is difficult to determine on the basis of the available information.[24]

Pastoralist activities, both in the form of "enclosed nomadism" and in the exploitation of the more marginal zones in the Negeb and the eastern slopes, almost certainly formed an important element of the economy as well, although this is difficult to quantify on the basis of archaeological materials.

Patterns of Labor

As has already been noted, the ecology and environment of the Israelite and Judean highlands were quite varied, with a number of ecological niches suitable for a number of different types of agricultural and pastoral exploitation. With a few exceptions, none of these zones was sufficiently extensive to allow for the type of mass labor forces thought to have been used in Mesopotamian irrigation agriculture, or for the largely temple- or palace-dominated basin agriculture of ancient Egypt.[25]

The societies of antiquity were typically composed of what economic anthropologists term "plural societies,"[26] that is, a variety of regional subcultures with differences in specific group lifestyles and economic roles is present. The nature of the interactions among these different groups and regions is varied—they might be relatively symbiotic, on the one hand, or even dysfunctional, on the other, depending on the specific circumstances. Society and economy tend to be held together in such settings by the elite and a rigid hierarchical social system.

The typical patterns of labor in the ancient Palestinian states are idealized in 1 Samuel 8:11–17, where the negative effects of centralized leadership are listed. In general, these are identified as involving severe restrictions in freedom and economic demands that will be imposed on the people by the king and his chosen elite. The implication is that their labor will be for the benefit of the king and the elite, rather than for themselves, and that the fruit of their labor will ultimately be taken over, again by the king and his chosen elite. Although this may be an exaggerated picture, it nevertheless reflects to some extent the type of economic relationships that probably existed between elites and the rest of the population.

With some exceptions (for example, land held by royalty and other elites), the primary production unit in settled agricultural communities in Iron Age II Israel and Judah was probably the individual (or possibly extended) family, who either worked an allotted share of land belonging to the extended family or land rented from a wealthy neighbor or absentee landlord. As is typical in peasant societies, these rural small landholders would have been subject in some way to the control of outsiders and to taxation, and would have had to exchange part of what they produced by farming for manufactured goods that they could not make themselves. But poorly developed managerial techniques would have limited the extent to which more politically powerful urbanites would have exerted their control.

Slavery, which assumed a variety of forms, was also an important part of the labor force in ancient economies, contributing especially to the generation of surplus. Elites, with land and political and military status, required slaves and/or serfs to work the land in order to attain and maintain status. Slavery is also suited to a redistributive economy.[27]

The extent to which Israel and Judah depended on corvée labor is difficult to assess, in spite of the implication in the biblical texts that it was one of the oppressive factors in the social system. It is likely that it was employed only at a moderate level, largely for unskilled work. Holladay, for example, argues that heavy use of corvée labor would have been counterproductive—labor taken from the villages would have had a significant negative impact on the viability of the communities that the elites depended on for productivity.[28]

Other forms of labor would also have been important in the economic system. These would have included, in particular, the work of artisans and individuals engaged in trading activities, as well as military service.

In contrast to peasants and slaves, nomads in pluralistic societies are relatively free from subjugation because of their mobility and their tendency to occupy peripheral zones. Economically, they are often linked in symbiosis with sedentary farmers, on whom they depend for agricultural produce and other commodities such as tools, which are exchanged for cattle and sheep. Nomads also contribute to the overall economy in some cases by participating in long-range trade. Through a blend of tribal reciprocity and redistributive estatist practices, they build up central storehouses and caravanseries that facilitate the passage of traders. They also sponsor and protect caravans, normally in return for "gifts" that establish a special guest-friend relationship between the traveler and the territorial clan involved. Although it is not possible to argue definitively that this pattern applied to the situation in Iron Age II Palestine, it is nevertheless likely, given its clear presence in other historical periods.

Systems of Exchange and Trade

It is unlikely, as some have argued, that market exchange in the form of capital markets operated on any large scale during Iron Age II, as capital markets require the existence of money (which was not available until the sixth century B.C.E.), as well as fairly general literacy.[29]

Although commerce and trade were certainly a part of the economy during this period, they probably remained agriculturally based and, at least in rural areas, continued to be based primarily on family and village self-sufficiency, and thus on a system of reciprocity. At the state level and in urban areas, redistribution (see below) would have been introduced as a form of exchange alongside reciprocity, which was the basic mode of exchange throughout antiquity. Even in economies dominated by redistribution, reciprocal and redistributive modes of exchange tended to be complementary and interactive.[30] Village farmers would have depended to some extent on the relatively modest urban-based markets, but this was probably rare. And the urban zone would have remained economically dependent on rural villages.[31] Villages in Iron Age II were still somewhat decentralized, even though their populations were held responsible for payment of debts, rents, tithes, and taxes. The harvests, flocks, and herds were probably still the property of individual households, which also would have had control of surpluses that, on the local level, were still exchanged on the basis of the principles of reciprocity.

Redistribution occurs as a form of exchange wherever a state dominates an area and monopolizes production and distribution. In this type of system, exchange is controlled by a central institution which bears responsibility for organizing production, storage, redistribution of goods, and trading (not marketing) produce.[32] Particularly when the forces of production are based on slave labor, the redistributive economy is a "political economy," in the sense that relationships in the system are dependent on power and status rather than maximizing profit. Some form of central storehouse complex (in Egypt and Mesopotamia, these were temple-centered) and scribal bureaucracy were necessary in this form of exchange, and large estates run by the elite were typical. Produce was redistributed to feed the state's and temple's nonagricultural workforce (for example, artisans and priests [see Deut. 18:1–8]), as well as the agriculturalists who produced it. From the perspective of the centralized bureaucracy, communities in this type of system were based on well-defined territories wherein residence (rather than kinship ties) conferred membership. Techniques had to be developed in this type of economy for coordinating workforces, food, and material for large building operations. These typically included the establishment of a corvée system of labor (see 1 Kings 9:15–22; 1 Kings 12:1–16), a bureaucracy (see 2 Sam. 8:15–18; 20:23–26; 1 Kings 4), and controls on transportation.

Taxation that involved politically or religiously induced extraction of a percentage of local production was an essential prerequisite for the redistributive system (cf. the system of tithing represented in Deut. 14:22–26 and Mal. 3:8–12; cf. 1 Samuel 8–10 and 1 Kings 12, where the redistributive system and its social consequences are opposed). State revenue would also in some cases have been collected through tribute and tolls. This system of exchange served to support the central administrative and religious institutions, as well as the military.

The late-eighth-century royal stamped jar handles, inscribed with *lmlk* ("belonging to the king"), suggest that a redistributive system was operating in Judah during the eighth century, and that the king was associated in some way with the production and distribution of goods, which would have been supervised by government officials.[33] The jars also bear place names, and some have private seals in addition to the official seals. The vessels apparently were royal property and served to provision official places in various locations, although it is not clear who was supplied with the provisions or where they originated. They may have been distributed to officials appointed by the crown or to troops in various parts of the state. If the cities identified on the seals were administrative centers, the goods transported in the jars may have been collected as taxes or tithes, which were stored in the administrative centers and sent out when required. The persons named on the private seals were perhaps royal tax officials.

The Samaria ostraca are also suggestive of a redistributive system in Israel, providing information about the receipt of oil and wine deliveries, apparently to the royal court. The recipients may have been court officials, but it is not clear whether the goods were meant for their personal use or were passed on to the court. In any case, the ostraca are probably documents that accompanied the taxes that were delivered, perhaps by individual families, to the royal house.[34]

Trade in preindustrial societies tends to be in luxury goods for elites and, in a redistributive system, operated under the aegis of the king, as was probably the case in Iron Age II Israel and Judah (see 1 Kings 10). Trade can be a major component in state formation and supports both the state's economic power and the maintenance of an elite class. Individuals engaged in trade activities were thus almost always emissaries of palace-centered economies, not independent entrepreneurs.[35] The larger urban centers would have been the centers for long-distance trade. Palestine's geographical location as a kind of land bridge between Egypt and Mesopotamia probably offered some economic advantage in terms of being in a position to collect taxes from, for example, caravans, but it is doubtful that at this time trade played any crucial role in the economy.[36]

Land Ownership and Distribution of Wealth

In centralized peasant or agrarian societies, land is the primary form of wealth, and social stratification, measured by differences in wealth and power, is pronounced.[37] One of the consequences of centralization during Iron Age II would have been the gradual development of a more diverse and specialized economy. With the resulting increase in competition among various elements of society, economic inequalities would also have become more pronounced. There is no middle class in such societies, and very few would have derived their wealth from trade and commerce. Wealth and high status usually went together; thus most of the wealthy would have been involved in some way with the court and/or administration.

The biblical traditions clearly speak of economic inequalities. Many of the laws and moral directives focus on concern for the poor (for example, Ex. 20:1–17; 21–23; Deut. 15:11), as do many of the prophetic traditions. As would be expected for an agrarian society, these concerns characteristically focus on land.[38] The jubilee and sabbatical legislation of Leviticus 25 and Deuteronomy 15, for example, point to the importance attached to land and family, even if these laws were merely ideals that were never enforced.[39] The low status accorded laborers and the prevalence of slavery are also represented (for example, Deut. 15:12, 16–17). The poor are also the focus of the laws stating that loans must never be made with interest (Ex. 22:25–27). The biblical ideal seems to be that too much debt endangered the community, although, again, it is impossible to determine the actual impact of such laws, or even whether they were ever actually enacted.

In his construct of the ancient Israelite economy, Max Weber emphasized the social differentiation and class antagonism between urban patricians, who owned large estates, and the great mass of rural farmers, who were debt-laden or deprived of land.[40] In a similar construct, Albrecht Alt proposed that even before the rise of monarchy a class of elite families arose, and their elders began to assume economic control over local communities.[41] Eventually, a large number of families were forced to give up their land, which was then redistributed among these more well-to-do elite families. Over time, the number of landowning families grew even smaller, while the landless class became more and more numerous. Eventually, according to Alt, the monarchy took the place of the local community and gained control of abandoned lands, seizing them for itself or parceling them out to its supporting elites and officials (in addition to acquiring land that had previously been owned by Canaanites). Local communities thus reached a point where they were constantly struggling against encroachment on their territory by the officials of the monarchy on whom such awards had been bestowed, rather than against the monarchy itself.

A number of recent studies draw essentially the same conclusions as Weber and Alt. Gottwald, for example, argues that once the egalitarian structure of the "intertribal confederacy" began to erode as a result of centralization, the upper classes began to purchase land and extend loans at interest, and to encroach in other ways on tribal institutions and ways of life. Gradually, as loans at interest were extended to the needy and their property mortgaged, many ended up as tenant farmers, debt servants, or landless wage laborers. Social divisions, impoverishment, and demoralization were further stimulated by foreign trade, diplomacy, war, and factional struggles among leaders.[42]

Other recent studies suggest, however, that although conflict between urban and rural, elite and peasant, certainly existed, it may not have been to the extent that Weber, Alt, and others have suggested.[43] Bendor, for example, argues that the network of kinship groups in rural communities would have been strong enough to defend and preserve their patrimony to a greater extent than these interpretations allow. He further concludes that the most important source for land acquisition by the monarchy would not have been land that was already held as patrimonies, but the conquest of new territories. He does not agree, then, that there was a huge gulf between a wealthy and corrupt minority and the vast majority of the population, who became more and more poverty-stricken over time. Neither does he subscribe to the view that such a polarity of class division was manifested in any sharp contrast between town and village, between urban landowning "patricians" and village "plebeians" who were mired in debt.[44]

Although he agrees that creditors and usury existed, and were catalysts in processes of enrichment and impoverishment, Bendor proposes that the principal reasons for resorting to creditors would have been related to famine or other natural disasters and to the necessity of paying taxes. Natural calamities and heavy pressure from the monarchy, therefore, would have caused many families that were self-sufficient to become impoverished. But for Bendor the most important dynamic was not that between wealthy elites and the suffering masses, but the *internal* dynamic of relationships in the kinship group. For example, a *bêt 'āb* might suffer hardships and "become poor," but this needs to be understood in terms of its relationship to the larger *mišpāḥāh*.[45]

This interpretation is grounded in Bendor's understanding of land ownership. Agreeing that this was the basis of wealth in ancient Israel and Judah, Bendor points out that it is not always clear in the biblical texts who the landowner was understood to be. According to his construct of the economy, the same land could belong to the *mišpāḥāh,* the *bêt 'āb,* and a specific nuclear unit simultaneously, but the nature of this ownership would have been construed differently in each context. Holding land, he argues, was understood more in terms of the right of *utilizing* it than of owning it; and immunity from having one's land used by others was more important than exclusive control over it.[46] Accordingly, socioeconomic differentiation in Iron Age II Palestine cannot, he believes, be understood in terms of the rigid type of class divisions that are common in contemporary individual-oriented societies, in which nuclear families are the basic unit of ownership. Socioeconomic differences surely existed among and within *bêt 'ābôt,* some being strong or wealthy, with a relatively stable patrimony, and others being weak or poor, with more unstable patrimonies.

Whether or not Bendor is correct in his assessment, the restructuring of the social order was probably related to changes in the conditions of property ownership. Kings typically needed large amounts of landed property in order to maintain their courts, and endowing land would have been one form in which elites were paid for their services.[47] This would necessarily contribute to changes in the social structure, even if, as Bendor argues, the basis of the economy was not altered to any great degree.

There are few references to royal property in the biblical texts. Only the description of David's decisions about property formerly belonging to Saul (cf. 2 Samuel 9; 16:1–14; 19:30) and the story of Naboth's vineyard (1 Kings 21) provide any direct insight into the legal issues associated with royal ownership of land. David is said to have restored to Meribbaal, the son of Jonathan and the last remaining member of Saul's line, a part of the property that had formerly belonged to Saul. And the story of Naboth's vineyard implies that, at least in this case, the king could not necessarily increase his property at will, but could possibly acquire the property of those who had been sentenced to crimes punishable by death.

Property belonging to the king, whatever its source or extent, was probably administered by royal officials. The list of officials in charge of different types of royal properties in 1 Chronicles 27:25–31 gives us some idea of how these responsibilities might have been delegated. In addition to details about the storage of provisions and supervision of the workers in this list, arable land, vineyards, plots of land with olive and fig trees, cattle, camels, donkeys, and small livestock are mentioned as the king's property.

In an argument similar in some respects to that of Bendor, Holladay points out that there is nothing in the archaeological record that clearly points either to a dramatic degradation of the living standards of most of those who lived in the large villages, towns, and cities that have been excavated, or to a striking rise in the living standards of a few "great houses." Rather, the present evidence, particularly that relating to patterns of residence, is unvarying from early Israel down to the late eighth century, and possibly even down to the final destruction of the Judean state. For this entire span of time, Holladay asserts, there is no evidence of one- or two-room hovels, or of structures that would have been used to house large numbers of workers. Aside from palaces and residences that are clearly governmental, there are also no residences from Iron Age II Palestine that are larger than the average "pillared" or "four-room house" by much more than a factor of two, or three at the most. There are some larger houses with adjoining courtyards and extra storerooms, and some smaller houses situated in tight spaces between larger ones. But in many cases it appears that the space for the smaller house takes up space in the courtyard, or the space of an adjacent larger house. The simplest and most probable explanation for situations such as these, according to Holladay, is that within the context of the *bêt 'āb,* an extra residence was created for a son or younger brother on family land in the midst of the increasingly densely packed village, where land must have been at a premium as families expanded.[48]

Whatever the extent of hardship endured by the rural farming population during Iron Age II, in economies based on a combination of reciprocity and redistribution, wealth was accumulated by the elites through collecting taxes, tolls, and in some cases tribute, not from the kinds of entrepreneurial activities associated with a market system of exchange. In the form of large estates, wealth was generally associated with political, military, or even religious power, not commercial or manufacturing activity. Possession of titled ancestors and landed estates is what was important.

Assyrian Dominance and the Judean Economy

Judah's reduction to vassal status by the Assyrians in the late eight century would have had a significant negative impact on its economy.[49] According to Hopkins, most of the goods required by the Assyrians as payment for tribute were not indigenous to Judah, and thus had to be procured through trade. In order to meet these needs, it was necessary to invest intensively in the few exportable products available—wine and oil. Demands for precious metals may also have encouraged a shift toward a monetary system, as suggested by the development of standardized shekel weights.

Hopkins suggests that periodic resistance to Assyrian dominance and attempts to achieve economic autonomy may also have affected the Judean economy. The increase in commodity production and interregional exchange very likely intensified social stratification, which would have made Judah more vulnerable to economic disruption. The devastation of the

Judean countryside, which is apparent in the archaeological record, resulted, Hopkins proposes, from administrative collapse as well as military action.

Technology

The major technological innovation during Iron Age II was the development and increased use of iron in the manufacture of tools and weapons.[50] By about 900 B.C.E., iron replaced bronze as the dominant metal used in manufacturing these utilitarian objects. In the archaeological record the number of iron objects increases almost twofold between the eleventh and the end of the tenth century, and the number of utilitarian iron objects surpasses that of bronze. There is also a greater variety of tool and weapon types.

Lack of, or decreased access to, tin, a necessary raw material for producing bronze, is the most widely accepted explanation for the increased use of iron between 1200 and 900 B.C.E. The proposal is that it was necessary to develop new resources, and because almost every region had some deposits of iron ore, iron could be used at a lower cost than bronze, which was growing scarce.

Regardless of the historical factors involved, it is fairly safe to assume that both technological and economic factors played a crucial role in determining the development of iron technology and the increased use of iron. Technologically, iron became a medium superior to bronze for manufacturing utilitarian objects only when it was carburized, and consistent application of the techniques of carburization in Palestine cannot be demonstrated for any period prior to the tenth century.

Another important element in the adoption of iron technology would have been human choice.[51] Adoption, or innovation, requires a conscious decision on the part of an individual or individuals to adopt one mode of undertaking a particular activity rather than another. Inventions become innovations only when they are adopted into industry. The process requires not only production and distribution of knowledge, but entrepreneurial decisions.

The social milieu into which a technological innovation is introduced also plays a primary role in both the acceptance of the innovation and the kinds of social changes that result.[52] Since any kind of technological change must be accepted by the members of a society, especially the leaders and/or those whose status renders their decisions legitimate, it cannot have any kind of social impact until they indicate approval.

If we apply these principles to the situation in Palestine, it might be characterized broadly as follows: The archaeological record suggests that the "invention" of ironworking, that is, the discovery of carburization and intentional application of the process, may have occurred sometime during the twelfth and eleventh centuries. However, an environment conducive to the innovation and adoption of the new discovery evidently did not exist prior to the late tenth century. In other words, there was a delay of one to two centuries before the discovery of ironworking was implemented in the economic activities of ancient Palestine. Unfortunately, the archaeological record does not supply us with conclusive evidence concerning why the peoples of ancient Palestine were so slow in taking advantage of the discovery.

SOCIOPOLITICAL ORGANIZATION AND STRUCTURE

Social Structure

The sociopolitical and economic changes introduced by centralization also led to structural transformations, as well as shifts and new tensions in the relationships among various groups. The two most prominent structural changes were associated with: (1) political centralization—Israel and Judah became states with taxing and conscripting powers, and developed standing armies and hierarchical bureaucracies; and (2) social stratification. One of the important questions to consider in relation to these changes is the extent to which there was continuity in social structure, particularly at the local level.

Comparison of textual and archaeological material with models suggests that there was some continuity in social structure from Iron Age I to Iron Age II, at least in rural settings. It is quite possible, for example, that the notion of tribe continued to play a part in people's self-understanding and their perceptions about how they related to others. If this was the case, then the associated notions of kinship would also have retained their significance.

Recent studies have shown that tribal organization is not necessarily independent of states, with tribes living only on their fringes and in conflict with them. Both now and in the past, tribes have sometimes been integrated into state systems, and many states have worked through tribes rather than against them.

There are four principal, often overlapping, ways in which people construct tribal identity in the contemporary Middle East, and three of the four are possibly applicable to the Iron Age II situation. The first construct involves the elaboration and use of explicit "native" ethnopolitical ideologies by the people themselves as a means of explaining their sociopolitical organization. The second consists of implicit *practical* notions held by people, which are not elaborated into formal ideologies. The third relates to concepts used by state authorities for administrative purposes. And the fourth relates to anthropological (analytical) concepts.[53] It is possible that each of the first three notions of tribal identity existed in Iron Age II—the first two to varying degrees among the general populace, and the third by those who participated in governing the state.[54]

Regardless of the exact dating of the tribal boundary lists in Joshua 13:1–21:42, tribal areas probably had some kind of administrative function in the Israelite and Judean states, as is typical in the Middle East today. The numerous examples of tracing tribal descent that occur in the texts relating to the monarchic period and after testify that the *concept* of tribe, at least, had not totally disappeared.

In his reconstruction of social structure, Bendor offers the following conclusions about the tribe during the monarchic period:[55] (1) Tribe was the term by which a certain territory was identified, usually as an administrative area. (2) The tribal names served as a means by which most of the populations living in particular areas were identified. (3) The population living in a tribal territory shared some common characteristics, expressed through notions of a common past and provenience, and perhaps some other distinguishing markers of tribal identity. (4) Rituals may have been maintained in cultic sites that were associated with specific tribal territories and populations. (5) The tribe provided support and a framework for the *mišpāḥôt* that composed it, and the "inheritance of the tribe" served as a sort of superstructure for the patrimony of the *mišpāḥôt* and *bêt 'ābôt*.

Pastoral nomadic groups probably also continued to coexist with settled populations throughout Iron Age II, although, with a few possible exceptions (for example, the Rechabites), they are not mentioned in the biblical texts relating to this period. As was noted in chapter 3, many Middle Eastern societies have had both nomadic and settled components, and political leadership and movements have frequently encompassed groups pursuing combinations of both forms of economic activity. Some nomadic groups have subsisted virtually as a state within a state, while others have been integrated to some extent into the wider political systems,[56] which was most likely the case in Iron Age II Palestine.

A number of scholars have postulated in strong terms that the institution of the monarchy and urbanization resulted in the complete breakdown of the kinship structure.[57] However, some recent studies consider the possibility that the basic social structure of Iron Age I may have continued to remain essentially intact, at least in rural settings, into Iron Age II.

Bendor, for example, argues that this structure "absorbed" and adapted to the pressure imposed by the monarchy and urbanization.[58] Kinship structure, in his estimation, was the "backbone" of society, even for the institution of the monarchy itself, which was based on the king's *bêt'āb* and *mišpāḥāh* and on the kinship units of its officials. The kinship structure, therefore, remained essentially the same, with the kinship unit maintaining its role as a self-sufficient economic unit. This would have been the case in spite of changes in the internal dynamic within and among kinship groups that resulted from the processes associated with centralization.

In contrast to arguments that the institution of the *mišpāḥāh* was replaced by communities in which kinship no longer played a role, even though their names survived, Bendor chooses to interpret the association of place names with social units as evidence that both the *mišpāḥôt* and the *bêt'ābôt* continued to define the populations of towns and villages and perhaps the cities.[59] The relationship between *mišpāḥāh* and village or town is also confirmed, Bendor believes, in the enumeration of tribal inheritances and boundaries in the book of Joshua, where the phrases "by their *mišpāḥôt*" or "by their *mišpāḥôt*—their cities and villages" occur. The concept behind these references for him is that both the inheritance and the localities are perceived in relation to *mišpāḥôt*.

The census lists in Numbers 1 and 26 and the genealogies in 1 Chronicles 2–8 are also cited by Bendor as verifying the continued existence and relevance of the *bêt'āb* and *mišpāḥāh*. Regardless of whether these lists represent real or fictitious lineages, they nevertheless reflect a conception that was either recently past or contemporaneous with their composition or compilation.[60] In addition to the functions outlined in chapter 3, according to Bendor's construct the *mišpāḥāh* would have been responsible during this period for fulfilling obligations to the monarchy in the form of taxes and conscription (both for labor and the army).[61]

Another issue that is raised in relation to social structure during this period, as in the case of Iron Age I, is the question of whether the basic socioeconomic unit was the nuclear or extended family, and whether it was the same for both commoners and elites. The archaeological record (clusters of two to three houses sharing the same courtyard) indicates the probability that extended families continued at least to reside together. And the consensus seems to be that the extended family continued to be the primary socioeconomic unit as well. In a study that focuses on ancient society in general, however, Carney suggests that although the extended family was the "ideal" in most of the societies of antiquity, it was not the norm, except perhaps among elites.[62] The poor, he argues, would not have had the resources to live in extended families and thus would have had looser, less contractual types of relationships than the elites, for whom the extended family was a resource base. Whether or not Carney's construct is applicable to ancient Israel and Judah is difficult to assess, particularly given the elite perspective that permeates the biblical texts, and the fact that the traditions themselves present quite an ambivalent picture.

In any case, whether it was the nuclear or the extended family, the family was certainly very important, both socially and economically, and the interests of individuals would have been subordinate to those of the family. Marriages, for example, were probably perceived not so much in relation to the benefits and happiness of individuals, but as compacts bonding family groups and assets together under carefully regulated conditions. Within the family, gender roles were probably more sharply defined than Meyers argues was the case in Iron Age I, with the woman's being more markedly inferior and subordinate. Age divisions, again primarily within the context of the family (whether nuclear or extended), and the power and responsibility that correspond to age, were probably also strongly demarcated.

Outside and above the level of the family, socioeconomic roles and statuses would have been based on division of labor and on social proximity to the ruling elites. In both cities and towns, society would have been subdivided into occupational groups, although in rural areas farming would have remained the primary occupation. The scholarly constructs of social stratification in Iron Age II Israel and Judah are based primarily on the biblical texts, comparisons of the biblical texts with other ancient Near Eastern texts, and, to a lesser extent, archaeological information.[63]

The lists of administrative offices in 2 Samuel 8:15–18 and 1 Kings 4:1–6 (cf. also the lists of deportees in 2 Kings 24 and 25) refer to government, cult, defense, and royal court offices. The particular offices mentioned include: priest, scribe, speaker, commander of the army, one who is in charge of the governors, friend of the king, one who is in charge of the house, and one who is in charge of forced labor. Apart from the offices mentioned in these lists, there are three others both mentioned in biblical texts and known from seals. These are: "son of the king," "the king's servant," and "ruler of the city." The latter is only mentioned in relation to Jerusalem and Samaria (1 Kings 22:26; 2 Kings 23: 8; 2 Chron. 34: 8). The functions of these offices are not explained, but we can assume with some certainty that those who filled them were in the upper echelon of the social hierarchy.[64]

Among these offices, the office of scribe and the question of whether scribal schools existed in ancient Israel and Judah have been the particular focus of scholarly attention.[65] Whatever form their training took, scribal activity was most likely sponsored and controlled by government authorities, and was probably confined primarily to the cities, particularly Jerusalem and

Samaria but also to other administrative centers. Scribes associated with the government administrative system would have been responsible for such activities as maintaining the royal archives, writing annals, conducting correspondence within the state as well as with neighboring states, and keeping commercial records.

Other professional classes outside the royal court possibly consisted of judges and local court officials, other administrators such as census takers, tax collecters, overseers of the corvée or forced labor that would have been used primarily for royal construction projects, district governors, and perhaps other officials who had responsibilities within the towns and villages, all of whom would have been answerable, directly or indirectly, to the king.

There was probably also a class consisting of noble families associated in some way with the royal court, and a class of wealthy landowners. There may also have been a class of merchants who attained wealth and achieved elite status through contributing goods or services to the king. Individuals involved in trading activities would also have been answerable, directly or indirectly, to the government. Whether or not there were professional lenders or other similar professionals and entrepreneurs, which are typical of market economies, is open to question. Such roles are thought to have been discouraged in redistributive economic systems.

Another group of social roles would have been associated with service in the military. These would have included officers, career professionals, enlistees and conscripts, mercenaries, various specialists like runners and charioteers, and possibly sailors.

The majority of the population probably consisted of an agricultural class, including not only the owners of large estates, but also small freeholders, family farmers, agricultural workers, and peasant farmers.

A number of roles were probably related to the "official" religion of the monarchy, at least in Jerusalem. The biblical construct includes high priests, ordinary priests, temple "doorkeepers" or supervisors, treasurers, scribes, musicians of various kinds, dancers, keepers of vestments, those "dedicated" to Temple service, interpreters of the law, and possibly prophets. It is particularly difficult, however, to distinguish the extent to which this construct actually reflects the situation during Iron Age II, as religious organization was a primary concern during the Persian period. The local or so-called "popular" cults would also have required religious specialists of various kinds, possibly including priests, diviners, and other types of intermediaries, although it is difficult to reconstruct from the biblical texts what these might have been.[66]

Artisans of various sorts would have played important socioeconomic roles during Iron Age II, although the locus of some craft production may have remained in the household in village contexts. It is possible that some artisan groups maintained a separate and marginal status, as may have been the case during Iron Age I. But others would have been more well integrated into the social structure,[67] some perhaps attached to the royal court, as seems to have been typical in other ancient Near Eastern states.[68] They may also have been organized in guilds in the cities and towns.[69] Types of artisans would have included stonemasons, builders, woodworkers, metalsmiths, jewelers, ivory and seal carvers, potters, leather workers, and weavers.

In his study of ancient Israelite society, Max Weber included artisans and metalsmiths among the *gērîm* ("sojourners" or "resident aliens"), and compared the status of the *gērîm* to the marginal social position of artisans and smiths, along with bards and musicians, among the modern bedouin. This changed, in Weber's estimation, only during the reconstitution of the postexilic Jewish community under Ezra and Nehemiah, when artisans were divested of their tribal foreignness, were organized into guilds, and were received into the Jewish confessional community organization.[70] Whether or not his line of reasoning is valid, Weber is probably correct in his assessment that the social status of artisans and smiths changed over time, particularly as the social structure became more hierarchical. They may have continued to be socially separated to some degree (as is suggested of the Rechabites in Jer. 35:8–10),[71] perhaps as endogamous families or guilds,[72] but this social separation would not have been as radical as it was during the premonarchic period (as is suggested in the traditions about the Kenites and Midianites). If the references in 2 Kings 24:14 and 16 (cf. Jer. 24:1; 29:2) to smiths and artisans as being among those of high status who were taken into exile by the Babylonians is correct, the integration may have occurred by the end of the monarchic period. Certainly by the second century B.C.E. artisans and smiths were highly regarded, as is apparent in Sirach 38:24–34, where they are identified as individuals whose skills are necessary for the maintenance of social stability and the stability of the "fabric of the world" (cf. Ex. 31:1–5; 1 Kings 7:13–14; 2 Chron. 2:13–14).

The lowest classes probably included resident aliens (*gērîm*), as well as indentured servants and slaves, many of them probably attached to agricultural lands. Widows, orphans, beggars, and other destitute or outcast persons may have also been perceived as having similar status.[73]

Comparative anthropological and historical evidence suggest that slaves are distinguished from other types of dependent laborers on the basis of their "outsider" status; that is, ideally, slaves were aliens (cf. Lev. 25:39–55). Types of slavery in the biblical construct of ancient Israel, however, range from the forced slavery of aliens to voluntary slavery of indigenous peoples.

According to the Hebrew Bible, the major factors contributing to self-enslavement, as distinct from the enslavement of aliens, were poverty and debt. In some cases these conditions left no alternative but to sell either oneself, or minor members of one's family such as a daughter, into servitude (e.g., Ex. 21:2–11; Lev. 25:39–55; Deut. 15:16–17; 2 Kings 4:1; Isa. 50:1; Amos 2:6; 8:6). In contrast to aliens, the laws stipulate that (ideally) "Israelites" could not be enslaved permanently or treated as harshly (Ex. 21:2–4; Deut. 15:12–17; Lev. 25: 39–55). The biblical construct also suggests that slaves were allowed to accumulate property, with which it was possible for them to purchase their freedom (2 Sam. 9:10; 16:4; 19:18, 30; Lev. 25:29).

In an anthropological study of the representations of slavery in the Bible, Gillian Feeley-Harnick points out that the status of slaves seems to have been somewhat ambiguous.[74] This is seen primarily, she suggests, in relation to kinship. On the one hand, slavery was the antithesis of kinship—that is, a slave was either an outsider who had no kin, community, or nation that served as the means of self-identity, or an "insider" who achieved this status out of necessity, a situation that, she argues, involved the destruction of kinship bonds (citing Neh. 5:5; Isa. 50:1; Amos 2:6; 8:6). On the other hand, according to her interpretation, slaves were more than kin, because by definition they did not have conflicting social ties.[75]

But slaves could nevertheless be incorporated into the kinship structure, especially when there was some need relating to production or reproduction. The biblical traditions, for example, refer to fathers who sell their daughters with the condition that the masters or their sons marry them, and to masters who have children by or adopt slaves in order to acquire heirs.

There is also some ambiguity associated with the roles of slaves. In theory, slaves were perceived as property and as "tools" to be used for carrying out the most lowly types of work (cf. Ex. 21:21; Sir. 33:24–29). But in spite of this, the legal traditions indicate that they were also perceived as fully human. In some cases they occupied positions of trust and had the potential of social mobility. The slave–master relationship, then, was not a simple matter of exploitation and domination, but manifested contradictions and ambiguity in concepts of authority, allegiance, and identity.[76]

Patron-Client Relationships

Another social institution that may have played an important role in the way in which ancient Israelite and Judean society was structured is the patron-client relationship, which was a dominant mode of relationship in the preindustrial societies of antiquity.[77] This type of relationship is typically found between individuals of differing social status at all levels of society, in both partly centralized and centralized societies.[78] In patronage societies political power structures are personalized because the society consists of only two groups—the "haves" and the "have-nots." The relationship between patron and client involves a kind of reciprocity, in which individuals with position and power use their influence to advance or protect individuals of inferior status, who thus become their clients. For example, in relation to the distribution of justice, patrons possess the ability to secure the rights of their clients. Without patrons, poor individuals have no access to official institutions that can ensure them fair treatment in, for example, conflicts with more influential members of society. Clients in turn owe their patrons loyalty, and reciprocate by providing them with resources or services. Ideally, the parties in the relationship are thus bound to ongoing mutual responsibilities. Along with the idea of loyalty, other concepts such as friendship and respect are a part of the relationship. The patron expects the client to be a friend and to show him respect as a way of expressing subordination. Potentially, the clients of powerful patrons can also become powerful and attract clients themselves.

Women

The biblical construct of women's lives suggests that women were regarded as having no independent legal status and as being subject to the authority of men, first their fathers' and then their husbands'.

Carol Meyers's study of women suggests that the shift to an urban setting during Iron Age II almost certainly had an impact on gender relations and women's status and roles, although there may have been less change in rural settings. In particular, the shift from the family household to a centralized government with a bureaucracy composed of male officials as the place where power resided would have resulted in males' being conferred more status and privilege than women. Other factors would have included the development of an economy in which both luxury items and basic goods were more readily available, and an increase in the types of services available outside the context of the household. These would have contributed to the loss of the household's status as a self-sufficient economic unit (at least in urban contexts). As a consequence, women would have become less essential and would have had fewer potential roles to fulfill, leading ultimately to an increase in gender differentiation and a corresponding decrease in women's power and status. Meyers postulates that if city households were composed of nuclear, rather than extended, families, as some have argued, the extent to which a woman was able to exercise authority would also have decreased.[79]

Nevertheless, women appear occasionally in leadership roles in the biblical texts (for example as queen mother, prophets, and wise women).[80]

Meyers suggests that these may represent a larger group of publicly active women whose identities were lost as the result of the male-controlled canonical processes.

POLITICAL INSTITUTIONS

Kingship and Government at the National Level

In a study of the monarchic period that remained the consensus until recently, Albrecht Alt argued that one of the major differences in the institution of kingship between Israel and Judah was the way in which leadership was manifested.[81] According to his construct, Judah's monarchy was characterized by the ideal of unified, stable dynastic leadership, whereas Israel's was characterized by a loosely connected, charismatic type of nondynastic leadership.

More recent studies argue, contra Alt, that the political instability of leadership in the north, represented in a number of coups d'état described in 2 Kings, was due to attempts on the part of opposing elites to place an individual outside the existing dynastic line on the throne; that is, both Israel and Judah had dynastic leadership.[82] Such conflicts may have arisen in part because the demographic composition of the population was fairly heterogeneous, allowing for the likelihood of conflict.[83] The instability of kingship represented in the traditions about Israel, then, is probably indicative of factional struggles among elites, some of which may have been grounded in geographical location and/or tribal identity. Such factional struggles among elites were typical of ancient agrarian societies.[84]

Royal propaganda was probably directed primarily toward such factions, as expressions of a dynasty's right to rule and as a means of denying counterclaims to the throne. Very often propaganda of this type asserted that the king had a right to rule by virtue of connections with the realm of the divine, which is certainly the case in the traditions preserved in the Hebrew Bible for both Israel and Judah. There is also typically an emphasis on the king's role as protector and guarantor of justice. Lemche suggests that this popular image of the "just king" is grounded in the patron-client model. In this sense, kings would have been considered the patrons of their states, and the common people their clients. Ideally, then, kings were entitled to expect and demand absolute loyalty from their subjects, but in turn had to provide them with recompense for their services.[85]

Ideally, then, the kings were subject to some restrictions in their use of power. Presumably, the pressures of other institutions (religious, economic, local tribal, legal), and expectations that they would abide by traditional customs and obligations, would have limited the extent to which they abused this power. It is nevertheless unlikely that the majority of the population could depend on legal protection from kings, as power was constructed by them, and by other elites, for their own benefit, not for the benefit of the larger populace.[86]

The development of the centralized states in Palestine, with their elites, factions, and bureaucrats, introduced a number of restraints on the general populace that almost certainly had not existed during Iron Age I. At the national level in preindustrial agrarian societies, political and economic power resided almost exclusively among the small percentage of the population constituting the elites—the royal family and the royal court, high civil and military officials, large landowners, religious leaders. This governing class would have controlled both the economic well-being and the legal and political status of the rest of the population, made up of a range of classes or professions with varying levels of status and power below the elites. In a political system such as this, where power was in the hands of such a small number of elites, the bulk of the population would have had little, if any, right of participation, whether directly or indirectly, in the ongoing administration of government at the national level.[87]

The royal bureaucracy was responsible for maintaining or enforcing the relationship between the center and the periphery of society. This involved regulating the subject population in the economic, as well as political, interests of the king, particularly through taxation and making demands in terms of production, military or labor conscription, property, and the like. Other bureaucratic functions would have included distributing agricultural surpluses and providing services, defense, and maintaining social order.[88] It is possible that these functions were carried out by government administrators appointed to districts, in a system perhaps set up according to the former tribal territories.[89]

Local Governance

Political activities would have been most prominent in the capitals, with towns and their residents generally playing more important roles in the political process than villages and rural areas. The power of the central government, therefore, would not have been equally influential in all areas—more control would have been maintained in cities and other important administrative towns, and less in rural and marginal regions. Populations in boundary areas would have been even less subservient, and their officials less subject to discipline and control, than those of the heartland or intermediate zones.

In a recent study on the Iron Age II political systems of Israel and Judah, Douglas A. Knight points to C. A. O. van Nieuwenhuijze's study of the ways in which state and local authorities interact in contemporary Middle Eastern village contexts as a useful model for understanding the situation in ancient Palestine.[90] This study indicates that villagers are typically reluctant to comply with the directives of government officials, whom they recognize as not being concerned so much about their well-being as they are about enforcing state decisions. In contrast to cities, the locus of national politics and economics, villages are relatively isolated both politically and economically from the wider realm of the nation-state, and from urban life in general, although as has been noted above they are economically interdependent.[91]

Although the centralized states of Israel and Judah and their governing classes certainly had some influence at every level, then, social and political life probably continued along traditional lines in contexts such as villages and perhaps lower-class urban neighborhoods, where traditional customs and norms probably continued to determine an individual's political status, with local power structure being more influential in regulating day-to-day life.[92]

Local politics, then, very likely operated in some respects quite independently of the national system of governance. If the segmented system of social organization was still in place in rural village contexts, the local systems of governance may have been similar to those of Iron Age I, with their own internal system of hierarchies and leaders based on position within the kinship network and other traditional patterns of status, honor, and custom. If this was the case, the centralized state, rather than displacing this structure, may have only been superimposed on it in such a way that it could continue to function relatively independently. As in the villages of Iron Age I, then, kinship relations, gender, age, profession, and property probably continued to affect the political standing of both individuals and groups. In the *bêt 'āb,* the male head of household would have had primary authority, and it is possible, as Carol Meyers has suggested, that women had some power as well within the context of the household. As a group, the male heads of households, or possibly lineages, comprised the local body of elders, who made decisions regarding judicial, religious, economic, and other local matters.[93] Although their authority would have been primarily related to maintaining internal order, it is possible that the elders also represented the town or village in relation to outsiders, and possibly to government officials.

The Judicial System

There is no consensus on the extent to which centralization altered the judicial systems that operated in Iron Age I villages. Nor is there a clear understanding of the king's role in establishing and maintaining laws or in meting out justice.

The past tendency on the part of biblical scholars has been to assume that the biblical laws are a reliable guide to the generally accepted norms of behavior in Iron Age II Israel and Judah, an assumption that is now being questioned. Although it is likely that there was some system of generally binding norms that was enforced by law and is reflected in these laws, there was probably also a wide range of expected behaviors that remained unregulated formally by the legal system.[94] Whether and to what extent the biblical laws were actually implemented, or whether they were merely statements of principles or ideals of behavior that were generally considered to be desirable, is impossible at this point to determine. If the latter is the case, then they cannot be regarded as an accurate reflection of the actual behavior of the peoples of Israel and Judah, or certainly not all of them. The ideals reflected in the Hebrew Bible and the actual practices in ancient Israelite and Judean society, then, did not necessarily coincide, particularly given the social diversity among various groups, many of whom would not necessarily have shared the same values.

Regardless of the extent to which the biblical laws reflect the reality of the situation in Iron Age II, once centralized leadership was established in Israel and Judah it is likely that the national government did exercise some control over the judicial system, although, again, the extent to which this was the case is unclear. A system of national laws and courts may have been set in place, as is suggested in Deuteronomy 17:2–13 and 2 Chronicles 19:4–11, although both of these texts probably reflect later judicial practice. The existence of such a system would have had an impact on the judicial authority of the local lineage systems, as is suggested in the elders' response to Jezebel's directive to charge Naboth with treason (1 Kings 21:8–14).[95]

Another factor that may have affected the judicial systems in Israel and Judah was their subjection at various times to foreign powers, especially Assyria and Babylonia. Given their dominant position, both may have influenced the development of law, and potentially also incited local conflict by imposing laws. But, again, the extent of this influence is difficult to discern on the basis of the present evidence.[96]

The development of centralized priesthoods, and the religious laws that were under their control, may also have had some influence on the judicial systems of both states. Many of these laws, however, especially those relating to technical matters of the cult, would have been of concern only to religious specialists, and thus would have had a history quite different from that of civil law.[97]

Although the former self-sufficiency of villages was limited to some extent by centralization, self-government probably essentially continued in matters of civil law on the local level, with justice being administered by local leaders on the basis of customary rules. In contrast to the national level, at this level individuals could probably count more on having their interests protected so long as they conformed to the social norms as expressed in these customary rules.[98] As was indicated in chapter 3, disputes in a segmented system are handled more effectively at the lower levels, where kinship ties are strong, than at the tribal or national levels, where communal consensus is more difficult to achieve. In villages, then, the legal system, like the political and economic systems, was probably community based, with the elders acting as judges and arbitrators. Those without strong kinship ties, such as widows and orphans, and perhaps resident aliens, probably had the least amount of protection in the system, although ideally, according to the legal traditions in the Bible, others were responsible for making certain that they were protected.

RELIGION

It is particularly difficult to determine the nature of religious beliefs and practices in Iron Age II Israel, because the biblical sources are almost exclusively Judean or transmitted in Judean versions, with only fragmentary, and heavily biased, information about the Northern Kingdom.

The authoritative dogma demanding adherence to a single, centralized form of worship presented in the canon as we now have it is widely acknowledged these days as being a much later construct. Recent studies have thus emphasized the strong probability that religion during this period was far from homogeneous, distinguishing particularly between official (national) and "popular" religions.[99] There is now little doubt that a variety of religious expressions existed in both kingdoms, ranging from dynastic cults to popular cults to women's cults.[100]

There is also some indication that, at least in some areas, Yahweh was associated with a consort. This is represented particularly clearly in the ninth-century B.C.E. Kuntillet 'Ajrud inscription that makes reference to Yahweh and his Asherah.[101] The large numbers of female figurines recovered from excavations also suggest the popularity of female deities, perhaps primarily in domestic contexts.

The "official" religion in Judah was probably, as is suggested in the biblical texts, closely associated with the Temple, whose construction is attributed to Solomon. It is possible that, as a symbol of the official religion, the Temple was connected to the palace and that the king had ultimate responsibility for the cult.[102] It is unlikely, however, that the Jerusalem Temple was considered by the priestly hierarchy to be the *only* legitimate cult site until either very late in the monarchic period or after the exile.

In contrast to Judah, there appears to have been no national cultic site in the capital of Samaria. If we are to believe the biblical construct, however, major shrines were established at Dan and Bethel. But, as in Judah, there would have been other places of worship as well, as is indicated by the archaeological evidence.

Religious Specialists: Diviners

Religious specialists mediate between humans and the divine, but in the ancient world they tended to have important roles in the maintenance of economic, political, social, and educational institutions as well as religion.

Corresponding to the varieties of religious expression that existed during Iron Age II would have been a variety of types of religious specialists.[103] Although apparently suppressed by the later editors of the texts, we can assume, particularly on the basis of texts that outlaw certain types of intermediaries, that they played a variety of roles, depending on the contexts in which they operated. These probably included, in addition to the priests and prophets who are legitimated in the biblical construct, various types of diviners and, perhaps, necromancers.[104]

Diviners, whose roles sometimes overlap with priests, commonly obtain "hidden" knowledge through either mechanical means or observations of nature. The deity replies through signs or tokens to questions posed by the diviner about past or future events, guilt, or other kinds of information that are hidden or obscure.

Divination was widely practiced in the ancient Near East.[105] In Mesopotamia, diviners were legitimate centralized religious specialists, some of whom functioned as advisers to kings. In the Hebrew Bible, on the other hand, diviners are likened to false prophets, and therefore were not considered to be legitimate intermediaries, at least by the final editors of the traditions. Divination was, however, acceptable when it was practiced by priests who used the Urim and Thummim, which apparently involved asking a question for which a yes or no answer was expected. The exact nature of these objects, which are said to have been kept in a particular pocket of the priest's garment, is not known, and there is no indication in the texts of what they were made of, what they looked like, or what techniques were involved in their use.

Religious Specialists: Priests

Anthropologically speaking, priests are full-time religious specialists who are typically found in socially stratified agricultural societies with complex political systems,[106] that is, in societies like monarchic Israel and Judah in which social complexity includes a division of labor. Priests function in institutions that are organized and permanent. The most common types of rituals performed by them are calendrical (based on agricultural cycles) and are communal and public, performed for the benefit of the entire community. A priest's authority may be either inherited or learned, derived from a standardized body of knowledge.

As specialists associated with permanent institutions, priests are rarely innovators, as they tend to be concerned with conserving and maintaining the status quo, that is, a traditional set of beliefs and practices. Thus, one of their functions is keeping cultural change and individual deviation from cultural norms at a minimum and within defined limits.

Priests in Jerusalem were clearly connected with an institution—the Jerusalem Temple. In addition to the hierarchy of priests associated with this Temple, there are clear indications also of priests in both Israel and Judah being associated with other shrines. Most priests, then, seem to have been associated with particular sanctuaries. Their office in the Jerusalem cult is portrayed in the biblical traditions as having been hereditary, traced back to Aaron as their eponymous ancestor and to the tribe of Levi. Their implied role as upholders and teachers of the Torah suggests that they supported the status quo of the monarchic state, with little or no interest in introducing any kind of social change. This is also suggested in the criticism that is directed toward them in some prophetic texts. Although it is not possible on the basis of the present information to discern what the exact nature of priesthood in Israel, and in shrines in Judah outside Jerusalem, would have been, it is likely that it was similar, at least in terms of having a hierarchical structure.

According to the biblical texts, there was a hierarchy of priests affiliated with the Jerusalem Temple, consisting, in descending order, of the high priest, the priests ("sons of Aaron"), and the Levites.[107] The high priest is represented as the only one allowed to enter the Holy of Holies. The chief functions of priests in general probably consisted of caring for the sanctuary, carrying out sacrificial duties and other ritual duties relating to major festivals (most of which were correlated with the agricultural calendar),[108] in general acting as teachers and custodians of sacred tradition, and keeping account of and administering Temple funds. They also apparently had authority in matters relating to religious law, although it is not clear whether, or to what extent, they had any role in administering justice.

In some traditions, the Levites are portrayed as subordinate cultic personnel, having charge of the lower-status duties of the Temple. These possibly included cleaning, preparing offerings, providing music, and acting as gatekeepers. They may also have had a teaching role as interpreters of the law. Both priests and Levites are said to have depended on offerings made by the general populace (tithes, portions of sacrifices, hides) for economic support.

Religious Specialists: Prophets

The origins of the institution of prophecy are traced in the biblical traditions to Moses (Deut. 18:9–22). In the Deuteronomistic picture of ideal society, prophets have central roles, along with judges, kings, and priests, in helping to maintain social stability. There is also an emphasis in many of the prophetic traditions on justice and righteousness, as they relate to the maintenance of right order and to social practices and judicial procedures that respect the rights of all classes. But we are still far from understanding the nature and functions of prophets in ancient Israel and Judah. Determining the nature of the relationship between prophets and other institutions, for example, is problematic, as is identifying the relationship between prophetic individuals and the texts that purport to contain their words or that describe their activities.

In anthropological studies of religious specialists,[109] prophets are distinguished from priests in the following ways: Prophets claim to have been individually called by a deity, that is, their vocation is customarily not inherited or taught, as is the case for priests. Prophets tend not to be associated with institutions. And prophets are less concerned than are priests with maintaining the status quo; that is, they are usually more involved in promoting dynamic social change as innovators and reformers. This type of intermediary also tends to arise during periods of crisis or social turbulence and change—for example, when class antagonisms increase or when a smaller-scale society is politically or economically threatened by a larger-scale society. Prophets are particularly powerful as leaders when their support groups (usually social groups that are alienated in some way) are numerically significant. They may stand outside the cultural system during such periods and propose new doctrines, ethics, and/or economic values.[110]

This type of prophet initiates what Anthony Wallace has called "revitalization movements."[111] A revitalization movement, according to his definition, is a "conscious, deliberate, organized effort on the part of some members of a society to create a more satisfying culture," that is, to transform society in some way. Wallace distinguishes a number of different types of revitalization movements. For some, the goal is to return to a former era of happiness, to restore a golden age ("revivalism"). For others, the goal may be to eliminate from the society undesirable aliens and/or cultural elements of foreign origin ("nativism"). In both types the goal is to revive or perpetuate certain aspects of native culture in the face of pressure to change. Frequently a movement will combine both goals. Certain current or remembered elements of the culture are normally selected for emphasis and attributed symbolic value.

Such movements occur in situations in which part of the population feels that the present cultural system is unsatisfactory. These are often situations of acculturation (often resulting from conquest or occupation by an alien society), economic distress, political subordination, rapid technological change, famine, and the like.

A prophet is typically responsible for formulating the code for such a movement, often as a result of a purported vision or religious experience in which he or she is given instruction by a supernatural being. The code includes a promise of salvation if its instructions are followed. It also defines what is wrong with the existing culture, and outlines a goal and plan for cultural transformation. The prophet communicates this revelation, promising salvation if the code is accepted. As special disciples and eventually mass followers join the prophet, the movement begins to be organized and to gain a support group. Often it is necessary at some point to modify the code. If the movement is successful (and very often they fail), there is some form of cultural transformation accompanying the acceptance of the code by the controlling portion of the population. As it becomes accepted, it becomes routinized and ceases to be a movement, becoming, for example, a church or political party—that is, it is institutionalized.

The messages of some of the biblical prophets seem to correspond in some respects with the goals of prophetic activity as outlined by anthropologists such as Turner and Wallace. Many of the prophetic figures in the Hebrew Bible understand themselves to have been individually called by God (some of the traditions describe a call vision—for example, Isaiah and Ezekiel). They are typically portrayed as addressing the problems and crises (political, economic, and religious) of their times. These include political crises such as threats from other nations (especially Assyria, Babylonia, Egypt), internal political conflict, social and economic injustice and oppression, and religious crises brought on by perceived corruption in the cult or syncretist religious practices.

Whether any of the biblical prophets actually led movements of the type encountered by anthropologists is not possible to determine on the basis of the biblical information. It is also difficult to discern the nature and extent of their support groups, although the fact that the traditions survived and were preserved suggests that they must have existed. Presumably, prophets who upheld the status quo (and thus were not associated with the types of movements described here) would have been supported by those in power, and peripheral prophets, who were critical of the status quo, by those who wanted some kind of change.

Robert Wilson has distinguished two general types of prophets in ancient Israel and Judah—"peripheral" prophets and "central" prophets.[112] Peripheral prophets are the most prominently represented type in the Hebrew Bible, and they fit Turner's and Wallace's definitions of a prophet in a way that central prophets do not. They tend to identify themselves with the lower classes and the oppressed, that is, they very likely had marginal or peripheral support groups and were not associated with institutions. These prophetic figures are portrayed as reformers who are concerned with promoting political, social, economic, and religious change. They are normally in conflict with leaders in the texts—kings, priests, members of the upper classes, central prophets (for example, Elijah, Micaiah ben Imlah, Jeremiah, Amos, Hosea).

Central prophets, on the other hand, appear to have been closely associated with the government and the institution of the monarchy, and are represented as being members of the royal court, serving as advisers to the kings in much the same way as diviners did in ancient Mesopotamia (see, for example, the traditions about Samuel, Nathan, and Isaiah). They are represented in the Hebrew Bible as upholders of the status quo—the monarchy, the socioeconomic and political situation, and the central religious institution—thus their messages tend to support the powers that be, even if they are sometimes critical of them. Prophets of this type are often, although not always, mentioned in contexts in which other prophets are in conflict with them.

Chapter 6

The Babylonian and Persian Periods

BIBLICAL INFORMATION

Persian period Judah is the most likely setting for the final construct of much of the material in the Hebrew Bible, even though many of the independent traditions originated in earlier periods. However, extracting information that may be relevant to the social situation during this time is like, to use Leach's metaphor, trying to unscramble an omelet. Even the material that is directly related to the Persian period poses difficulties, particularly because much of it appears to be propagandistic in nature.[1] Some of it is possibly a response to the Persian imperial strategy of encouraging the development of local religious and ethnic identities,[2] and much of it is almost certainly related to the social and ideological tensions that developed in the reconstituted community, particularly between indigenous and immigrant, urban and rural populations, and those with differing religious orientations.

The emphases in the Persian period texts include the importance of reconstructing Jerusalem and establishing a temple center there, instituting religious law and a "covenant" relationship with a single deity, and promoting ethnic consciousness, all features that are clearly related to a process of self-definition (or redefinition).

The literate class of this new society, usually regarded as having been composed of those who had returned from Babylonia, appear, then, to have generated a kind of ideological superstructure in which they created an identity and heritage that were continuous with the Iron Age II kingdoms of Israel and Judah. Written into this "history" was an "Israel" that promoted their own self-interests and explained their own situation, over against those of others such as the "people of the land," that is, those who had remained behind, and peoples from other regions such as Samaria.[3]

The biblical texts assert, for example, that there was a wholesale removal of all classes of "significant" people, and that only the poorest "people of the land" remained behind (2 Kings 24:14; 25:12; Jer. 39:10; 52:15), or that during the period of exile, the land was essentially emptied of people (2 Chron. 36:17–21). When the deportees returned, according to this construct, they met with opposition from the "people of the land," who are regarded as polluting and as having no legitimate claims in the new community (Ezra 4:1–5; 10:1–17). This "myth of the empty land," it has been suggested, is not supported by the archaeological evidence, and is most likely an ideological construct intended to benefit those who had returned from exile.[4]

Many of the social-scientific studies of the Persian period focus on issues relating to the traditions recorded in Ezra-Nehemiah.[5] These include the question of what Ezra's and Nehemiah's respective positions were in relation to the Persian authorities, the nature and effects of their "reforms," and issues having to do with Jewish self-definition and conflict within the "community."

Although they purport to contain records relating to this period and earlier, there are a number of problems interpreters face in attempting to reconstruct the history and society of fifth-century Judah using these traditions as sources. One has to do with their propagandistic orientation. Another relates to the uncertainty regarding whether Ezra went to Judah before or after Nehemiah, or whether he was there at all, and which Artaxerxes appointed them.[6] One commentator remarks: "I very much suspect the text of Ezra-Nehemiah to be a highly fictionalized account with little historical worth."[7]

Others nevertheless believe it is possible to reconstruct, at least in broad outline, the events of the period. Even Philip Davies, who is particularly wary of reconstructing earlier periods on the basis of the biblical texts, suggests that for this period the nonbiblical data seem in general to confirm some of the basic processes described in Ezra-Nehemiah, although he is careful to point out that this is not an argument for or against their historicity.[8]

Ezra is said in the text to have been authorized by the Persian authorities to return to Judah in order to institute religious reforms, and to have introduced a set of strict laws prohibiting intermarriage. He is also said to have presided over a ceremony of covenant renewal, during which he read from the "Book of the Torah of Moses," which some scholars believe was the Torah that is now the core of the Jewish canon.

According to the biblical text, Nehemiah was sent to Jerusalem by the Persian emperor Artaxerxes to serve as governor there, and to have been responsible for rebuilding the city walls and introducing a number of reforms.[9] These reforms are portrayed as having included strict enforcement of a policy of exclusivism, according to which membership in the community was determined by birth, support of the Temple, an emphasis on purity and strict conformity to the laws of the Torah, and strict prohibition of intermarriage.

The prophetic traditions, which tend to support the diaspora Jews as the legitimate heirs of "Israel," also give some indication of Judah's situation under Persian domination. Haggai, for example, suggests that the economic and social conditions during the time of Zerubbabel and Joshua were miserable. And the Malachi and Trito-Isaiah traditions reflect social and religious tensions and conflict. Malachi makes reference to inferior sacrificial offerings and the practice of withholding tithes and offerings, and to Jewish men who are divorcing their wives in order to marry "foreign" women.

The construct of "Israel's" "history" in Chronicles reflects the Persian period context in that it is strongly biased in favor of Judah, Jerusalem, and the people who remained faithful to the Jerusalemite cult as comprising the true "Israel."

As has been indicated above, in general the biblical texts relating to the Persian period suggest that there were various sorts of conflict within the Persian province of Judah—conflicts, for example, between the returned exiles and those who had remained behind in Palestine (the "people of the land"); religious conflict pertaining to what constituted "legitimate" beliefs and practices; conflict with the Samaritans to the north who had built their own temple on Mt. Gerizim and tried to halt construction on the Temple in Jerusalem.

EXTRABIBLICAL LITERARY INFORMATION

There are a number of sources that document the history of the Babylonian and Persian periods. They are too numerous to list here, but among them are Babylonian and Persian documents and inscriptions relating to the reigns of kings, documents from Egypt, and from the Greek world the histories of Herodotus, Thucydides, and Xenophon, who were near contemporaries of Ezra and Nehemiah (according to the biblical chronology).[10] Cuneiform records relating to the Neo-Babylonian and Persian empires include the Wiseman chronicles, the Weidner texts, the Nabonidus chronicle, which describes the fall of Babylon and the rise of Cyrus, the "Verse Account of Nabonidus," the Cyrus Cylinder, and the Behistun inscription describing the first few years of Darius's reign. Many of these are very likely propagandistic. Elamite texts from Persepolis provide some insight into the economy of the Persian Empire. And a number of Aramaic documents from various places, most in Egypt, provide information on both Persian history in general and the history of specific Jewish communities. Among the texts from Egypt are Jewish documents from Elephantine.[11]

ARCHAEOLOGICAL INFORMATION

Although the archaeological evidence from the period of the Babylonian exile is limited, sites such as Jerusalem, Tel Beit Mirsim, and Lachish were clearly destroyed toward the beginning of the sixth century B.C.E. However, evidence from other sites in the northern part of Judah and Benjamin, some with continued occupation (for example, Tell el-Fôl, En-Gedi, Gibeon, Tell en-Nasbeh, Bethel) and some new, suggests that some portions of the Judean population were not affected by the Babylonian campaigns there, and in fact were prospering in the late sixth century. The continued use of burial caves in the Hinnom Valley is cited as evidence for the continued occupation of Jerusalem during the exile.[12]

The Persian period has been referred to as one of the most neglected periods in Syro-Palestinian archaeology, although more attention has been given to it in recent years.[13] Relatively few sites dating to this period have been excavated, and for those that have been, the Persian period levels have commonly been of less interest to the excavators than other periods. It is perhaps significant in this regard that several of the most recent surveys of Palestinian archaeology do not go beyond Iron Age II in their discussions.[14] Interpretations of Persian period material in the past also suffered from a relative lack of sophistication in pottery typology and architectural chronology. As a consequence of these factors, it is not possible to rely to any great extent on archaeological material for reconstructing Persian period Judean society. In some respects, however, the archaeological data we do have do seem to be consistent with some elements of the biblical construct.

The material evidence points, for example, to a period of transition in the sixth century. This is apparent in the persistence, although deteriorated in quality, of typical Iron Age II ceramic forms, the subsequent appearance of transitional forms in mid-sixth-century contexts, and their gradual replacement by pottery that is more distinctively Persian. There is also enough material evidence to postulate a change in Judah's status during the course of the fifth and fourth centuries. One type of evidence, perhaps representing a new phase in imperial policy, is a series of fortresses or garrisons whose construction is dated to the mid-fifth century.[15] These were typically located in elevated areas, and extended from the Mediterranean to the Jordan River, and down into the Negeb, following the major trade routes. They were apparently abandoned shortly after their construction. This brief period of occupation is interpreted as having been associated with an intensification of Persian military presence in response either to a challenge posed by Greece on the Mediterranean seaboard and trade routes and/or unrest resulting from an Egyptian revolt (ca. 464–454 B.C.E.). If this was the case, the fortresses would then have been abandoned when they were no longer necessary.[16]

Destruction layers found at various sites suggest that there was some instability during the Persian period. Some sites (for example, Hazor) were not occupied throughout the entire period. And there are a number of sites that appear to have had two or more phases of occupation dating to the Persian period (for example, Akko, Jaffa, Gezer, Lachish, En-Gedi, Ashdod). There is also evidence that toward the end of the fifth century B.C.E. there was widespread destruction in the southern part of Samaria and the traditional area of Benjamin, and about a century later in the Shephelah and Negeb. The latter may be related to the efforts on the part of Egypt to extricate itself from Persian control. Destruction is also apparent in some sites dating to the years toward the end of the period.

Other evidence of change includes an increase in the number of seals dating to the late fifth century, and in coins from early fourth-century contexts. Attic ware also became more common, suggesting that Greece was exerting more cultural influence, although the nature and extent of this influence is not clear.[17] A number of new rural settlements were also established beginning in the late fifth or early fourth centuries, some of them yielding a mix of Persian and Hellenistic pottery.

SOCIOHISTORICAL CONTEXT

The Babylonian Exile

There is very little information, biblical or extrabiblical, relating to the exilic period or the conditions under which the deportees and those left behind in Judah lived during the period of Babylonian domination, although there is some archaeological evidence that at least some of those who remained in Judah were able to prosper to some extent. Jeremiah and Ezekiel provide glimpses of how the early years of the exiles were perceived, and Deutero-Isaiah the latter years. There are also references in Babylonian texts to the rations provided for Jehoiachin of Judah and to prosperous Jews who were later running businesses in Babylonia. And we know that centuries later there was still a Jewish community there. In light of this scarcity of information, it is interesting that scholarly constructs have created such a forceful picture of intensive religious and literary activity, particularly on the part of the exiles. Again, Philip Davies is particularly skeptical of such constructs:

> Biblical scholarship . . . has painted an entirely fanciful portrait of religious fervour and furious literary creativity among Judaeans in Babylonia. There

is little biblical evidence for any such activity and it goes against everything that we know or can infer about deported populations.[18]

> Biblical historians . . . fondly imagine the deportees hugging their copies of Deuteronomy or transcripts of the oracles of Jeremiah to their chests, and spending evenings in Tel Abib ruminating on their plight and preserving the faith, developing their literature into long histories and bodies of law and huge collections of oracles.[19]

Davies suggests that the official archives of the Judean monarchy would probably have been either confiscated by the Babylonians or left behind in Judah, and that the deportees therefore would not have had access to them. Neither would they have been allowed to take with them even private scrolls, given the likelihood that one of the intentions behind the deportation was to alienate them from their homeland.[20]

Regardless of the nature and extent of literary activity, however, the Babylonian policy of allowing exiled groups to settle in their own separate communities almost certainly facilitated their being able to maintain a sense of group identity, something that may have been of less concern for those who remained behind and were able to hold on to their ties to the land. Some of the basic substructures of society, such as the institution of the elders, also seem to have remained intact, as is suggested in Jeremiah and Ezekiel and in the continuity implied in postexilic texts. The importance of maintaining a separate identity while living among the Babylonians may have contributed to the Priestly emphasis in the biblical traditions on markers of social identity such as circumcision, sabbath observance, and dietary laws.

The time between the first deportation (598/97) and the edict of Cyrus (538/37) is especially poorly documented. Presumably there was widespread disruption and depopulation as a result of the Babylonian campaigns and deportations, possibly including the encroachment of the Edomites on the territory of Judah, as is suggested in the exilic prophetic traditions and the archaeological evidence.

After the fall of Jerusalem, we are told in the biblical texts, the Babylonians appointed a native governor by the name of Gedaliah, who resided at Mizpah (presumably because Jerusalem was devastated) and was later assassinated during a revolt that resulted in further deportations. Land was probably redistributed among those who remained behind, creating a situation that apparently affected their relationship with the exiles once they returned following Cyrus's edict.

Several recent studies have argued that the destruction of Jerusalem and the exile of elites most likely had only a minimal impact on those who remained in Judah, and that the social order remained essentially intact.[21] In his construct of Persian period social history, Jon Berquist argues that the destruction of Jerusalem probably did not affect the rural or poor who remained behind to the extent that it would have affected the elites in exile. The latter were not only geographically displaced but removed from their traditional sources of power and the basis of their self-identification, including landed property. On the basis of references in Ezekiel and Deutero-Isaiah, Berquist postulates that some of the exiles (particularly those with governmental experience, including Temple service) lived in the capital and were involved in governmental activities in the Babylonian palace and temple systems, while others were primarily agricultural and rural.[22]

There seems to have been only a low-level Babylonian administrative presence in Judah itself, with the social structure basically remaining intact and village elders remaining influential in organizing and regulating local life. Family life, cultural traditions, economic strategies, traditional values, and local religious rituals probably also remained relatively constant. It is also possible that the destruction of the temple had little effect on the practice of religion in rural areas. If this was the case, religious practice would have continued relatively unchanged, at outlying shrines and/or within villages. Trade probably endured as well, but at a much reduced level.[23]

The Persian Period

Among the most recent and comprehensive analyses of the sociohistorical context of Persian-period Judah is Berquist's *Judaism in Persia's Shadow*.[24] According to Berquist, the basic organization set in place by the Babylonians was not changed by Cyrus (550–530 B.C.E.), who allowed most regional administrators under the Babylonian system to retain their administrative roles.[25] However, in contrast to the Babylonian administrative strategy of centralizing and intensifying resources by moving populations toward its own center, which kept the periphery weak, the administrators of the early Persian Empire encouraged their movement back toward the peripheries, partly as a means of securing the boundary areas of the empire, and partly to increase potential sources of tribute. The resulting movement of populations was also accompanied by territorial expansion. Support was provided by the Persians for rebuilding religious institutions in peripheral areas, primarily because of the roles they played in collecting tribute and taxes and in providing an ideological base for the populations of the provinces.

If we are to believe the biblical texts, however, the actual political and religious restoration of Judah, at least in Jerusalem, did not really begin in earnest until the reign of Darius (522–486 B.C.E.), and, as the exiles began to return, the internal stability of the province seems to have been affected by steadily increasing tensions between the native and immigrant populations.

After Cyrus, Cambyses (530–522 B.C.E.) introduced little apparent change in imperial structure or activity. Judah was probably fairly stable during his reign, but there may also have been some social change as the returning exiles began to assimilate, particularly in terms of internal stratification. The relative absence of imperial attention during this period, Berquist suggests, probably allowed Judah a certain amount of autonomy in terms of establishing its own identity and pursuing its own goals.[26]

The impact of Persian rule on Judean society and religion appears to have been stronger during Darius's reign.[27] He is believed, for example, to have sponsored the publication of laws throughout the empire and, therefore, possibly to have supported the codification of Jewish law. In the early part of his reign, he is also said to have suppressed a number of revolts that had been initiated toward the end of Cambyses' reign, and to have reorganized the empire into twenty provinces (satrapies), requiring a fixed amount of annual tribute from each one. Persian officials, including governors, were assigned to each satrapy, and local administrators who were loyal to the Persian authorities supplied internal structural unity. Under Darius, then, imperial power became more centralized and more of its administrative functions were transferred to the provinces. But native officials held positions of authority only at the will of the Persian administration. Darius's policies also allowed for the Jerusalem Temple to be rebuilt. According to the biblical traditions, he sent Zerubbabel to Judah to act as governor of Jerusalem, accompanied by Joshua, who had been appointed high priest (520 B.C.E.). Zerubbabel served the interests of the Persian Empire, Berquist argues, by encouraging Temple construction and the production of surplus food to support the Persian army.

Imperial support was withdrawn again during Xerxes' reign (486–465 B.C.E.). Funding for construction projects and for the Temple decreased, while at the same time economic pressure in the form of taxation to provide for imperial expenses increased. Among the changes in policy introduced by Xerxes was the replacement of local authorities with Persians. Although the Jerusalem Temple continued to play a major role in provincial politics, it became, according to Berquist, the locus for Persian imperial agents, such as provincial governors and financial administrators. It may also have been the focus of some internal economic and political conflicts. One of the consequences of the combination of Xerxes' policies and conflicts internal to Judah seems to have been a significant deterioration in the economy, possibly exacerbated by a depletion of local resources and a decline in trade with

Greece. The authority of the local power bases may also have been reduced.[28] The instability of this period is also suggested by the destruction apparent in sites in Samaria and Benjamin.[29]

Economic pressure in the form of increased taxation continued during the reign of Artaxerxes I (465–423 B.C.E.), resulting, Berquist suggests, in widespread bankruptcy and loss of land among the local populations, with Persians in many cases becoming the new landowners. Judah's orientation at this time also seems to have begun to shift from east to west, as the result of increasing influence on the part of the Greek city-states and other Mediterranean powers.[30]

Because of pressures from Egypt and Greece, the Persian Empire was also concerned during Artaxerxes' reign with strengthening its colonies along the Mediterranean. This was facilitated by the construction of a number of fortifications along the major communication and trade routes. One of the other consequences of this concern, Berquist proposes, was the fortification of Jerusalem, as recorded in Ezra-Nehemiah.[31] Yet another was the reinstatement of funding for religious institutions and a renewed support of local religious leaders, presumably as a means of influencing the local population in favor of the Persian authorities and of keeping other local authorities under control. Once the Egyptian and Greek threats were alleviated, however, attention to the outlying provinces again declined.

In general, the Persian Empire underwent significant political and economic decline during the course of the late Persian period (423–333 B.C.E.). Although there is no written evidence that clearly relates to Judah during this period, Berquist postulates that internally pluralism in Judah increased, particularly as the result of the increasing, and mixed, cultural influences of both Greece and Persia. There are no records pointing to any major restructuring in Persian colonial administration for this period. Governance within Judah probably continued in a form similar to that of the prior century—that is, local governors assisted by appointed priests and other officials.[32]

JUDAH AS A PERSIAN PROVINCE

The extent to which the Persian Empire affected local structures and economies is not very clear from the sources, although Berquist is more than likely correct in suggesting that this fluctuated over time. Berquist argues that, in general, the greatest political influences in Judah were external, but that the local population nevertheless continued to adhere to its own traditions and customs and to maintain some degree of political self-determination.

Thus, there was a dynamic of external pressures combined with internal factors of continuity and opposition, neither of which was primary.[33]

Berquist's study is concerned primarily with the question of how Judean society and religion changed as a result of Judah's situation as a province (or colony) in the Persian Empire, and how the new form of religion that developed functioned both to maintain and to oppose the society in which it took its shape.[34] He argues that because the colony of Judah and the Persian Empire constituted an intricately connected social system, it is important to take into account Persian imperial history and society as influential factors in the colony's internal development. He therefore works from a model of an imperial core (Persia) and its interrelationship with a colonial periphery and semiperiphery (Judah and Jerusalem respectively). The various forces of this relationship are examined primarily in relation to the ancient textual information (biblical and extrabiblical).[35] Subsumed under this overarching model are several others that include considerations of secondary state development, the interrelationship among core, periphery, and semiperiphery in empires, and the ways in which societies are constructed and maintained.

Berquist's overarching model is dependent in large part on Shmuel Noah Eisenstadt's work on the processes associated with institution building in empires.[36] Arguing that humans tend to use ideology, power, and material resources in constructing the boundaries of social systems, he further suggests that regulative mechanisms such as bureaucracies, laws, and rituals are also necessary. Such constructed social boundaries are reinforced by institutions, which in turn are dependent on the level and distribution of resources. In their struggle for control of resources, society's elites, using ideology and rhetoric, are able to exercise control through institutions as well as by coercion. The resulting inequality in access to resources results in heterogeneity and conflict, which then requires further measures on the part of elites to maintain control and enforce the boundaries they have constructed.

According to Eisenstadt, the extent of social complexity required for an empire to develop necessarily leads to a high degree of social differentiation, including the development of a class of imperial political elites. The goals of this class of elites include harnessing and controlling the new resources available to them, which they use to consolidate control over the larger society. Typically, the empire's more traditional power bases attempt to limit access to resources, whereas the more entrepreneurial elites diffuse the new culture throughout the empire's geographic area. Elites who are supported by religion, which in imperial situations tends to be highly politicized, become particularly powerful.

The growth of such an elite class eventually results in a clearly delineated center and periphery and the development of multiple autonomous centers. Normally the cities of the empire form the area in which the elite and their new power bases are concentrated, and traditional authority continues to operate in the more rural agricultural areas. The colonial periphery, according to some models, often consists of rudimentary states that lack sufficient authority or ability to govern themselves and their populations, thus facilitating the governing authority of the imperial center. Peripheral colonies nevertheless maintain some local control, although the authority of their leaders is based less on material resources (which are controlled by the imperial authorities) than on symbolic forms of legitimation such as religion. Thus colonies and colonial administration do not necessarily derive all of their power from the empire.

Colonies are considered by Berquist to constitute one type of secondary state formation.[37] According to the models on which he depends, empires allow the growth of limited power bases in colonies because of their need to maintain order and to control and exploit as fully as possible the resources they provide.

The core or center of the empire, then, is the locus of the greatest power, wealth, and privilege. In the periphery (particularly among peasants), trade is typically scarce, taxation leads to the removal rather than accumulation of local resource surpluses, and there is no control over military power. Often there is also an area that constitutes a kind of "semiperiphery" and provides core-periphery mediation (for example, Jerusalem in Judah).

In Berquist's estimation, the most influential political changes as Judah developed into a secondary state were its reurbanization and the introduction of a class of urban elites. Together, these shifted the bases of political power and culture from those who had been living in the land over the course of the exile in favor of those who had had experiences in Babylonia and Persia. The introduction of this urban population, which had different ethnic connections, regional experiences, political affiliations, occupations, and financial bases, resulted eventually in a significant shift in Judah's social character.[38]

Taking into account this dynamic between center and periphery, then, the "restoration" of Judah was possibly based on a deliberate Persian strategy to reorganize the empire. This was carried out through resettlement, founding new settlements, restoring or building new temples, and sometimes establishing law codes. The combined effect of these three initiatives in the case of Judah was the creation of a society and a new ethnic identity whose core had come into the land from outside.[39]

DEMOGRAPHY AND SETTLEMENT PATTERNS

Biblical scholars and archaeologists have traditionally appealed to lists in Ezra-Nehemiah in their attempts to define the boundaries of the Persian province of Judah—the list of returnees in Ezra 2 and Nehemiah 7; the list of "districts" and "subdistricts" that sent delegations to work on the walls of Jerusalem in Nehemiah 3; the list of cultic officials in Nehemiah 11; and the list of singers in Nehemiah 12. Taken together, these lists suggest a fairly large area, extending from Kadesh-Barnea in the south to Hazor in the northeast, and Lod, Hadid, and Ono on the northwest coastal plain. As Charles Carter has pointed out, however, the intentions behind the creation of these lists were not to delineate boundaries. What is more likely is that they were meant either to identify sites to which the diaspora Jews returned or those at which they had ancestral connections, whether or not they were within the boundaries of the province (that is, the extent of Jewish settlement in Palestine rather than the extent of the province itself).[40]

In addition to the biblical lists, three types of archaeological data have been used as the basis for reconstructing the province's borders: seal impressions, coins, and fortresses. Ephraim Stern,[41] for example, argues that any site at which seals or coins bearing the names of Judah or Jerusalem have been found should be considered Judean, and interprets the fifth-century fortresses as boundary fortifications. One of the problems with the former argument is that there are any number of different reasons for the presence of a particular artifact type. And the problem with the latter, as Carter points out, is that some of the fortresses are situated well beyond the limits of even the maximal reconstructions of the province, and thus would not necessarily have functioned to defend provincial boundaries.[42] The more likely proposal (already introduced above), especially given the brevity of time during which these fortresses apparently functioned, is that they represent a concern on the part of the Persian authorities to protect the trade routes and communication lines that were necessary for maintaining control of the empire.[43]

In a study based on recent surveys of Judah and Benjamin, Carter addresses a number of demographic issues relating to Persian-period Judah. These include the size and population of the province and the number, size, and distribution of sites.[44]

Carter's approach is historical and geographical, and agrees with recent proposals that the natural geographical divisions of Palestine were often the bases of distinct geopolitical entities, and that empires tended to divide their provinces into such geographically self-contained units. Using central-place theory as a model, he proposes that the core of Judah the Persian province was located in the central hills, and did not include either the Shephelah, which was itself a self-contained geographic entity, or the coastal plain. He places the western boundary at the edge of the central hill country, with the eastern boundary possibly extending as far as the Dead Sea and, to the north, the Jordan River. The northern and southern boundaries are more difficult to establish, but on the basis of the former tribal boundaries of Judah and Benjamin, Carter suggests that the northern boundary extended toward the hill country of Ephraim, and the southern border from En-Gedi, on the shore of the Dead Sea, northwest toward Hebron, and farther west to the edge of the hill country. The area of the province according to this construct would have been approximately 1,700 square kilometers or 620 square miles.

The results of surveys conducted by Kochavi in 1967 and 1968 indicated that there was a 25 percent increase in the number of occupied settlements toward the end of the sixth century in Judah.[45] Carter's more recent study of site distribution, based on both excavations and surveys, identifies a total of 111 occupied sites within the province that may date to the Persian period. Most of these sites were very small (31 percent) or small (36 percent), that is, two-thirds of the Persian-period sites were five dunams or less in area (four dunams = one acre), with populations of less than 125. Twenty-three percent of the sites were of medium size, with populations ranging from 125 to 300, and approximately 11 percent were large (10 percent) or very large (less than 1 percent), with populations of more than 300. Of the latter, only four sites were more than 20 dunams in area, and only Jerusalem exceeded 25 dunams. Most of the population (69 percent), according to this study, was concentrated in the central hills, 18 percent on the western slopes, 12 percent in the desert fringe, and 3 percent in the Judean desert.[46] In his survey, Kochavi notes that nearly all the new settlements were unwalled villages. Two-thirds of them had not been inhabited during Iron Age II, and one-fourth had never been previously inhabited.[47] These new sites were most likely built as Judah was repopulated during the reigns of Cyrus and his successors, and may point to an economic policy of deliberate ruralization on the part of the Persian authorities.

Carter estimates that the population of the province ranged from a low of 11,000 in the late-sixth/early-fifth centuries to a high of 17,000 in the late-fifth/early-fourth centuries,[48] an estimate that is considerably lower than the 42,000 returnees in Ezra 2/Nehemiah 7. According to Carter's estimates, then, the province of Judah was relatively small and relatively poor for much of the Persian period. This accords, he argues, with the general picture presented in the biblical texts, especially Haggai and Nehemiah.

There was also a slow influx of population into the Jerusalem area over the course of the period, as it gradually regained its prominence following its destruction by the Babylonians. Carter estimates on the basis of excavations that its population eventually reached about fifteen hundred, and its size between 130 and 140 dunams, with the Temple Mount covering about eighty dunams (but probably about half this size in the early part of the period).[49]

ECONOMY

Subsistence Strategies and Patterns of Labor

The large number of rural sites in Judah dating to the Persian period indicate that the basic subsistence strategies—subsistence farming based on a household economy—remained the same as for previous periods. As has been suggested above, however, there may have been a deliberate strategy of ruralization on the part of the Persian authorities, which served as a means of creating a larger tax base for their exploitation. As a result, much of what was produced was probably turned over to the Persian authorities as taxes, contributing to an increase in poverty in the rural areas. Much of the land may also have been claimed as imperial domain, in which case many of the rural peasants would have labored on land that was no longer associated with the traditional patrimonies. The passage of military troops near Judah may also have resulted in the rural areas' being responsible for additional labor to provide for the military as well as Judah's elites.[50]

Systems of Exchange and Trade

Although it was relatively rare in antiquity, it is possible, as the result of increased trade, especially with Greece, that a market form of exchange began to operate in Jerusalem during the course of the Persian period. Reciprocity and redistribution probably remained the dominant form of exchange,[51] however. Market exchange requires a marketplace and an institutionally protected arena in which goods and services are bartered and wealth is exchanged directly with the aim of maximizing returns to both buyers and sellers. As was noted in chapter 5, such markets require the existence of money, which after it began to be used during the sixth century B.C.E., was primarily available to, and in the hands of, the political elites. But because its abstract value was only rudimentary at this stage, it would not have eliminated the need for personal exchanges between trading parties.

Money also facilitated long-distance commerce and trade, which because of its potentially disruptive social effects was normally insulated from local commerce. For the sake of economic security, then, local political leaders typically prevented the incorporation of local markets into long-distance trade networks. Because control or ownership of land was the most desirable commodity for ancient elites as well as the material basis for household security, those who acquired wealth through commerce, or by any other means, would have continued to invest it in land, as had been the case for previous periods.

The Temple, in addition to its religious functions once it was rebuilt, very likely functioned as an administrative and economic center with its own bureaucracy for redistributing resources and wealth.[52] This would have included issuing loans, controlling and collecting taxes, tribute, and other types of income from the land, and supporting priests, scribes, Temple servants, and other individuals necessary to its continued functioning.

The material evidence from the Persian period indicates that there was an expansion in international trade from the sixth century onward.[53] This is apparent particularly in increasing amounts of imported pottery from Greece. It is also possible that trade resulted in Greek settlement in Palestine and Phoenicia, although this possibility is still open to debate. In any case, Greece began to play an important role in trade and other economic spheres in Judah; nevertheless, the economy seems to have continued to decline throughout the period.

Land Ownership and Distribution of Wealth

Still open to debate also is the question of land ownership. Some scholars argue that land continued to be owned primarily by the Jews themselves. This is the assumption underlying arguments that there were conflicts over land between the returning exiles and those who remained behind, the latter presumably having taken over land that had originally constituted the patrimonies within the families of the exiles. It is also apparent in the argument (see below) that the *bêt 'ābôt* replaced the *bêt 'āb* as the primary social unit associated with land ownership.

Others have argued that much of the land became the domain of the Persian authorities.[54] Regardless of who owned the majority of the land, the economic well-being of the local population in Persian-period Judah seems to have declined progressively over time, with the development of a high degree of poverty, particularly in rural areas, resulting in some cases in an inability to pay off debts, and consequently the necessity of selling off land to the more wealthy. This was most likely caused in part by the Persian government's depletion of the rural economy through heavy taxation, and in part by the fact that the taxes had to support the local elites as well as the empire. Presumably, the elites in Jerusalem, especially those supported by the Persian government, fared better than the general population.

Berquist suggests that the rebuilding of Jerusalem's walls during the time that Nehemiah served as governor exacerbated the separation between the rich and the poor by creating a physical barrier between the urban elites and the rural population,[55] but that Nehemiah recognized this and attempted financial reforms to curb the problem of extreme poverty.

SOCIAL ORGANIZATION WITHIN THE PROVINCE

In his study of Persian-period Judah, J. P. Weinberg postulates that Judah constituted what he calls a "citizen-temple community" (*Bürger-Tempel-Gemeinde*), in which the Temple was an essential and central institution, and the social structure was based on a unified organization of community members and the Temple priesthood.[56] Within this citizen-temple community, the primary social unit was the *bêt 'ābôt,* which consisted on average of eight hundred to one thousand men and was distinct from the preexilic *bêt 'āb* and *mišpāḥāh.* Weinberg postulates that the *bêth 'ābôt*

> is an agnatic band . . . which unified a number of families that were related (either genuinely or fictionally). The essential characteristics of the *bêt 'ābôt* are a large quantitative composition and a complicated inner structure, an obligatory genealogy and inclusion of the name of the *bêt 'ābôt* in the full name of each of its members and a conscious solidarity based on communal ownership of lands.[57]

This construct is based in part on Weinberg's understanding of the *gôlāh* lists in Ezra 2, Nehemiah 7, and 1 Esdras 5, which he views as sources for understanding how the social organization of the local population in the Persian period differed from that of previous periods. The citizen-temple community was grounded in the leadership of the collective of *bêt 'ābôt,* which was directly involved in the administration of property that, Weinberg suggests, belonged communally to the constituent members of the "community." An essential feature of the community in his construct is the inalienable property (which formally belonged to God) of the *bêt 'ābôt,* which was divided into parcels for use by the separate families comprising it.[58]

Towns were the center of economic activity, and together the temple and the town formed a loose horizontal network of interacting and counterbalancing institutions. This combination of socioeconomic interests and religious affiliation ensured land rights and citizenship within the community, and is important, Weinberg argues, for understanding the nature of the crises depicted in Ezra-Nehemiah. This structure was essentially related to agriculture, manufacturing modes of production, and the appearance of money economies, and was a response to increased urbanization, the Persian taxation system, and the practice by the Persian rulers of distributing estates among its elites. In the face of these Persian policies, the local community structure provided its members with an organizational unity and a means of collective self-government, as well as internal political, social, and economic welfare.[59] Persian-period Judah, then, according to Weinberg's construct, was a society composed of "free and fully-enfranchised people who were socially and politically relatively similar, and who strictly distanced themselves from all those who were not community members."[60] Weinberg's citizen-temple community thus did not comprise the whole population of the Judean province, only those who sought separation from the royal sector and unification with the Temple.[61] It is this structure and the associated concerns for boundary maintenance that account for the tensions depicted in Ezra-Nehemiah.

Although the essential place of the Temple and priesthood are generally held to have had a central role in Judean society during this period, as Weinberg argues, other aspects of his construct have been disputed. Joseph Blenkinsopp, for example, challenges Weinberg's conclusions about the relationship of the community to Persian authority, arguing that the elite were intentionally recruited from among the returnees by the Persian government, who encouraged their loyalty to the empire.[62] The temple community, then, was semiautonomous and was controlled by this group of loyal elites. Blenkinsopp's construct is similar to Weinberg's in the sense that the returnees organized the community according to ancestral houses, and the community was composed of free, property-holding citizens and Temple personnel. Leadership consisted of tribal elders and an imperial representative. This cohesive social entity was jealously protective of its status and privileges. To sustain this structure, the immigrants had to regain land previously distributed to the peasants and also rebuild and secure control of the Temple.

Another study that gives attention to social structure is Daniel L. Smith's *The Religion of the Landless*.[63] Smith's study focuses on the social developments in the community of exiles as a community in crisis. The models he uses for understanding these developments, illuminating the social realities reflected in the biblical texts, and proposing hypotheses, are related to group crisis, minority behavior, and contact between ethnic groups in situations of unequal power distribution. He points in particular to structural adaptation as one of the survival mechanisms of the exiles. He argues that the exilic material from the Bible reveals both continuity and change in various aspects of the social life of the exilic community. In his construct, continuity with the past is reflected in the continuing authority of the elders, while structural adaptation is represented in the demographic changes of the *bêt 'āb/ bêt 'ābôt,* with the *roš* (see "Social and Political Institutions" below) as the communal leader.[64] This structural adaptation was intended to preserve identity, facilitate self-management, and cope with the economic and political demands of the Babylonian conquerors.

The replacement of the *bêt 'āb* and *mišpāḥāh* with the *bêt 'ābôt* was the primary structural adaptation to social organization that was introduced among the exiles but continued to persist into the postexilic period. In terms of size and function, this new social unit resembled the preexilic *mišpāḥāh,* but while the *mišpāḥôt* were based on "blood" lineage, the *bêt 'ābôt* was more artificial in the sense that there were criteria other than "blood" lineage that were determinative for its construction, one of which was probably common residence in exile. The *bêt 'ābôt,* then, was an exilic unit that was fairly large and included the smaller *bêt 'ābs*, but also some individuals who adopted a familial fiction, most likely as an expression of social solidarity with other exiles.

Smith suggests that this structural change was a response to the social crisis brought on by the Babylonian resettlement, along with Babylonian economic policies and possibly labor needs (that is, the need for large numbers of laborers for building projects).

Social Stratification

Most studies of Persian-period Judah emphasize a sharp division between a class of elites, usually identified as deriving from the exilic population, and a poorer rural population composed of the "people of the land" (normally identified with the population who had remained behind in Judah during the Babylonian exile). Contrary to Weinberg's arguments, many scholars now agree that during much of the period of Persian dominance the elite class was loyal to, and was supported to some extent by, the Persian authorities, whose self-interests would have been served by such a relationship. If this was in fact the case, the Jewish elites would have been in a somewhat ambiguous position in relation to the rest of the Jewish population, who on the one hand had to depend on them for support and protection, but on the other would have viewed them with hostility because of their relative wealth and privilege.

The composition of the elite class was probably similar in some respects to that of the monarchic period, with the major exceptions being that there were no royal family or officials directly connected to the king's residence. Jewish officials among the elite would have been answerable to Persian rather than local authorities. Another consequence of Persian dominance seems to have been an increase in the authority of priests and of scribes, many of whom also may have been priests.

Classes of elites clearly represented in the postexilic literature include: professional members of the cult, including Aaronic and Levitical priests (Neh. 7:1, 39, 43; 8:1–9), singers (Neh. 7:1, 23, 45), Temple servants (Neh. 3:26, 31; 7:46; 11:19), and gatekeepers (Neh. 7:1, 23, 45); a scribal class (Ezra 8:1, 9); the provincial governor, who would also have had officials serving under him (perhaps "Solomon's servants" of Neh. 11:57–60); and "men of the guard" (Neh. 4:23; 7:3). Artisans may also have been counted among the elite during this period (Neh. 3:8, 21–22; Ezra 3:7).

CONFLICT IN THE POSTEXILIC COMMUNITY

It is clear from the biblical texts that there were internal conflicts and tensions within the province of Judah during this period. But scholarly opinion has varied with respect to its nature and extent. A number of studies focus on this issue in relation to tensions that arose between the returning exiles and the "people of the land," especially during and after the reign of Darius, who appears to have sent exiles to Judah expressly for the purpose of organizing it more effectively for Persian benefit. The tensions may also have been associated with a related conflict between urban and rural populations.[65]

Another level of conflict portrayed in the texts is rivalry between Judah and Samaria. This rivalry is also represented in Genesis through Kings in the schism between Israel and Judah, with Israel represented as the defecting branch of the true "Israel," whose religion is focused in Jerusalem.

The nature and source of the tensions internal to Judah are constructed in a number of different ways. Paul Hanson,[66] for example, emphasizes the rise of competitive power groups within the Judean community as the basis for the development of apocalypticism. In his reconstruction, after the exile a party of ruling priests supported by a Persian mandate returned to Judah with the express purpose of building the Temple, and quickly gained the advantage in the local struggle for power. The disciples of prophets, with more egalitarian ideals, responded by challenging priestly authority. This opposition, Hanson argues, was the major source of conflict in the early postexilic period—especially as the priestly class became increasingly concerned with secular interests and their own power—and resulted in a bitter struggle for community control. The priestly class had the upper hand in this struggle, because they had the support of Persian authorities, and were able to some extent to influence Persian policy.[67]

Using Mary Douglas's work,[68] Daniel Smith considers the issue of conflict in light of group crisis models and the role of ritual behavior, especially purity legislation, as a means of protecting and maintaining social boundaries among colonized peoples. The exilic and postexilic elaboration of purity laws, and the emphasis on maintaining separation from the unclean, Smith argues, are related to concerns about the transfer of pollution from foreigners. This concern for boundary maintenance in relation to foreigners is represented most clearly in the dissolution of mixed marriages in Ezra-Nehemiah.[69]

Smith also considers the conflict between the returning exiles and those still in the land in light of group crisis models, arguing that the "sectarian" consciousness of the returned exiles is consistent with the social development of groups experiencing stress. His argument is that the survival of the exiles as a minority group in exile depended on their success in creating a solid community with well-defined social boundaries. The solidarity that was established in exile contributed to the later sense of separation from the population that did not share in the exile experience. The resulting conflict, then, did not reflect the "degeneration" of religious faith on the part of those left in Palestine so much as it did different responses to the crisis, which ultimately led to different social configurations. This perceived separation is represented in the continued emphasis in the postexilic community on purity boundaries and delimiting identification markers like "remnant," "holy seed," and "sons of the exile." For Smith, then, the *economic* conflicts between the exiles and those who remained behind exacerbated, but did not cause, this conflict.[70]

In her study of the nature of kinship and marriage in Genesis (which she analyzes from the perspective that the final redaction of these traditions dates to the Persian period), Naomi Steinberg also draws conclusions about how and why boundaries were defined in the postexilic community.[71] One of the goals of the study is to investigate how the interrelationship among inheritance, descent, and marriage were conceptualized in the postexilic context. She concludes that the ancestral stories in Genesis are metaphors for establishing identity and defining community boundaries, that is, the kinship structures in the texts are metaphors for social structure. More specifically, the narrative genealogy functions to establish family membership in *bêt 'ābôt,* the primary postexilic kinship group. Only those able to trace their genealogy back to the family of Jacob—that is, to those who were removed from the land and were in exile—constituted the true "Israel," according to this biblical construct. Family, or genealogy, was thus a means of legitimating status and the power structure in postexilic community organization. Because those who had been in exile were the ones who could trace their genealogy back to the patrilineal name "Israel," they were entitled to membership in the restored community. Ability to demonstrate inclusion within the *bêt 'ābôt* was a requirement both for membership and for defining the group's character.

The ancestral stories in Genesis, then, were intended as rationalizations for a particular social "reality" or construct. The legitimation of community boundaries is further represented in the stories' emphasis on entering into an "appropriate" marriage (Genesis 12–36), which excludes foreigners. That foreign wives are "inappropriate" spouses is also an idea expressed in Ezra 9–10. Steinberg suggests that this concern is related to different standards in the exilic and in the postexilic communities—that is, while in exile people could marry whomever they wanted (since Joseph did; Genesis 36–50), but "appropriate" wives are necessary when living in the land of inheritance.

WOMEN AND BOUNDARY DEFINITION

As is indicated above, establishing identity, and the boundaries that define self-identity, are clearly significant issues in the Persian-period biblical literature. This is particularly apparent in the passages in Ezra 9–10 and Nehemiah 13, where intermarraige with "foreign" women is strongly discouraged. But there are a number of problems confronted if we try to sort out what the meaning and significance of these references are. As Tamara Eskenazi and Eleanore Judd point out, we are missing important information about these charges against mixed marriages: we are not told what constituted "foreignness," what proportion of the community was guilty of having married these "foreign" women, why men would have married such women, whether women also married "foreign" men, or what, if anything, happened to these marriages. Most importantly, it is not clear who counts as a "foreigner" or who counts as a legitimate member of "Israel."[72]

Given what they do know about the demographic composition of Judah in the Persian period, Eskenazi and Judd suggest that these women could have been identified with any of the following groups: (1) They could have been Judahites or Israelites who had not been in exile or who differed ethnically and socioeconomically from the returnees. If this was the case, the controversy would have concerned how Jewishness was defined, particularly on the basis of ancestry or participation in the exilic experience (perhaps also implying a conflict over land rights). (2) The women could have been members of foreign nations. (3) The women could have come from Judahite and Israelite families in the land who engaged in religious practices and beliefs different from those of the returnees. If the latter was the case, the conflict would have been related to Judaism as a religion rather than as peoplehood.

Claudia Camp makes a similar observation, noting that the terms *zār* and *nokrî* have a variety of (sometimes overlapping) meanings. They can refer to persons of foreign nationality, but they are also used to designate persons outside one's own household or family, persons who are not members of the priestly caste, or deities or practices that fall outside the covenant relationship with Yahweh.[73]

In an earlier study, Eskenazi suggests that the opposition to mixed marriages in Ezra 9–10 was related to socioeconomic issues, especially a concern about losing inherited land.[74] One of the functions of marriage was related to transferring property and social status from one group to another. Prohibition of marriage outside the group, she suggests, was a means of assuring that property and kinship related rights remained within a closed group. If this is correct, the problem of mixed marriages would make most sense if women were able to inherit property. Because foreign wives ("foreignness" is not defined) posed a socioeconomic danger to the community, opposition to intermarriage with them was also an affirmation of women who did belong to the group.

Eskenazi draws these conclusions on the basis of her examination of the sixth- to fourth-century B.C.E. texts from the Jewish community in Elephantine. One of the aims of her study is to challenge the view that women's status declined in the postexilic period, arguing rather that conditions similar to the premonarchic period (as constructed by Carol Meyers) recurred in the postexilic period. This was partly due to a renewed emphasis on the family as the fundamental socioeconomic and political unit, which resulted in a more equitable distribution of power for women. She suggests this as a background for understanding the problem of foreign wives in Ezra 9–10.

The Elephantine texts show that women in the Jewish community there were able to initiate divorce, hold property, buy and sell, and inherit property even when there was a son. Eskenazi contends that there was continuity in the practices in Jewish communities of this period, since they were all under the same Persian imperial government and would have had frequent contact and communication. References in Ezra-Nehemiah indirectly support for her the view that wives in Judah had some similar rights.

Claudia Camp argues that the marriage prohibitions related to two major issues for the returned exiles: (1) a need for family stability as a survival mechanism and to establish claims to land and political power; and (2) a need to promote the pure and proper worship of Yahweh.[75] From her perspective, these two issues were closely linked, and crisis was reached when some men began marrying into foreign families. These marriages threatened the stability of the authority structure, particularly because intermarriage for the purpose of attaining upward mobility could bring outside challenges to the power of the leadership group (Ezra 10; Neh. 13:26–27; cf. Mal. 2:10–12). The focus on *wives* rather than husbands may, Camp proposes, represent a situation in which Judean men were marrying foreign women but not allowing their daughters to marry foreign men, possibly because the foreign brides brought as dowries actual land holdings that were claimed by members of the *gôlāh* community.

Berquist's study of Judah in the Persian period also deals with this issue.[76] He draws a distinction between the ways in which intermarriage is regarded in the Ezra and the Nehemiah passages, although there is a concern in both for economic and political consequences. The focus in the Ezra passage is on leadership, and there is some indication that inheritance was at least part of the problem (Ezra 9:12). Jewish men, including priests, Levites, and officials, were marrying women from neighboring areas (Ezra 9:1–2). Nehemiah presents the problem differently. Whereas Ezra deals with *all* foreign women, Nehemiah focuses on marriages with the traditional enemies of Israel—Ashdod, Ammon, Moab (Neh. 13:23). The more specific problem identified here is that the children of such marriages speak only the languages of their mothers (Neh. 13:24). The implication, Berquist suggests, is that without a knowledge of Hebrew or Aramaic they would not be capable of assuming leadership positions within the community. Nehemiah also seems to be concerned with preventing interference in the Jewish community by foreign officials (Neh. 13:28).

Berquist also points out that the solutions to the problems differ. Nehemiah recommends discontinuing the practice, whereas Ezra recommends divorce. Berquest questions the interpretation that ethnic purity is the issue, especially in light of the fact that neither Ezra nor Nehemiah appears to be concerned with ethnic issues when dealing with the Persian court, with which both of them must have had some connection. The primary issues in Berquist's construct are matters of regional competition and economic differentiation *within* Judah. In both respects Judah was isolating itself from other geographic and political entities, while at the same time the ruling elite were distancing themselves from the economic concerns of the masses. In a situation in which economic depletion and competition from other regions were harsh realities, regulations against intermarriage would have emphasized a sense of Jewish solidarity over against other regions as a means of solidifying political control and economic security within the elite stratum of Jerusalem society. In this context, there would also have been an emphasis on marrying within one's own class, particularly as related to control over land and wealth. In this respect, Ezra's injunction may refer not to foreign women per se but to women who were socially distant from the elites in terms of wealth and status. The *economic* consequences of intermarriage with those outside one's class, then, would have been a further depletion of already scarce resources, and the *political* effects of marrying outsiders would have included interference from other regional governments.

Eskenazi and Judd's study, referred to above, focuses on understanding the intermarriage problem in relation to ethnic groups and how ethnicity is defined.[77] They consider both systems theory—which views society as a system of tension management between dominants and subordinates in which the dominants have responsibility as well as privilege—and power conflict theory—which also views society in terms of dominants and subordinates, but assumes groups whose interests clash over scarce resources such as economic goods, prestige, and power. In both approaches, intermarriage is integral to understanding ethnic groups, and is identified as a classic example of crossing ethnic boundaries. In some cases crossing boundaries has positive value—for example, when it assists in cementing alliances. In other cases it is viewed negatively, as a violation of group integrity.

On the basis of social-scientific models, Eskenazi and Judd recommend considering three processes: (1) the structure and function of the social norms, that is, concepts associated with who benefits and how; (2) the source of deviations from those norms, that is, actual practices; and (3) the *pattern* of deviation, especially in terms of religion, race, and class.

As is the case in the other studies cited above, Judah is viewed as an immigrant community in transition, adjusting to a new situation. This required a reevaluation of norms in light of the new circumstances and, as a part of this process, establishing new boundary markers. The conflict over intermarriage in Ezra 9–10, then, needs to be evaluated in terms of the complex network of intricate variables that shape such communities in periods of transition. Eskenazi and Judd further suggest that developments in twentieth-century Israel provide a useful model for understanding Ezra-Nehemiah, pointing to the potential value of comparing with Persian-period Judah the tensions between Jews from different ethnic backgrounds, between Jews and non-Jews, and between orthodox and nonorthodox Jews. Eskenazi and Judd focus on the third type and agree with some of the constructs introduced above that the "foreign" women of Ezra 9–10 could very well have been Judahites or Israelites who, in the process of redefinition, came to be regarded as outsiders. Thus, although they may have been viewed as appropriate marriage partners by the early returnees, by the time of Ezra they were considered to be outside the newly defined boundaries.

In his analysis of this problem, Daniel L. Smith-Christopher agrees with other studies in viewing it in relation to land tenure and economic associations.[78] Where he deviates from other conclusions, however, is in his argument that the returned exiles, rather than constituting a privileged elite, were a threatened minority who regarded themselves as being in a disadvantaged position, socially and economically, in relation to those who had not gone into exile. In his interpretation of Ezra, those who were considered guilty in the intermarriage problem would have been men who were attempting to "marry up" as a means of exchanging their low status as "exiles" for participation in aristocratic society. The consciousness of "us" and "them," then, is related to a threatened minority group (the returned exiles) that was intent on its internal affairs and survival over against the majority ("foreigners"—that is, those who had no connection with the returned exiles). He also deals with the question of *who* would have regarded the marriages as "mixed" and suggests the possibility that it was only Ezra and his supporters, not necessarily the married persons themselves. The priests would have been singled out (Ezra 9:1), then, because they disagreed with Ezra about what constituted a marriage that was actually mixed. Essentially the only basis for Ezra's objection is that the foreigners were simply Jews who had not been in exile.

In Nehemiah, on the other hand (as Berquist suggests), the chief danger is perceived as coming from outside Judah, not from an internal struggle. Here political considerations predominate, particularly in the form of "power-grabbing" on the part of the leadership through strategic marriages.

The value of these studies, whether or not they agree, is that they provide some insight into the complexities associated with group and boundary definition and its interrelationship with economic and political as well as social and religious dynamics.

SOCIAL AND POLITICAL INSTITUTIONS

Governance and Leadership on the Level of the Empire

Scholarly opinion has varied with respect to the question of the extent of Persian influence in governance of the province of Judah. Berquist is probably correct in proposing that it varied throughout the period, and that at times Persia's influence was more direct and oppressive, while at others it was more removed and tolerant.[79] What is clear is that the Jews were no longer politically independent, existing now as an administrative unit within the Persian Empire. Judah no longer had a king, could no longer conduct on its own any kind of foreign policy, and depended on the Persian Empire as a whole to maintain its own power.

The Persian king had supreme authority, and his imperial administration appointed officials both to oversee financial operations and to ensure political stability. Through the Persian officials and the local officials who were answerable to them, taxes were collected and redistributed, and imperial law was enforced.

Local Governance and Leadership

Because loyalty and internal peace were central to maintaining the stability of the province, in most periods Judah seems to have been given as much autonomy in its internal affairs (for example, in issuing its own currency, policing its own territory, collecting its own tribute and taxes) as still allowed the Persian Empire to gain the maximum amount of tax revenue and resources from it. The biblical construct indicates that local officials were sometimes appointed to important positions, particularly as governor or high priest (for example, Zerubbabel, Joshua, Ezra, Nehemiah). Day-to-day administration seems in part to have been the responsibility of the priesthood, which, locally, wielded enormous political and economic power. But both governor and priest were nevertheless answerable to the Persian authorities, and appear to have cooperated with them in their internal administration of the province.[80]

In addition to Persian administrators, then, Judah had its own centralized government agencies, embodied in the person of the governor and located in Jerusalem, possibly working out of the rebuilt Temple and supported by the Temple's personnel,[81] including the high priest. Berquist suggests that most of the appointed local governors, and possibly the high priests, may have served at least some time in foreign courts, especially the Persian imperial court.[82]

Whatever externally validated authority the Persian-appointed governors may have had, most scholars agree that there continued also to be a system of governance that operated on the local level which included the traditional elders and perhaps a new type of leader related to the postexilic form of the *bêt 'ābôt* called the *rošîm,* or "heads."[83]

Both Ezekiel and Jeremiah speak of "elders" operating as leaders among the exiles in Babylonia (Ezek. 8:1; Jer. 29:1), implying that groups of exiles were able to organize themselves into some form of self-government in which the elders made decisions with relative autonomy. It is possible that the prominence of elders in self-government both during and after the exile related as much to encouragement on the part of the Babylonians and Persians, as a means of maintaining social stability within the dominated populations, as it did to intentional preservation of a traditional political system on the part of the Jews.

The use of the term *roš* in reference to communal leaders in the postexilic materials constitutes another possible indication of change in social structure, signifying the development of a new concept of leadership based on the *bêt 'ābôt.* Smith suggests the possibility that the *rošîm* were a select group of elders who were the leaders of the large resident units (the *bêt 'ābôt*) and had more authority than other elders in the community.

The Judicial System

Judah was apparently allowed to keep its own judicial system somewhat intact, with local law codes and norms, including those governing the upkeep and correct performance of the cult, generally remaining in force. If this was the case, the system would have been supported by the Persian government.

But just as domination by the Assyrians and Babylonians during Iron Age II probably had some effect on Judah's judicial system, so the Persian presence must have carried some new influences. One of the consequences may have been a clash between foreign-imposed and local laws.[84] Another seems to have been an increase in the power of the priesthood, and a corresponding rise in attention to religious law, which was probably not as greatly influenced by outside forces as civil law would have been. A distinction seems to have been made between the two types of law, with one under the control of the priests, and the other under the control of the Persians (2 Chron. 19:4–11). Although the nature of the interaction between these two legal systems remains unclear, the distinction itself may be significant in terms of its having contributed to the survival of Jewish identity during the various periods of domination. In the long run, it was the Priestly law, given final form in the Torah, that gave the "Israelite" legal system its distinctive stamp and shaped Jewish communities for generations to come. But the question of whether and to what extent this legal material reflects actual laws in the Persian period itself is still open to debate, some arguing that it was an important part of the judicial system,[85] and others that at this point it was still in many respects theoretical.[86]

Berquist has argued that Darius in particular was responsible for affecting local judicial systems in the province, as he moved the empire toward a stronger, more standardized legal base. This was effected by charging the provincial governors and local officials from various regions to codify laws that were based on local traditions, which would then have been enforced by Persian authorities. The value of enforcing such a codification of local legal traditions would have been related to the aim of standardizing the imperial administrative and legal systems. Judah, then, very likely possessed its own laws within the Persian Empire, as did other provinces, in addition to the imperial laws imposed from outside. Berquist suggests that these legal documents may have been used intentionally as a means of both maintaining social order and defining the Jewish population.

For most of Judah's population, written law would have had little effect, as very few villagers and occupants of rural areas would have been literate. The upper classes and those who lived in Jerusalem, on the other hand, would have had higher rates of literacy, or at least access to those who could read. It was in their day-to-day lives that the standardization introduced by written law would have had some kind of significant influence. This would presumably have produced a situation in which there was a differentiation in power between those who could read and had access to the written legal documents, and were therefore more knowledgeable about the rules, and the poor and rural populations who had no access to them, even though the laws controlled their behavior. There was likely some abuse of this power, in the sense that those who could read could interpret the laws in ways that benefited their own social class. Standardization of social norms, on the other hand, could also have contributed to a stronger sense of identity among those who shared the laws.

RELIGION

Because of their loss of national independence, self-identity among the peoples of postexilic Judah was probably grounded more in religious beliefs and practices than had been the case during the monarchic period. One of the ways in which identity was constructed, at least among the elites, was on the basis of establishing and affirming religious continuity with the "past." This was accomplished institutionally by rebuilding the Temple and reestablishing its services of prayer and sacrifice, along with the festivals and rituals that had presumably continued to be celebrated to some extent during the exile, both in Babylonia and in Judah itself. It was also supported literarily by creating a coherent body of sacred literature that was composed in part of earlier traditions, which were reinterpreted in light of the present situation, and in part of newer traditions.

The nature of the deity also seems to have been given new definition, and in the "official" religion of the urban elites the belief in a single, universal deity replaced the local national God of the monarchic period. Some groups, perhaps including the "people of the land," were presumably excluded from this religion, which was centered in the Jerusalem Temple. The Temple appears to have become a symbol of the superiority of the ruling class and a means by which they could facilitate economic exploitation, both on the part of the local elites and the Persian authorities who supported it. The establishment of the Temple and the priesthood, a system for identifying "insiders" versus "outsiders," and an ideology of holiness to support the insiders, all apparently supported to some extent by the Persian authorities, thus were interrelated with other means of political control.

The Temple

The Jerusalem Temple was the center of elite religion in Persian-period Judah. But it also had other roles within the culture[87]—it was a symbol for the "unity" of the populace (a belief that not everyone would have subscribed to), a ground for contesting power, a place from which the province was administered, a locus for the collection and redistribution of taxes, and the seat of the highest concentration of educated persons. It also served as a symbolic legitimation of the relationship between Judah and Persia. In this respect, construction of the Temple was probably influenced as much by motivations relating to Persian policies and goals as it was by the motivations of the local population, although even within the local population there were probably a variety of opinions and responses to it. Some, for example, would have supported the need to maintain a cult that was agreeable to the Persian overlords. Others would have preferred religious independence despite political domination. Yet others may have viewed politics as irrelevant as long as Temple worship was restored. And many were probably ill-served by the Temple, in the sense that it contributed to their exploitation.[88]

The Priesthood

The priesthood during the Persian period appears to have been involved as much in political and economic concerns as in those associated with religious beliefs and practices.[89] As an official probably appointed by the Persian government, the high priest in particular would have been responsible for encouraging loyalty and obedience to the Persian Empire as one of his official functions. Priests, and probably other Temple functionaries, were also counted among the elite in Jerusalem, and presumably received significant financial reward for their services in the Temple, enough that they would have been considered to be among the wealthy. The political power and centralization of the priesthood also brought priests into close contact with other political leaders of Judah, such as the governor, with whom they would have both shared and contested power. It is likely that writing was also controlled by the priesthood, giving them even more power. In contrast to the monarchic period, however, because the priests were no longer answerable to a local king, there was probably more separation between government and religion, to the extent that the priesthood was able to establish itself more completely as a distinct system of power and authority.

The biblical construct suggests that the high priesthood was hereditary, beginning at least during the Persian period. Socially, this would have meant that they constituted a portion of the local aristocracy.

"Legitimate" Religion and Pluralism

In the biblical construct, alternative religious orientations may be represented in the apocalyptic and Wisdom writings.[90] Berquist suggests that in the late Persian period in particular, when Persian control mechanisms were breaking down and Persian interference in local affairs may have declined, religious pluralism may have increased.[91] But even before this, various groups within Judah would have related to the official religion of the Jerusalem Temple and priesthood in different ways.

The official religion called for popular acceptance of the governors as divinely chosen figures who spoke the will of God and the policies of the emperor, as well as encouraging adherence to the priestly, Temple forms of religion. It was primarily the elite, however, who would have had constant and easy access to the Temple and its leadership, as well as sufficient wealth to participate in the most lavish of the Temple celebrations. Others, who worshiped at the Temple more sporadically because of limitations imposed by lack of proximity to Jerusalem or insufficient wealth, would not have had the luxury of identifying themselves closely with the official religion.[92] At times the boundary definitions may have allowed for them to be included among those considered to be insiders, but at other times the in-group would have been more narrowly defined by those with more consistent contact with the Temple. Those who never worshiped in the Temple and claimed no adherence to the worship of Yahweh, of course, would have been perceived as being completely outside the Temple system. The kinds of concerns we see expressed in the postexilic literature about boundary definition, then, were probably related to religious as well as economic issues, with which they were interrelated. The biblical construct also implies that there were mechanisms in place for maintaining the insider/outsider distinctions. Those who were perceived as having violated the laws of the official religion, for example, could be declared unclean and thus kept outside the system of Temple worship, as could others who were considered socially deviant in some respect. Priests could also control the insider/outsider definitions through the religious-juridical system. Through the application of such mechanisms, a social and religious hierarchy was established.

Alternative forms of religion, then, would probably have been associated in some way with social groups that did not fully reap the benefits of the official religion. Some of these, Berquist suggests, may even have come from among the elite themselves. The roots of the wisdom traditions, he suggests, were connected with an optional form of religious expression associated with Jerusalem's intellectual circles, which existed alongside the religion centered in the Temple but over time became increasingly distinct from it. This may have been due in part to a disagreement over the issue of the final authority of the traditions in the Torah. The alternative for this group, Berquist postulates, was a search for religious truths that transcended the particularities of the Jerusalem Temple and its associated legal tradition, although they did not necessarily completely reject the Temple system.[93]

Apocalypticism has also been connected in recent studies to the elite rather than to a persecuted and economically deprived social group on the fringes of society.[94] Davies, for example, argues that there was no "apocalyptic group," suggesting that the appeal in the apocalyptic literature to esoteric knowledge, heavenly revelation, and the use of myth are all characteristic of the methods used by ruling factions to justify their status and exercise ideological control. Berquist makes a similar argument, indicating that, as a genre, apocalyptic could have flourished only within circles of individuals with sufficient education to produce literature with this level of sophistication. These individuals may have been scribes, government officials, and/or others with similar status within Jerusalem society, perhaps with lesser status and prestige than those who employed them, who were frustrated and dissatisfied in some way both with the system of leadership and with the distribution of wealth. In this construct, apocalyptic represents a kind of "rhetoric of desperation" that resulted from such things as a perceived inability to participate in decision making.

Chapter 7

In Retrospect

Looking over the last two decades of studies that have focused on reconstructing the society of ancient Israel, one of the conclusions we can draw with certainty is that they have not provided definitive answers that can be "proved" to be correct. Nor have they established any real consensus on *specific details* relating to the various questions that have been raised about the nature and development of ancient Israelite society. There are many, often conflicting, theories and hypotheses. This is not by any means a negative evaluation of their value, however. In particular, the application of social-scientific methods, models, and theories has significantly expanded the field of questions it is possible to ask about the nature of ancient society. These questions in and of themselves have more than anything else raised our awareness of the complexities that are associated with understanding society in general, and the nature of Israelite society in particular.

In spite of the fact that there is no clear consensus on the issue of what exactly the "Israel" of Iron Age I was, and how it came into being, for example, there is now general agreement, even if not about specific details, that there was much more to its development than the movement of a single horde of people across the ancient landscape, and a sweeping conquest of a homogeneous indigenous population, or a semipeaceful settlement among them. If there is no consensus on the exact composition of Iron Age I Israel, or on the specific factors that gave rise to it, there is certainly a general consensus that a variety of factors contributed—factors relating to the environment, to the economy, to technology, to subsistence strategies, to settlement patterns, to interregional forces—in addition to the actions and goals of individuals. It is also now widely accepted that the highland population of Iron Age I Palestine was probably composed primarily of indigenous peoples from a variety of social backgrounds—urban, nomadic, seminomadic, semisedentary, sedentary villages, all types of societies—which would in one way or another have been engaged in symbiotic relationships with one another. Most reconstructions now also emphasize gradual evolution and cultural continuity, rather than "destruction" or "collapse." In spite of the fact that the models are elaborated to different degrees and contain different emphases, the reconstructions are not in total disagreement, sharing certain fundamental perspectives both in their approaches and in their interpretations. Similar cases are made for the transition to statehood and the transitions that occurred as the result of Babylonian and Persian domination. The general shifts in emphasis that are apparent in these recent studies relate very directly to the new questions that are being asked on the basis of social-scientific models and theories.

Another important factor in recent studies of the social world of ancient Israel is a shift in the way "history" is perceived. As was emphasized in chapter 1, the images of the past that we tend to accept as more, or less, reliable are a matter of consensus, but that consensus is continually shifting. In this respect, history has come to be understood more as an "ongoing conversation" between past and present than as what "really" happened in the past, or what we *know* or *think we know* about past events and peoples. In a sense, then, history is what historians can convince us "probably" happened. But this "probably" is always subject to revision. Interpretations are thus recognized as hypotheses that can never be identified as "true" or "false," but are subject to change as new information or different methods of interpretation are applied. All we can say with confidence is that one or another hypothesis or theory seems more or less convincing or plausible or adequate in light of the evidence, or offers the most appropriate guides for further reflection.

Disputes and disagreements among scholars have been an integral part of the developments in social world studies. In spite of the fact that they have sometimes been overly vicious (in, for example, the "minimalist" vs. "maximalist" debate), they are nevertheless healthy in the sense that they keep scholarship from stagnating and force us to rethink the way we ask questions, and thus the possible range of answers.

A number of factors account for the wide variety, and sometimes radically different, constructions of ancient Israelite history and society. The types of questions interpreters have asked, as well as their biases and presuppositions (for example, presuppositions about the relative value of particular types of information), have certainly affected how they have gone about doing their research and ultimately what conclusions they have come to. Sometimes these are apparent or consciously identified, but in most cases they are not. In some cases, political or religious orientation or related ideologies have had a significant influence on how sources have been evaluated and the conclusions drawn. Conclusions also vary widely according to the interpreters' theoretical orientations, and to changes in "interpretive fashion" (sometimes this is a matter of a sort of scholarly "generation gap").

The choices scholars make about what models are most appropriate to the task at hand have also had a significant effect on the conclusions they have drawn. There is no general agreement among biblical scholars about which models are most relevant for reconstructing ancient Israelite society; nor is there necessarily any agreement on how they should be used. Thus we end up with, for example, conflicting constructs of the rise of the state—some propose that there is evidence for chiefdoms in the tenth century B.C.E., and others say that the evidence points not to chiefdoms, but to the initial stages of the early state. These differences stem in large part from the models that are applied to the evidence and confusion about how to define terms such as "tribe," "chiefdom," "city," "state," and so forth. They also relate to how different scholars understand the nature of the evidence and the interplay between different kinds of evidence and between the evidence and the models. For example, the question of *when* centralization became a reality in Palestine has recently arisen as an issue because, from the perspective of some scholars, there are no *clear* signs of full centralization in the archaeological record until the eighth century. This concern relates not only to the nature of the information, but also to the models with which these scholars have chosen to work. A responsible scholar recognizes, however, that there is always a complex interrelationship among interpreter, evidence, and models, is aware of the limitations of models (which themselves are hypothetical entities, and are not "real"), and remains open to the possibility that a model may eventually need to be updated or refined. Most perspectives, regardless of their presuppositions or choice of models, are in my estimation worth considering, and reconsidering, as we engage in the task of constructing, and reconstructing, the social history of ancient Israel.

One of the recent debates that has arisen in response to the application of social-scientific approaches in biblical scholarship has to do with the the issue of whether biblical historians are qualified to apply social-scientific methods and models. But even though there are certainly risks that are taken in crossing over the disciplinary boundaries into what for some are the murky waters of social-scientific methods, theories, and models, there are nevertheless enormous benefits. Those who have taken these risks have generated new theories and fresh ways of conceptualizing the nature of, and interrelationships among, various types of social phenomena in ancient Palestine—social organization and structure, kinship systems, gender relations, social stratification, the economy, the relationship between rural and urban populations, governmental institutions, leadership—and how these related to social processes, opening up new perspectives on the ancient information in a way that traditional approaches do not. The significance of this approach for the historian of ancient Israel lies, therefore, *not* in providing evidence or new data for "filling in the gaps," but rather in providing "tools" for analyzing and raising questions about the ancient information.

This is not to say that we should not be cognizant of the problems that have so often been pointed out—for example, that models and theories are often used uncritically, reducing that which is complex to simplistic explanations; treating models and theories as if they were *data* for "filling in the gaps" rather than hypothetical entities; the danger of drawing conclusions that are so abstract or general that it is difficult to relate them to anything specific. These types of criticisms are in many respects valid in relation to particular studies, and in some cases the problems they point to are unavoidable. But our response to them should be to consider them as possible correctives rather than as reasons to abandon the approach altogether.

If we do not take the leap in crossing the traditional disciplinary boundaries, we cannot know *how* to ask the questions that are appropriate to understanding societies in all their complexity. It is one thing to be able to say that early Israel was a tribal society because that is what the texts tell us; it is another to be able to pose the appropriate questions about "what" tribal societies are, and about how models of tribal or segmented societies can contribute to gaining a better sense of the ancient Israelite situation and its complexity. We cannot, of course, impose particular anthropological models of tribal or segmented societies on the ancient situation in such a way that we are forcing the ancient information to fit them. But we can say, "These are the characteristics of tribes or segmented systems as they have been identified by anthropologists"; "these are the complex ways in which tribes are conceptualized"; and "these are the ways in which state systems incorporate tribal structures"; and as a result have a better sense of the possibilities for the ancient situation.

Another example: It is one thing to say that the primary units in the ancient Israelite social organization were the *bêt 'āb, mišpāḥāh,* and *šēbeṭ/maṭṭeh* because that is what they are called in the biblical texts. It is another thing to try to come to some understanding of what these term may have *meant,* and what their composition and interrelationships may have been, both "on the ground" and in the minds of the writers who used them throughout the course of Israel's history. Even if we cannot necessarily come up with "the" definitive answers (Does *bêt 'āb* refer to the nuclear family or the extended family? Does *mišpāḥāh* refer to the extended family, the clan, the lineage?), by looking at the ways in which societies at similar stages of development are organized we can postulate possibilities, while recognizing that part of the reason that there is so much difficulty in trying to come up with "the answer" to these questions is that social organization in *every* society is difficult to force into any neat system of classification, that social organization in *every* society is complex and fluid to some extent and tends to change as circumstances change. The fact that we have moved beyond identifying and defining the specific terms that refer to social units in simplistic ways, to talking about social complexity, is a major step forward in our understanding of the nature of ancient Israelite society—in spite of the fact that different scholars understand this complexity in different ways.

The application of social-scientific models also allows us to postulate answers to questions for which the the biblical texts provide no explicit information for any period. For example, although we get a very strong sense from the biblical texts that disparities in wealth existed, that land ownership was important, that slavery and forced labor existed, and so forth, there is no explicit description of the economy and how it differed from period to period. What were the subsistence strategies, strategies for spreading risk, patterns of labor, and systems of exchange in various periods? How did they relate to urban populations, rural populations, nomadic and seminomadic populations, social structure, kinship relations, politics, religion? To what extent were surpluses generated in the various periods, and what were they used for? Were there significant shifts in land ownership patterns from period to period? What was the nature and extent of the economic gulf between the upper-class urban populations and the rural populations? What kind of impact did outside dominance during the Persian period have on the economy in Judah?

Social-scientific models are also particularly suited to dealing with questions having to do with the complex issues associated with identity and conflict—for example, the ways in which "Israel" may have been conceptualized in various situations and periods in relation to issues of ethnicity and boundary definition, and how religion related to these processes—and how to evaluate both the textual and material evidence in relation to these issues. By applying social-scientific models, we can begin to understand why it is that notions about what it meant to be "Israelite" appear to have been so different in Iron Age I, Iron Age II, and the Persian period.

Attention to demography and settlement patterns have had a particularly significant impact on the ways in which we view both the social processes involved in the major social transitions in ancient Israel's history and the ways in which social structure and group interaction can be understood in various periods, particularly in relation to social complexity. As in contemporary Middle Eastern societies, social groups in ancient Palestine probably did not always fall readily into neat classificatory niches such as villagers, pastoral nomads, or city dwellers.

In spite of the clear reference to leaders in the biblical stories, it is difficult to identify on the basis of their vague and stylized constructions what roles and statuses such leaders might have had in various periods, particularly during Iron Age I and in the transition to statehood. Here again, anthropological models have proved useful in determining the possible nature and function of leadership during various periods.

Ultimately, we can argue that social-scientific approaches to reconstructing the world of ancient Israel have provided an important corrective to the traditional historical reconstructions that present history as consisting of stories about deliberate actions of particular individuals or groups. That is, they introduce a stronger concern for the general as well as the specific, for the social world as well as isolated events and single individuals. They also balance the traditional tendency of biblical historians to concentrate almost solely on Israel's political and religious history by shifting attention to the broader, and in a sense more mundane, complexities of economic, social, technological, and other factors associated with daily life, and to consideration of social processes as well as political or religious events. Finally, social-scientific approaches allow us to ask questions about the *interconnectedness* of individuals and events, social, political, and economic relations, values, and the structures of ideas portrayed in the biblical traditions. What emerges as a result of these approaches are more detailed and nuanced pictures of an ancient social world (or social "worlds") that was likely as complex and diffuse as our own.

Notes

Chapter 1. "Unscrambling Omelets" and "Collecting Butterflies"

1. On the problem of defining "Israel," see chap. 2.

2. Edmund Leach, "Anthropological Approaches to the Study of the Bible during the Twentieth Century," in Edmund Leach and D. Alan Aycock, eds., *Structuralist Interpretations of Biblical Myth* (Cambridge: Cambridge University Press, 1983), 7–32; idem, *Rethinking Anthropology* (London: Athlone, 1971). For a concise discussion of Leach's positions, see James W. Flanagan, *David's Social Drama: A Hologram of Israel's Early Iron Age*, SWBAS, 7 (Sheffield: Almond Press, 1988), 40–44.

3. See, e.g., James Luther Mays, David L. Petersen, and Kent Harold Richards, eds., *Old Testament Interpretation: Past, Present, and Future. Essays in Honor of Gene M. Tucker* (Nashville: Abingdon Press, 1995), 7.

4. Among the recent general works dealing with the social world of ancient Israel and those dealing with method are: Bernhard Lang, ed., *Anthropological Approaches to the Old Testament* (Philadelphia: Fortress Press, 1985); Victor H. Matthews and Don C. Benjamin, *Social World of Ancient Israel, 1250–587* B.C.E. (Peabody, Mass.: Hendrickson, 1993); R. E. Clements, ed., *The World of Ancient Israel: Sociological, Anthropological and Political Perspectives* (Cambridge: Cambridge University Press, 1989); J. W. Rogerson, *Anthropology and the Old Testament* (Atlanta: John Knox Press, 1978); Norman K. Gottwald, *The Hebrew Bible: A Socio-Literary Introduction* (Philadelphia: Fortress Press, 1985); idem, *The Hebrew Bible in Its Social World and Ours* (Atlanta: Scholars Press, 1993); Robert R. Wilson, *Sociological Approaches to the Old Testament* (Philadelphia: Fortress Press, 1984); Thomas W. Overholt, *Cultural Anthropology and the Old Testament* (Minneapolis: Fortress Press, 1996); Robert C. Culley, "Exploring New Directions," in Douglas A. Knight and Gene M. Tucker, eds., *The Hebrew Bible and Its Modern Interpreters* (Philadelphia and Chico, Calif.: Fortress Press and Scholars Press, 1985), 167–200; Dale B. Martin, "Social Scientific Criticism," in Stephen L. McKenzie and Stephen R. Haynes, eds., *To Each Its Own Meaning: An Introduction to Biblical Criticisms and Their Application* (Louisville, Ky.: Westminster/John Knox Press, 1993), 103–19.

5. See J. Maxwell Miller, "Reading the Bible Historically: The Historian's Approach," in McKenzie and Haynes, *To Each Its Own Meaning,* 12.

6. See James W. Flanagan, "Finding the Arrow of Time: Constructs of Ancient History and Religion," *Currents in Research: Biblical Studies* 3 (1995): 50–51, 72. For a

series of studies that deal intentionally with issues of cultural bias, see Daniel Smith-Christopher, ed., *Text and Experience: Towards a Cultural Exegesis of the Bible* (Sheffield: Sheffield Academic Press, 1995).

7. See, e.g., Philip R. Davies, *In Search of "Ancient Israel,"* JSOTSS, 148 (Sheffield: Sheffield Academic Press, 1995).

8. Victor Turner, "Social Dramas and Stories about Them," in W. J. T. Mitchell, ed., *On Narrative* (Chicago: University of Chicago Press, 1981), 137–64.

9. For an interesting study of the complex interplay between the oral and the written, see Susan Niditch, *Oral World and Written Word: Ancient Israelite Literature,* Library of Ancient Israel (Louisville, Ky.: Westminster John Knox Press, 1996).

10. See, e.g., Davies, *In Search of "Ancient Israel,"* 19–20; idem, *Scribes and Schools: The Canonization of the Hebrew Scriptures* (Louisville, Ky.: Westminster John Knox Press, 1998). On literacy, see also Niditch, *Oral World and Written Word.*

11. See, e.g., Frank S. Frick, "*Cui Bono?*—History in the Service of Political Nationalism: The Deuteronomistic History as Political Propaganda," *Semeia* 66 (1994): 79–92; Mario Liverani, "Propaganda," in David Noel Freedman, ed., *The Anchor Bible Dictionary* (New York: Doubleday, 1992), 5:474–77.

12. See Flanagan, "Finding the Arrow of Time," 61–62.

13. Miller, "Reading the Bible Historically," 14.

14. For recent evaluations of the historical value of the Bible, see, for example: Davies, *In Search of "Ancient Israel"*; John Van Seters, *In Search of History: Historiography in the Ancient World and the Origins of Biblical History* (New Haven, Conn.: Yale University Press, 1983); Marc Brettler, *The Creation of History in Ancient Israel* (New York: Routledge, 1996); Robert Morgan and John Barton, *Biblical Interpretation* (Oxford: Oxford University Press, 1988); Keith W. Whitelam, "Recreating the History of Israel," *JSOT* 35 (1986): 45–70; idem, *The Invention of Ancient Israel: The Silencing of Palestinian History* (New York: Routledge & Kegan Paul, 1996); Baruch Halpern, *The First Historians: The Hebrew Bible and History* (San Francisco: Harper & Row, 1988); idem, "Erasing History: The Minimalist Assault on Ancient Israel," *BRev* XI/6 (1995): 26–35, 47.

15. Leach, "Anthropological Approaches," 7–32.

16. Ibid., 21.

17. Davies, *In Search of "Ancient Israel."* Davies's book, as well as several other recent works that call into question the usefulness of the Bible as a historical source, has stimulated some harsh criticism. See, e.g., Iain W. Provan, "Ideologies, Literary and Critical: Reflections on Recent Writing on the History of Israel," *JBL* 114 (1995): 585–606. See also the responses by Davies and Thomas L. Thompson in the same volume: Thomas L. Thompson, "A Neo-Albrightean School in History and Biblical Scholarship?" *JBL* 114 (1995): 683–98; Philip R. Davies, "Method and Madness: Some Remarks on Doing History with the Bible," *JBL* 114 (1995): 699–705. Cf. William G. Dever, "Revisionist Israel Revisited: A Rejoinder to Niels Peter Lemche," *Currents in Research: Biblical Studies* 4 (1996): 35–50.

18. Davies, *In Search of "Ancient Israel,"* 29.

19. Ibid., 36–37.

20. Ibid., 16–17.

21. Whitelam, "Recreating the History of Israel"; idem, "Prophetic Conflict in Israelite History: Taking Sides with William G. Dever," *JSOT* 72 (1996): 25–44. Cf.

William G. Dever, "The Identity of Early Israel: A Rejoinder to Keith W. Whitelam," *JSOT* 72 (1996): 3–24.

22. Halpern, "Erasing History."

23. A number of articles have appeared recently on the "house of David" inscription. See, e.g., Avraham Biran and Joseph Naveh, "An Aramaic Stela Fragment from Tel Dan," *IEJ* 43 (1993): 81–98; Frederick H. Cryer, "A 'BETDAWD' Miscellany: DWD, DWD' or DWDH?" *SJOT* 9 (1995): 52–58; idem, "Of Epistomology, Northwest-Semitic Epigraphy and Irony: The '*BYTDWD*/House of David' Inscription Revisited," *JSOT* 69 (1996): 3–17; Niels Peter Lemche and Thomas L. Thompson, "Did Biran Kill David? The Bible in the Light of Archaeology," *JSOT* 64 (1994): 3–22; Ehud Ben Zvi, "On the Reading '*bytdwd*' in the Aramaic Stele from Tel Dan," *JSOT* 64 (1994): 25–32; Philip R. Davies, "'House of David' Built on Sand," *BARev* 20/4 (1994): 54–55; Baruch Halpern, "The Stela from Dan: Epigraphic and Historical Considerations," *BASOR* 296 (1994): 63–80.

24. Roland de Vaux, *Ancient Israel,* vol. 1: *Social Institutions.* (New York: McGraw-Hill, 1961), viii.

25. A number of recent studies deal explicitly with this issue. In particular, William G. Dever has published a number of articles in which the focus is the relationship between biblical and archaeological material. They are too numerous to list here, but see, e.g., William G. Dever, "Unresolved Issues in the Early History of Israel: Toward a Synthesis of Archaeological and Textual Reconstructions," in David Jobling, Peggy L. Day, and Gerald T. Sheppard, eds., *The Bible and the Politics of Exegesis* (Cleveland: Pilgrim Press, 1991), 195–208; idem, "'Will the Real Israel Please Stand Up?' Part I: Archaeology and Israelite Historiography," *BASOR* 297 (1995): 61–80.

26. See, e.g., Neil Asher Silberman, "Power, Politics and the Past: The Social Construction of Antiquity in the Holy Land," in Thomas E. Levy, ed., *The Archaeology of Society in the Holy Land* (New York: Facts on File, 1995), 9–23.

27. For bibliography on Albright see, e.g., R. Gnuse, "New Directions in Biblical Theology: The Impact of Contemporary Scholarship on the Hebrew Bible," *JAAR* LXII (1994): 893–918.

28. See, e.g., P. J. Ucko, "Foreword," in Ian Hodder, ed., *The Meaning of Things: Material Culture and Symbolic Expression* (London: HarperCollins, 1989), ix–xvii.

29. Dale F. Eickelman, *The Middle East: An Anthropological Approach,* 2d ed. (Englewood Cliffs, N.J.: Prentice-Hall, 1989), 20 n. 20.

30. Ibid., 228.

31. See, e.g., Clifford Geertz, *The Interpretation of Cultures: Selected Essays* (New York: Basic Books, 1973); Victor Turner, *Dramas, Fields, and Metaphors: Symbolic Action in Human Society* (Ithaca, NY: Cornell University Press, 1974); James W. Fernandez, *Persuasions and Performances: The Play of Tropes in Culture* (Bloomington: Indiana University Press, 1986). Examples of studies of ancient Israelite religion that look at symbols and patterns of meaning include: Howard Eilberg-Schwartz, *The Savage in Judaism: An Anthropology of Israelite Religion and Ancient Judaism* (Bloomington: Indiana University Press, 1990); Leach and Aycock, *Structuralist Interpretations of Biblical Myth;* Paula M. McNutt, *The Forging of Israel: Iron Technology, Symbolism, and Tradition in Ancient Society,* SWBAS, 8 (Sheffield: Almond Press, 1990).

32. See, e.g., Jan Vansina, *Oral Traditions as History* (Madison: University of Wisconsin Press, 1985).

33. Ronald M. Spores, "Research in Mexican Ethnohistory," in Richard E. Greenleaf and Michael C. Meyer, eds., *Research in Mexican History* (Lincoln: University of Nebraska Press, 1973), 25; cf. idem, "New World Ethnohistory and Archaeology, 1970–1980," *ARA* 9 (1980): 575–603.

34. See, e.g., Frank S. Frick, *The Formation of the State in Ancient Israel,* SWBAS, 4 (Sheffield: Almond Press, 1985); idem, "Social Science Methods and Theories of Significance for the Study of the Israelite Monarchy: A Critical Review Essay," *Semeia* 37 (1986): 9–52.

35. See, e.g., Herbert H. Hahn, *The Old Testament in Modern Research* (Philadelphia: Fortress Press, 1966); Rogerson, *Anthropology and the Old Testament;* Flanagan, *David's Social Drama,* 31–76; Norman K. Gottwald and Frank S. Frick, "The Social World of Ancient Israel," in Norman K. Gottwald, ed., *The Bible and Liberation: Politics and Social Hermeneutics* (Maryknoll, N.Y.: Orbis Books, 1983), 149–65.

36. See, e.g., Eilberg-Schwartz, *The Savage in Judaism,* 31–86.

37. William Robertson Smith, *Lectures on the Religion of the Semites* (London: Adam and Charles Black, 1894). See also idem, *Kinship and Marriage in Early Arabia* ([1885] Boston: Beacon Press, 1967). On Robertson Smith see, for example, T. O. Beidelman, *W. Robertson Smith and the Sociological Study of Religion* (Chicago: University of Chicago Press, 1974); William Johnstone, ed., *William Robertson Smith* (Sheffield: Sheffield Academic Press, 1995); Eickelman, *The Middle East,* 35–40.

38. See, e.g., Antonin Causse, *Du groupe ethnique à la communauté religieuse* (Paris, 1937); idem, *Les "pauvres" d'Israël* (Strasbourg, 1922); idem, *Les prophètes contre la civilisation* (Alençon, 1913).

39. Max Weber, *Ancient Judaism,* trans. Hans H. Gerth and Don Martindale ([orig. publ. 1916–19] New York: Free Press, 1952).

40. Johannes Pedersen, *Israel: Its Life and Culture,* 4 vols. (London: Oxford University Press, vols. 1 and 2, [1920] 1926; vols. 3 and 4, [1934] 1940). See also the recent reprint of these volumes with an introduction by James Strange (Atlanta: Scholars Press, 1991).

41. Roland de Vaux, *Ancient Israel,* 2 vols. ([1958] New York: McGraw-Hill, 1961).

42. See, e.g., Hermann Gunkel, *The Legends of Genesis: The Biblical Saga and History,* trans. W. H. Carruth ([1901] New York: Schocken, 1964). For a more recent translation of the original *Die Sagen der Genesis,* see idem, *The Stories of Genesis,* trans. John Scullion and William R. Scott (Vallejo, Calif.: BIBAL Press, 1994). See also idem, *The Psalms: A Form-Critical Introduction,* trans. Thomas M. Horner ([1926] Philadelphia: Fortress Press, 1967); Sigmund Mowinckel, *The Psalms in Israel's Worship,* 2 vols., trans. D. R. Ap-Thomas ([1951] New York: Abingdon, 1962).

43. Adolphe Lods, *Israel from Its Beginnings to the Middle of the Eighth Century,* trans. S. H. Hooke ([1930] New York: Alfred A. Knopf, 1932); idem, *The Prophets of Israel,* trans. S. H. Hooke (New York: E. P. Dutton, 1937).

44. For example, Albrecht Alt, *Essays in Old Testament History and Religion,* trans. R. A. Wilson ([1953] Sheffield: JSOT Press, 1989); Martin Noth, *Das System der zwoelf Staemme Israels* (Stuttgart: Kohlhammer, 1930); idem, *The History of Israel,* 2d ed., trans. P. R. Ackroyd ([1950] New York: Harper & Row, 1960).

45. For example, William Foxwell Albright, *From the Stone Age to Christianity:*

Monotheism and the Historical Process (Garden City, N.Y.: Doubleday, 1957); idem, *History, Archaeology, and Christian Humanism* (New York: McGraw-Hill, 1964).

46. See S. H. Hooke, *Myth and Ritual: Essays on the Myth and Ritual of the Hebrews in Relation to the Culture Pattern of the Ancient East* (London: Oxford University Press, 1933); idem, *The Labyrinth: Further Studies in the Relation between Myth and Ritual in the Ancient World* (New York: Macmillan, 1935); idem, *Myth, Ritual and Kingship: Essays on the Theory and Practice of Kingship in the Ancient Near East and Israel* (Oxford: Clarendon, 1958); A. M. Hocart, *Kingship* (London: Oxford University Press, 1927); idem, *Kings and Councillors: An Essay in the Comparative Anatomy of Human Society* (Cairo: Paul Barbey, 1936).

47. For example, Émile Durkheim, *The Elementary Forms of Religious Life,* trans. Joseph Ward Swain ([1915] New York: Free Press, 1954).

48. See, For example, Branislaw Malinowski, *Magic, Science and Religion, and Other Essays* (New York: Free Press, 1948); A. R. Radcliffe-Brown, *Structure and Function in Primitive Society* (New York: Free Press, 1952).

49. See, e.g., A. D. H. Mayes, *The Old Testament in Sociological Perspective* (London: Marshall Pickering, 1989).

50. See, for example, Gottwald and Frick, "The Social World of Ancient Israel."

51. See, e.g., Fernand Braudel, *The Mediterranean and the Mediterranean World in the Age of Philip* II, vols. 1 and 2 (London: Collins, 1972); idem, *On History* (Chicago: University of Chicago Press, 1980).

52. Norman Yoffee, "Conclusion: A Mass in Celebration of the Conference," in Levy, *The Archaeology of Society in the Holy Land,* 542–48.

53. See, e.g., Miller, "Reading the Bible Historically," 25; Gary A. Herion, "The Impact of Modern and Social Science Assumptions on the Reconstruction of Israelite History," *JSOT* 34 (1986): 3–33.

54. See Morgan and Barton, *Biblical Interpretation,* 1–43.

55. Ian Hodder, "Post-Modernism, Post-Structuralism and Post-Processual Archaeology," in Ian Hodder, ed., *The Meaning of Things: Material Culture and Symbolic Expression* (London: HarperCollins, 1989), 67.

56. Ucko, "Foreword," xii–xiii.

57. Ibid., xii–xiii.

58. Yoffee, "Conclusion," 544.

59. Christopher Tilley, *Reading Material Culture* (Oxford: Basil Blackwell, 1990), vii; cf. idem, "Interpreting Material Culture," in Hodder, *The Meaning of Things,* 185–94.

60. Flanagan, *David's Social Drama,* 72–73.

61. For a discription of various types of analytic models, see, e.g., T. F. Carney, *The Shape of the Past: Models and Antiquity* (Lawrence, Kans.: Coronada Press, 1975), 11–20. Among the types of models identified by Carney are: descriptive models, normative models, static models, dynamic models, ideal type models, and cross-cultural models.

62. Ibid., 34–38.

63. Norman K. Gottwald, "Recent Studies of the Social World of Premonarchic Israel," *Currents in Research: Biblical Studies* 1 (1993), 165.

64. For a succinct discussion of the developments of cross-disciplinary endeavors in the last twenty years, and various reactions to them in biblical studies, see Flanagan, "Finding the Arrow of Time."

65. See Flanagan, *David's Social Drama,* 77–116.

66. For a thorough discussion of the analytical distinction between actions and notions, see Flanagan, *David's Social Drama,* 96–103.

67. Ibid., 99.

68. Ibid., 112–16.

69. Eilberg-Schwartz, *The Savage in Judaism,* 88–89.

70. Ibid., 93.

71. Ibid., 95–98.

72. S. Talmon, "The Comparative Method in Biblical Interpretation: Principles and Problems," *VTS* 29 (1977): 356.

73. Ibid.

74. J. D. Martin, "Israel as a Tribal Society," in Clements, *The World of Ancient Israel,* 97.

75. Robert P. Carroll, "Prophecy and Society," in Clements, *The World of Ancient Israel,* 205.

76. Ibid, 205–6.

77. Ibid., 219.

78. Leach, *Rethinking Anthropology,* 1–4.

79. Eilberg-Schwartz, *The Savage in Judaism,* 90.

80. Robert R. Wilson (*Sociological Approaches to the Old Testament,* 28–29) offers a set of ideal guidelines for using comparative materials.

81. Leach, "Anthropological Approaches," 8–12.

82. Eilberg-Schwartz, *The Savage in Judaism,* 119.

Chapter 2. Iron Age I: The Origins of Ancient "Israel"

1. For a good, concise discussion of issues associated with ethnicity, see Eickelman, *The Middle East,* 207–27.

2. See Fredrik Barth, *Ethnic Groups and Boundaries* (Boston: Little, Brown and Co., 1969). Although Barth's general observations about the nature of ethnic boundaries are basically accepted, it has been noted that he does not give adequate attention to how social processes are related to the production of the cultural conceptions with which people distinguish themselves from "other" ethnic categories. See Eickelman, *The Middle East,* 209–10.

3. G. W. Ahlström, *Who Were the Israelites?* (Winona Lake, Ind.: Eisenbrauns, 1986).

4. Davies, *In Search of "Ancient Israel,"* 47–50.

5. On the problem of defining Canaanites, see, e.g., Niels Peter Lemche, *The Canaanites and Their Land: The Tradition of the Canaanites* (Sheffield: JSOT Press, 1990). For a more recent consideration of ethnicity by Lemche, see *The Israelites in History and Tradition* (Louisville, Ky.: Westminster John Knox Press, 1998).

6. For example, Davies, *In Search of "Ancient Israel."* Cf. Keith W. Whitelam, "The Identity of Early Israel: The Realignment and Transformation of Late Bronze–Iron Age Palestine," *JSOT* 63 (1994): 84.

7. In the stories about David, which claim the largest territory, Israel is approximately 565 km north to south and 120 km west to east.

8. C. Nicholas Raphael, "Geography and the Bible (Palestine)," in Freedman, ed., *The Anchor Bible Dictionary,* 3:965.

9. Ibid.; cf. Dennis Baly, *The Geography of the Bible,* rev. ed. (New York: Harper & Row, 1974). Raphael (see n. 8) includes a sixth zone, the Sinai Peninsula, which is not included here. For other summaries of the geography of Palestine, see, e.g., David C. Hopkins, *The Highlands of Canaan: Agricultural Life in the Early Iron Age,* SWBAS, 3 (Sheffield: Almond Press, 1985); Frick, *The Formation of the State,* 100–128; Flanagan, *David's Social Drama,* 120–37.

10. For example, Davies, *In Search of "Ancient Israel"*; David W. Jamieson-Drake, *Scribes and Schools in Monarchic Judah: A Sociological Approach,* SWBAS, 9 (Sheffield: Almond Press, 1991).

11. Judges 5 is normally accepted as an early tradition, dating to sometime in Iron Age I, and thus as preserving some fragmentary social information related to some isolated groups in Iron Age I Palestine. See, for example, Lawrence E. Stager, "The Song of Deborah—Why Some Tribes Answered the Call and Others Did Not," *BARev* XV (1989): 50–64.

12. For a recent survey of scholarship on the Deuteronomic History, see, for example, Douglas A. Knight, "Deuteronomy and the Deuteronomists," in Mays et al., *Old Testament Interpretation,* 61–79.

13. For a recent summary of various interpretations, see Michael G. Hasel, "*Israel* in the Merneptah Stela," *BASOR* 296 (1994): 45–61.

14. For example, William G. Dever, "How to Tell a Canaanite from an Israelite," in Herschel Shanks, ed., *The Rise of Ancient Israel* (Washington, D.C.: Biblical Archaeology Society, 1992), 26–56; Hasel, "*Israel* in the Merneptah Stela."

15. For example, Ahlström, *Who Were the Israelites?* 37–43; G. W. Ahlström and D. Edelman, "Merneptah's Israel," *JNES* 44 (1985): 59–61. For a critique of Ahlström's interpretation, see Anthony J. Frendo, "Five Recent Books on the Emergence of Ancient Israel: Review Article," *PEQ* 124 (1992): 145.

16. G. W. Ahlström, "The Origin of Israel in Palestine," *SJOT* 2 (1991): 19–34; D. Edelman, "Who or What Was Israel?" *BARev* 18/2 (1992): 21, 72–73.

17. For example, Niels Peter Lemche, *Ancient Israel: A New History of Israelite Society* (Sheffield: JSOT Press, 1988); Robert B. Coote, *Early Israel: A New Horizon* (Minneapolis: Fortress Press, 1990); W. Stiebing Jr., *Out of the Desert? Archaeology and the Exodus/Conquest Narratives* (Buffalo: Prometheus, 1989); J. Bimson, "Merneptah's Israel and Recent Theories of Israelite Origins," *JSOT* 49 (1991): 3–29.

18. Lawrence E. Stager, "The Archaeology of the Family in Ancient Israel," *BASOR* 260 (1985): 1–35; Dever, "How to Tell a Canaanite from an Israelite."

19. See Hasel, "*Israel* in the Merneptah Stela," 52–53.

20. See Frank J. Yurco, "3,200-Year-Old Picture of Israelites Found in Egypt," *BARev* 16/5 (1990), 20–38.

21. For example, Norman K. Gottwald, *The Tribes of Yahweh: A Sociology of the Religion of Liberated Israel, 1250–1050 B.C.E.* (Maryknoll, N.Y.: Orbis Books, 1979), 474–85; Lemche, *Ancient Israel,* 85–91.

22. Gottwald, *The Tribes of Yahweh,* 419–25, 489–97; Marvin L. Chaney, "Ancient Palestinian Peasant Movements and the Formation of Premonarchic Israel," in David Noel Freedman and David Frank Graf, eds., *Palestine in Transition: The Emergence of Ancient Israel,* SWBAS, 2 (Sheffield: Almond Press, 1983), 73–83; Ahlström, *Who Were the Israelites?* 16–19.

23. Publications on the material culture of Iron Age I Israel are too numerous to

include a comprehensive list here. For recent summaries, see, for example, Israel Finkelstein, *The Archaeology of the Israelite Settlement* (Jerusalem: Israel Exploration Society, 1988); Israel Finkelstein and Nadav Na'aman, eds., *From Nomadism to Monarchy: Archaeological and Historical Aspects of Early Israel* (Jerusalem: Israel Exploration Society, 1994); Volkmar Fritz, *The City in Ancient Israel* (Sheffield: Sheffield Academic Press, 1995), 50–75; Stager, "The Archaeology of the Family in Ancient Israel"; Dever, "How to Tell an Israelite from a Canaanite"; idem, "Archaeological Data on the Israelite Settlement: A Review of Two Recent Works," *BASOR* 284 (1991): 77–90; idem, *Recent Archaeological Discoveries and Biblical Research* (Seattle: University of Washington Press, 1990), 37–84.

The two other typical Iron Age I assemblages, that associated with the Philistines found primarily in the southern coastal plain and the Shephelah, and that associated with the lowland areas where the Late Bronze Age traditions continue, are not included in the survey of material culture in this chapter.

24. See, for example, Donald B. Redford, *Egypt, Canaan, and Israel in Ancient Times* (Princeton, N.J.: Princeton University Press, 1992); Itamar Singer, "Egyptians, Canaanites, and Philistines in the Period of the Emergence of Israel," in Finkelstein and Na'aman, *From Nomadism to Monarchy,* 282–338.

25. For the most recent information from excavations and surveys on site distribution, see Finkelstein, *The Archaeology of the Israelite Settlement,* 332–33; Finkelstein and Na'aman, *From Nomadism to Monarchy.*

26. Israel Finkelstein, "The Emergence of Israel: A Phase in the Cyclic History of Canaan in the Third and Second Millennia B.C.E.," in Finkelstein and Na'aman, *From Nomadism to Monarchy,* 160.

27. Finkelstein, *The Archaeology of the Israelite Settlement,* 330–35. See also M. Broshi, "The Population of Iron Age Palestine," in Avraham Biran and Joseph Aviram, eds., *Biblical Archaeology Today, 1990,* Proceedings of the Second International Congress on Biblical Archaeology; Supplement: Pre-Congress Symposium: Population, Production and Power (Jerusalem: Ketepress Enterprises, Ltd., 1993), 14–18. Broshi estimates the population for *all* of Iron Age Palestine (including the coastal regions) to have been about 60–70,000 in 1200 B.C.E., about 150,000 in 1000 B.C.E., and about 400,000 by 734 B.C.E.

28. Finkelstein, *The Archaeology of the Israelite Settlement,* 192–93.

29. Fritz, *The City in Ancient Israel,* 69–70; cf. Stager, "The Archaeology of the Family," 17–23; Finkelstein, *The Archaeology of the Israelite Settlement,* 238–54.

30. There are a few Iron Age I sites outside the central hill country proper that do not fit this pattern. A good example is Tel Masos. See chapters 3 and 4.

31. See, for example, Stager, "The Archaeology of the Family," 11–23; Finkelstein, *The Archaeology of the Israelite Settlement,* 254–59; Fritz, *The City in Ancient Israel,* 73–75.

32. Fritz, *The City in Ancient Israel,* 73–75.

33. See Rafael Frankel, "Upper Galilee in the Late Bronze Age–Iron I Transition," in Finkelstein and Na'aman, *From Nomadism to Monarchy,* 18–34.

34. For example, Dever, *Recent Archaeological Discoveries and Biblical Research;* idem, "Archaeological Data on the Israelite Settlement"; idem, "How to Tell a Canaanite from an Israelite."

35. For example, Finkelstein, *The Archaeology of the Israelite Settlement,* 270–91;

Israel Finkelstein and Nadav Na'aman, "Introduction: From Nomadism to Monarchy—The State of Research in 1992," in Finkelstein and Na'aman, *From Nomadism to Monarchy,* 9–17.

36. See Hopkins, *The Highlands of Canaan,* for a thorough discussion of the impact of various technologies on agriculture in Iron Age I Palestine. Hopkins challenges interpretations that place too much emphasis on cistern and terracing technologies as explanations for the increase in agriculture. He reconstructs a more complex picture, which takes into account diversity among ecosystems, labor resources, and risk-spreading strategies.

37. See, for example, Jane C. Waldbaum, *From Bronze to Iron: The Transition from the Bronze Age to the Iron Age in the Eastern Mediterranean* (Göteborg: Paul Åströms Förlag, 1978); Theodore A. Wertime and James D. Muhly, eds., *The Coming of the Age of Iron* (New Haven, Conn.: Yale University Press, 1980); T. Stech-Wheeler, J. D. Muhly, K. R. Maxwell-Hyslop, and R. Maddin, "Iron at Taanach and Early Iron Metallurgy in the Eastern Mediterranean," *AJA* 85 (1981): 245–68; McNutt, *The Forging of Israel,* 97–211.

38. Ucko, "Foreword," x–xi.

39. There is a fairly extensive literature on the issue of ethnic identity and its relationship to material culture by both anthropologists and archaeologists. See, for example, Hodder, *The Meaning of Things;* idem, *Symbols in Action: Ethnoarchaeological Studies of Material Culture* (Cambridge: Cambridge University Press, 1982); idem, *Symbolic and Structural Archaeology* (Cambridge, Cambridge University Press, 1982); S. Shennan, ed., *Archaeological Approaches to Cultural Identity* (London: Unwin Hyman, 1989).

40. See, e.g., Peter Parr, "Pottery, People, and Politics," in Roger Moorey and Peter Parr, eds., *Archaeology in the Levant: Essays for Kathleen Kenyon* (Warminster: Aris & Phillips, 1978), 202–9; Gloria London, "A Comparison of Two Contemporaneous Lifestyles of the Late Second Millennium B.C.," *BASOR* 273 (1989): 37–55.

41. See, e.g., Yigal Shiloh, "The Four-Room House: Its Situation and Function in the Israelite City," *IEJ* 20 (1970): 180–90; G. Ernest Wright, "A Characteristic North Israelite House," in Moorey and Parr, *Archaeology in the Levant,* 149–54.

42. See, e.g., Moawiyah Ibrahim, "The Collared Rim Jar of the Early Iron Age," in Moorey and Parr, *Archaeology in the Levant,* 116–25; Finkelstein, *The Archaeology of the Israelite Settlement,* 281–82.

43. See, e.g., William G. Dever, "Ceramics, Ethnicity, and the Question of Israel's Origins," *BA* 58 (1995): 200–213.

44. Israel Finkelstein, "The Great Transformation: The 'Conquest' of the Highlands Frontiers and the Rise of the Territorial States," in Levy, *The Archaeology of Society in the Holy Land,* 365. Cf. idem, *The Archaeology of the Israelite Settlement,* where Finkelstein's earlier criterion for labeling an Iron Age I site as "Israelite" was that the later inhabitants considered themselves to be Israelites.

45. For bibliographies of works supporting these hypotheses, see Gnuse, "New Directions in Biblical Theology," 894; Dever, *Recent Archaeological Discoveries and Biblical Research,* 37–84; George W. Ramsey, *The Quest for the Historical Israel* (Atlanta: John Knox, 1981).

46. See, for example, William Foxwell Albright, "Archaeology and the Date of the Hebrew Conquest of Palestine," *BASOR* 58 (1935), 10–18; idem, "The Israelite

Conquest of Canaan in the Light of Archaeology," *BASOR* 74 (1939): 11–23; cf. G. Ernest Wright, "The Literary and Historical Problem of Joshua 10 and Judges 1," *JNES* 5 (1946): 105–14.

47. Alt, *Essays in Old Testament History and Religion,* 133–69.

48. Noth, *The History of Israel,* 53–84; Manfred Weippert, *The Settlement of the Israelite Tribes in Palestine: A Critical Survey of Recent Scholarly Debate,* Studies in Biblical Theology 21 (Napierville, Ill.: Alec R. Allenson, 1971).

49. George E. Mendenhall, "The Hebrew Conquest of Palestine," *BA* 25 (1962): 66–87; idem, "The Hebrew Conquest of Canaan," in Edward F. Campbell and David Noel Freedman, eds., *Biblical Archaeologist Reader III* (Garden City, N.Y: Doubleday, 1970), 100–120.

50. Gottwald, *The Tribes of Yahweh.*

51. Cf. Gottwald, "Recent Studies," 167.

52. Gottwald, *The Tribes of Yahweh,* 25–29.

53. Ibid., xxiii.

54. Ibid., 398–408; cf. Baruch Halpern, *The Emergence of Israel in Canaan* (Chico, Calif.: Scholars Press, 1983), 50–63.

55. See, e.g., Gottwald, "Recent Studies," 163–89; idem, in Shanks, *The Rise of Ancient Israel,* 70–75.

56. Gottwald, *The Tribes of Yahweh,* 72–125, 883–84.

57. Ibid., 658–59.

58. Finkelstein, *The Archaeology of the Israelite Settlement,* 306–14.

59. Niels Peter Lemche, *Early Israel: Anthropological and Historical Studies on the Israelite Society before the Monarchy* (Leiden: E. J. Brill, 1985), 411–35; cf. idem, *Ancient Israel,* 75–117; idem, "Early Israel Revisited," *Currents in Research: Biblical Studies* 4 (1996), 9–34.

60. Lemche, *Ancient Israel,* 90.

61. Robert B. Coote and Keith W. Whitelam, "The Emergence of Israel: Social Transformation and State Formation following the Decline in Late Bronze Age Trade," *Semeia* 37 (1986): 107–47; idem, *The Emergence of Early Israel in Historical Perspective,* SWBAS, 5 (Sheffield: Almond Press, 1987). Cf. Whitelam, "The Identity of Early Israel"; Coote, *Early Israel.* Coote's reconstruction focuses heavily on the issue of early Israel's dependency on Egypt during the Late Bronze Age.

62. Coote and Whitelam, *The Emergence of Early Israel,* 11–26.

63. Another study that focuses on long-term trends is Thomas L. Thompson's *Early History of the Israelite People: From the Written and Archaeological Sources* (Leiden: E. J. Brill, 1992). Thompson maintains that the period of transition from the Late Bronze Age to Iron Age I in Palestine should be understood as reflecting the ways in which various regions of Palestine were affected by and responded to prolonged drought and famine brought on by a major climatic change. Thompson's study has been considered by many to be somewhat problematic. See, for example, Whitelam, "The Identity of Early Israel," 79–81. Whitelam agrees that climate is an important factor, but argues that sociopolitical factors are more important in understanding settlement shifts and that famine is frequently the result of sociopolitical factors rather than drought.

64. For example, Braudel, *The Mediterranean and the Mediterranean World;* idem, *On History.*

65. Whitelam, "The Identity of Early Israel," 80–83.

66. Gerhard and Jean Lenski, *Human Societies: An Introduction to Macrosociology,* 3d ed. (New York: McGraw-Hill, 1978). A fifth edition of this book was published in 1987.

67. Coote and Whitelam, *The Emergence of Early Israel,* 27–80. Cf. Finkelstein and Na'aman, "Introduction: From Nomadism to Monarchy," 14. Finkelstein and Na'aman identify Early Bronze I, Middle Bronze II, and Iron I as "waves of settlement," Early Bronze II, Middle Bronze III, and Iron II as periods associated with the foundation of large urban centers and extensive territorial formations, and the Intermediate and Late Bronze Ages as times of collapse into a severe settlement crisis.

68. Coote and Whitelam, *The Emergence of Early Israel,* 88–115.

69. Ibid., 128–29.

70. See especially Finkelstein, *The Archaeology of the Israelite Settlement;* idem, "The Emergence of Israel," 150–78; idem, *Living on the Fringe: The Archaeology and History of the Negev, Sinai and Neighboring Regions in the Bronze and Iron Ages* (Sheffield: Sheffield Academic Press, 1995); idem, "The Great Transformation," 349–65. Cf. Volkmar Fritz, "Conquest or Settlement? The Early Iron Age in Palestine," *BA* 50 (1987): 84–100; A. Kempinski and Volkmar Fritz, "Excavations at Tel Masos (Khirbet el Meshash), Preliminary Report on the Third Season, 1975," *Tel Aviv* 4 (1977): 136–58.

71. A number of other studies also argue that a major component of the Iron Age I settlers was from a nomadic background, primarily on the basis of references to the *shasu* in Egyptian New Kingdom texts. See, for example, Redford, *Egypt, Canaan, and Israel in Ancient Times,* 257–80; Anson F. Rainey, "Unruly Elements in Late Bronze Canaanite Society," in David P. Wright, David Noel Freedman, and Avi Hurvitz, eds., *Pomegranates and Golden Bells: Studies in Biblical, Jewish, and Near Eastern Ritual, Law, and Literature in Honor of Jacob Milgrim* (Winona Lake, Ind.: Eisenbrauns, 1995), 481–96. Cf. David C. Hopkins, "Pastoralists in Late Bronze Age Palestine: Where Did They Go?" *BA* 56 (1993): 200–211. For a general discussion of the processes of sedentarization and nomadization, see also Israel Finkelstein and Avi Perevolotsky, "Processes of Sedentarization and Nomadization in the History of Sinai and the Negev," *BASOR* 279 (1990): 67–88.

72. Finkelstein, *The Archaeology of the Israelite Settlement,* 20–21.

73. Ibid., 342–46.

74. In his 1995 study ("The Great Transformation," 354), Finkelstein explicitly identifies his work with the concept of *la longue durée.*

75. See, for example, M. Rowton, "Enclosed Nomadism," *Journal of the Economy and Social History of the Orient* XVII (1974): 1–30.

76. Finkelstein, *The Archaeology of the Israelite Settlement,* 336–51.

77. Cf. Fritz, *The City in Ancient Israel,* 71–72.

78. Finkelstein, *The Archaeology of the Israelite Settlement,* 198–234, 336–51.

79. Ibid., 244–50.

80. Ibid., 257. Cf. Volkmar Fritz, "The Israelite 'Conquest' in the Light of Recent Excavations at Khirbet el-Meshâsh," *BASOR* 241 (1981): 61–73. This proposal is not one that is generally accepted—see, e.g., Dever, "Archaeological Data on the Israelite Settlement," 79; Fritz, *The City in Ancient Israel,* 59.

81. Finkelstein, *The Archaeology of the Israelite Settlement,* 274.

82. Finkelstein, *The Archaeology of the Israelite Settlement,* 198–234, 336–51; idem, "The Emergence of Israel," 160–62; cf. Adam Zertal, "'To the Land of the Perrizites and the Giants': On the Israelite Settlement in the Hill Country of Manasseh," in Finkelstein and Na'aman, *From Nomadism to Monarchy,* 47–69; Avi Ofer, "'All the Hill Country of Judah': From a Settlement Fringe to a Prosperous Monarchy," in Finkelstein and Na'aman, *From Nomadism to Monarchy,* 106–9.

83. Finkelstein, "The Great Transformation," 352.

84. See, for example, Dever, *Recent Archaeological Discoveries,* 74–79; idem, "Archaeological Data on the Israelite Settlement."

85. Ibid., 86.

86. See also Finkelstein's *'Izbet Ṣarṭah: An Early Iron Age Site Near Rosh Ha'ayin, Israel,* BARIS, 299 (Oxford: BAR, 1986). Finkelstein and Na'aman's *From Nomadism to Monarchy* is now the most up-to-date synthesis of the archaeological material.

87. For reviews of the most recent models, see, e.g., Gnuse, "New Directions in Biblical Theology"; Gottwald, "Recent Studies"; Frendo, "Five Recent Books on the Emergence of Ancient Israel"; Dever, "Archaeological Data on the Israelite Settlement."

88. Gottwald, "Recent Studies," 165.

Chapter 3. Iron Age IA and B: The "Tribal" Period

1. Gottwald, *The Tribes of Yahweh.*

2. See, e.g., Halpern, *The Emergence of Israel,* 20–24.

3. See Halpern, *The Emergence of Israel,* 24–32. Halpern suggests that although these traditions in and of themselves should not be used to reconstruct history, they may nevertheless help corroborate reconstructions that have been deduced separately, if their origin and context can be identified. Halpern himself assumes an early date for these traditions.

4. Cf. Halpern, *The Emergence of Israel,* 172. Halpern asserts that this does not mean there was no tribal confederacy, just that its organizational structure may have been loose and decentralized.

5. For example, Halpern, in ibid.

6. See, e.g., Stager, "The Archaeology of the Family."

7. Much of the relevant archaeological information has been presented in chapter 2 and is only summarized here. As in that chapter, the summaries focus on highland sites.

8. Stager, "The Archaeology of the Family," 17–22; cf., e.g., Dever, "'Will the Real Israel Please Stand Up?'" 61–80.

9. See, e.g., Stager, "The Archaeology of the Family," 11–18.

10. See, e.g., Finkelstein, *The Archaeology of the Israelite Settlement,* 41–46; idem, "Arabian Trade and Socio-political Conditions in the Negev in the Twelfth–Eleventh Centuries B.C.E.," *JNES* 47 (1988): 241–52. Because of its uniqueness, Finkelstein does not include Tel Masos among the sites he considers to have been "Israelite." Cf. William G. Dever, "Archaeology and Israelite Origins: Review Article," *BASOR* 279 (1990): 89–95. Dever argues that there are problems with the stratigraphy and dating of Tel Masos, and that perhaps the date of the stratum identified as eleventh-

century by the excavators should be adjusted downward to at least the mid-tenth century.

11. See, e.g., Dever, "How to Tell a Canaanite from an Israelite," 43.

12. See, e.g., P. Kyle McCarter Jr., "The Origins of Israelite Religion," in Shanks, *The Rise of Ancient Israel,* 119–41.

13. Beno Rothenberg, *Timna: Valley of the Biblical Copper Mines* (London: Thames & Hudson, 1972), 183–84.

14. See, e.g., Finkelstein, *The Archaeology of the Israelite Settlement,* 212–20, 231–33.

15. See Adam Zertal, "An Early Iron Age Cultic Site on Mt. Ebal: Excavation Seasons 1982–1987," *Tel Aviv* 13–14 (1986–87), 105–65.

16. For arguments against the interpretation that it is a cult site, see, e.g., Aharon Kempinski, "Joshua's Altar—An Iron Age I Watch Tower," *BARev* January/February (1986): 43, 49–53; Dever, "How to Tell a Canaanite from an Israelite," 32–34.

17. For example, Finkelstein, *The Archaeology of the Israelite Settlement,* 82–85.

18. See, e.g., Amihai Mazar, "The 'Bull Site'—An Iron I Open Cult Place," *BASOR* 247 (1982): 27–41; Finkelstein, *The Archaeology of the Israelite Settlement,* 86–87.

19. Eickelman, *The Middle East,* 54–55.

20. On settlement patterns in the Negeb, see, e.g., Baruch Rosen and Israel Finkelstein, "Subsistence Patterns, Carrying Capacity and Settlement Oscillations in the Negev Highlands," *PEQ* 124 (1992): 42–58.

21. See Finkelstein, "The Great Transformation," 353.

22. Eickelman, *The Middle East,* 54.

23. The most extensive analysis of ancient Israel's subsistence system, incorporating analysis of biblical, archaeological, and cross-cultural data, appears in David Hopkins's *The Highlands of Canaan.* Hopkins shows that early Iron Age farmers in Palestine made use of a complex and diversified strategy, in which the economic base combined cultivation of grains, horticulture, and viticulture with stockbreeding and transhumant animal husbandry, demonstrating how complex, capital- and labor-intensive, and risky such an enterprise was. Hopkins gives particular attention to issues having to do with risk spreading. See also Frank S. Frick, "Ecology, Agriculture and Patterns of Settlement," in Clements, *The World of Ancient Israel,* 67–93.

24. Finkelstein argues that the highland frontier zones were inhabited by pastoralists in all periods of the third and second millennia B.C.E. See Finkelstein, "The Great Transformation," 353.

25. For a list of studies on pastoral nomadism in the Middle East, see Eickelman, *The Middle East,* 75 n. 2.

26. For a good discussion of the relations between nomadic and settled populations, see A. M. Khazanov, *Nomads and the Outside World,* trans. Julia Crookenden (Cambridge: Cambridge University Press, 1984).

27. Gottwald, *The Hebrew Bible,* 279.

28. For example, Lemche, *Ancient Israel,* 93–95.

29. For example, Gottwald, *The Tribes of Yahweh,* 292; S. Bendor, *The Social Structure of Ancient Israel* (Jerusalem: Simor Ltd., 1996); Stager, "The Archaeology of the Family," 20.

30. See Gottwald, *The Tribes of Yahweh,* 253.

31. Carney, *The Shape of the Past,* 141, 168–69.

32. Finkelstein, "Arabian Trade."

33. Cf. Dever, "Archaeology and Israelite Origins," 93. Dever argues that the high percentage of cattle bones recovered from Tel Masos indicates that the Iron Age I settlers there must have been experienced stockbreeders, who had been sedentary, not nomadic, for some time.

34. Lemche, *Early Israel,* 196–98.

35. Bendor, *The Social Structure of Ancient Israel,* 135–40.

36. For a comprehensive list of the types of tools and utensils produced with these technologies, see, e.g., Coote, *Early Israel,* 14–15.

37. See, e.g., Waldbaum, *From Bronze to Iron;* Wertime and Muhly, *The Coming of the Age of Iron;* Stech-Wheeler et al., "Iron at Taanach"; McNutt, *The Forging of Israel.*

38. Cf. the references to twelve-tribe associations among the Ishmaelites (Genesis 17; 25), the Aramaeans (Genesis 22), and the six Arab tribes (Genesis 25).

39. Cf. Frick, "Ecology, Agriculture and Patterns of Settlement," 78–79. Frick assumes that while these boundary descriptions do reflect later administrative divisions under the monarchy, they derive from a source representing tribal claims during the late premonarchic period. Cf. Halpern, *The Emergence of Israel.* Halpern also suggests the possibility that the notion of a twelve-tribe system antedates the early monarchy (p. 12), and that there was a full-blown tribal confederacy by the twelfth century (as indicated by Judges 5) (pp. 91–92).

40. See Lemche, *Early Israel,* 202–4.

41. See, e.g., Eickelman, *The Middle East,* 151–78.

42. See, e.g., Marshall D. Johnson, *The Purpose of Biblical Genealogies* (Cambridge: Cambridge University Press, 1969); Abraham Malamat, "Tribal Societies: Biblical Genealogies and African Lineage Systems," *Archives europées de sociologie* 14 (1973): 126–36; Robert R. Wilson, "The Old Testament Genealogies in Recent Research," *JBL* 94 (1975): 169–89; idem, *Genealogy and History in the Biblical World* (New Haven, Conn.: Yale University Press, 1977); James W. Flanagan, "Genealogy and Dynasty in the Early Monarchy of Israel and Judah," *Proceedings of the Eighth World Congress of Jewish Studies* (Jerusalem, 1982), 23–28; idem, "Succession and Genealogy in the Davidic Dynasty," in H. B. Huffmon et al., eds., *The Quest for the Kingdom of God: Studies in Honor of George E. Mendenhall* (Winona Lake, Ind.: Eisenbrauns, 1983), 35–55.

43. See Flanagan, "Genealogy and Dynasty," 24–25.

44. The concept of segmentation can be traced back to Émile Durkheim's *The Division of Labor in Society,* trans. George Simpson ([orig. 1893] New York: Free Press, 1933), 175. E. E. Evans-Pritchard's *The Nuer* (Oxford: Clarendon Press, 1940) contains the most thorough application of segmentary theory to an African society. For a review of issues of segmentation in the Middle East, see, e.g., Eickelman, *The Middle East,* 131–38; Paul Dresch, "Segmentation: Its Roots in Arabia and Its Flowering Elsewhere," *Cultural Anthropology* 3 (1988): 50–67; Steven Caton, "Power, Persuasion, and Language: A Critique of the Segmentary Model in the Middle East," *International Journal of Middle East Studies* 19 (1987): 77–102. See also Marshall D. Sahlins, "The Segmentary Lineage: An Organization of Predatory Expansion," *Anthropological Quarterly* 63 (1961): 322–46; Khazanov, *Nomads and the Outside World,* 144–48; Ernest Gellner, *Saints of the Atlas* (Chicago: University of Chicago

Press, 1969); idem, "Introduction to Nomadism," in Cynthia Nelson, ed., *The Desert and the Sown* (Berkeley: University of California Press, 1973), 1–10.

45. Gellner, "Introduction to Nomadism," 4; cited in Flanagan, *David's Social Drama,* 278–79.

46. Evans-Pritchard, *The Nuer,* 147.

47. Reference to the minimal sections as "lineages" is avoided, since patrilineal ties cannot be traced with precision.

48. Eickelman, *The Middle East,* 87–89.

49. Eickelman (ibid., 132–35) emphasizes that these notions are cultural *principles,* not directly observable "actual" social actions. The *principle* of segmentation and associated notions of person, responsibility, and honor serve in a sense as "native" models of the social order.

50. Gellner, "Introduction to Nomadism," 4.

51. Eickelman, *The Middle East,* 141–44.

52. See, e.g, Flanagan, *David's Social Drama,* 278–88; J. W. Rogerson, "Was Early Israel a Segmentary Society?" *JSOT* 36 (1986): 17–26; D. Fiensy, "Using the Nuer Culture of Africa in Understanding the Old Testament: An Evaluation," *JSOT* 38 (1987): 73–83; Gottwald, *The Tribes of Yahweh,* 322–33; F. Crüsemann, *Der Widerstand gegen das Königtum: Die antiköniglichen Texte des Alten Testamentes und der Kampf um den frühen israelitischen Staat* (Neukirchen-Vluyn: Neukirchener Verlag, 1978), 201–15; Frick, *The Formation of the State,* 51–69; Lemche, *Early Israel,* 202–30.

53. Eickelman, *The Middle East,* 133–35; cf. Lemche, *Early Israel,* 223–31; Rogerson, "Was Early Israel a Segmentary System?" Lemche and Rogerson argue that *segmentary lineage theory* is inadequate for understanding the situation in early "Israel."

54. Eickelman, *The Middle East,* 147.

55. See, e.g., Morton H. Fried, *The Notion of Tribe* (New York: Ramdom House, 1975); idem, *The Evolution of Political Society: An Essay in Political Anthropology* (New York: Random House, 1967).

56. This is perhaps the case in the Israelite monarchic construct of twelve tribal districts.

57. Eickelman, *The Middle East,* 128–29. For a thorough discussion of the types of relationships that exist among nomadic tribes and states, see., e.g., Khazanov, *Nomads and the Outside World.* The variety of ways in which tribes and states interrelate in contemporary Middle Eastern societies is also the subject of Philip S. Khoury and Joseph Kostiner, eds., *Tribes and State Formation in the Middle East* (Berkeley: University of California Press, 1990).

58. Østein S. LaBianca and Randall W. Younker, "The Kingdoms of Ammon, Moab and Edom: The Archaeology of Society in Late Bronze / Iron Age Transjordan (ca. 1400–500 B.C.E.)," in Levy, *The Archaeology of Society in the Holy Land,* 405.

59. Eickelman, *The Middle East,* 73.

60. LaBianca and Younker, "The Kingdoms of Ammon, Moab and Edom," 404.

61. Lemche, *Early Israel,* 111.

62. Eickelman, *The Middle East,* 128.

63. Lemche, *Early Israel,* 112–15.

64. Ibid., 116–18.

65. For example, Pedersen, *Israel;* de Vaux, *Ancient Israel.*

66. C. H. J. de Geus, *The Tribes of Israel: An Investigation into Some of the Presuppositions of Martin Noth's Amphictyony Hypothesis* (Assen: Van Gorcum, 1976). Although his study was not intended so much to present a social-scientific analysis of ancient "Israel" as it was to critique Martin Noth's amphictyonic hypothesis, and in retrospect is problematic in some respects, it was nevertheless important for providing the groundwork for further studies (for example, Gottwald's *The Tribes of Yahweh*). For critiques of de Geus's construct, see, e.g., Lemche, *Early Israel,* 66–76; James D. Martin, "Israel as a Tribal Society," in Clements, *The World of Ancient Israel,* 96.

At about the same time, George Mendenhall considered the issue of the nature of tribes and their social organization in Iron Age I Palestine. See George E. Mendenhall, *The Tenth Generation: The Origins of the Biblical Tradition* (Baltimore: Johns Hopkins University Press, 1973). Using only Elman Service's study of the evolution of society (Elman R. Service, *Primitive Social Organization* [New York: Random House, 1962]), however, and arguing that no form can have the same function in two different societies, Mendenhall concludes that although there are *some* incidental similarities between the early Israelite tribes and the characteristics of tribes as identified by anthropologists, ultimately the anthropological category of "tribe" does not fit the situation in ancient Palestine.

67. Cf. Halpern, *The Emergence of Israel,* 109–33, 145–63. Halpern makes a similar argument in his detailed discussion of the regional, historical, cultural, linguistic, and economic differences among the tribes.

68. Gottwald, *The Tribes of Yahweh,* 245–92.

69. Gottwald, *The Tribes of Yahweh,* 345–86; idem, *The Hebrew Bible,* 281–84. Cf. idem, "Recent Studies," in which he concedes that such a tribal organization may not have existed.

70. Gottwald, *The Tribes of Yahweh,* 338.

71. Ibid., 339.

72. For a thorough critique of Gottwald's reconstruction, see Lemche, *Early Israel.* Cf. Martin, "Israel as a Tribal Society."

73. Lemche, *Early Israel,* 282–90; idem, *Ancient Israel,* 98–109.

74. For example, Bendor, *The Social Structure of Ancient Israel,* 39.

75. In many cases *'eleph* refers to the number one thousand, but in some cases it appears to be used synonymously with *mišpāḥāh,* usually in military contexts. Gottwald (*The Tribes of Yahweh,* 270–76) defines it as a military unit based on the *mišpāḥāh*.

76. For a review of passages in which *bêt 'āb* and *mišpāḥāh* occur, see, e.g., Lemche, *Early Israel,* 245–72; Gottwald, *The Tribes of Yahweh,* 257–70, 285–92; Bendor, *The Social Structure of Ancient Israel,* passim.

77. Lemche in particular concludes that the *bêt 'āb* is used to refer to a variety of social groupings, ranging from the nuclear family up to and including the lineage.

78. For example, Gen. 18:19; 24:38; 24:40; 28:21.

79. For example, Gen. 24:38, 40, 41; Judg. 9:1; 2 Sam. 16:5.

80. For example, Deut. 29:17; 1 Sam. 9:21; 1 Sam. 10:21.

81. For example, the genealogies in Genesis 10 and 36 and Ex. 6:14–25; the description of the apportionment of land in Joshua 13–21; the census/genealogy list in Numbers 26; the census list in Num. 1:1–47. Bendor (*The Social Structure of Ancient*

Israel, 47) argues that the census lists and genealogical records, even though schematic, reflect to some extent the social pattern that existed in a number of different situations.

82. Ibid. Bendor's analysis is based primarily on the biblical texts, with some attention to anthropological models. For other reconstructions see, e.g., de Geus, *The Tribes of Israel;* Gottwald, *The Tribes of Yahweh,* 245–92; Lemche, *Early Israel,* 245–90.

83. Bendor, *The Social Structure of Ancient Israel,* 31.

84. A sib is a unilineal, usually exogamous, kin group based on a traditional common descent. The use of this particular term as a translation for *mišpāḥāh* is problematic, in that the ideal marriage pattern relating to this grouping in the biblical traditions appears to be endogamy rather than exogamy.

85. Although it does not enter into Bendor's discussion, another perspective may be represented in the occasional occurrence of *bêt 'ēm* ("mother's house"—e.g., Gen. 24:28; Judg. 9:1; Ruth 1:8; S. of Sol. 3:4; 8:2). With the exception of Judg. 9:1, the perspective represented is that of a woman. See Carol Meyers, "To Her 'Mother's House': Considering a Counterpart to the Israelite *Bêt 'āb,"* in Jobling et al., *The Bible and the Politics of Exegesis,* 39–51.

86. Bendor, *The Social Structure of Ancient Israel,* 40–41.

87. Evans-Pritchard, *The Nuer.*

88. Cf. Gottwald's argument that the *bêt 'āb* refers to the nuclear family and that the residential unit (which was not the *bêt 'āb* alone) contained up to five generations. Lemche notes in his review of contemporary Middle Eastern tribal societies that he did not come across any instances of a residential unit that large.

89. See, for example, Lev. 18:6–18; 20:11–12; Deut. 22:30; 27:20.

90. Lemche, *Early Israel,* 250–51; cf. Carney, *The Shape of the Past,* 89–92. Carney argues that in ancient societies, although the extended family was the norm among elites, the poor did not have the resources to live in extended families.

91. Lemche, *Early Israel.* The biblical material used to support this interpretation is cited on pp. 48–54 and 120–24.

92. Bendor, *The Social Structure of Ancient Israel,* 31. Passages Bendor identifies as clearly referring to the nuclear family include Gen. 42:19, 33; 45:18; Judg. 14:19. Other examples of passages in which *bêt 'āb* occurs are noted on pp. 45–47.

93. Num. 27:1–11 and 36:1–12 refer to surviving daughters' inheriting land in the absence of sons, with the stipulation that they must marry within their own *mišpāḥāh.*

94. Bendor, *The Social Structure of Ancient Israel,* 129–33.

95. Ibid., 202. Cf. Gottwald's assumption (in *The Tribes of Yahweh*) that a segmentary society is egalitarian.

96. See also Lemche, *Early Israel,* 120–24.

97. Bendor, *The Social Structure of Ancient Israel,* 118, 202–3.

98. Ibid., 118, 141–64.

99. For example, ibid., 31; de Geus, *The Tribes of Israel.* For this level of society, see also Lemche, *Early Israel,* 260–72; Gottwald, *The Tribes of Yahweh,* 249–51, 257–70, 282–84.

100. For example, de Geus, *The Tribes of Israel.*

101. For example, Lemche, *Early Israel,* 245–90.

102. For example, Bendor, *The Social Structure of Ancient Israel.*

103. Gottwald, *The Tribes of Yahweh,* 340. Protection of the *bêt 'āb* by the *mišpāḥāh,* in Gottwald's construct, consisted of supplying a male heir if necessary, safeguarding and preventing the alienation of the *bêt 'āb*'s property, redeeming its members from enslavement, and executing blood vengeance. These actions, according to Gottwald, were taken only in emergency situations, in order to return the *bêt 'āb* to its normal state as an autonomous unit. In ordinary circumstances the *mišpāḥāh* served essentially as a reassurance for the *bêt 'āb* within it. Arguing against the view that the *mišpāḥāh* was a clan, Gottwald asserts that it provided a social fabric with some of the bonding virtues of the true clan, but without placing restrictions on the family's primacy, and that it did not have the typical characteristics of a clan—that is, it was neither an exogamous unit nor a unilineal descent group.

104. Ibid., 318–21.

105. Bendor, *The Social Structure of Ancient Israel,* 84–86.

106. Lemche, *Early Israel,* 96–97, 231–44.

107. For example, Gen. 11:29; 20:12; 24:15; 29.

108. See, for example, Gen. 34:12; Ex. 22:16–17; Deut. 22:28–29; 1 Sam. 18:25.

109. See Bendor, *The Social Structure of Ancient Israel,* 67–79.

110. Ibid., 80–82.

111. Lemche, *Early Israel,* 269–72; idem, *Ancient Israel,* 95.

112. For example, Bendor, *The Social Structure of Ancient Israel,* 31, 36, 87–89; Lemche, *Early Israel;* de Geus, *The Tribes of Israel,* as noted above. Bendor does not include discussions of the nature of the tribe or of tribal society, nor does he address the problem of the tribe prior to the period of settlement or monarchy.

113. Joan M. Gero and Margaret W. Conkey, eds., *Engendering Archaeology: Women and Prehistory* (Oxford: Basil Blackwell, 1991).

114. Andrea Cornwall and Nancy Lindisfarne, eds., *Dislocating Masculinity: Comparative Ethnographies* (London: Routledge & Kegan Paul, 1994).

115. Peggy L. Day, ed., *Gender and Difference in Ancient Israel* (Minneapolis: Fortress Press, 1989).

116. Carol Meyers, *Discovering Eve: Ancient Israelite Women in Context* (Oxford: Oxford University Press, 1988); cf. idem, "Everyday Life: Women in the Period of the Hebrew Bible," in Carol Newsom and Sharon H. Ringe, eds., *The Women's Bible Commentary* (Louisville, Ky.: Westminster/John Knox Press, 1992), 244–51.

117. For example, M. K. Whyte, *The Status of Women in Preindustrial Societies* (Princeton, N.J.: Princeton University Press, 1978).

118. Meyers, *Discovering Eve,* 24–46.

119. Ibid., 139–64.

120. Ibid., 157–64.

121. For example, the myth of Cain and traditions about the Kenites and Midianites; see Paula M. McNutt, "The Kenites, the Midianites, and the Rechabites as Marginal Mediators in Ancient Israelite Tradition," *Semeia* 67 (1994): 109–32.

122. Turner, *Dramas, Fields, and Metaphors,* 233.

123. See, e.g., A. C. Hollis, *The Masai* (Oxford: Oxford University Press, 1905); G. W. B. Huntingford, "Free Hunters, Serf-Tribes and Submerged Classes in East Africa," *Man* 31 (1931): 262–66; William A. Shack, "Notes on the Occupational Castes among the Gurage of Southwest Ethiopia," *Man* 54 (1964): 50–52.

124. See, e.g., Carelton Stevens Coon, *Tribes of the Rif* (Cambridge, Mass.: Peabody Museum of Harvard University, 1931), 64–74, 92–95; idem, *The Story of the Middle East* (New York: Henry Holt, 1951), 200, 209, 248; H. R. P. Dickson, *The Arab of the Desert: A Glimpse into Badawin Life in Kuwait and Sau'di Arabia* (London: George Allen & Unwin, 1951), 515–25; Alois Musil, *The Manners and Customs of the Rwala Bedouins* (New York: American Geographic Society, 1928), 136–37, 281–82; C. A. O. van Nieuwenhuijze, *Social Stratification and the Middle East* (Leiden: E. J. Brill, 1965), 31–36; idem, ed., *Commoners, Climbers and Notables: A Sampler of Studies on Social Ranking in the Middle East* (Leiden: E. J. Brill, 1977); Raphael Patai, *The Kingdom of Jordan* (Princeton, N.J.: Princeton University Press, 1958), 161–63; idem, *Golden River to Golden Road: Society, Culture, and Change in the Middle East* (Philadelphia: University of Pennsylvania Press, 1967), 18, 90, 251–66.

125. See, e.g., Albright, *From the Stone Age to Christianity,* 257; idem, "Jethro, Hobab and Reuel in Early Hebrew Tradition," *CBQ* 25 (1963); idem, *Archaeology and the Religion of Israel,* 5th ed. (Garden City, N.Y.: Anchor Books, 1968), 96; de Vaux, *Ancient Israel,* 478–79; Baruch Halpern, "Kenites," in Freedman, ed., *The Anchor Bible Dictionary,* vol. 4.

126. In African mythology, smiths often play the role of culture hero. See, for example, Germaine Dieterlen, "A Contribution to the Study of Blacksmiths in West Africa," in Pierre Alexandre, ed., *French Perspectives in African Studies* (London: Oxford University Press, 1973), 40–61; Marcel Griaule, *Conversations with Ogotemmêli: An Introduction to Dogon Religious Ideas* (Oxford: Oxford University Press, 1965); Marcel Griaule and Germaine Dieterlen, "The Dogon," in Daryll Forde, ed., *African Worlds: Studies in the Cosmological Ideas and Social Values of African Peoples* (London: Oxford University Press, 1954), 83–110.

127. See, e.g., McNutt, "The Kenites, the Midianites, and the Rechabites"; B. Mazar, "The Sanctuary of Arad and the Family of Hobab the Kenite," *JNES* 24 (1965): 302–3; Yohanan Aharoni, "Nothing Early and Nothing Late: Rewriting Israel's Conquest," *BA* 39 (1976): 60; Frank Moore Cross, *Canaanite Myth and Hebrew Epic: Essays in the History of the Religion of Israel* (Cambridge, Mass.: Harvard University Press, 1973), 201–2, 206; Halpern, "Kenites," 19–20.

128. See Weber, *Ancient Judaism.*

129. See, e.g., Lemche, *Early Israel,* 118–20.

130. Eickelman, *The Middle East,* 90–91.

131. See, e.g., Frick, *The Formation of the State;* James W. Flanagan, "Chiefs in Israel," *JSOT* 20 (1981): 47–73; idem, *David's Social Drama;* Lemche, *Early Israel,* 277–79. Frick comes to this conclusion primarily on the basis of archaeological material, Lemche on the basis of texts, and Flanagan on the basis of both archaeological and textual materials.

132. Lemche, *Ancient Israel,* 96.

133. Ibid., 100–102.

134. Robert R. Wilson, "The Role of Law in Early Israelite Society," in Baruch Halpern and Deborah W. Hobson, eds., *Law, Politics and Society in the Ancient Mediterranean World* (Sheffield: Sheffield Academic Press, 1993), 90–99.

135. For recent discussions of religion in the Iron Age I period that consider archaeological information and/or give attention to the relationship between religion and society, see especially Rainer Albertz, *A History of Israelite Religion in the Old*

Testament Period, vol. 1: *From the Beginnings to the End of the Monarchy* (Louisville, Ky.: Westminster John Knox Press, 1994); J. Andrew Dearman, *Religion and Culture in Ancient Israel* (Peabody, Mass.: Hendrickson, 1992); Patrick D. Miller, Paul D. Hanson, and S. Dean McBride, eds., *Ancient Israelite Religion: Essays in Honor of Frank Moore Cross* (Philadelphia: Fortress Press, 1987); Hershel Shanks, ed., *The Rise of Ancient Israel* (Washington, D. C.: Biblical Archaeology Society, 1992); Finkelstein, *The Archaeology of the Israelite Settlement;* William G. Dever in numerous articles—see, e.g., "'Will the Real Israel Please Stand Up?' Part II: Archaeology and the Religions of Ancient Israel," *BASOR* 298 (1995): 37–58.

136. Robert R. Wilson, *Prophecy and Society in Ancient Israel* (Philadelphia: Fortress Press, 1980).

Chapter 4. Iron Age IC: The Rise of Monarchy

1. See, e.g., Halpern, *The Emergence of Israel in Canaan;* idem, *The Constitution of the Monarchy in Israel* (Chico, Calif.: Scholars Press, 1981). For more recent arguments, see, e.g., idem, "The Construction of the Davidic State: An Exercise in Historiography," in Volkmar Fritz and Philip R. Davies, eds., *The Origins of the Ancient Israelite States* (Sheffield: Sheffield Academic Press, 1996), 44–75. Halpern's argument in this article is not so much for the historicity of the biblical "Davidic-Solomonic" empire, as that the early sources in Samuel point to a more limited, though historically real, "united monarchy." For a more social-scientifically oriented argument in favor of the reliability of the biblical texts, see Christa Schäfer-Lichtenberger, "Sociological and Biblical Views of the Early State," in the same volume (pp. 78–105).

2. See Flanagan, *David's Social Drama,* 225–35.

3. See, e.g., James W. Flanagan, "The Relocation of the Davidic Capital," *JAAR* 47 (1979): 223–44; idem, "Social Transformation and Ritual in 2 Samuel 6," in Carol Meyers and Michael P. O'Connor, eds., *The Word of the Lord Shall Go Forth* (Winona Lakes, Ind.: Eisenbrauns, 1983), 362–72.

4. See, e.g., Flanagan, "Chiefs in Israel"; idem, "Succession and Genealogy"; idem, *David's Social Drama,* 242–46.

5. Ibid., 208.

6. On the lack of extrabiblical written sources for this period, see, e.g., Redford, *Egypt, Canaan, and Israel in Ancient Times,* 299–309.

7. For recent reviews of the tenth-century archaeological information, see, e.g., Flanagan, *David's Social Drama,* 119–88; Frick, *The Formation of the State;* John S. Holladay Jr., "The Kingdoms of Israel and Judah: Political and Economic Centralization in the Iron IIA–B (Ca. 1000–750 BCE)," in *The Archaeology of Society in the Holy Land,* 368–98.

8. E.g., Frick, *The Formation of the State,* 155–68; Stager, "The Archaeology of the Family," 23; cf. also Finkelstein, *The Archaeology of the Israelite Settlement;* Herzog, "The Beer-Sheba Valley: From Nomadism to Monarchy," in Finkelstein and Na'aman, *From Nomadism to Monarchy,* 122–49. Cf. Holladay ("The Kingdoms of Israel and Judah," 395 n. 14), who notes the recent lowering of the dates from Tel Masos by some interpreters.

9. On monumental architecture and the process of urbanization, see, e.g., Yigael Yadin, "Solomon's City Wall and Gate at Gezer," *IEJ* 8 (1958): 82–86; William G. De-

ver, "Monumental Architecture in Ancient Israel in the Period of the United Monarchy," in T. Ishida, ed. *Studies in the Period of David and Solomon,* (Winona Lake, Ind.: Eisenbrauns, 1982), 269–306; Holladay, "The Kingdoms of Israel and Judah"; Fritz, *The City in Ancient Israel,* 76–120.

10. Halpern, "The Construction of the Davidic State," 73.

11. See, e.g., D. Milson, "The Design of the Royal Gates at Megiddo, Hazor, and Gezer," *ZDPV* 102 (1986): 87–92; Ze'ev Herzog, "Settlement and Fortification in the Iron Age," in A. Kempinski and R. Reich, eds., *The Architecture of Ancient Israel: From the Prehistoric to the Persian Periods* (Jerusalem: Israel Exploration Society, 1992), 231–46.

12. See, e.g., D. Ussishkin, "Was the 'Solomonic' Gate at Megiddo Built by King Solomon?" *BASOR* 239 (1980): 1–18.

13. See, e.g., G. J. Wightman, "The Myth of Solomon," *BASOR* 277–78 (1990): 5–22; Israel Finkelstein, "On Archaeological Methods and Historical Considerations: Iron Age II and Samaria," *BASOR* 277–78 (1990): 109–19; idem, "Penelope's Shroud Unravelled: Iron II Date of Gezer's Wall Established," *Tel Aviv* 21 (1994): 276–82. Cf. William G. Dever, "On Myths and Methods," *BASOR* 277–78 (1990): 121–30; R. W. Younker, "A Preliminary Report of the 1990 Season at Tel Gezer: Excavations at the 'Outer Wall' and the 'Solomonic' Gateway (July 2–August 10, 1990)," *AUSS* 29 (1991): 19–60; A. Ben Tor, "Tel Hazor, 1994," *IEJ* (1995): 65–68. For an overview of the issues, see P. J. Ray, "The Great Controversy: The 'Outer Wall' at Gezer," *NEASB* 38 (1993): 39–52.

14. See Finkelstein, *The Archaeology of the Israelite Settlement,* 330–35; Broshi, "The Population of Iron Age Palestine"; M. Broshi and Israel Finkelstein, "The Population of Palestine in Iron Age II," *BASOR* 287 (1992): 50–53.

15. See Ofer, "'All the Hill Country of Judah,'" 13–14.

16. Ibid., 106.

17. See Ze'ev Herzog, "The Beer-Sheba Valley.

18. See, e.g., A. Mazar, "Iron Age Fortresses in the Judean Hills," *PEQ* 114 (1982): 87–109; R. Cohen, "The Iron Age Fortresses in the Central Negev," *BASOR* 236 (1981): 93–101; cf. Kenneth G. Hoglund, *Achaemenid Imperial Administration in Syria-Palestine and the Missions of Ezra and Nehemiah,* SBLDS, 125 (Atlanta: Scholars Press, 1992), 165–205. Hoglund dates a number of the Negeb fortresses to the fifth rather than the tenth century (see chapter 6 below). The interpretation of these sites as "fortresses" has also been questioned. See, e.g., Israel Finkelstein, "The Iron Age 'Fortresses' in the Negev and Wilderness of Beersheba," *Tel Aviv* 11 (1984): 189–209; idem, "Arabian Trade," 241–52; idem, *Living on the Fringe,* 104–29. Finkelstein suggests that these sites reflect the sedentarization of the local population.

19. There are numerous recent publications on the material culture of the Sea Peoples. For a fairly comprehensive, although not completely up-to-date, review of Philistine material culture, see Trude Dothan, *The Philistines and Their Material Culture* (New Haven, Conn.: Yale University Press, 1982). For a more recent summary, see, e.g., Lawrence E. Stager, "The Impact of the Sea Peoples in Canaan (1185–1050 BCE)," in *The Archaeology of Society in the Holy Land,* 332–48.

20. For recent reviews of the general state of scholarship on the United Monarchy and the evolution of the state, see, e.g., Israel Finkelstein, "The Emergence of the Monarchy in Israel: The Environmental and Socioeconomic Aspects," *JSOT* 44

(1989): 43–74; Gary N. Knoppers, "The Vanishing Solomon: The Disappearance of the United Monarchy from Recent Histories of Ancient Israel," *JBL* 116 (1997): 19–44.

21. On the issue of the historicity of the Court History, see, e.g., Flanagan, *David's Social Drama,* 35–40; David M. Gunn, *The Story of King David* (Sheffield: Almond Press, 1978), 30–33. On the district list, see, e.g., Paul S. Ash, "Solomon's? District? List," *JSOT* 67 (1995): 67–86.

22. Jamieson-Drake, *Scribes and Schools.* Jamieson-Drake draws this conclusion on the basis of an analysis of the archaeological evidence. The key variables in his analysis are: (1) evidence of centralized administrative control, (2) evidence of social stratification, and (3) evidence of the presence of full-time nonagricultural specialists. The archaeological correlates he identifies for these variables are: settlement patterns, public works, luxury items, and evidence of writing. Other arguments for a later date can be found in Davies, *In Search of Ancient "Israel,"* 64–66; G. Garbini, *History and Ideology in Ancient Israel* (London: SCM Press, 1988); Redford, *Egypt, Canaan, and Israel;* Niels Peter Lemche, "From Patronage Society to Patronage Society," in Fritz and Davies, *The Origins of the Ancient Israelite States,* 106–20; Thompson, *The Early History of the Israelite People.*

23. Ibid., 105.

24. For studies that focus on the effects of increased wealth and social stratification, see, e.g., Marvin L. Chaney, "Systematic Study of the Israelite Monarchy," *Semeia* 37 (1986): 53–76; Norman Gottwald, "The Participation of Free Agrarians in the Introduction of the Monarchy to Ancient Israel: An Application of H. A. Landsberger's Framework for the Analysis of Peasant Movements," *Semeia* 37 (1986): 77–106; Holladay, "The Kingdoms of Israel and Judah," 376–79.

25. Waldbaum, *From Bronze to Iron;* Wertime and Muhly, *The Coming of the Age of Iron;* McNutt, *The Forging of Israel,* 192–205.

26. E.g., Fried, *The Evolution of Political Society;* Elman R. Service, *Origins of the State and Civilization* (New York: W. W. Norton, 1975); Henri J. M. Claessan and Peter Skalnik, *The Early State* (The Hague: Mouton, 1978); idem, *The Study of the State* (The Hague: Mouton, 1981); Ronald Cohen and Elman R. Service, eds., *Origins of the State* (Philadelphia: Institute for the Study of Human Issues, 1978). For a more recent collection of studies of state formation in the Middle East, see Khoury and Kostiner, *Tribes and State Formation.*

27. See, e.g., Fried, *The Evolution of Political Society,* 227–42; Barbara J. Price, "Secondary State Formation: An Explanatory Model," in Cohen and Service, *Origins of the State,* 161–86; William T. Sanders and David Webster, "Unilinealism, Multilinealism and the Evolution of Complex Societies," in eds., C. L. Redman et al., *Social Archaeology: Beyond Subsistence and Dating* (New York: Academic Press, 1978), 249–302.

28. Flanagan, "Chiefs in Israel"; idem, *David's Social Drama;* Frick, *The Formation of the State.* In addition to the studies cited below, other recent studies that accept chieftaincy as a stage in the movement toward statehood in ancient Palestine include, for example, Finkelstein, "The Great Transformation"; Holladay, "The Kingdoms of Israel and Judah"; Juval Portugali, "Theoretical Speculations on the Transition from Nomadism to Monarchy," in Finkelstein and Na'aman, *From Nomadism to Monarchy,* 203–17.

29. Flanagan, "Chiefs in Israel." Saul's reign was referred to as a chiefdom earlier—see George E. Mendenhall, "The Monarchy," *Interpretation* 29 (1975): 155–70.

30. See also James W. Flanagan, "Succession and Genealogy in the Davidic Dynasty," in Huffmon et al., *The Quest for the Kingdom of God,* 35–55.

31. Colin Renfrew, "Beyond a Subsistence Economy: The Evolution of Social Organization in Prehistoric Europe," in Charlotte B. Moore, ed., *Reconstructing Complex Societies* (Cambridge, Mass.: American Schools of Oriental Research, 1974), 69–85.

32. Frick, *The Formation of the State;* cf. idem, "Social Science Methods and Theories of Significance for the Study of the Israelite Monarchy: A Critical Review Essay," *Semeia* 37 (1986): 9–52. In this article, Frick defines Saul's reign and the early days of David as an inchoate state, the later days of David as a typical state, and the reign of Solomon as a transitional early state on the threshold of a full-blown state. This contrasts with the earlier book in which he defines the kingdom of Saul and the early days of David as a chiefdom.

33. Frick, *The Formation of the State,* 9–11.

34. Ibid., 13–50.

35. R. N. Adams, *Energy and Structure* (Austin: University of Texas Press, 1975).

36. The conflict approach is represented by Fried (e.g., *The Evolution of Political Society*) and others who focus on change and assume that dissent and conflict are the fundamental features of social systems. From this perspective, centralization can arise out of either internal or external conflicts, although conflict between states and nonstate polities are the most significant cause of the emergence of secondary states.

37. This is a structural-functional approach, represented by Service and others, in which societies are generally regarded as basically stable, homeostatic systems. It focuses on the capacity of the emerging state system to coordinate and organize large numbers of people.

38. Price, "Secondary State Formation."

39. Sanders and Webster, "Unilinealism, Multilinealism, and the Evolution of Complex Societies."

40. Colin Renfrew, "Systems Collapse as Social Transformation: Catastrophe and Anastrophe in Early State Societies," in Colin Renfrew and K. L. Cooke, eds., *Transformations: Mathematical Approaches to Culture Change* (New York: Academic Press, 1979), 481–506.

41. Frick, *The Formation of the State,* 71–97.

42. D. Webster, "Warfare and the Evolution of the State: A Reconsideration," *American Antiquity* 40 (1975): 464–70.

43. On patron-client relationships and the evolution of the state, see also Lemche, "From Patronage Society to Patronage Society"; idem, "Kings and Clients: On Loyalty between the Ruler and the Ruled in Ancient 'Israel,'" *Semeia* 66 (1994): 119–32. Other studies that propose the significance of patron-client relationships in this period include Finkelstein, "The Great Transformation," 361–62; idem, "The Emergence of the Monarchy"; Flanagan, *David's Social Drama.*

44. C. S. Peebles and S. M. Kus, "Some Archaeological Correlates of Ranked Societies," *American Antiquity* 42 (1977): 421–48.

45. T. K. Earle, *Economic and Social Organization of a Complex Chiefdom: The Halelea District, Kahua'i, Hawaii* (University of Michigan Museum of Anthropology Paper No. 63, 1978).

46. Frick, *The Formation of the State,* 99–189.

47. Leon Marfoe, "The Integrative Transformation: Patterns of Sociopolitical Organization in Southern Syria," *BASOR* 234 (1979): 1–42.

48. Holladay ("The Kingdoms of Israel and Judah," 395 n. 14) argues that recent reevaluations of the archaeological material, particularly the lowering of the dates for Tel Masos by some interpreters, have compromised Frick's use of some of the archaeological materials.

49. Frick, *The Formation of the State,* 191–204.

50. Coote and Whitelam, *The Emergence of Early Israel,* 139–66; cf. idem, "The Emergence of Israel."

51. For another reconstruction based on the *longue durée* perspective, see, e.g., Finkelstein, "The Great Transformation." Finkelstein argues in this article that it was not the "Israelite Settlement," but the emergence of monarchy, that was the "exceptional event" in the late second to early first millennium, and that the later direct rule of foreign empires brought to an end the cyclical processes of the third and second millennia that were associated with local ecological and socioeconomic factors (362).

52. R. L. Carneiro, "A Theory of the Origins of the State," *Science* 169 (1970): 733–38.

53. Cf. Hopkins, *The Highlands of Canaan.*

54. R. Cohen, "State Origins: A Reappraisal," in Claessen and Skalnik, *The Early State,* 31–75; idem, "Evolution, Fission, and the Early State," in Claessen and Skalnik, *The Study of the State,* 87–115.

55. For a recent study on the formation of the "state" in Ammon, Moab, and Edom, see LaBianca and Younker, "The Kingdoms of Ammon, Moab and Edom," 399–415. Using evidence of food systems as a barometer of local-level social organization, LaBianca and Younker propose that the political entities of Ammon, Moab, and Edom were not true states, but rather are better described as "tribal kingdoms"—polities that gave greater prominence to the cooperative networks customarily forged by tribal peoples as a means of countering external threats to their territories (p. 399). Their argument that these kingdoms are best understood as "tribal kingdoms" rather than "states" is based in part on what they view as the *absence* of a number of essential features which typify true states. In true states, such as those of Late Bronze Age western Palestine, the role of kinship relations is diminished, religion and political authority are typically separate, the ruler usually maintains a standing army, a significant amount of the population is settled in urban centers that are part of a pronounced settlement hierarchy, and there is a significant amount of ethnic plurality and social differentiation (p. 409).

56. Renfrew, "Systems Collapse as Social Transformation," 499.

57. Stager, "The Archaeology of the Family," 18–23; Frick, *The Formation of the State,* 160–61.

58. Flanagan, *David's Social Drama.*

59. Ibid., 77–88.

60. On the analytical distinction between the domains of actions and notions, see ibid., 89–103.

61. Flanagan cites many of the anthropological studies included also in Frick's and Coote and Whitelam's analyses. Among the other studies cited by Flanagan, those which stand out most prominently are works by Ernest Gellner, Jack Goody, Ladislav Holy and Milan Stuchlik, Anatolii Khazanov, Edmund Leach, Roy A. Rappaport, and Victor Turner.

62. Flanagan, *David's Social Drama,* 9.
63. Ibid., 119–88.
64. Ibid., 168.
65. Ibid., 185–87.
66. Ibid., 196–272.
67. For another recent examination of the different models of David in the biblical texts, see Walter Brueggemann, *David's Truth in Israel's Imagination and Memory* (Philadelphia: Fortress Press, 1985).
68. Flanagan, *David's Social Drama,* 271.
69. Ibid., 275–318.
70. Ibid., 276.
71. Moiety refers to the division of a society into halves. In many societies membership in a moiety is ascribed by unilineal descent, and each half is exogamous.
72. Roy A. Rappaport, *Ecology, Meaning and Religion* (Richmond, Calif.: North Atlantic Books, 1979).
73. Christa Schäfer-Lichtenberger, "Sociological and Biblical Views of the Early State," in Fritz and Davies, *The Origins of the Ancient Israelite States,* 78–105.
74. Ibid., 94–105.
75. Ibid., 90–91.

Chapter 5. Iron Age II: The Period of the Monarchy

1. For a survey of some potentially useful models of agrarian societies for studying the monarchy, see Marvin L. Chaney, "Systematic Study of the Israelite Monarchy," *Semeia* 37 (1986): 53–76.
2. Lemche, *Ancient Israel,* 122. For reviews of recent evaluations of the historical worth of these books, see, e.g., Knight, "Deuteronomy and the Deuteronomists"; Robert R. Wilson, "The Former Prophets: Reading the Books of Kings," in Mays et al., *Old Testament Interpretation,* 83–96.
3. See, e.g., Giorgio Buccellati, *Cities and Nations of Ancient Syria: An Essay on Political Institutions with Special Reference to the Israelite Kingdoms* (Rome: Instituto di Studi del Vicino Oriente, 1967); Tryggve Mettinger, *Solomonic State Officials: A Study of the Civil Government Officials of the Israelite Monarchy* (Lund: CWK Gleerup, 1971).
4. See references in chapter 1.
5. For recent summaries of the social information provided by Iron Age II archaeological materials, see, e.g., Holladay, "The Kingdoms of Israel and Judah"; William G. Dever, "Social Structure in Palestine in the Iron II Period on the Eve of Destruction," in Levy, *The Archaeology of Society in the Holy Land,* 416–31. For Judah, see also Jamieson-Drake, *Scribes and Schools.*
6. For a succinct summary, see the table identifying archaeologically discernible characteristics of the state in Holladay, "The Kingdoms of Israel and Judah," 373.
7. Ibid., 394 n. 4; Dever, "Social Structure in Palestine," 419.
8. Dever, "Social Structure in Palestine," 422–23.
9. Holladay, "The Kingdoms of Israel and Judah," 373.
10. See, e.g., Dever, "Social Structure in Palestine," 421; and especially Elizabeth Bloch-Smith, *Judahite Burial Practices and Beliefs about the Dead* (Sheffield: JSOT

Press, 1992) where full treatment of Israelite and Judean burial customs appears; cf. idem, "The Cult of the Dead in Judah: Interpreting the Material Remains," *JBL* 111 (1992): 213–24.

11. Dever, "Social Structure in Palestine," 424.

12. See, e.g., Niditch, *Oral World and Written Word.*

13. Magen Broshi and Israel Finkelstein, "The Population of Palestine in Iron Age II," *BASOR* 287 (1992): 47–60; cf. Broshi, "The Population of Iron Age Palestine," who estimates an increase from about 60–70,000 in 1200 B.C.E. (including the coastal regions) to about 150,000 in 1000 B.C.E., to about 400,000 by the middle of the eighth century. Finkelstein's 1988 study (*The Archaeology of the Israelite Settlement*) estimates 28,000+ for Benjamin, Ephraim, and Manasseh in the tenth century. For Jerusalem and its outskirts, Yigal Shiloh estimates a population of 25–40,000 by the end of the eighth century; see Yigal Shiloh, "Judah and Jerusalem in the Eighth–Sixth Centuries B.C.E.," in Seymour Gitin and William G. Dever, eds., *Recent Excavations in Israel: Studies in Iron Age Archaeology* (Winona Lake, Ind.: Eisenbrauns, 1989), 97–106. If Broshi and Finkelstein are anywhere near correct in their estimates of the total population, this figure is very high.

14. See, e.g., Carney, *The Shape of the Past,* 84–85.

15. Lemche, *Early Israel,* 164–201; cf. Douglas A. Knight, "Political Rights and Powers in Monarchic Israel," *Semeia* 66 (1994): 99; Frank S. Frick, *The City in Ancient Israel,* SBLDS, 36 (Missoula, Mont.: Scholars Press, 1977), 91–97.

16. Dever, "Social Structure in Palestine," 418.

17. Fritz, *The City in Ancient Israel,* 117–20; cf. Frick, *The City in Ancient Israel,* 136–42. Frick distinguishes store cities, chariot cities / cities for defense, and Levitical cities (which he suggests may have been administrative and fiscal centers).

18. Fritz, *The City in Ancient Israel,* 130.

19. Ibid., 152.

20. David Hopkins, "Bare Bones: Putting Flesh on the Economics of Ancient Israel," in Fritz and Davies, *The Origins of the Ancient Israelite States,* 124.

21. See, e.g., Stager, "The Archaeology of the Family"; Hopkins, *The Highlands of Canaan.*

22. Hopkins, *The Highlands of Canaan,* 245–54.

23. See Carney, *The Shape of the Past,* 99.

24. See, e.g., Hopkins, "Bare Bones," 128; Holladay, "The Kingdoms of Israel and Judah," 390.

25. Ibid., 391.

26. Carney, *The Shape of the Past,* 193–204.

27. Ibid., 214–15.

28. Holladay, "The Kingdoms of Israel and Judah," 382.

29. See Carney, *The Shape of the Past,* 176–77; M. I. Finley, *The Ancient Economy* (Berkeley: The University of California Press, 1973); Douglas E. Oakman, *Jesus and the Economic Questions of His Day* (Lewiston, N.Y.: Edwin Mellen Press, 1986). The authors of the studies argue that even by the time of the Roman period, there was little, if any, market competition. Cf. Morris Silver, *Prophets and Markets: The Political Economy of Ancient Israel* (Boston: Kluwer-Nijhoff Publishing, 1983). Silver, who is an economist, argues that the Israelite economy during the eighth and seventh centuries was ". . . a living economy whose entrepreneurs . . . responded positively and

rationally to market economies" (p. 24). In support of this argument, Silver cites archaeological evidence of "industrial installations" for the manufacture of ceramics, textiles, olive oil, wine, and metalworking (pp. 13–18), and biblical references to the export of commodities to Egypt and Phoenicia (e.g., Hos. 12:2; Ezek. 27:17; 1 Kings 5:20–25; 2 Chron. 2:9; Ezra 3:7). He also interprets the Samaria ostraca and *lmlk* stamps on storage jars as evidence of a market economy (see below). I do not find Silver's arguments convincing. The "industrial installations" used as evidence for a market economy, for example, could just as easily point to the presence of workshops and storehouses that were part of a system based on reciprocity and redistribution.

30. Carney, *The Shape of the Past,* 204.

31. Hopkins, "Bare Bones," 124–25.

32. See Carney, *The Shape of the Past,* 141, 172–75, 204.

33. See, e.g., Hopkins, "Bare Bones," 127–28; Dever, "Social Structure in Palestine," 424; cf. Silver, *Prophets and Markets,* 29–34. Silver argues that these stamps are evidence of commerce, refuting the interpretation that they were royally owned. For him, they reflect the existence of private brands of wine, oil, or pottery, that is, organized private enterprise, and the reference to the king on the stamps merely suggests that the products were "fit for kings or even the gods" (p. 34).

34. See, e.g., Dever, "Social Structure in Palestine," 424; Fritz, *The City in Ancient Israel,* 170; cf. Silver, *Prophets and Markets,* 35–38. Silver argues that the location of the warehouses in the citadel, where the ostraca were found, is not conclusive evidence of ownership and management by the monarchy. He suggests, rather, that they were private warehouses, located within the walled area of the city for security reasons.

35. Carney, *The Shape of the Past,* 172–75.

36. See Jamieson-Drake, *Scribes and Schools,* 126–28. Jamieson-Drake notes that there is little in the way of evidence for any significant amount of foreign trade in Judah. With the exception of Jerusalem, and possibly Lachish, his survey indicates that for the eighth to seventh centuries, all the evidence for imports comes from forts.

37. The classic works that consider economy in peasant societies are Eric R. Wolf, *Peasants* (Englewood Cliffs, N.J.: Prentice-Hall, 1966) and Robert Redfield, *Peasant Society and Culture* (Chicago: University of Chicago Press, 1956). For a more recent work, see, e.g., Gerhard and Jean Lenski, *Human Societies: An Introduction to Macrosociology.* 5th ed. (New York: McGraw-Hill, 1987).

38. For a recent evaluation of the biblical ideals associated with land ownership, see, e.g., Eryl W. Davies, "Land: Its Rights and Privileges," in Clements, *The World of Ancient Israel,* 349–69.

39. Marvin L. Chaney suggests that debt easement was associated with factionalism among elites. See Marvin L. Chaney, "Debt Easement in Israelite History and Tradition," in Jobling et al., *The Bible and the Politics of Exegesis,* 127–39.

40. Weber, *Ancient Judaism,* 56–57.

41. See Bendor's discussion of Alt in *The Social Structure of Ancient Israel,* 270–79.

42. Gottwald, *The Hebrew Bible,* 323–25; cf., e.g., idem, "Social Class as an Analytic and Hermeneutical Category in Biblical Studies," *JBL* 112 (1993): 3–22; Chaney, "Systematic Study of the Israelite Monarchy."

43. For example, Bendor, *The Social Structure of Ancient Israel,* 268–70.
44. Ibid., 209–10.
45. Ibid., 244.
46. Ibid., 36.
47. Mettinger suggests that there would have been two types of government-controlled land: (1) government-managed land farmed under the direction of governmental functionaries; and (2) govenment land assigned to officials, priests, nobles, and other elites. But Mettinger also argues that there is no evidence of a serious clash between the former tribal conception of landed property and the royal prerogatives introduced by centralization. Mettinger, *Solomonic State Officials,* 80–87.
48. Holladay, "The Kingdoms of Israel and Judah," 390–93.
49. See Hopkins, "Bare Bones," 138–39.
50. See, e.g., Waldbaum, *From Bronze to Iron;* Wertime and Muhly, *The Coming of the Age of Iron;* Stech-Wheeler et al., "Iron at Taanach"; McNutt, *The Forging of Israel.*
51. See Colin Renfrew, "The Anatomy of Innovation," in *Approaches to Social Archaeology* (Edinburgh: Edinburgh University Press, 1984), 390–418; cf. Lenski and Lenski, *Human Societies,* 58–72.
52. See Dennis Heskel and Carl Clifford Lamberg-Karlovsky, "An Alternative Sequence for the Development of Metallurgy: Tepe Yahya, Iran," in Wertime and Muhly, *The Coming of the Age of Iron,* 229–65.
53. Eickelman, *The Middle East,* 127; cf. LaBianca and Younker, "The Kingdoms of Ammon, Moab and Edom," 405.
54. Cf. Lemche, *Ancient Israel,* 150–51. Lemche argues that the tribe no longer had any political role, the state assumed all the former functions of the tribe. Kinship groups continued to exist, but had no significance outside local communities.
55. Bendor, *The Social Structure of Ancient Israel,* 92.
56. See Lemche, *Early Israel,* 111.
57. For example, Weber, *Ancient Judaism;* de Vaux, *Ancient Israel;* Gottwald, *The Hebrew Bible.*
58. Bendor, *The Social Structure of Ancient Israel,* 32–33, 165–67, 216–28. Cf. Lemche, *Ancient Israel,* 151; idem, *Early Israel,* 261, 265; Halpern, *The Constitution of the Monarchy,* 215–16. Lemche argues that the local significance of the kinship group was eventually *reduced,* as local administrators were introduced in connection with the development of a national administration, but that the lineage system continued to function, in spite of the decline in the political significance of the tribe. Halpern suggests that tribal organization continued to exist alongside national administration, and that the kinship system did not break down.
59. Ibid., 98–99, 219.
60. Ibid., 102–3.
61. Ibid., 118.
62. Carney, *The Shape of the Past,* 89–92; cf. Frick, *The City in Ancient Israel,* 105–6.
63. See especially Mettinger, *Solomonic State Officials,* and de Vaux, *Ancient Israel.*
64. The most extensive analysis of these terms and the functions of individuals who filled these offices is Mettinger's, *Solomonic State Officials.* Mettinger's study is

primarily a text-critical examination that considers the terms in relation to possible foreign prototypes. His analysis suggests a considerable amount of Egyptian influence. Cf. E. W. Heaton, *Solomon's New Men: The Emergence of Ancient Israel as a Nation State* (New York: Pica Press, 1974). Heaton argues that these offices were a conscious imitation of Egyptian civil servants. Cf. also Donald B. Redford, "Studies in Relations between Palestine and Egypt During the First Millennium B.C.E.: The Taxation System of Solomon," in J. Wevers and D. B. Redford, eds., *Studies in the Ancient Palestinian World* (Toronto: University of Toronto Press, 1972), 141–56. Redford disagrees with the proposal that the system of court officials was modeled after that of Egypt, but agrees that the system of taxation was influenced by Egypt.

65. See, e.g., Mettinger, *Solomonic State Officials,* 140–57; André Lemaire, *Les Écoles et la formation de la Bible dans l'ancien Israël* (Göttingen: Vandenhoeck & Ruprecht, 1981); James L. Crenshaw, "Education in Ancient Israel," *JBL* 104 (1985): 601–15; Jamieson-Drake, *Scribes and Schools;* Joseph Blenkinsopp, *Sage, Priest, Prophet: Religious and Intellectual Leadership in Ancient Israel* (Louisville, Ky.: Westminster John Knox Press, 1995), 9–65.

66. For recent social-science-oriented studies of these roles, see Lester L. Grabbe, *Priests, Prophets, Diviners, Sages: A Socio-Historical Study of Religious Specialists in Ancient Israel* (Valley Forge, Pa.: Trinity Press International, 1995); Blenkinsopp, *Sage, Priest, Prophet.*

67. See McNutt, *The Forging of Israel,* 235–49; idem, "The Kenites, the Midianites, and the Rechabites."

68. On artisans in Mesopotamia, see, e.g., Ann C. Gunter, ed., *Investigating Artistic Environments in the Ancient Near East* (Washington, D. C.: Arthur M. Sackler Gallery, Smithsonian Institution, 1990).

69. Frick, *The City in Ancient Israel,* 127–35.

70. Weber, *Ancient Judaism,* 28–29.

71. See Frank S. Frick, "The Rechabites Reconsidered," *JBL* 90 (1971): 279–87; idem, "Rechab," in Freedman, ed., *The Anchor Bible Dictionary,* 5:630–32; Halpern, "Kenites"; McNutt, *The Forging of Israel,* 243–49; idem, "The Kenites, the Rechabites, and the Midianites." The interpretation that the Rechabites may have been smiths is based on a genealogical link with the Kenites in 1 Chron. 2:55.

72. Guild organization in the Persian period is suggested in 1 Chron. 2:55; 4:14, 21; and Neh. 3:8, 31.

73. For a recent study of those with low status, see, e.g., Paula S. Hiebert, "'Whence Shall Help Come unto Me?' The Biblical Widow," in Day, *Gender and Difference,* 125–41.

74. Gillian Feeley-Harnick, "Is Historical Anthropology Possible? The Case of the Runaway Slave," in Gene M. Tucker and Douglas A. Knight, eds., *Humanizing America's Iconic Book* (Chico, Calif.: Scholars Press, 1982), 95–126.

75. Ibid., 108–9.

76. Ibid., 125.

77. See Carney, *The Shape of the Past,* 171; Lemche, "From Patronage Society to Patronage Society"; idem, "Kings and Clients"; cf. Coote, *Early Israel,* 20–25.

78. Lemche ("Kings and Clients," 120; "From Patronage Society to Patronage Society," 110–11) suggests that patron-client relationships do not exist in bureaucratic states unless they are beginning to fall apart.

79. Meyers, "Everyday Life," 250–51; idem, *Discovering Eve,* 186–96. Anthropological studies cited by Meyers include Laurel Bossen, "Women and Economic Institutions," in Stuart Plattner, ed., *Economic Anthropology* (Stanford, Calif.: Stanford University Press, 1989), 318–50; Carol R. Ember, "The Relative Decline in Women's Contribution to Agriculture with Intensification," *American Anthropologist* 85 (1983): 285–304; Irene Silverblatt, "Women in States," *Annual Review of Anthropology* 17 (1988): 427–60. Cf. Grace I. Emmerson, "Women in Ancient Israel," in Clements, *The World of Ancient Israel,* 371–94. Emmerson offers a generally positive evaluation of women's status.

80. See, e.g., Athalya Brenner, *The Israelite Woman: Social Role and Literary Type in the Biblical Narrative* (Sheffield: JSOT Press, 1994).

81. Alt, *Essays in Old Testament History and Religion,* 239–59.

82. See, e.g., Buccellati, *Cities and Nations,* 200–208; Lemche, *Ancient Israel,* 147–48; Tomoo Ishida, *The Royal Dynasties in Ancient Israel: A Study on the Formation and Development of Royal-Dynastic Ideology* (New York: Walter de Gruyter, 1977), 171–82; Knight, "Political Rights and Powers," 101–2. Alt's hypothesis was refuted particularly forcefully by Giorgio Buccellati, although it is still affirmed in many general introductions and histories. Buccellati's study focuses in large part on refuting Alt's proposal that the Northern Kingdom was characterized by the ideal of charismatic leadership, and his assertions that both Jerusalem and Samaria were city-states during the monarchic period. Although there are problems with Buccellati's study—e.g., his assumptions that Israel evolved out of a nomadic background, and that the biblical traditions contain essentially accurate historical information—his refutations of Alt's hypotheses are nevertheless convincing.

83. See, e.g., Lemche, *Ancient Israel,* 146; Finkelstein, "The Great Transformation," 362.

84. See Carney, *The Shape of the Past,* 115–21; Keith W. Whitelam, "The Symbols of Power: Aspects of Royal Propaganda in the United Monarchy," *BA* 49 (1986): 166–73; idem, "Israelite Kingship: The Royal Ideology and Its Opponents," in Clements, *The World of Ancient Israel,* 119–39.

85. See, e.g., Lemche, "Kings and Clients"; Keith W. Whitelam, *The Just King: Monarchical Authority in Ancient Israel* (Sheffield: JSOT Press, 1979); idem, "Symbols of Power"; Liverani, "Propaganda."

86. Knight, "Political Rights and Powers," 103–4.

87. Ibid., 102; Carney, *The Shape of the Past,* 115–21.

88. Ibid., 73–74; Frick, *The City in Ancient Israel,* 114–15.

89. See, e.g., Mettinger, *Solomonic State Officials,* 111–27.

90. C. A. O. van Nieuwenhuijze, "The Near Eastern Village: A Profile," *The Middle East Journal* 16 (1962): 295–308.

91. Knight, "Political Rights and Powers," 105–9.

92. Ibid., 109–10.

93. Ibid., 105–9. On the roles of elders, see also, e.g., Frick, *The City in Ancient Israel,* 116–27; Halpern, *The Constitution of the Monarchy,* 198–206.

94. See, e.g., Eryl W. Davies, "Ethics of the Hebrew Bible: The Problem of Methodology," *Semeia* 66 (1994): 43–53; Bernard S. Jackson, "Ideas of Legal Administration: A Semiotic Approach," in Clements, *The World of Ancient Israel,* 185–202;

Lyn M. Bechtel, "Shame as a Sanction of Social Control in Biblical Israel: Judicial, Political, and Social Shaming," *JSOT* 49 (1991): 47–76.

95. Wilson, "The Role of Law," 96–97.

96. Ibid.

97. Ibid.

98. Knight, "Political Rights and Powers," 105–9.

99. On the problem of defining "popular religion," see J. Berlinerblau, "The 'Popular Religion' Paradigm in Old Testament Research: A Sociological Critique," *JSOT* 60 (1993): 3–26. For recent studies that deal with popular religion, see, e.g., Mark S. Smith, *The Early History of God: Yahweh and the Other Deities in Ancient Israel* (New York: Harper & Row, 1990); Albertz, *A History of Israelite Religion.*

100. On the question of women's religious expressions, see, e.g., Phyllis A. Bird, "The Place of Women in the Israelite Cultus," in Miller et al., *Ancient Israelite Religion,* 397–419; idem, "Israelite Religion and the Faith of Israel's Daughters: Reflections on Gender and Religious Definition," in Jobling et al., *The Bible and the Politics of Exegesis,* 97–108; Susan Ackerman, "'And the Women Knead Dough': The Worship of the Queen of Heaven in Sixth-Century Judah," in Day, *Gender and Difference,* 109–24; idem, *Under Every Green Tree: Popular Religion in Sixth-Century Judah* (Atlanta: Scholars Press, 1992); idem, "The Queen Mother and the Cult in Ancient Israel," *JBL* 112 (1993): 385–401; Karl van der Toorn, *From Her Cradle to Her Grave. The Role of Religion in the Life of the Israelite and the Babylonian Woman* (Sheffield: JSOT Press, 1994).

101. See, e.g., Michael D. Coogan, "Canaanite Origins and Lineage: Reflections on the Religion of Ancient Israel," in Miller et al., *Ancient Israelite Religion,* 115–29; P. Kyle McCarter, "Aspects of the Religion of the Israelite Monarchy: Biblical and Epigraphic Data," in Miller et al., *Ancient Israelite Religion,* 137–55; J. H. Tigay, *You Shall Have No Other Gods: Israelite Religion in the Light of Hebrew Inscriptions* (Atlanta: Scholars Press, 1986); William G. Dever, "Asherah, Consort of Yahweh? New Evidence from Kuntillet 'Ajrûd," *BASOR* 255 (1984): 29–37.

102. See, e.g., Grabbe, *Priests, Prophets, Diviners, Sages,* 20–40.

103. The most recent and comprehensive studies of religious specialists that are social-scientific in orientation are Grabbe, *Priests, Prophets, Diviners, Sages,* and Blenkinsopp, *Sage, Priest, Prophet.* See also Robert R. Wilson, *Prophecy and Society in Ancient Israel* (Philadelphia: Fortress Press, 1980); Robert C. Culley and Thomas W. Overholt, eds., *Anthropological Perspectives on Old Testament Prophecy, Semeia* 21 (1981); Thomas W. Overholt, *Channels of Prophecy: The Social Dynamics of Prophetic Authority* (Minneapolis: Fortress Press, 1989).

104. There are repeated prohibitions in the Hebrew Bible against practicing types of intermediation that are identified as lacking legitimacy. Deuteronomy 18:9–14, for example, lists divination, soothsaying, augury, sorcery, and necromancy, among others (cf. also, for example, 1 Samuel 28; Ezek. 13:17–23). The presence of such prohibitions, however, probably indicates that these practices were fairly popular and widespread.

105. See, e.g., Wilson, *Prophecy and Society,* 90–98; Grabbe, *Priests, Prophets, Diviners, Sages,* 119–51.

106. See, e.g., Victor W. Turner, "Religious Specialists," in Arthur C. Lehmann and James E. Myers, eds., *Magic, Witchcraft, and Religion: An Anthropological Study of the Supernatural,* 4th ed. (Mountain View, Calif.: Mayfield, 1997), 78–85.

107. There is a great deal of confusion among the texts with regard to such issues as the origin and significance of the Zadokites and the position of the Levites at various periods. Some texts, for example, emphasize the position of the Zadokites as presiding priests, and others include all Levites as priests. It is likely that the confusion is the result of power struggles among various priestly factions, although the history behind these struggles is difficult to sort out.

108. Although space does not permit any full consideration of the ritual systems of ancient Israel and Judah, it is worth noting that rituals were closely interrelated with the economy—described by some as a kind of "divine economy" in which the firstfruits and tithes that represent God's investment in the system are given to the priests to support the Temple and the priestly establishment, as well as ensuring the fertility of the land. Sacrifice is another way of maintaining this "economy."

109. See, e.g., Turner, "Religious Specialists."

110. Cf. Grabbe, *Priests, Prophets, Diviners, Sages,* 116–18. Grabbe deemphasizes the role of prophets as innovators of change.

111. See, e.g., Anthony F. C. Wallace, "Revitalization Movements," *American Anthropologist* 58 (1956): 264–81.

112. Wilson, *Prophecy and Society,* 135–295. Wilson's identification of central prophets with southern traditions and peripheral prophets with northern traditions is less convincing than the distinction he makes between the two types.

Chapter 6. The Babylonian and Persian Periods

1. For recent discussions of the Persian period literature, see, e.g., Philip R. Davies, *In Search of "Ancient Israel"*; Lemche, *Ancient Israel,* 173–75; Giovanni Garbini, "Hebrew Literature in the Persian Period," in Tamara C. Eskenazi and Kent H. Richards, eds., *Second Temple Studies 2: Temple and Community in the Persian Period* (Sheffield: Sheffield Academic Press, 1994), 180–88.

2. Philip R. Davies, *In Search of "Ancient Israel,"* 31.

3. Ibid., 84.

4. Robert P. Carroll, "The Myth of the Empty Land," *Semeia* 59 (1992): 79–93; Hans M. Barstad, *The Myth of the Empty Land: A Study of the History and Archaeology of Judah during the "Exilic" Period* (Oslo: Scandinavian University Press, 1996). Carroll suggests that this "myth" should be read in conjunction with the conquest narratives that portray the land as having been polluted by its Canaanite inhabitants.

5. For a review of problems and recent studies, see, e.g., Tamara C. Eskenazi, "Current Perspectives on Ezra-Nehemiah and the Persian Period," *Currents in Research: Biblical Studies* 1 (1993): 59–86; Jon L. Berquist, *Judaism in Persia's Shadow: A Social and Historical Approach* (Minneapolis: Fortress Press, 1995), 105–20.

6. For recent studies on the problems of dating Ezra-Nehemiah, see, e.g., Sarah Japhet, "Composition and Chronology in the book of Ezra-Nehemiah," in Eskenazi and Richards, *Second Temple Studies 2,* 189–216; Lester Grabbe, *Judaism from Cyrus to Hadrian,* vol. 1: *The Persian and Greek Periods* (Minneapolis: Fortress Press, 1992), 30–46.

7. Robert P. Carroll, "So What Do We *Know* about the Temple? The Temple in the Prophets," in Eskenazi and Richards, *Second Temple Studies 2,* 45–46.

8. Philip R. Davies, *In Search of "Ancient Israel,"* 83.

9. For an evaluation of Nehemiah in light of anthropological studies of "revitalization movements," see Kenneth D. Tollefson and H. G. M. Williamson, "Nehemiah as Cultural Revitalization: An Anthropological Perspective," *JSOT* 56 (1992): 19–39.

10. For reviews and evaluations of these materials, see, e.g., Hoglund, *Achaemenid Imperial Administration;* Grabbe, *Judaism from Cyrus to Hadrian,* 53–67.

11. See, e.g., Eskenazi, "Current Perspectives," 61–62.

12. Barstad, *The Myth of the Empty Land,* 47–55.

13. The most comprehensive survey of archaeological material relating to this period, although somewhat out of date, is Ephraim Stern, *Material Culture of the Land of the Bible in the Persian Period* (Warminster: Aris and Phillips, 1982); for more recent summaries, see, e.g., idem, "Between Persia and Greece: Trade, Administration and Warfare in the Persian and Hellenistic Periods," in Levy, *The Archaeology of Society in the Holy Land,* 432–45; Hoglund, *Achaemenid Imperial Administration;* Grabbe, *Judaism from Cyrus to Hadrian,* 67–73; Charles E. Carter, "The Province of Yehud in the Post-Exilic Period: Soundings in Site Distribution and Demography," in Eskenazi and Richards, *Second Temple Studies 2,* 106–45; Eric M. Meyers, "Second Temple Studies in the Light of Recent Archaeology, Part I: The Persian Period," *Currents in Research: Biblical Studies* 2 (1994): 25–42; Jane C. Waldbaum, "Greeks *in* the East or Greeks *and* the East? Problems in the Definition and Recognition of Presence," *BASOR* 305 (1997): 1–17.

14. See Waldbaum, "Greeks *in* the East," 4–5.

15. See especially Stern, *Material Culture,* 250; Kenneth G. Hoglund, "The Achaemenid Context," in Philip R. Davies, ed., *Second Temple Studies 1: Persian Period* (Sheffield: Sheffield Academic Press, 1991), 63–64; idem, *Achaemenid Imperial Administration,* 202–5.

16. Hoglund, "The Achaemenid Context," 63–64.

17. See especially Waldbaum, "Greeks *in* the East"; cf. Carter, "The Province of Yehud," 120; Stern, *Material Culture;* Meyers, "Second Temple Studies."

18. Philip R. Davies, *In Search of "Ancient Israel,"* 77.

19. Ibid., 55.

20. Ibid., 76.

21. For example, Barstad, *The Myth of the Empty Land;* Berquist, *Judaism in Persia's Shadow,* 13–17.

22. Berquist, *Judaism in Persia's Shadow,* 13–17.

23. Ibid., 17–18. See also Barstad, *The Myth of the Empty Land.*

24. See also Hoglund, *Achaemenid Imperial Administration;* Grabbe, *Judaism from Cyrus to Hadrian.* The most up-to-date and comprehensive study of the history of the Persian Empire is Pierre Briant's *Histoire de l'empire perse de Cyrus à Alexandre* (Paris: Fayard, 1996).

25. Berquist, *Judaism in Persia's Shadow,* 23–44; cf. also Grabbe, *Judaism from Cyrus to Hadrian,* 79–83, 115.

26. Berquist, *Judaism in Persia's Shadow,* 45–50.

27. Berquist, *Judaism in Persia's Shadow,* 51–86; Grabbe, *Judaism from Cyrus to Hadrian,* 115–16.

28. Berquist, *Judaism in Persia's Shadow,* 87–103.

29. Grabbe, *Judaism from Cyrus to Hadrian,* 129.

30. Berquist, *Judaism in Persia's Shadow,* 105–20.

31. For this period, see also Hoglund, *Achaemenid Imperial Administration;*

idem, "The Achaemenid Context." Hoglund also argues that the reforms of Ezra and Nehemiah were initiated by Persian policies aimed at controlling outlying territories more tightly.

32. Berquist, *Judaism in Persia's Shadow,* 121–27.

33. Ibid., 10.

34. Ibid., iv.

35. Berquist's model is outlined in *Judaism in Persia's Shadow,* 241–55.

36. For example, Shmuel Noah Eisenstadt, *The Political Systems of Empires: The Rise and Fall of Historical Bureaucratic Societies* (New York: Free Press, 1969); idem, *Revolution and the Transformation of Societies: A Comparative Study of Civilizations* (New York: Free Press, 1978).

37. For a list of factors leading to Judah's formation as a secondary state, see Berquist, *Judaism in Persia's Shadow,* 140.

38. Ibid., 140.

39. See, e.g., Philip R. Davies, *In Search of "Ancient Israel,"* 82; Berquist, *Judaism in Persia's Shadow,* 26.

40. Carter, "The Province of Yehud," 109–11.

41. Stern, *Material Culture,* 245–49.

42. Carter, "The Province of Yehud," 112–13.

43. For example, Hoglund, *Achaemenid Imperial Administration,* 202–3.

44. Carter, "The Province of Yehud in the Post-Exilic Period." Cf. Avi Ofer, "'All the Hill Country of Judah': From a Settlement Fringe to a Prosperous Monarchy," in Finkelstein and Na'aman, *From Nomadism to Monarchy,* 106.

45. M. Kochavi, ed., *Judea, Samaria, and the Golan: Archaeological Survey 1967–1968* (Jerusalem: Archaeological Survey of Israel, 1972).

46. Carter, "The Province of Yehud," 129–33, 135.

47. Kochavi, *Judea, Samaria, and the Golan.*

48. Carter, "The Province of Yehud," 108, 133–35; cf. J. P. Weinberg, *The Citizen-Temple Community,* trans. D. Smith-Christopher (Sheffield: JSOT Press, 1992), 132. Weinberg estimates the size of the Jewish community in Judah to be 150,000 after 458–57 B.C.E.

49. Carter, "The Province of Yehud," 127–29, 135.

50. Berquist, *Judaism in Persia's Shadow,* 62; Grabbe, *Judaism from Cyrus to Hadrian,* 115–16.

51. The Greeks developed a market system in the fifth century B.C.E., but even after this, redistribution and reciprocity continued to dominate. On market economies, see, e.g., Carney, *The Shape of the Past,* 141, 176–77.

52. See, e.g., Berquist, *Judaism in Persia's Shadow,* 26.

53. See, e.g., Stern, "Between Persia and Greece," 436–37; Waldbaum, "Greeks *in* the East."

54. For example, Philip R. Davies, *In Search of "Ancient Israel."*

55. Berquist, *Judaism in Persia's Shadow,* 113–14.

56. Weinberg, *The Citizen-Temple Community.* For evaluations of Weinberg's construct, see, e.g., Eskenazi, "Current Perspectives," 67–69; Daniel L. Smith, *The Religion of the Landless: The Social Context of the Babylonian Exile* (Bloomington, Ind.: Meyer-Stone Books, 1989); Joseph Blenkinsopp, "Temple and Society in Achaemenid Judah," in Philip R. Davies, *Second Temple Studies 1,* 22–53.

57. Weinberg, *The Citizen-Temple Community,* 61.

58. Ibid., 28.

59. Ibid., 22–26.

60. Ibid., 29.

61. Ibid., 34–48.

62. Joseph Blenkinsopp, "Temple and Society in Achaemenid Judah," in Philip R. Davies, *Second Temple Studies 1,* 22–53; cf. also, e.g., Lemche, *Ancient Israel,* 188; Berquist, *Judaism in Persia's Shadow.*

63. Smith, *The Religion of the Landless.*

64. Ibid., 93–126, 201–16. Cf. Bendor, *The Social Structure of Ancient Israel,* 228. Bendor emphasizes the fact that in the book of Nehemiah the *bet 'āb* and the *mišpāḥāh* are still mentioned as fundamental units of the community (Neh. 4:13; 10:35 [10:34]).

65. See, e.g., Berquist, *Judaism in Persia's Shadow,* 78–79.

66. Paul D. Hanson, *The Dawn of Apocalyptic: The Historical and Sociological Roots of Jewish Apocalyptic Eschatology* (Philadelphia: Fortress Press, 1979).

67. Cf. Berquist, *Judaism in Persia's Shadow,* 8. Berquist notes that despite the persuasiveness of Hanson's reconstruction and the extent of its acceptance, more recent historians have emphasized the *external influences* of the Persian Empire on the Jerusalem community. Cf. also Philip R. Davies, "The Social World of Apocalyptic Writings," in R. E. Clements, ed., *The World of Ancient Israel,* 251–71; Stephen L. Cook, *Prophecy and Apocalypticism: The Postexilic Social Setting* (Minneapolis: Fortress Press, 1995). Davies's criticism (p. 252) of Hanson's construct is that one cannot infer a type of society from a type of literature (apocalyptic), which is what Hanson does. In contrast to Hanson, Cook suggests that the social locus of early apocalyptic writings was possibly the priestly class that was at the center of power in postexilic Judah, not those on the social fringes who were opposed to it.

68. Mary Douglas, *Purity and Danger: An Analysis of the Concepts of Pollution and Taboo* (London: Routledge & Kegan Paul, 1966).

69. Smith, *The Religion of the Landless,* 64–65, 203.

70. Ibid.

71. Naomi Steinberg, *Kinship and Marriage in Genesis: A Household Economics Perspective* (Minneapolis: Fortress Press, 1993). See especially her conclusions on pp. 135–47.

72. Tamara C. Eskenazi and Eleanore P. Judd, "Marriage to a Stranger in Ezra 9–10," in Eskenazi and Richards, *Second Temple Studies 2,* 266–85.

73. Claudia V. Camp, "What's So Strange about the Strange Woman?" in *The Bible and the Politics of Exegesis,* 17–38.

74. Tamara C. Eskenazi, "Out from the Shadows: Biblical Women in the Postexilic Era," *JSOT* 54 (1992): 25–43. See also Harold C. Washington, "The Strange Woman of Proverbs 1–9 and Post-exilic Judean Society," in Eskenazi and Richards, *Second Temple Studies 2,* 217–42. Washington supports Eskenazi's conclusions in his analysis of Proverbs 1–9.

75. Camp, "What's So Strange about the Strange Woman?"

76. Berquist, *Judaism in Persia's Shadow,* 117–18.

77. Eskenazi and Judd, "Marriage to a Stranger in Ezra 9–10."

78. Daniel L. Smith-Christopher, "The Mixed Marriage Crisis in Ezra 9–10 and

Nehemiah 13: A Study of the Sociology of the Post-Exilic Judean Community," in Eskenazi and Richards, *Second Temple Studies 2,* 243–65.

79. See Berquist, *Judaism in Persia's Shadow,* 131–46.

80. Cf. Weinberg, *The Citizen-Temple Community.* Weinberg presents a construct in which the Jewish community was much more autonomous.

81. Davies notes that there is confusion in the texts in this respect. There may have been a provincial administration that was separate from the Temple administration, but if so the two were probably not in tension. He suggests that it is most likely that there was a unified ruling elite. Philip R. Davies, *In Search of "Ancient Israel,"* 101–3.

82. Berquist, *Judaism in Persia's Shadow,* 154.

83. See, e.g., Smith, *The Religion of the Landless,* 93–99.

84. See Wilson, "The Role of Law," 97–98.

85. See, e.g., Berquist, *Judaism in Persia's Shadow,* 138.

86. For example, Philip R. Davies, *In Search of "Ancient Israel,"* 144.

87. See, e.g., Berquist, *Judaism in Persia's Shadow,* 147–59.

88. See, e.g., ibid., 63–64; David J. A. Clines, "Haggai's Temple, Constructed, Deconstructed and Reconstructed," in Eskenazi and Richards, *Second Temple Studies 2,* 60–87.

89. See, e.g., Berquist, *Judaism in Persia's Shadow,* 151–56.

90. Cf. Cook, *Prophecy and Apocalypticism.* Cook argues that some of the protoapocalyptic texts were written by members of the priestly class.

91. Berquist, *Judaism in Persia's Shadow,* 121.

92. See, e.g., ibid., 150–51; Clines, "Haggai's Temple."

93. Berquist, *Judaism in Persia's Shadow,* 161–76.

94. For example, ibid., 177–92; Cook, *Prophecy and Apocalypticism;* Philip R. Davies, "The Social World of Apocalyptic Writings."

Selected Bibliography

Chapter 1

Brettler, Marc. *The Creation of History in Ancient Israel*. New York: Routledge, 1996.

Carney, T. F. *The Shape of the Past: Models and Antiquity*. Lawrence, Kans.: Coronada Press, 1975.

Clements, R. E., ed. *The World of Ancient Israel: Sociological, Anthropological and Political Perspectives*. Cambridge: Cambridge University Press, 1989.

Eilberg-Schwartz, Howard. *The Savage in Judaism: An Anthropology of Israelite Religion and Ancient Judaism*. Bloomington: Indiana University Press, 1990.

Flanagan, James W. "Finding the Arrow of Time: Constructs of Ancient History and Religion." *Currents in Research: Biblical Studies* 3 (1995): 37–80.

Gottwald, Norman K. *The Hebrew Bible: A Socio-Literary Introduction*. Philadelphia: Fortress Press, 1985.

———. *The Hebrew Bible in Its Social World and Ours*. Atlanta: Scholars Press, 1993.

Halpern, Baruch. *The First Historians: The Hebrew Bible and History*. San Francisco: Harper & Row, 1988.

Jobling, David, Peggy L. Day, and Gerald T. Sheppard, eds. *The Bible and the Politics of Exegesis*. Cleveland: Pilgrim Press, 1991.

Lang, Bernhard, ed. *Anthropological Approaches to the Old Testament*. Philadelphia: Fortress Press, 1985.

Levy, Thomas E., ed. *The Archaeology of Society in the Holy Land*. New York: Facts on File, 1995.

Matthews, Victor H., and Don C. Benjamin. *Social World of Ancient Israel 1250–587 B.C.E.* Peabody, Mass.: Hendrickson, 1993.

Morgan, Robert, and John Barton. *Biblical Interpretation*. Oxford: Oxford University Press, 1988.

Overholt, Thomas W. *Cultural Anthropology and the Old Testament*. Minneapolis: Fortress Press, 1996.

Rogerson, J. W. *Anthropology and the Old Testament*. Atlanta: John Knox Press, 1978.

Van Seters, John. *In Search of History: Historiography in the Ancient World and the Origins of Biblical History*. New Haven, Conn.: Yale University Press, 1983.

Vaux, Roland de. *Ancient Israel*. 2 vols. New York: McGraw-Hill, 1961.

Whitelam, Keith W. "Recreating the History of Israel." *JSOT* 35 (1986): 45–70.

———. *The Invention of Ancient Israel: The Silencing of Palestinian History*. New York: Routledge, 1996.

Wilson, Robert R. *Sociological Approaches to the Old Testament.* Philadelphia: Fortress Press, 1984.

Chapter 2

Ahlström, G. W. *Who Were the Israelites?* Winona Lake, Ind.: Eisenbrauns, 1986.

Coote, Robert B., and Keith W. Whitelam. "The Emergence of Israel: Social Transformation and State Formation following the Decline in Late Bronze Age Trade." *Semeia* 37 (1986): 107–47.

Coote, Robert B., and Keith W. Whitelam. *The Emergence of Early Israel in Historical Perspective.* SWBAS, 5. Sheffield: Almond Press, 1987.

Davies, Philip R. *In Search of "Ancient Israel."* JSOTSS, 148. Sheffield: Sheffield Academic Press, 1995.

Finkelstein, Israel. " *'Izbet Ṣarṭah: An Early Iron Age Site Near Rosh Ha'ayin, Israel.* BARIS, 299. Oxford: BAR, 1986.

———. *The Archaeology of the Israelite Settlement.* Jerusalem: Israel Exploration Society, 1988.

Finkelstein, Israel, and Nadav Na'aman, eds. *From Nomadism to Monarchy: Archaeological and Historical Aspects of Early Israel.* Jerusalem: Israel Exploration Society, 1994.

Freedman, David Noel, and David Frank Graf, eds. *Palestine in Transition: The Emergence of Ancient Israel.* SWBAS, 2. Sheffield: Almond Press, 1983.

Fritz, Volkmar. *The City in Ancient Israel.* Sheffield: Sheffield Academic Press, 1995.

Gottwald, Norman K. *The Tribes of Yahweh: A Sociology of the Religion of Liberated Israel, 1250–1050 B.C.E.* Maryknoll, N.Y.: Orbis Books, 1979.

———. "Recent Studies of the Social World of Premonarchic Israel." *Currents in Research: Biblical Studies* 1 (1993): 163–89.

Lemche, Niels Peter. *The Israelites in History and Tradition.* Louisville, Ky.: Westminster John Knox Press, 1998.

Mendenhall, George E. "The Hebrew Conquest of Palestine." *BA* 25 (1962): 66–87.

———. "The Hebrew Conquest of Canaan." In *Biblical Archaeologist Reader III,* edited by Edward F. Campbell and David Noel Freedman, 100–120. Garden City, N.Y.: Doubleday, 1970.

Raphael, C. Nicholas. "Geography and the Bible (Palestine)." In *The Anchor Bible Dictionary, Vol. 3,* edited by David Noel Freedman, 964–77. New York: Doubleday, 1992.

Shanks, Herschel, ed. *The Rise of Ancient Israel.* Washington D.C.: Biblical Archaeology Society, 1992.

Stager, Lawrence E. "The Archaeology of the Family in Ancient Israel." *BASOR* 260 (1985): 1–35.

Thompson, Thomas L. *Early History of the Israelite People: From the Written and Archaeological Sources.* Leiden: E. J. Brill, 1992.

Weippert, Manfred. *The Settlement of the Israelite Tribes in Palestine: A Critical Survey of Recent Scholarly Debate.* Studies in Biblical Theology, 21. Napierville, Ill.: Alec R. Allenson, 1971.

Chapter 3

Albertz, Rainer. *A History of Israelite Religion in the Old Testament Period.* Vol. 1, *From the Beginnings to the End of the Monarchy.* Louisville, Ky.: Westminster John Knox Press, 1994.

Bendor, S. *The Social Structure of Ancient Israel.* Jerusalem: Simor Ltd., 1996.

Dearman, J. Andrew. *Religion and Culture in Ancient Israel.* Peabody, Mass.: Hendrickson, 1992.

Geus, C. H. J. de. *The Tribes of Israel: An Investigation into Some of the Presuppositions of Martin Noth's Amphictyony Hypothesis.* Assen: Van Gorcum, 1976.

Hopkins, David C. *The Highlands of Canaan: Agricultural Life in the Early Iron Age.* SWBAS, 3. Sheffield: Almond Press, 1985.

Lemche, Niels Peter. *Early Israel: Anthropological and Historical Studies on the Israelite Society Before the Monarchy.* Leiden: E. J. Brill, 1985.

McNutt, Paula M. *The Forging of Israel: Iron Technology, Symbolism, and Tradition in Ancient Society.* SWBAS, 8. Sheffield: Almond Press, 1990.

Meyers, Carol. *Discovering Eve: Ancient Israelite Women in Context.* Oxford: Oxford University Press, 1988.

———. "Everyday Life: Women in the Period of the Hebrew Bible." In *The Women's Bible Commentary,* edited by Carol Newsom and Sharon H. Ringe, 244–51. Louisville, Ky.: Westminster John Knox Press, 1992.

Miller, Patrick D., Paul D. Hanson, and S. Dean McBride, eds. *Ancient Israelite Religion: Essays in Honor of Frank Moore Cross.* Philadelphia: Fortress Press, 1987.

Rogerson, J. W. "Was Early Israel a Segmentary Society?" *JSOT* 36 (1986): 17–26.

Wilson, Robert R. *Genealogy and History in the Biblical World.* New Haven, Conn.: Yale University Press, 1977.

Wilson, Robert R. "The Role of Law in Early Israelite Society." In *Law, Politics and Society in the Ancient Mediterranean World,* edited by Baruch Halpern and Deborah W. Hobson, 90–99. Sheffield: Sheffield Academic Press, 1993.

Chapter 4

Chaney, Marvin L. "Systematic Study of the Israelite Monarchy." *Semeia* 37 (1986): 53–76.

Finkelstein, Israel. "The Emergence of the Monarchy in Israel: The Environmental and Socioeconomic Aspects." *JSOT* 44 (1989): 43–74.

Flanagan, James W. "Chiefs in Israel." *JSOT* 20 (1981): 47–73.

———. *David's Social Drama: A Hologram of Israel's Early Iron Age.* SWBAS, 7. Sheffield: Almond Press, 1988.

Frick, Frank S. *The Formation of the State in Ancient Israel.* SWBAS, 4. Sheffield: Almond Press, 1985.

———. "Social Science Methods and Theories of Significance for the Study of the Israelite Monarchy: A Critical Review Essay." *Semeia* 37 (1986): 9–52.

Fritz, Volkmar, and Philip R. Davies, eds. *The Origins of the Ancient Israelite States.* Sheffield: Sheffield Academic Press, 1996.

Gottwald, Norman K. "The Participation of Free Agrarians in the Introduction of the Monarchy to Ancient Israel: An Application of H. A. Landsberger's Framework for the Analysis of Peasant Movements." *Semeia* 37 (1986): 77–106.

Knoppers, Gary N. "The Vanishing Solomon: The Disappearance of the United Monarchy from Recent Histories of Ancient Israel." *JBL* 116 (1997): 19–44.

Schäfer-Lichtenberger, Christa. "Sociological and Biblical Views of the Early State." In *The Origins of the Ancient Israelite States,* edited by Volkmar Fritz and Philip R. Davies, 78–105. Sheffield: Sheffield Academic Press, 1996.

Chapter 5

Blenkinsopp, Joseph. *Sage, Priest, Prophet: Religious and Intellectual Leadership in Ancient Israel.* Louisville, Ky.: Westminster John Knox Press, 1995.

Buccellati, Giorgio. *Cities and Nations of Ancient Syria: An Essay on Political Institutions with Special Reference to the Israelite Kingdoms.* Rome: Instituto di Studi del Vicino Oriente, 1967.

Culley, Robert C., and Thomas W. Overholt, eds. *Anthropological Perspectives on Old Testament Prophecy. Semeia* 21.

Frick, Frank S. *The City in Ancient Israel.* SBLDS, 36. Missoula, Mont.: Scholars Press, 1977.

Grabbe, Lester L. *Priests, Prophets, Diviners, Sages: A Socio-Historical Study of Religious Specialists in Ancient Israel.* Valley Forge, Pa.: Trinity Press International, 1995.

Heaton, E. W. *Solomon's New Men: The Emergence of Ancient Israel as a Nation State.* New York: Pica Press, 1974.

Jamieson-Drake, David W. *Scribes and Schools in Monarchic Judah: A Sociological Approach.* SWBAS, 9. Sheffield: Almond Press, 1991.

Knight, Douglas A. "Political Rights and Power in Monarchic Israel." *Semeia* 66 (1994): 93–117.

Lemche, Niels Peter. "Kings and Clients: On Loyalty between the Ruler and the Ruled in Ancient 'Israel.'" *Semeia* 66 (1994): 119–32.

Mettinger, Tryggve. *Solomonic State Officials: A Study of the Civil Government Officials of the Israelite Monarchy.* Lund: CWK Gleerup, 1971.

Overholt, Thomas W. *Channels of Prophecy: The Social Dynamics of Prophetic Authority.* Minneapolis: Fortress Press, 1989.

Wilson, Robert R. *Prophecy and Society in Ancient Israel.* Philadelphia: Fortress Press, 1980.

Chapter 6

Barstad, Hans M. *The Myth of the Empty Land: A Study of the History and Archaeology of Judah during the "Exilic" Period.* Oslo: Scandinavian University Press, 1996.

Berquist, Jon L. *Judaism in Persia's Shadow: A Social and Historical Approach.* Minneapolis: Fortress Press, 1995.

Briant, Pierre. *Histoire de l'empire perse de Cyrus à Alexandre.* Paris: Fayard, 1996.

Cook, Stephen L. *Prophecy and Apocalypticism: The Postexilic Social Setting.* Minneapolis: Fortress Press, 1995.

Davies, Philip R., ed. *Second Temple Studies 1: Persian Period.* Sheffield: Sheffield Academic Press, 1991.

Eskenazi, Tamara C. "Current Perspectives on Ezra-Nehemiah and the Persian Period." *Currents in Research: Biblical Studies* 1 (1993): 59–86.

Eskenazi, Tamara C., and Kent H. Richards, eds. *Second Temple Studies 2. Temple and Community in the Persian Period.* Sheffield: Sheffield Academic Press, 1994.

Grabbe, Lester. *Judaism from Cyrus to Hadrian.* Vol. 1, *The Persian and Greek Periods.* Minneapolis: Fortress Press, 1992.

Hanson, Paul D. *The Dawn of Apocalyptic: The Historical and Sociological Roots of Jewish Apocalyptic Eschatology.* Philadelphia: Fortress Press, 1979.

Hoglund, Kenneth G. *Achaemenid Imperial Administration in Syria-Palestine and the Missions of Ezra and Nehemiah.* SBLDS, 125. Atlanta: Scholars Press, 1992.

Smith, Daniel L. *The Religion of the Landless: The Social Context of the Babylonian Exile.* Bloomington, Ind.: Meyer-Stone Books, 1989.

Steinberg, Naomi. *Kinship and Marriage in Genesis: A Household Economics Perspective.* Minneapolis: Fortress Press, 1993.

Stern, Ephraim. *Material Culture of the Land of the Bible in the Persian Period.* Warminster: Aris and Phillips, 1982.

Weinberg, J. P. *The Citizen-Temple Community.* Trans. D. Smith-Christopher. Sheffield: JSOT Press, 1992.

Index of Biblical References

Index of Authors

Index of Subjects